REBUILDING BRITAIN'S BLITZED CITIES

REBUILDING BRITAIN'S BLITZED CITIES

Hopeful Dreams, Stark Realities

Catherine Flinn

BLOOMSBURY ACADEMIC
LONDON • NEW YORK • OXFORD • NEW DELHI • SYDNEY

BLOOMSBURY ACADEMIC
Bloomsbury Publishing Plc
50 Bedford Square, London, WC1B 3DP, UK
1385 Broadway, New York, NY 10018, USA

BLOOMSBURY, BLOOMSBURY ACADEMIC and the Diana logo are trademarks of
Bloomsbury Publishing Plc

First published in Great Britain 2019

A catalogue record for this book is available from the British Library.

A catalog record for this book is available from the Library of Congress.

ISBN: HB: 978-1-3500-6762-2
ePDF: 978-1-3500-6763-9
eBook: 978-1-3500-6764-6

Typeset by Newgen KnowledgeWorks Pvt. Ltd., Chennai, India
Printed and bound in Great Britain

To find out more about our authors and books visit www.bloomsbury.com
and sign up for our newsletters.

CONTENTS

ACKNOWLEDGEMENTS

I owe enormous debts of gratitude to many people. First, to my primary supervisor Glen O'Hara, who has always given endlessly of his time and advice, his expertise, his library and more – massive thanks. And to my second supervisor Steve Ward, who also gave more time than I suspect he realizes, is a vast source of knowledge on the ins and outs of British planning and is kind and generous and told me all sorts of interesting facts I never could have uncovered in an archive. Next, to an amazing colleague: Peter Larkham is an absolute superstar. He has always opened his files and shared his knowledge, providing as much help as if I was his own student! Peter is a great example of why I love my field: so many are both collegial and kind. Likewise, thanks to Mark Clapson for heroic assistance with this and much else. Next, a big thank you hug to George Gosling-Page for reading, suggestions, advice and general moral support. Also grateful thanks to Thomas, Julie and Matt for help, advice and support. Special thanks to Martin Daunton and John R. Gold, who have been generous with time and helpful in a myriad of ways and are both lovely people to boot.

Research-wise Ed Hampshire (formerly at the National Archives) was terrific in helping me navigate the vagaries of the British civil service, pointing me down the archival paths at Kew to help me find what I needed most. Also at TNA, Julie Ash and Dave Lilley have been wonderful to me. At the Bodleian Library, many people put up with several years of questions, always with a kind answer: thanks to Jim, Nick, Paul and Lee and – now departed – Mikko, Simon and Anne. The staffs of many archives were terrific, in particular: Darren at the Labour Party Archive, Jeremy at the Conservative Party Archive, Carol at the Hull History Centre, David Cornforth in Exeter, Michaela at the University of Liverpool archives and Laura formerly at Newcastle's Sharp archive. Thanks also to the colleagues of those above as well as the Liverpool Record Office, West Country Studies Library and Devon Record Office.

The wonderful Gladstone's Library provided a scholarship to help finish the book and I am especially grateful to them. Thanks also to the Economic History Society and Oxford Brookes University for financial support of my research. Thanks for permission to quote or reproduce material go to the Town & Country Planning Association, Liverpool City Council Planning Department and Exeter Memories; and for material reproduced from Harold Macmillan's archive with the kind permission of the Trustees of the HM Book Trust. The publication of the many illustrations has been made possible by a grant from the Scouloudi Foundation in association with the Institute of Historical Research. Thanks also to all the people at Bloomsbury who have helped along the way.

Finally there are those who are very close to my heart and without whom I never would have attempted this work, much less completed it. I might never have started without the encouragement of Professors Geoff Smith and Roberta Hamilton, who believed in my ability, and contributed both directly and indirectly to this book. Further support from the family side includes Veronica Permuy, Pam Dunfield and Ralph Wood, and I am grateful for their love and encouragement. Here in the United Kingdom, thanks also to Alan and Alice who have treated me like family and helped keep me sane.

But of course my biggest debt is to my family: my parents, my brother and my husband. From proofreading to transcription, from photography to patience, you have all been supportive in so many ways. Thank you to Mom and Dad who instilled in me the desire for learning, passed on a sense of humour and above all supported me with more than just their love. Likewise, in the latter stages of this work, my husband Mark – I love you to infinity and beyond!

They will understand though that I dedicate this book to Dr. Harman Van Peeke – 'Cousin Van' – who encouraged me, inspired me and set a fantastic example in determination. Sadly he will not see the final product. Thank you, Van, for believing in me!

ABBREVIATIONS

BOD-CPA	Conservative Party Archive, Bodleian Library
BOD-MSS	Modern Political Papers, Bodleian Library
BT	Board of Trade
CAB	Cabinet Records
CEPS	Central Economic Planning Staff
CPO	Compulsory Purchase Order
DO	Declaratory Order
DRO	Devon Records Office
ECCM	Exeter City Council Minutes
EPC	Economic Planning Committee
HCCM	Hull City Council Minutes
HHC	Hull History Centre
HICCS	Hull Inc. Chamber of Commerce & Shipping
HLG	Housing & Local Government
HO	Home Office
IPC	Investment Programmes Committee
LCC	London County Council
LNER	London & Northeast Railway
LPA	Labour Party Archive
LRO	Liverpool Record Office
LSE	London School of Economics
LSE-BLPES	London School of Economics, British Library of Political and Economic Studies
LVCCM	Liverpool City Council Minutes
MAG	Municipal Affairs Group (Hull)
MEA	Ministry of Economic Affairs
MHLG	Ministry of Housing & Local Government
MLGP	Ministry of Local Government & Planning
MP	Member of Parliament
MTCP	Ministry of Town & Country Planning
PWRASC	Post-War Redevelopment Advisory (Special) Committee (Liverpool)
RCSC	Reconstruction Coordinating Special Committee (Hull)
SAUN	Thomas Sharp Archive, Newcastle University
T	Treasury
TNA	The National Archive (UK)
ULA	University of Liverpool Archive
WCSL	West Country Studies Library
WDC	War Damage Commission
WORK	Ministry of Works

PERSONS AND AFFILIATIONS

Reconstruction Ministries

List of Ministers and Dates

Lord Reith	Minister of Works and Buildings	1940–11 Feb 1942
	Minister of Works and Planning	11 Feb 1942–22 Feb 1942
Lord Portal	Minister of Works and Planning	22 Feb 1942–Feb 1943
	Minister of Works	Feb 1943–Nov 1944
Wm Morrison	Minister of Town and Country Planning	
		Feb 1943 (creation of ministry)–July 1945
Duncan Sandys	Minister of Works	21 Nov 1944–25 May 1945
	and Caretaker Government	25 May 1945–26 July 1945
A. Greenwood	Minister without Portfolio	11 May 1940–22 Feb 1942
Sir William Jowitt	Solicitor General	May 1940–March 1942
	Paymaster General	March–Nov 1942
	Minister without Portfolio (Reconstruction Committees chair until 11 Nov 1943)	Nov 1942–Oct 1944
	Minister of National Insurance	Oct 1944–May 1945
Lord Woolton	Minister for Reconstruction (Lord President in Caretaker Government with same responsibilities for Reconstruction)	11 Nov 1943–23 May 1945

Leadership and Roles in the Treasury

Chairmen of IPC

E. Plowden, temporary committee	Aug–Oct 1947
H. T. Weeks	Dec 1947–Apr 1948
W. Strath	29 Apr 1948–18 Nov 1949 (originally 'pro tem')
F. F. Turnbull	18 Nov 1949–dissolution late 1953

Key Civil Servants

Sir E. Plowden	Chief Planning Officer, CEPS Mar 1947–1953

Government Ministers

Labour

Chancellor of the Exchequer	H. Dalton	27 Jul 1945–13 Nov 1947
	Sir S. Cripps	13 Nov 1947–19 Oct 1950
	H. Gaitskell	19 Oct 1950–26 Oct 1951
Minister for Economic Affairs	Sir S. Cripps	29 Sep 1947–13 Nov 1947
	(joint with Chancellor position to Feb 1950)	
	H. Gaitskell	Feb 1950–Oct 1950

President of the Board of Trade	Sir S. Cripps	27 Jul 1945–29 Sep 1947
	H. Wilson	29 Sep 1947–24 Apr 1951
	Sir H. Shawcross	24 Apr 1951–26 Oct 1951

Conservative

Chancellor of the Exchequer	R. A. Butler	28 Oct 1951–5 Apr 1955
Minister for Economic Affairs	Sir A. Salter	31 Oct 1951–24 Nov 1952
President of the Board of Trade	P. Thorneycroft	30 Oct 1951–5 Apr 1955

Leadership and Roles in the Planning Ministry

Ministers

Minister, Town and Country Planning	W. S. Morrison	Feb 1943–July 1945
	L. Silkin	July 1945–28 Feb 1950
	H. Dalton	28 Feb 1950–26 Oct 1951
	(changed to 'Local Government & Planning' Jan 1951)	
Housing & Local Government	H. Macmillan	30 Oct 1951–18 Oct 1954
	D. Sandys	18 Oct 1954–9 Jan 1957

Civil Servants

Whiskard	Geoffrey, Sir	Permanent Secretary – inception to August 1946
Sheepshanks	Thomas, Sir	Permanent Secretary from Aug 1946 to 1955
Sharp	Evelyn, Dame	Deputy Secretary (later Permanent)
Neal	Lawrence	Deputy Secretary
Pepler	G.L.	Technical planning officer
Beaufoy	S.L.G.	Planning/technical
Dodd	K.S.	Planning/technical
Gatliff	?	Planning/technical
Kennedy	R.T.	Planning/technical
Mann	Leonard	Planning/technical
Vince	W.B.	Planning/technical
Walsh		Planning/technical
Wells	H.W.	Planning/technical

Local Authorities – Key Figures

Kingston-Upon-Hull

Body, Adrian	City councillor
Bullock	Town clerk
Cameron[?]	City engineer
Abercrombie, Sir Patrick	Planning consultant (external)

Exeter

Newman, C. W.	Town clerk
Gayton, Harold	Chief planning officer
Sharp, Thomas	Planning consultant (external)

Liverpool

Shennan, Alfred	Alderman (and private practice architect)
Keay, L. H.	City architect
Hamer, Herbert	City engineer

ILLUSTRATIONS

PREFACE: IN SPITE OF PLANNING

[T]here is a story to be told about the world as it appears not because of, but *in spite of*, planning.[1]

Why does the world around us look the way it does? A number of years ago, during my studies in architectural history, I was assigned to lead a seminar on 'speculative office building', focusing on twentieth-century London. I was excited to investigate the numerous buildings from the 1950s and 1960s that I walked past daily, and to find out why they were – to me, then – so unattractive. What I learnt, but did not yet have enough knowledge or sophistication to explain, was that they were the products of complex factors – economics, changing societal behaviour, the business culture – and that above all, they were designed to generate income.

Years later, after a long time spent working in the building industry itself, I came back to this topic but with a new goal: to understand the deeper backstory of those buildings from the 1950s and 1960s. I soon discovered that John R. Gold's call to look beyond the plans in investigating the built environment has only been partially heeded. A few historians have investigated the successes and failures of planning and architecture in the post–Second World War period. But generally, there is still a gap in scholarship regarding the evolution of Britain's architectural landscape to the present. How did cities go from plans to reality? These are complex stories that require broad, difficult, multidisciplinary work. Studies interrogating the economic and political underpinnings of the built environment are rare in general history, and even in the specialized fields of architectural and landscape history.

Urban places – with certain exceptions such as Celebration in Florida or Canary Wharf in the London Docklands or even Plymouth to some extent – are not built straight from the designs and plans of architects and town planners, although they are frequently discussed in that way. Why do plans rarely translate into reality? Postwar Britain offers a unique opportunity to examine what happened after plans were made. Many cities made plans – radical and less radical, by costly consultants or little-known in-house staff – that were never built. I wanted to look at what they *did* build, and why and how this happened.

The perspective taken in this book comes from many years' employment in the building professions and involvement in the process of building, from single projects to urban areas such as Canary Wharf. My passion for history combined with hands-on experience in the building industry created a desire to expose the *whole* process of building, versus examining design alone. Postwar reconstruction in Britain offers the ideal template: studying the planning of cities and the rhetoric of reconstruction, followed by examining the actions of officials in central and local government and other involved players, to expose the underlying realities within the built environment. And though this environment continues to change, the stories behind the initial steps are illuminating.

This book studies examples of the process of reconstructing cities after enormous destruction, looking at as many factors and influences as practically possible. The source material is strongly archival: central government and local files, national and local press, personal papers and other similar materials have helped here to elucidate the story of postwar blitzed British cities. What emerges is even more complex than initial impressions. The impact of people, power, decision-making and circumstances on building and rebuilding cities in a market economy comes to light.

I have endeavoured to look at British built environments in a fresh way: not via a traditionalist view of local building through the centuries, or of famous buildings, but of the everyday built products of a modern society. This book aims to offer a small step forward towards a more integrated and accessible history of our built environment.

Chapter 1

INTRODUCTION: A BLESSING IN DISGUISE, OR AN OPPORTUNITY SQUANDERED?

Hitler at least has brought us to our senses. We, the British public, have suddenly seen our cities as they are! After experiencing the shock of familiar buildings disembowelled before our eyes – like an all too real Surrealism – we find the cleared and cleaned up spaces a relief. In them we have hope for the future, opportunities to be taken or lost.

– Max Lock, architect and town planner (1943)[1]

You have, ladies and gentlemen, to give this much to the Luftwaffe: when it knocked down our buildings, it didn't replace them with anything more offensive than rubble. We did that.

– Charles, Prince of Wales (December 1987)[2]

Rebuilding after war is a huge challenge faced by many places over centuries of destructive human action. In the Second World War, the German air force heavily bombed British cities. Although this campaign – popularly called 'The Blitz' – was less devastating than the Allied or German bombing on the continent, for many cities the damage was not insignificant. From early in the war effort was made around the country and in central government to plan for reconstruction. Materials and funding were promised. Legislation was passed on compensation but also eventually to require all areas to make plans, whether bombed or not. The rise of expertise in urban planning and the growth of the planning profession were important results of these factors. Plans produced were modern, optimistic and forward-looking. Yet, despite the optimism, none of the plans was fully implemented. This book examines why.

Despite frequent praise in the contemporary press, later opinion on what was built in the 1940s and 1950s has been quite negative. Since the 1980s the postwar built environment in Britain has been condemned mainly as a failure. However, blaming architects and planners for this fails to consider the context in which rebuilding happened. This perception of failure looms especially large in light of the huge gap between what was hoped for and what was realized. Such judgements are mainly shaped by recent values, tastes and expectations. During and after the war those who created plans for the future focused on hope and potential, publishing modernist visions of new city centres.[3] Planning is supposed to shape the urban environment for the better, and it is therefore important to study its impacts, but in the postwar period many plans never went much further than the paper they were drawn on. And if the rebuilt city centres were indeed failures, we need to look deeper than just appearance to understand why.

I. *The Challenge of Rebuilding*

The scale of the challenges facing Britain in 1945 was largely understood at the time. Although the Great War left behind huge amounts of physical destruction in 1918, most was on the European continent – mainly in France and Belgium. The Second World War saw the advent of a widespread use of aerial warfare and regular attacks on civilians, factories and dockyards in addition to military targets.[4] Though Britain avoided invasion, German bombers inflicted a huge amount of damage on the physical environment, mainly in cities. 'The Blitz' lasted through the years 1940 and 1941, even though bombing did not cease completely until 1945. From the start of the Blitz, citizens and local officials were thinking and talking about plans for reconstruction. Additionally, some cities – such as Coventry – had been planning for modernization and redevelopment of their centres for many years prior to 1939.[5]

Planning for the future was certainly a way to stay positive about fighting the war and to visualize potential victory. Local and national governments were aware of this and many encouraged planning from early on, as with the oft-cited example of Lord Reith, who – as Minister for Works and Planning – famously told officials to 'plan boldly' for their city's future.[6] In many places the bombing was discussed as 'a blessing in disguise' – an event that would help transform cities by removing outdated cores and allowing new and better infrastructure to arise.[7] Churchill even called it an 'opportunity'.[8] However, there was a marked lack of pragmatism and little discussion around who would pay for these updated street layouts and shiny new buildings.

Within the new planning ministry, as well as among local authorities, the expectation that not just priority but specific and direct assistance would be given to cities was apparent. In 1943 a ministry official wrote: '[T]here will be no lack of capital for building reconstruction which will be, together with basic industries [and "housing" added by hand] the first to receive quotas of materials and labour.'[9] However, while cities were praised during the war for their fortitude, the promises of preference were not kept. Indeed, despite the plans made, these cities soon became a rhetorical footnote. After the war the profession of town planning had taken off, in part due to the need for plans; in part because of new legislation that compelled every county and city borough to create and submit plans; and in part due to the rise of the expert alongside new or expanding programmes to train planners.[10] It is striking, therefore, that cities most affected by the Blitz only partially implemented the plans they made. In fact, as mentioned, none of the plans were implemented completely. The following chapters tell the story of what happened instead.

British postwar plans also are intriguing to compare with European examples. Today many cities in Poland and Germany, as well as a number of other European cities, are well known not just for the scale of destruction but also for their restored appearance. Warsaw and Dresden particularly come to mind. Why – with a few exceptions – did British cities stick to modern plans and build modern new buildings, rather than reconstructing historic city centre streetscapes in the same way several places in continental Europe did? After all, cities such as Dresden, Gdansk and Warsaw are well known for their 'preserved' (or really, restored) sense of history. In the many records examined for this study, British officials showed little to no inclination to do the same. Planning in Britain was modernist, forward-facing and vehicle-oriented, while tourism was largely ignored.

As we know, Britain's urban environments – like others around the world – have been created through actors (city councillors, developers, etc.), circumstances and myriad external factors such as national and local economics, political machinations and more. To understand the world around us, and perhaps to judge it in a kinder way, we can look at examples in postwar Britain and learn more about ourselves, our sense of belonging and our true heritage: but not just the 'heritage' that has created an industry around our past.[11] This is about our heritage of everyday life and everyday politics, of local desires and priorities as they played out after one of the most destructive conflicts ever seen on British soil.

Postwar reconstruction is particularly important to study because the uniqueness of wartime destruction followed by rebuilding has affected – and will surely continue to affect – so many places: from the Great Fire of London to Hurricane Katrina to the tsunamis and earthquakes of 2004 and 2011 to the current destruction of historic sites in the Syrian conflict.[12] All nations and/or cultures deal with the aftermath of disasters, both man-made and natural. What can we learn from post–Second World War Britain about this process, particularly in its immediate aftermath?

As part of this study we need to examine various aspirations for the rebuilding of cities. Also, we need to ask how various cities coped with conflicts between ambitions and priorities. In this postwar period there is a greater role of central government, and this is more directly important in shaping local aspirations across the country than ever before. There are also significant issues around constraints: many barriers existed to block either, and sometimes both, sets of objectives. Within central government problems were caused by the shortage of resources, which also meant political wrangling over those scarce resources. Both politicians and civil servants had to work on balancing physical reconstruction needs against the wider needs of the economy – and the pressures of the growth of the welfare state – even more during the peace.

The postwar period was also one of tensions between central and local governments over priorities for reconstruction. Within the cities themselves – as will be demonstrated in the examples used here – there were further struggles. As the agenda of physical reconstruction evolved, competing and conflicting interests arose or were highlighted by the rebuilding process. Among these conflicts were factors such as the resurgence of the property sector, the desire for modernization of cities, the protection of heritage (or lack of) and topping all these perhaps were individual vested interests such as local property owners and businesses. We need to understand these national and local conflicts with their individual interests and aspirations to better appreciate how today's cities have evolved.

II. *Background*

Since the 1980s, historians have been paying increasing attention to post-1945 urban reconstruction. This has produced an important body of work, but also left some important questions unanswered.[13] We have since learned quite a lot about *planning* the postwar world, but know rather less about the process of implementing the plans made. Most of the published work on physical reconstruction is made up of local studies with a few histories having a national focus. Several histories have used case studies to investigate issues in some of the larger blitzed cities and have revealed the importance of local politics and political players, and of the relationship between local authorities and central government, while using postwar planning as an example.[14] These histories analyse a number of individual cities, draw out a number of stories around the plans of the 1940s and 1950s and have provided crucial pieces in building our understanding of postwar city planning. Yet looking for answers as to what was implemented and how, as well as why the plans were often shelved, there are details still to be uncovered in order to move towards a more complete assessment of postwar cities.

There are also a number of histories that have contributed to our understanding of the political and economic context of the reconstruction. While not studies of physical planning, these histories show us that as rebuilding went forward priorities quickly shifted to focusing on economic – rather than physical – reconstruction.[15] Physical reconstruction seems to have become an afterthought for central government. Urban historians, while not specifically addressing reconstruction itself, have also examined some of the social and cultural contexts of reconstruction. For example, past work has helped locate societal changes and priority shifts within planning, policy and development, as well as some of the impacts of changing demographics and expectations of everyday citizens.[16]

In a different genre but similar vein, there are histories of business in the postwar era that have contributed to a further understanding behind the physical growth of cities after the war. Such writing tells us about the kinds of players, particularly large multiples and property development corporations, who were responsible for actually building new shops, offices and other city centre institutions.[17] We also know quite a lot about planning and building design in the immediate postwar era. Responses to demand for both public and private work, changes in building technology, influence from outside Britain carrying forward from prewar trends, as well as changing ideologies and priorities in the postwar world – these are additionally enlightening in understanding postwar urban change.[18] Work in this area has also helped us learn where early ideas originated and about the people involved in the designs and plans and their responses to the new demand for literal – rather than vague – plans for cities.[19]

Still, our understanding of physical reconstruction in the immediate postwar period has mainly existed within the realms of 'planning' history. *Rebuilding Britain's Blitzed Cities* brings additional external factors into its investigation of the built environment, where most historians have mainly examined the visual. In 1999 a small but important piece of work by Peter Mandler asked for a wider scope of enquiry, similar to Gold's 'In Spite of Planning' cited in the Preface. Mandler attempted to push discussion forward by reminding us that postwar rebuilding should be seen within a broader picture. His chapter 'New Towns for Old: The Fate of the Town Centre' in *Moments of Modernity* takes note of the 'surprisingly limited' role of the planner and planning, and he argues that thus far historians have not produced integrated studies of urban development and that they therefore treat events beyond planning as 'epiphenomenal', or secondary.[20] His awareness of the role of politics as well as economics, and the actual process of development, points towards a clearly evolving understanding, if not of the process itself then at least of the need to expose the process. His vision of the outcome and its 'modernity' understands postwar Britain to have been led by a market-driven model, a political response to public needs tied with consumer demands, or – in his words – a result of the 'unexpected consequences of "consumer sovereignty"'.[21] Of all the work by planning and urban historians of the past fifty years, this approach provides one of the clearest pictures of the issues needing to be addressed to help us understand the evolution of Britain's postwar cities.[22] This book takes up Mandler's challenge.

The discussions that surround the making of urban history – an evolving genre that is intrinsically interdisciplinary – focus mainly on this potential for more comprehensive perspectives.[23] Historians are encouraged to use these connecting approaches of political, cultural, economic and social history even if the kind of synthesis found in histories of earlier periods might still be yet to come. This book takes the first postwar decade and attempts to synthesize the evidence found, revealing that a combination of economic factors, legislative changes and local issues, as well as the interactions and decisions of many actors, combined to override physical plans in almost every city. Planners, builders, developers and local councils all had to work in the context of political and economic factors that they did not control. Numerous constraints both delayed rebuilding and dictated what could be built, so even though wartime discourse prioritized rebuilding blitzed cities, neither the 1945 Labour government nor its Conservative successors followed through. This book helps develop explanations of the gap between planning and implementation – and dreams and reality – by starting with the wider political and economic picture and then focusing on how central government decision-making played out in many blitzed cities. The detailed stories of reconstruction in these cities can then help us understand the shaping of Britain's built environment. Inspired by J. B. Jackson's study of American vernacular, such as strip malls and highway business development, these stories give us some sense of where the everyday urban features around us come from.[24]

Throughout the book, the term 'blitzed cities' usually refers to the list of eighteen badly bombed cities drawn up by the planning ministry as most deserving of attention and assistance. This is not to say there were not several deserving cities left off this list, as explained in Chapter 4. Furthermore, the huge number of actors in the central government alone – from politicians to civil servants and more – can be very confusing. Therefore, a list is provided at the start to clarify names and positions. The stories here fascinated me and I hope that readers might be similarly drawn in, particularly in places where moral or reasonable choices seem at best overlooked and at worst taken deliberately. Readers will no doubt find shortcomings in the story. The depth of information on city councils in Chapter 5 is frustrating, from a political standpoint as well as around personal interactions. Meeting minutes are normally the only official source available, but they are often brief and usually impersonal, while newspaper stories can be biased or exaggerated or both. Additionally, while the files in the National Archives are full of information, there are clear gaps in what was saved, on top of the impossibility of reading absolutely everything there. I have done my best to cover all these areas as deeply as possible throughout.

III. *Structure*

In the following chapters this book attempts to use the perspective discussed above to produce a broad contextual history of the early stages of postwar reconstruction. Chapter 2 investigates both the wide and narrow background to postwar reconstruction. It covers three key areas: first, the rhetoric of reconstruction as found in print (magazines, pamphlets, etc.), in exhibitions, on radio, in film and in political material. Second, it looks in depth at the machinery of government around reconstruction and how the coalition government made frequent changes to the organization it attempted to set up to plan for the future. This is the first account that tries to unravel the way 'reconstruction' unfolded in an official capacity, included here to both provide clarity and show the difficulties brought on by poor organization and, to some extent, a lack of consensus. Finally, it looks at the physical realities that were to be faced after the war, such as logistical issues and the amount of destruction. These aspects of postwar Britain have never been analysed together specifically in regards to physical reconstruction, nor used to produce an analysis of the ideologies held, the machinery in place or the logistical situation in 1945. Taken together we have a good picture of the expectations that had been set and the wheels that had been put in motion (or not), and a starting point for physical reconstruction becomes clearer. This chapter provides context for the details and analysis that follow.

Chapter 3 examines the reconstruction issues and their background in the Cabinet and Treasury. Importantly it investigates how the postwar government(s) attempted to put controls on capital spending, including on labour and materials, while also exploring the machinations of government and civil servants in economic planning. Here we see the complexity of the economic planning apparatus within the Attlee government, which has not always been clear in other histories. Within that framework, we look at the Investment Programmes Committee (IPC): what it was and why it is important to study. This is the first in-depth assessment of the IPC, outside of some earlier research by historian Martin Chick.[25] Chapter 3 also looks into the institutional infrastructures created, as well as the personalities within those and their influence. The IPC was created to help control investment within the economic planning policies of the postwar government, but it worked inside a confusing and overly complex 'structure'. Here we see its impact on the blitzed cities, and how they had to fight for any kind of allowances to be able to begin rebuilding. The chapter concludes with an assessment of the influence of economic planning through 1954 on the cities.

Chapter 4 is a study of the newly formed planning ministry and how its officials presented and implemented legislation – particularly the 1947 Town and Country Planning Act – and how they supported and championed blitzed cities. From a background on planning in Britain before the war to an assessment of the planning structures in place in 1945, Chapter 4 examines the creation of a planning ministry, its role and its importance. It then looks at the early stages of reconstruction planning from the perspective of central government and how relations with local government played out. It concludes by showing how individuals in the ministry, and the relationships they established with the cities, had such a significant impact on physical plans – on top of the economic issues already discussed.

The book then sets out three case studies of blitzed cities after the war – Hull, Exeter and Liverpool – and details how each city made plans and then began rebuilding. Each city is studied via several aspects: looking at local government, interaction with central government, and local participation and intervention. Through these examples, we can then see how the national picture covered in the previous chapters actually played out locally. Hull was chosen as a northern port city and primary target – most of the southern port cities having been either well-researched or in progress – and it had so far only been covered by one book chapter in a political history.[26] Exeter was selected initially because at the start of the research project it had not yet been investigated and its core was possibly the most devastated.[27] Third, Liverpool was chosen as a city that has not had its reconstruction examined even while it was the most heavily bombed area outside London.[28] Chapter 5 demonstrates how each city had a unique experience in both their plan-making and their relations with central government. Further, it shows how the issues within each city – both physically and among city officials and others – had huge impacts on the results of the eventual rebuilding.

The penultimate chapter is a discussion of early reconstruction in terms of architecture, local economies and reactions to what happened. The answers also help explain how the process has reverberated, affecting today's cities. This is not an 'architectural history' as such, but in examining the architecture of reconstruction this chapter uses the case study cities, and the initial results of rebuilding therein, to look at several aspects – for example, the role of private investment as well as the constraints of cost, coordination and government restriction on building – to see how these played out in a physical form. The chapter also makes comparisons with European cities who rebuilt in a much different idiom. Whereas British cities were all about the modern, others rebuilt historic cores or neighbourhoods. Why did this not happen in Britain? Finally, we look briefly at the public reception of the reconstruction.

IV. *Summary*

Taking on this project poses several challenges: contemporary history draws from an unprecedented amount of material; narrowing the evidence and analysing it is therefore problematic. Material in this book was drawn from numerous sources: from the National Archives at Kew to several local archives; from parliamentary records to city council minutes; from contemporary pamphlets and publications found in political party archives to material from sound archives; from archives of architectural publications from the 1940s and 1950s to current discussions found on radio or television, and more. Developing an interpretation of postwar urban reconstruction in the recent past requires complex interdisciplinary historical methods. In the present work such interpretation means contextual analysis of the economic, political and social setting, in addition to the visual and physical setting. Recent history can also be more prone to preconceptions, especially when that history is within living memory.[29]

Finally, it is worth reiterating an issue that was aptly noted by Gold: there is a 'case for the contribution that an understanding of planning history and changing urban form can make when exploring related aspects of political, socioeconomic, and cultural change'. The chapters that follow endeavour to explore postwar reconstruction in Britain first through its political and economic context, and then through the local background. In other words, this book attempts to build an analysis from this *towards* the built environment, rather than *from* it, by looking at how politics, economics and related changes affected planning and eventually urban form. In this respect, it highlights Gold's statement that 'there is a story to be told about the world as it appears not because of, but *in spite of*, planning'.[30]

Chapter 2

CONSIDERING RECONSTRUCTION, 1940–45

There is so much now to plan for, to prepare for.
A whole shining world is possible.
Is there for the asking if we choose to make it:
Is ours if we will.
We are the shapers of our environment.
We are the makers of our own destiny.
We are the creators of our own happiness.
If truly we desire it we can build
A new and noble world for generous living.
. . .
Such towns as these are ours if we choose.
Sheer shining towns of beauty and delight:
Towns so proudly urbane
That there will be no need for anyone to escape from them.

– Thomas Sharp[1]

These words written in 1941 by the town planner Thomas Sharp epitomize the tone taken by planners and many others after the start of the Blitz: positive, forward-looking and optimistic about the opportunity to shape new and more modern cities. The rubble of war ('blitz') could be cleared, along with inner-city slums ('blight'), and as such there would be a silver lining to the bombing by the Luftwaffe. Cities would remake themselves with 'modern' amenities such as wider streets for cars and 'modern' buildings made of steel and glass and concrete, removing cramped and twisted medieval thoroughfares and outdated shops and offices.[2] In wartime Britain plans were made, alongside a huge variety of publications. Discussions took place through such media as radio, film and exhibitions. Administrative machinery was created and implemented both to study and to initiate this new order for the postwar built environment.

Although the following chapters will show why plans were rarely implemented in postwar Britain, the first step in looking at the plans is to visit the context in which they were created. This chapter focuses on the rhetorical background of wartime. The influences around planning – particularly bold planning – and the discourse of priority for those who suffered the worst of German bombing emerge as a significant backdrop to the reality after 1945. This rhetoric is analysed here through various media forms, as well as through the machinery of government. It will show that the platform on which authorities in the bombed cities began the postwar period was justifiably hopeful, if not expectant.

Reconstruction became a hot topic as early as 1940–41 when heavy bombing raids started. In the broader sense this applied to economic and social reconstruction as well as physical reconstruction. In fact the word 'reconstruction' has varying, if sometimes ambiguous, uses. The word is readily recognized, but its application – particularly by historians – varies widely.[3] In wartime Britain, the word was used for many purposes: in political discussions it was frequently used to refer to the time anticipated after the war, including visions of the future in a socioeconomic context.[4] First World War discussions of 'reconstruction' had focused on housing, reorganization of government, employment and health care. But changes brought about by worldwide political upheaval, societal changes, the economic issues of the 1920s and 1930s and mass bombing gave the word a new meaning by 1940.[5]

As a clear demonstration of the wide scope of meaning intended, witness the creation of a 'Ministry of Reconstruction' in 1943, whose brief covered everything from health care to taxation, from local and central government organization to postwar business and trade issues, to building or rebuilding itself.[6] Its remit was vast, at times too all-encompassing, and it seemed on occasion as if the ministry itself might simply exist to keep morale centred on the assumption of a positive outcome to the conflict.[7] This chapter will, after a discussion of the language of reconstruction, investigate the origins, functions and work of the wartime administrative machinery that addressed the subject within the Coalition government. The stop and start nature of the administrative solutions and the impact on town and country planning will be seen in the brief attempts to convene committees to examine reconstruction issues in the blitzed cities. In addition to the discussion of Whitehall administration the final section of the chapter contains a synopsis of the impact of air raid destruction on the building industry and sets out the general scenario at war's end in order to give a sense of the physical issues that were faced in late 1945.

Throughout this book the term 'reconstruction' is mainly used to mean physical building that would – and did – take place at a later time in cities and towns where bomb damage occurred. Yet to understand how the discussions played out in the period from 1945, it is important to examine how 'reconstruction' was perceived during the war itself.[8] Wartime discourse shows how complex the questions – and more importantly the answers – would be, that is, how to organize demobilization, how to reform social services and, crucially, how to manage the economy to prevent the problems of the previous postwar period. Furthermore, how would Britain rebuild its bombed cities? Labour and materials issues were anticipated, but – as will be shown – discussion went ahead in a positive tone. This chapter looks at how the British public, politicians, planners and officials talked about physical reconstruction. It is not concerned with documenting and detailing all wartime reconstruction publications and propaganda – and in any case this has already been done in many books, theses and articles[9] – instead the intent here is to provide an overview and an understanding of the rhetoric of reconstruction: the words, the meaning and the tone of what wartime Britain expected, or wanted, to happen when the time for physical rebuilding eventually arrived.

I. *Perceptions of Reconstruction: Public Rhetoric and Propaganda*

Throughout the war – in newspapers, magazines and books, on radio and in films and exhibitions, in speeches and political material in and out of Whitehall – discussion centred around both fighting the war and 'winning the peace'.[10] Great energy was clearly expended on beating Hitler, but discourse on the postwar world was plentiful. This section uses examples from various places where the rhetoric of reconstruction can be found and will elicit a general sense of what kinds of discussion took place around reconstruction during the war.

Printed Sources

An array of published material during wartime discussed the future of Britain after the war. Much of it, from whole books to pamphlets, focused on physical reconstruction. Even with paper rationing and shortages, a significant amount of material appeared, written by authors who ranged from serious academics to trained architects and town planners to poets and essayists.[11] Architectural periodicals arguably had very little else to write about during the war, and the subject of physical reconstruction was also covered in the popular press. The largest and most frequently cited wartime publication discussing ideas for the postwar period is *Picture Post*, a popular and accessible magazine which was considered fairly progressive and left-leaning, though not party affiliated.[12] In 1941 the editors brought out an issue in which prominent figures contributed essays on important ideas for the future. 'A Plan for Britain: The Britain We Hope to Build When the War Is Over' included essays from sources such as the architect Maxwell Fry on physical planning – 'The New Britain Must Be Planned' – and several others.[13] Newspaper articles on reconstruction were plentiful: hundreds, if not thousands, of opinions, discussions and letters to the editor appeared during the war.[14]

The range of choice in private books and pamphlets was huge, and included titles such as *Homes, Towns and Countryside*; *Our Towns: A Close Up*; *Britain's Cities Tomorrow: Notes for Everyman on a Great Theme*; *The City of Our Dreams*; and more.[15] As the titles show, the rhetoric of these publications was upbeat, looking forward to a better postwar world. While those publications authored by professional planners possibly carried more authority, there were also many untrained civilians writing on the topic, though one wonders who their readership might have been. Many associations and groups such as the Co-operative Permanent Building Society also jumped on the reconstruction bandwagon. From 1942 to 1945 they published a series called 'Design for Britain', including titles such as *Plan for the New Architecture, Here Comes Tomorrow, Post-War Building*,

National Planning and Redevelopment, New Towns for Old and *Houses and Towns After the War*.[16] There was even a market for material directed at children.[17]

Additionally, of course, there were organizations with vested interests in the rebuilding process, such as the Town and Country Planning Association (TCPA) which sponsored a 1943 series called *Rebuilding Britain*.[18] Most examples of this type come from professional association publications in the same vein and include other professional groups or professionally affiliated publications, who also trumpeted their thoughts and suggestions. Examples include the Architectural Press, which printed a pamphlet entitled *Planning for Reconstruction* (1944) (see Figure 2.1), as well as numerous others including *Architectural Review*, and the

Figure 2.1 *Planning for Reconstruction*, Architectural Press, 1944.

Institution of Municipal and County Engineers.[19] While perspectives, specific topics and affiliations of authors varied, the overriding theme of discussion was the need for more and better planning and the imminent postwar potential to 'fix' or 'improve' the built environment, which perhaps also displayed a form of confidence in the growing welfare state. As the Royal Institute of British Architects (RIBA) booklet accompanying its 1943 exhibition stated:

> Rebuilding is concerned with the whole framework in which we spend our lives, whether we are rich or poor, young or old, and whether we work in the fields or in an office. We have the means at our disposal to make this framework gay and lovely, to make of it something in which human beings can expand and enjoy themselves, and in which the human spirit can flower as never before ... 'We can do it better than ever it has been done before if we really care enough about it, and we can do it more widely, so that we can all enjoy the benefits.'[20]

Though not as plentiful as private publications, official publications provide examples of postwar ideas for physical planning, at least as distributed by the coalition government. A number were presented through the Army Bureau of Current Affairs (ABCA), which published pamphlets and booklets for service men and women. A booklet issued in September 1942 focused on 'Town Planning', and advocated the need for physical planning and a 'positive planning policy'.[21] It discussed land use planning in layman's terms, and included drawings of 'The Way It Might Be'. An ABCA booklet titled 'Social Security' also included a section on rebuilding towns and cities: 'We have one large immediate task in the replanning and rebuilding of our cities and towns. This will make a very great call on all our resources ... but it is also an immense opportunity.'[22] Although purportedly objective, Conservatives perceived the ABCA publications as having a left-wing viewpoint.[23] In any case, the Conservative party used their own series of pamphlets 'Looking Ahead' to outline official party visions of the future, while Labour also produced similar propaganda.[24] Other bodies publishing on reconstruction included the Ministry of Information which often – rather than write and produce their own work – either sponsored private publication of approved documents (mainly pamphlets) or, more frequently, paid for print runs and then distributed works themselves. These publications were popular from the outset, and were mainly distributed within the civil service. Examples include the Faber series for the TCPA on 'Rebuilding Britain' in 1941.[25]

Seen throughout the multitude of printed matter during wartime is a constant optimism and acceptance of making plans for a bigger and better-built environment in Britain. This discussion was equally local and national in scope, just as the parameters around rebuilding would be framed. Considering the rationing of paper during wartime, surely the plethora of material published – hundreds of plans and reports of various sizes and shapes alone – suggests the importance of the discussion of reconstruction and physical planning existed in both civilian and official circles.[26] Even experts from other fields, such as the influential economist

G. D. H. Cole, wrote about physical planning.[27] In almost every case the tone was positive and gave a clear impression of the perceived importance of physical planning.

Beyond the more general works that ranged from dialogues on landscape, countryside and rural outlook, to city and town planning ideas and ideologies, there were also publications focused on specific cities, some official and some unofficial.[28] Official plans were seen with regularity during the war because many blitzed cities took advice from Coalition ministers to initiate plans, to prepare for the postwar period and to get ahead so as not to delay the actual reconstruction once peace arrived. However, amateur and professional planners also published their own ideas. In every case the focus was on potential for change and improvement.[29] Wartime plans for cities throughout Britain were so numerous that even today a comprehensive study of the subject is ongoing, and the list continues to grow beyond the hundreds.[30] The sheer number of plans points to a recognized importance for rebuilding or at least replanning. The language of the plans and their visual qualities also made them suitable for promotional material for cities as well, further demonstrating the very positive language of wartime planning.[31]

Beyond the printed matter that was available, in wartime Britain the public was introduced to ideas about the postwar period and an imagined future – reconstruction in all its forms or meanings – through other media as well. Discussions occurred on radio, in film and through public exhibitions. Such media included a great deal of information about the built environment: on rebuilding war damage, the future provision of housing and the planning and improvement of towns and cities.

Exhibitions

Public exhibitions in Britain have a colourful and robust history both in production and attendance of large-scale events. With mid-eighteenth-century origins – beginning with the predecessor of the Royal Society of Arts – a long history exists around public displays of varying purposes. While possibly at their strongest in the later nineteenth century, exhibitions proved the best way to get information – particularly in a physical form – to the masses, in a pre-television age.[32] Although the war meant there was no new construction, the public could still attend displays designed to provide ideas and provoke discussion on the postwar physical Britain.[33]

In February 1943 the RIBA sponsored *Rebuilding Britain*.[34] The exhibit focused on participation – what individuals could do to be involved in making their 'new Britain'. It described the 'problems' seen in both urban and rural areas – much of it blamed on industry and lack of planning. It made suggestions for a better environment and encouraged public involvement. It was also meant to inform the non-expert about ideas for planning legislation, architecture and even new building methods. The *Rebuilding Britain* exhibit was the largest and most comprehensive exhibit focused on the built environment during wartime[35] (see Figure 2.2).

More specific exhibitions were held locally: mainly – though not exclusively – in blitzed cities such as Coventry, which held the 'Coventry of Tomorrow' exhibit

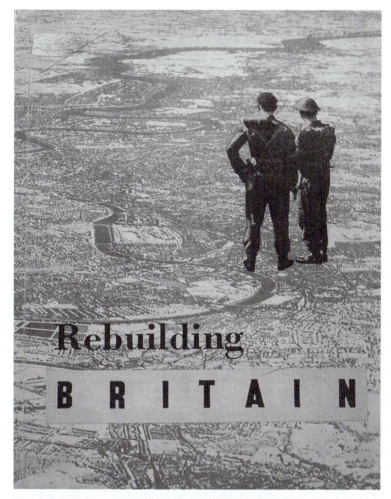

Figure 2.2 RIBA exhibition brochure: *Rebuilding Britain* (London, 1943). Courtesy of RIBA.

in summer 1940 and a further exhibit, 'Coventry of the Future', in October 1945.[36] At least one provincial city, Exeter, exhibited their plans locally but followed it with a visit to London.[37] In a comprehensive look at wartime exhibitions, research from Lilley and Larkham reveals that at least sixty-two exhibits were held in the provinces and a further twenty-five in London and its boroughs.[38]

To some the visual aspects of reconstruction planning have been seen as 'future gazing' and such exhibitions and publications were about people being asked to put their trust in experts – although not all agreed.[39] One viewpoint particularly looks at the visuals of planning from 1940 as an aspect of the changing nature of 'Englishness', but emphasizes the grandiose language used, and the ongoing promotion of a better, more modern England.[40] Another – though more negative – view of this rhetoric is that from the mid-nineteenth to the mid-twentieth century, while the varying exhibitions that promoted a changing architecture made their ambitions clear, 'cities planned by the few for the many ... were bound to alienate'.[41] Yet the public reaction at the time seems not to have been so negative. Some have argued that the expert-driven model was promoted, and visitors seen often as merely consumers.[42] However, the exhibits can still be seen as high profile, frequent and well-attended. And the rhetoric of the potential for a newly rebuilt Britain remained positive and forward-looking. The popularity of exhibitions in addition to print media again points strongly towards an outlook where 'reconstruction' was important.

Radio

Radio discussion of reconstruction was also regular and much came from various wartime 'talks'. Shows were produced in London and then more frequently in the provinces as the bombing increased after 1940. The BBC invited various writers and other public figures to discuss their views on postwar Britain, as part of a variety of wartime programming. The best known of these presenters were the poet John Betjeman and the author J. B. Priestley.[43] Non-technical, but censored, they espoused their own views of what should happen after the German and Japanese were defeated. Priestley did so in a socialist vein, but with positive rhetoric: '[W]e can march forward – not merely to recover what has been lost, but to something better than we've ever known before'.[44] His talks, though hugely popular, lasted only eight months.[45]

Betjeman was apparently an entertaining and opinionated speaker who had been an early champion of modern architecture. Naturally then, he had more (even than Priestley) to say on aspects of physical planning. However, his earlier modernistic and futuristic views had been tempered – perhaps by war – and by 1943 had evolved into something more nostalgic. Betjeman advocated caution first and foremost. 'Planning is very much in the English air now. Let the planners be careful ... I do not believe we are fighting for the privilege of living in a highly developed community of ants'.[46] He claimed also that the 'broad sweep of England's beauty ... is so easily destroyed, not by bombs but by witless local councillors' as well as developers, utilities, progressive road schemes and so on – 'the wrong sort of planner'.[47]

While historians suggest that Priestley's controversial cancellation by the BBC was due to a policy of avoiding reconstruction topics as too political, one notable exception was the BBC series of broadcasts in the winter of 1941–42, entitled 'Making Plans'.[48] The broadcasts were organized, and often presented by, F. J. Osborn, a reformer and propagandist for planning, and an officer in the Town and Country Planning Association.[49] With the BBC Talks Department he put together groups made up of a mixture of private citizens, planning experts and local government officials. Twenty-four weekly talks were broadcast and topics ranged from 'The New House' and 'The New Factory' to 'Planning the Countryside' and 'The Right Use of Land' as well as a talk headed by Professor William Holford on

'The Reconstruction of the Old Town'.[50] Talks on socioeconomic 'reconstruction' had caused ripples of controversy but 'Making Plans' did not. The need for physical planning was clearly considered non-controversial, even in some respects apolitical.[51] There was an all-party consensus that a lack of planning had been the primary reason for the unfortunate ribbon development and loss of much green/ agricultural land in the interwar period, and discussions on how best to avoid the same mistakes were encouraged from all political angles. Osborn, ever the promoter for town planning, played on this in stating: 'No more important subject was ever chosen for a series by the BBC than the twenty-four talks on "Making Plans".'[52]

Nevertheless, the talks themselves were certainly not filled with consensus about the manner of planning and problem-solving that should take place after the war. Pointing to imminent problems with agreeing on the details of planning legislation, several leading public figures disagreed with each other about the best methods of control.[53] On top of this, the citizens participating were invited to ask tough questions of the 'experts'. The de facto producer, Osborn, was pleased though and considered the discussions productive, helpful and a good starting point for the inevitable debate to come about methods, goals and legislation.[54] Again, the rhetoric was positive, but the reality would be far more complex than simply getting planners to agree. Within the talks though there was a high level of agreement on the positive nature of planning, suggesting that, again, the war would bring opportunity to fix what was wrong and create a better physical environment for all:

There is an extraordinary opportunity coming out of all this devastation. The destruction at the hands of the enemy has provided an opportunity of getting on with what has, in fact, always been a necessity. (L. H. Keay, city architect, Liverpool)[55]

If physical reconstruction is to be the grand setting for a fuller and more purposeful life after the war, it's most important that every single building project is co-ordinated with local and national plans.

What is the nation fighting for anyway? Is it not to remain a free and independent people capable of shaping its own destiny, and is not the shaping of that destiny part of our war effort? (H. Manzoni, city surveyor, Birmingham)[56]

This question of 'what is the nation fighting for' brings the discussion of rhetoric back to the issue that dominated official discourse, the importance of positive language in boosting the national morale. One of the best speech-makers in this vein was, of course, Winston Churchill. Again, here is his comment from the introduction to *Making Plans*:

Nothing must be permitted to divert our energies from the urgent war duties that are imposed upon us ... Neither, however, must we be taken unawares when victory on the field of battle has at last been won. It is right and desirable that informed forethought should be given to the complex problems of rehabilitation and reconstruction that will await solution when the perils that now threaten us daily are ever past.[57]

Radio was a primary media outlet for speeches from government leaders. They too often restated publicly this same positivist idiom, if only perhaps using it to strengthen morale. Here again is the Prime Minister: 'We have one large immediate task in the replanning and rebuilding of our cities and towns. This will make a very great call on all our resources in material and labour. But it is also an immense opportunity.'[58]

Film

Though radio was a popular and frequently used media source in wartime, ideas for reconstruction were perhaps better discussed in visual terms, and adding a visual element to the vocal expression of reconstruction was the medium of film. A number of short films appeared during the war on the subject of physical reconstruction, both officially made or sponsored and – though less frequently – privately funded. This brief overview examines the films as another form of the wartime discourse about the new ideas on planning and cities, in yet another media form. Although much was simply propaganda, the content remains important. Academics have previously studied how and why the films were made, as well as setting them in context, but these studies – which are extremely informative, if not invaluable – have not set the films alongside all the other media types while also examining their rhetoric.[59]

Wartime films were primarily – though not wholly – produced by the Ministry of Information, or other official bodies like the ABCA. While generally focused on housing – known to be a top issue for the general public – the films looked towards the new Britain. Some films, such as *London and Coventry – The Plan and the People* (1945), *Proud City* (1945) and *A City Reborn* (1945), explain plans for specific cities. Other films discussed general planning issues and promoted the ideology of modernism: rebuilding would be new, sleek and would accommodate automobiles and people together. They provided not just an addition to the wartime film 'diet of escapism and fantasy', but they also gave 'fragmentary glimpses of the shining new future'.[60] The films contained a combination of approaches: they demonstrated the current (urban) situation and/or perceived problems, they presented solutions – promoting mainly the professional solutions, and they appealed for support. Whereas much of the rhetoric on radio was straightforward promotion of planning, film of the period attempted to suggest what civilian reaction might be.

New Towns for Old (1942) was the 'first MOI film to be dedicated to the reconstruction of the built environment'.[61] The script by Dylan Thomas encouraged the public's involvement: 'When this war's won we've got to rebuild all our big towns.' 'Who's going to see that they don't stay just plans? Who's going to make them come true? You are. It's your town.'[62] Thomas's next film, *When We Build Again* (1943), a private venture underwritten by the Cadbury Brothers, addresses the reconstruction of Birmingham. Based on the book published by Lord Cadbury in 1941, mainly focused on housing and siting of industry, it too retained the positive attitude of future possibilities, and closed with 'Nothing is too good for people; the future will belong to them.'[63]

A City Reborn, written by an apparently very busy Dylan Thomas, is an MOI-sponsored film focused on the rebuilding of Coventry. It uses an invented documentary format, with actors playing the roles of citizens – a soldier, his girlfriend, a munitions worker, an engineer and the like. The film features dramatic music from the outset, underlining its importance, though also giving a feeling of doom, should the past be repeated. 'After the war [there should be] no thinking of returning to the good old days [of] crippling streets.' 'This will happen again if we don't plan!'[64] The film emphasizes the fact that Coventry had prepared one of the earliest plans for rebuilding, and 'in this plan the centre of the city – largely destroyed – is to be rebuilt entirely'. It further promotes the plan as something that will create 'a good decent pleasant [city] to live in', with 'a proper peoples' plan'. 'Coventry is going to be a place to live in where people believe that human life can be good and pleasant.'[65]

The ABCA included a film on physical reconstruction in their wartime series: 'Town and Country Planning', made during the war, but released just after in 1946. It trumpeted about the postwar possibilities: 'Yes and we are going to do it right this time' … 'The whole bag of tricks located and designed according to a proper plan.'[66] But this contrasted somewhat starkly with the contemporary – and more realistic – private film by Jill Craigie, *The Way We Live* (1946). Also made in wartime, the Craigie film is about the planning and rebuilding of Plymouth. It employed a similar documentary style, with actors, as *A City Reborn*. It begins with tempered optimism: 'This film is made for the peoples of the Blitz in the hope that their newly-built cities will be worthy of their fortitude'[67] (see Figure 2.3).

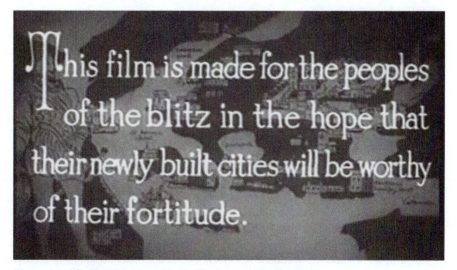

Figure 2.3 *The Way We Live*, 1946 (still); directed by Jill Craigie.

And like *When We Build Again* it looked chronologically backwards in pointing out past problems, calling living conditions in the city 'conditions like the Middle Ages'. The plan was presented in a positive and practical manner, but realism is again injected when the father figure asks of the plan: 'But is it practical?' And the film continued to address potential issues the planners foresaw – that is, that small traders were afraid the new city centre would favour larger stores. Furthering the incorporation of practical questions, Craigie's future husband, the (then) local candidate for MP, Michael Foot, stated that it is 'unfair that the burden of rebuilding the blitzed cities should fall on their hands' in suggesting they have a right to central government support.[68]

Although many examples exist, four other titles deserve mention here. *Proud City* was a publicity piece by the MOI promoting the Abercrombie and Forshaw *County of London* plan of 1943, of which the MOI also made a dramatized version, *The People and the Plan* (1945).[69] A positive future was promoted in the film *They Came to a City* (1944), adapted from a J. B. Priestley play, with a plot that concerned the experiences of various people coming to their 'ideal' city.[70] Finally, a 1946 film called *Land of Promise* had started production as a planning film under director Paul Rotha with Thomas Sharp, the eminent planner, as writer, but increased its scope to encompass a vision of the postwar society as well as the built environment, treating it 'as one aspect of a fully planned economy'.[71] Film in this period tended to the dramatic in its expression and dialogue, compared to later work, but much of this was still positive, with few films asking the very practical questions included in *The Way We Live*. The future complexity of reconstruction was perhaps realized, if rarely discussed. Clearly however, film – like radio, print and exhibitions – gave a definite impression that physical reconstruction was both important and offered positive possibilities for the postwar future.

Political Material

While film reached many people, if not as many as radio, the impending general election of 1945 brought door-to-door literature in the form of campaign propaganda. Unsurprisingly, this media included an increase in the use of emotion and sentiment about the impending postwar future – the reconstruction period – to win votes in the coming election. Labour, Conservatives and Liberals all issued printed materials touting their vision of a postwar Britain. Most of the rhetoric was focused on the social and economic ideologies of the parties, but there were party leaflets and pamphlets discussing town planning and, in particular, housing. All parties understood that building houses would be a selling point,[72] and the posters and literature sold party ideas both to women – discussing future homes – and to the wider public on general housing reconstruction.[73]

Interestingly, while an abundance of publications emerged in wartime about the impending challenges of physical rebuilding beyond the issue of housing, within the election materials physical reconstruction generally is virtually ignored. For example, research undertaken in the Labour and Conservative party archives reveals an extensive amount of rhetoric directed at housing and employment, but

Cirencester & Tewkesbury Division

THE RT. HON.
W. S. MORRISON
M.C., K.C., Minister of Town and Country Planning,
NATIONAL CONSERVATIVE
CANDIDATE.

Town and Country Planning.

I have been engaged for the last two years in setting up the new Ministry of Town and Country Planning and arming it with the powers necessary for its purpose. The Act of 1943 brought all land in England and Wales under Planning Control. The Act of 1944 provided local authorities with new powers to acquire land for the reconstruction, according to proper plans, of bomb-damaged and obsolete towns. We shall bring forward in the new Parliament proposals for improving the law with regard to compensation and betterment, so as to secure for the future the best use of land in the public interest, including proper reservation of open spaces and the best location of industry and housing.

For these concrete proposals for peace abroad and orderly progress at home, I ask for your support.

I am, Ladies and Gentlemen,

Yours sincerely,

W. S. MORRISON.

The Manor House,
Withington, Glos.

Figure 2.4 W. S. Morrison (Conservative) election material, 1945. Labour Party Archive (LPA), Manchester. *Courtesy of Conservative Party Archive and LPA.*

essentially nothing on rebuilding blitz damage. This is particularly striking in light of the fact that such mention – even cursory – was missing from candidates in blitzed cities themselves, such as Coventry, Plymouth, Southampton and so on[74] (see Figure 2.4 for the only example found, from the Minister of Town and Country Planning, W. S. Morrison). The parties had not ignored the issue during the war however, and the Conservative Party in particular added to the plethora of wartime literature with a series including some discussion of physical reconstruction. Their series 'Looking Ahead' covered the topic, as did the Conservative Women's Reform Group with 'When Peace Comes'. And Lord Woolton himself, a strong Tory activist, brought out his own publication – *The Adventure of Reconstruction* – based on his ministerial experiences, which are discussed below.[75] Clearly both parties – if not their electoral candidates – as well as many other institutions had spent time in the war thinking about, talking about and writing about reconstruction.

Further Rhetorical Examples

Beyond the official and unofficial publications mentioned, which discussed the subject of reconstruction in fairly specific terms, were also various contributions from diverse angles – if in a less specific way. Non-experts voiced diverse opinions. For example, the essayist and journalist George Orwell discussed his postwar vision of Britain in *The Lion and the Unicorn*. Much of Orwell's wartime writing has to do with a broader vision, not specifically focused on the built environment, yet he did make relevant comments. Arguing in favour of the potential of land nationalization, he stated that without such state ownership 'any *real* reconstruction is impossible'.[76] Likewise John Betjeman worried about what reconstruction would look like. As an essayist – rather than in a radio broadcast – he commented on reconstruction planning in his 1943 work *English Cities and Small Towns*. 'Much rubbish about "opening up vistas", "rural slums", "post war reconstruction", has been appearing lately in the press … These old towns of England are numerous enough to survive a decade of barbarian bombing. But their texture is so delicate that a single year of over enthusiastic "post war reconstruction" may destroy the lot.'[77] From the earliest bombing raids of 1940, the focus of a large number of publications – and of radio, film, exhibitions and more – had been the discussion of a future physical environment. This discourse centred almost entirely on a positive view of the new possibilities ahead and the potential for a greatly modernized Britain: redesigned roads with more space for cars, buildings that were made of new materials and functioned more comfortably (i.e., were air-conditioned). Tempered with economic realism in places, and with a small and growing nostalgia for historic Britain, by the end of the war the focus of the rhetoric was shifting.[78] The physical environment under discussion centred increasingly upon housing, and among politicians (at least publicly) the idea of building newer and better cities from the rubble had also mostly been left behind for both this issue and postwar employment.

If 'experts', planners, architects, surveyors, government officials and elected leaders were all pro-planning, why in the run-up to the general election did so much of the discussion turn away from reconstruction generally and onto housing and employment? Certainly it seems that politicians were aware that the voting public cared most about where they would live and that they preferred houses to flats though 'planners' might have suggested the expediency and cost-effectiveness of building bigger buildings housing more people.[79] By mid-1945, rhetoric was all about getting the votes, and the people were impatient to get their lives back to 'normal'.[80]

II. *Official Wartime Machinery of Reconstruction*

Alongside talk of reconstruction is the question of administrative action. The Coalition government initiated such machinery, but – as will be shown – in a complex manner with a complete lack of continuity. While the make-up of the Cabinet changed numerous times during the war, so too did the administrative set up that was meant to prepare Britain for a multitude of postwar issues. In the Great War there had been a Ministry of Reconstruction, but it was not reconstituted at the outset of the next war. Instead, a cabinet committee on reconstruction was established in 1940. Considering the phony war had just ended and the 'real' war begun, this was an optimistic stance taken by Churchill's cabinet. Yet the issues it would cover were seen right away to be crucial both to avoid the mistakes of the prior postwar period, and to keep the homefront morale pointed in a positive direction.[81] Discussion of 'reconstruction' had become politically and practically unavoidable. The original committee's brief stemmed from the work of Sir John Reith, as Minister of Works, whose primary ministerial concern was with the physical environment, but the work subsequently travelled through the hands of Arthur Greenwood (Minister without Portfolio), William Jowitt (successor to Greenwood but in a slightly different capacity) and finally Lord Woolton (as the first Minister of Reconstruction since the 1920s). All of these ministers had a much broader scope for their studies of reconstruction than simply repairing bomb damage. Under Jowitt and Woolton particularly, the term 'reconstruction' was weighted far more to the economic and social postwar ideologies than to the repair of the built environment. Nevertheless, the broader discussion originated with Reith's proposals to the war cabinet.[82]

The Committee on Reconstruction Problems developed after the work of the non-permanent Committee on War Aims concluded a very broad wartime machinery was needed for both successful prosecution of the war and to prepare goals for peacetime.[83] The impetus for the initial machinery of reconstruction discussion came to the Cabinet via Sir John (later Lord) Reith. Although fairly new to the House of Commons, in October 1940 Reith was elevated to the Lords and given the position of Minister of Works and Buildings: a non-Cabinet position, but with serious responsibilities.[84] Reith was to oversee not just repair of war damage and the strict control of building materials, but he also received the first remit to look into postwar reconstruction in the physical sense.[85]

In December 1940 Lord Reith presented the war cabinet with a paper titled the 'Reconstruction of Town and Country'.[86] While focused on the topic of the title, the paper took into account the perceived need for both control of land use and for central planning. Reith laid out his perceived objectives for reconstruction, the principles behind them and the preparatory work he thought should be undertaken. Clearly written, it was a document with great foresight, though only implemented in pieces at best. It is worth noting that Reith also captured the spirit of public feeling and competently projected the tone that accompanied most wartime discussion of reconstruction, as seen above. 'Public attention is now directed on prospects of reconstruction not just because of opportunities in restoration of damaged property but in hope of a fresh start in a new spirit of co-operation and with the high objective of a better Britain.'[87] The memo, while focused on physical reconstruction, managed to persuade Churchill that a larger committee to oversee this important subject was necessary. But Lord Reith was difficult to work with and – perhaps for that reason – he was not able to push his ideas very far into action. In a memo about Churchill's reaction to the Reith document, the Cabinet Secretary Edward Bridges wrote, 'Lord Reith threatens to come and see me. Indeed I narrowly escaped discussing the matter with him.'[88] As Bridges had a reputation for bringing people together and working well with all, this was a revealing comment about Reith's ability to work with others. In the end, however, Reith happily corresponded with Bridges about the committee membership, and deferred to his judgement – an apparently rare display of respect for judgement outside his own.[89]

Churchill soon followed the Reith memo with a cabinet minute stating that 'provision must now be made for the study of postwar problems. It is unnecessary to set up a grandiose Ministry of Reconstruction', and assigned Arthur Greenwood, Minister without Portfolio, to the chair.[90] Bridges had intended for John Anderson, Lord President, to have the chair, but was overridden by Churchill. This appears to be one of several manifestations of Churchill's reluctance to put much effort into reconstruction planning while still in the early stages of the war, and he had said to Bridges: 'We must be very careful not to allow these remote post-war problems to absorb energy which is required, maybe for several years, for the prosecution of the war.'[91] Publicly, however, Churchill stated:

> I must say a word about the functions of the Minister charged with the study of post-war problems and reconstruction. It is not his task to make a new world, comprising a new Heaven, a new earth, and no doubt a new hell (as I am sure that would be necessary in any balanced system). It is not his duty to set up a new order or to create a new heart in the human breast. These tasks must be undertaken by other agencies. The task of my right hon. Friend is to plan in advance a number of large practical steps which it is indispensable to take if our society is to move forward, as it must, which steps can be far larger and taken far more smoothly if they are made with something of the same kind of national unity as has been achieved under the pressure of this present struggle for life.[92]

Illustrating further the complexity that could already be found in postwar issues, the Committee on Reconstruction Problems was soon given a much broader scope of work than Reith had probably envisioned. As well as the task of looking at 'practical schemes of reconstruction', the stated purpose of the committee included the lofty goal 'to prepare a scheme for a post-war European and world system', even suggesting they work towards 'a durable international order'.[93] This had been part of the original remit of the War Aims committee, now absorbed in the new reconstruction committee. Reith's original intent for the committee brief would eventually have to be picked up in various subcommittees. It seems clear that this was essentially a committee of compromise between Labour's loftier social goals, Churchill's war aims and Reith's postwar practicalities. It was probably more short-sighted than originally intended by Reith since the terms of reference stated that the aim was to 'arrange for the preparation of practical schemes of reconstruction, to which effect can be given in a period of, say, three years after the war'.[94] Reith would probably have known that three years was unrealistically brief.

As Reith's diaries show, he expected, after discussion with Bridges, that Anderson as Lord President would chair the committee but then found that Churchill had insisted on Greenwood 'possibly to get [him] shelved'.[95] He also whined about the new structure 'apparently absorbing Attlee's fatuous committee', referring presumably to War Aims. Reith revealed his agreement with Anderson that the choice of committee chair seemed a 'Labour racket', and opined that the Labour ministers were 'wanting to collar the kudos of my job'.[96] Here Reith displays an awareness that Labour was hoping to be seen as the party of planning and foresight, that is, the party for the postwar era.

Smaller additional committees were set up by Reith in 1941, again showing the complexity in postwar planning. One committee – known as the Interdepartmental Advisory Committee on Reconstruction – aimed to keep various ministries from overlap in their work, already a problem in the new structure.[97] Lord Reith, like many others of his time – Labour ministers in particular – saw a need for central planning and hoped to leave his mark on Britain in a tangible way. But he was not politically savvy and though he managed to get the function of physical planning shifted from the Ministry of Health to the Ministry of Works (becoming Works and Planning), he lost his ministerial post – as did Greenwood – in a cabinet shake-up on 22 February 1942.[98]

The office of Minister without Portfolio lapsed and the chairmanship of the reconstruction committee was given to Sir William Jowitt, Paymaster General. In December 1942 Jowitt's appointment was extended and the title of Minister with Portfolio officially added.[99] At this point, the organization for reconstruction discussion became more streamlined, although it also took on a broader scope, with the number of committees increasing, and their various remits made more specific.[100] Jowitt was not well thought of by some of his fellow ministers – Hugh Dalton called him 'weak' and 'useless'[101] – but he knew the law and legislation, having practiced as a barrister and held the post of solicitor-general, and he took a great interest in social reconstruction, particularly the work of the Beveridge report.[102] Jowitt commissioned a survey on public opinion about issues to be faced after the war, the results of which supported the Beveridge recommendations, published in November 1942. The Cabinet then chose to separate the functions of the main reconstruction committee into two areas: 'problems' and – relating to the Beveridge report – 'priorities'.[103] Even if the administrative organization of planning for reconstruction was unstable, the Cabinet felt it important to start working on postwar strategies. In this sense physical planning and socioeconomic planning were not treated as separate issues in the sphere of reconstruction.

In keeping with the wartime culture of secrecy, documents from the reconstruction committees were circulated for internal discussion, not shared with the public, or with Parliament even though popular opinion favoured such discussion – as evidenced by the success of the Beveridge report.[104] Jowitt and the members of the reconstruction committees knew that their work could carry weight and importance, particularly in terms of social and economic reconstruction. Beginning in March 1943, Jowitt had his office compile the committee work into a series of quarterly reports. Only three were produced before yet more changes were to disrupt the reconstruction committee machinery, but they were a barometer of the issues committee members, and ministers, felt were important.[105] At the same time, Churchill told his Cabinet that preparation should start right away on 'rebuilding our shattered dwellings and cities, on which there is or may be found a wide measure of general agreement'.[106] The reports covered two sections labelled 'internal' and 'external'. They dealt with subjects ranging from international relief and military obligations, to the Beveridge plan, a future health service and education. They also covered issues such as labour, industry, food and agriculture, housing and – to a limited extent – town and country planning. In hindsight it is clear the committee remits were far too vast: the complexity of reconstruction planning was enormous. At the time few recognized this though one who did was Lord Cherwell, Paymaster General. His October 1943 cabinet memo stated:

> BEFORE discussing the need for decisions on reconstruction plans we must set out what questions need to be decided. To a certain extent, it is true, all problems are interrelated. Nevertheless, they must be divided into categories and dealt with separately. Otherwise we should have to work out a complete plan for our post-war Utopia, and the only decision needed would be whether to take it or leave it.[107]

This showed a clear understanding that the remit was too large and there was a need for better organization. After nearly three years, the discussion had returned to approximately where Lord Reith had left it. Possibly it was felt Jowitt was not the person to provide the organization. In November 1943 Churchill finally agreed to set up a ministry devoted to reconstruction, appointing a minister – not Jowitt – who would also have a seat in the war cabinet. The appointment was given to Lord Woolton, probably as a compromise with Labour since he was officially 'non-party'.[108] This was to be a better-organized entity for reconstruction strategy, with responsibility for interdepartmental task monitoring, avoiding overlap and identifying problems not yet being covered by any officials. But the primary responsibility for plan-making stayed with the existing departments, and Woolton did not intend to create an executive group or gather a large staff.[109] However, the minister's responsibilities still encompassed the whole field of reconstruction policy, if primarily as a coordinating body.[110]

After numerous ministerial and administrative changes, the subject of reconstruction finally found a stable home in Whitehall. Having been under Reith and Greenwood, Anderson and then Jowitt, Lord Woolton remained at the helm until the end of the Coalition in 1945.[111] The staff of the Office of the Minister of Reconstruction was small but in its eighteen months produced numerous reports on health, social services, housing, employment and other subjects.[112] Though short-lived, this Office provided a more organized and comprehensive approach to the subject of reconstruction planning which went right back to that advocated originally by Lord Reith in 1940. Planning would not disappear, and as victory looked more certain it seemed to take on increased significance.

Although there was still some conflict between departments with overlapping roles the organization under Woolton at least helped clarify and delineate postwar ministerial, or departmental, responsibilities for postwar reconstruction. For example, the Ministries of Works, of Health and later of Town and Country Planning, all had some role in the provision of housing, as well as varying levels of departmental interest in land use itself. Government leaders appear to have realized that if 'planning' was going to happen there would need to be comprehensive clear organization, good coordination and a consensus, wherever possible, on priorities. The following section describes the key aspects of issues identified under the various reconstruction entities as they related to physical reconstruction, and how they were managed.

III. *Considering Physical Reconstruction: Town Plans and Planning*

Town and country planning at a national level has its origins in nineteenth-century public health legislation. But not until the early twentieth century was there further general legislation containing planning law as distinct from housing provisions. Legislation in 1909 permitted local authorities to draw up plans for schemes, usually in connection with the development of new housing areas. In 1932 the provisions were extended to almost any type of land, whether developed or as yet untouched.[113] Under the 1909 Act, the central authority for planning was the Local Government Board but from 1919 this function moved to the Ministry of Health. Generally speaking, the planning efforts of the interwar period, and particularly the 1930s, were more focused on improving living conditions, or creating new places (i.e., garden cities), than about replanning city centres as they then existed.

The recognition of the need for controls on development and industrial location had prompted creation of a Royal Commission in 1937 chaired by Justice Barlow, tasked with reporting on this issue. Such an 'advance towards a new conception of planning under positive central direction' set the stage for Reith's wartime work.[114] The Barlow Report was issued in 1940, and in October it came to partial fruition with the transition of the small department called the Office of Works into the Ministry of Works and Buildings. Under Reith's leadership, two further reports were commissioned in 1941, one under Lord Justice Scott to study rural land use, and the other under Lord Justice Uthwatt to study the issue of compensation and betterment which would arise from state control of land use.[115] The Uthwatt Report would be key in regards to postwar reconstruction.[116] It is worth noting that these reports did not emerge without debate and disagreement around the recommendations. While reconstruction rhetoric tended to optimism, the detailed practicalities of compensation, betterment and land use would continue to be hotly contested.[117]

Reith's new ministry was also given responsibility for coordinating the planning of postwar reconstruction, following his December 1940 cabinet memo, although the Ministry of Health retained its statutory planning functions. Specifically directed at physical reconstruction and town planning in bombed cities was a panel of experts Reith created in early 1941 called the Consultative Panel on Physical Reconstruction.[118] The Panel was to prepare for the formulation of legislation for planning machinery and to advise on the 'interrelationship' between parts of this work, as well as to make suggestions for best practices. The group was set up as a body of specialists from the fields of business and planning, all with experience in planning and reconstruction. They were meant to be consulted individually, according to the insistence of the Lord President, Sir John Anderson. Reith made sure they met twice, however, in April and October 1941.[119] Reith also appointed a subcommittee called the Reconstruction Areas Group, composed partly of members of the panel, formed to generate expert advice on problems and issues foreseen in the redevelopment of bomb-damaged cities. The group brought local authority and central government officials together, and while they might have played a significant role in the preparation for rebuilding blitzed cities, neither entity lasted longer than Reith's brief tenure.[120]

Lord Reith's impetus for early planning – including his infamous encouragement to 'plan boldly and comprehensively' – set the tone for town planning and land use planning for the remainder of the war.[121] Though Reith did not stay in his position past February 1942, the very able Lord Portal followed him in his role at the renamed Works and Planning.[122] In 1942 the functions related to postwar physical reconstruction, and the staff of the Town Planning Division, had been transferred to the Ministry of Works and Buildings which became Works and Planning.[123] Less than two weeks after this formal change the ministry was assigned to Lord Portal when Lord Reith was moved out of government. Lord Portal was a competent if less dynamic leader than Reith.

Planning for reconstruction during wartime was clearly an administrative merry-go-round. The government machinery changed with regularity, although probably often improving from a town planner's perspective.[124] Portal stayed at the Ministry of Works when in February 1943 the Ministry of Town and Country Planning (hereafter MTCP) was established by an act of the same name. So, with the statutory planning functions transferred to it, a body now completely focused on planning was created. The new ministry was also charged with 'securing consistency and continuity in the framing and execution of a national policy concerning the use and development of land in England and Wales'.[125] The MTCP would remain essentially unchanged until the end of the first Attlee government in 1950. Early on the three main areas of departmental responsibility included: liaising with local planning authorities, approving planning schemes, formulating a national planning policy and drafting legislation to facilitate wartime control – and later further controls – of development as well as oversight for the planning of postwar redevelopment in both war-damaged and blighted areas.[126]

The first planning minister appointed was the Conservative MP William Morrison. The initial brief for Morrison was to implement the Uthwatt Report. He was therefore responsible for taking the initial wartime Town and Country Planning Act through parliament. While it was considered 'a milestone in legislation for building control' – though apparently Morrison had had little to do with its gestation – he was caught in the crossfire between Labour MPs who wanted more intervention and Conservatives who wanted as little as possible.[127] Morrison stayed at this post in the Caretaker government of May 1945, remaining until Labour came into office in July of that year.

Under Morrison's leadership an advisory group for blitzed cities was again formed. Similar to the body that had briefly been gathered under Reith, the

Advisory Panel on Redevelopment of City Centres was appointed in May 1943.[128] Civil servants who had worked in planning throughout the war (originally in the Ministry of Health) were aware that the government was late in organizing machinery for assisting the blitzed cities after the war, and encouraged Morrison to approve the panel. The terms of reference were: '[To] examine the main planning issues involved in the redevelopment of city centres which have been devastated by bombing, to define and measure the problems of finance and organisation connected therewith and to set out the relevant considerations on which central and local Government policy in regard to such development should be based.'[129] The Panel spent the next year surveying seven cities. The survey work was thorough, involving numerous city visits, discussions with local authorities, reviews of plans where they existed and concluded with a report, produced in August 1944.[130] Suggestions were made for financial assistance to the cities, and for planning beyond the provisions of the concurrently drafted Town and Country Planning Act of 1944.

Side by side with the Panel's activities under the new ministry, a technical planning section – moved from the Ministry of Health – had begun work on an advisory publication. Though most of the work was apparently completed during wartime the publication, titled *The Redevelopment of Central Areas*, was not actually published until 1947.[131]

Clearly by the end of the war a great deal of energy, thought, manpower and time had been spent thinking about postwar and the impending issues of reconstruction. By 1943 there was a permanent planning structure in place, and a clear leadership established. But throughout the war constant changes also resulted in disconnected preparations and the potential for any kind of 'corporate memory' was missing until the MTCP was created. The issues of reconstruction were very clearly multifaceted, and were seen as such, but the Coalition government went through so many changes in internal leadership and organization that much valuable time was wasted. And while government was disorganized, the complexity of organizing reconstruction issues in the war still foreshadowed the actual complexity of the postwar period.

IV. *Physical Realities Faced After War*

One task undertaken by the several advisory groups and panels that worked under the planning flag in wartime was collecting information on the condition of Britain's blitzed cities. In order to clarify the foundations of postwar problems in bombed areas, some description of the destruction is necessary. What kind of physical destruction was wrought by the German bombers? What was the state of the postwar economy, both national and local? What might be the postwar issues with building materials and availability of labour?

German raids caused the majority of wartime destruction in 1940 and 1941, with later raids in 1942 for emotional effect only.[132] Bombing was estimated to have destroyed 75,000 shops, 42,000 commercial properties and 25,000 factories.[133] Additionally the government estimated that 450,000 homes were destroyed or made uninhabitable.[134] At a 1945 Cabinet meeting, Sir John Anderson, Chancellor of the Exchequer, stated that the cost of damage from bombing was estimated at £1,150 million.[135] This was a growing figure: Anderson had already stated in Commons the previous year that the estimated cost of reconstructing war damage would be £50 million per year for two years and then less going forward.[136]

The MTCP surveyed each of their administrative regions for bomb damage statistics in the larger towns and cities. The totals appear in Table 2.1. Statistics were created on an estimated basis, using numbers of houses destroyed and an average acreage per house.[137] With much scattered damage not included, the total of over 2,500 acres included only destruction in thirty-five urban areas.[138] The MTCP had additionally surveyed cities before the end of the war, attempting to count numbers of destroyed and damaged (without differentiating) shops, offices and commercial buildings, as well as factories, including warehouses.[139] In neither case were numbers accurate. Later, in a 1954 article on the rebuilding of bombed cities, *The Architects' Journal* cited statistics gathered from local authorities in the provincial cities themselves.[140] The journal created a table of central area bomb damage, comparing eight major provincial cities by loss of square footage per head of population. The estimated range was from three to just over twenty square feet per head. The estimated cost of rebuilding was not given, nor was it estimated by the MTCP (see Table 2.1 on next page for statistics).

The destruction of buildings was a particular problem due to the comparatively long durable life of building stock versus goods and machinery. Though the bombing destroyed plenty of both, buildings have a much longer life – easily by fifty times that of machinery, or more.[141] Therefore replacing building stocks in a normal economy would use a lower percentage of labour as it happens less often, so in a postwar situation far more labour would be needed. In a non-war situation typically more labour is involved in the production of shorter-lived goods and machinery. Yet in this postwar era there would be a higher demand on the resources of the building industry, including labour, for many years to come. Once stock had been replaced to either prewar or (then) current demand levels, the building industry would likely be facing the opposite condition of having too much labour, and possibly too many materials, for the lower demands. Such demands are very difficult to predict.

Losses covered a wide range of building types. Industry and major transport were clearly the primary targets, but the destruction of shops, offices, warehouses, factories, churches and other institutions was widespread. The destruction of housing was vast and very much in the public eye, and as a basic need would command a high priority when it came time to rebuild.[142] By the end of the war, building houses was clearly more important to the public than building shops, offices and possibly even industry. But the government occupied a difficult position: the postwar economic situation imposed such a terrible burden in the balance of payments (primarily to the Dollar Area) that production of exports

Table 2.1 Bomb damage stats by county borough (London boroughs not listed)

County borough	Acres damaged (est.)
Cities on MTCP blitz list (18)	
Liverpool C.B.	208
Plymouth C.B.	168
Portsmouth C.B.	165
Coventry C.B.	160
Southampton C.B.	145
Hull C.B.	136
Bristol C.B.	121
Sheffield C.B.	108
Norwich C.B.	78
Exeter C.B.	68
Manchester C.B.	61
Birmingham C.B.	60
Great Yarmouth C.B.	50
Swansea C.B.	42
Canterbury C.B.	26
Dover M.B.	25
South Shields C.B.	19
Lowestoft C.B.	15
Cities not on list of 18	
Birkenhead C.B.	76
Salford C.B.	65
Bath C.B.	55
Wallasey C.B.	43
Sunderland C.B.	40
Grimsby C.B.	24
Barrow-in-Furness C.B.	23
Folkestone M.B.	20
Teignmouth C.B.	20
Gosport [C.B.?]	17
Eastbourne C.B.	15
Hastings C.B.	15
Nuneaton C.B.	15
Tynemouth C.B.	15
Weston-Super-Mare	13
	2,111

Notes: Birmingham was shown at 495, but included blight, which has been removed. For purposes of selecting the 18 cities, Birkenhead and Wallasey may have been included with Liverpool; Salford with Manchester; Sunderland with Newcastle; Grimsby with Hull; Nuneaton with Coventry. All figures from HLG 71/601 and 602.

became a top priority.[143] Britain needed to build more production facilities but the materials produced, including building supplies, would need to be shared between exports and domestic use.

The local economic situation in provincial blitzed cities had as much or more impact on local authorities as the national situation. Local authorities suffered the loss of rates payable from the bombed out businesses and homes, with the scale of loss dependent on types of buildings as well as amount destroyed.[144] It proved nearly impossible to collect rates on premises that were uninhabitable. Additionally, the cities had to replace infrastructure damaged or destroyed by bombing: roads, sewers, power lines, water, telephone and more were all badly affected. How could a city pay to rebuild its infrastructure when it also had significantly less income because of the loss of rates from bomb damage? Even if the cities possessed the funds to rebuild the infrastructure, where would they obtain the materials? Steel shortages would be severe and, as much as the country could manufacture, there was – as mentioned – a necessity to export large amounts. Timber was always a large import product, mainly used for housing and household goods, and imports could further affect the dollar trade deficit. Concrete, bricks and other materials needed for building roads, sewers, shops, warehouses, offices, factories, schools and houses were all in short supply, yet had to come from the same stocks, preferably domestic. The world economy was precariously balanced, and Western Europe in particular depended on rebuilding to start a recovery and move towards some level of equilibrium. Britain was only a piece of this larger picture, and while the circumstances would filter into all industries, they were very possibly felt most significantly by the building industry.[145] The issue of labour availability to carry out the rebuilding was also to be key, particularly in the immediate postwar. Demobilization would be slow and therefore labour shortages would severely affect the building industry.

With Britain's provincial cities suffering severe losses to their infrastructure and buildings, the replacement costs would be high and the time frame for rebuilding slow. The incoming 1945 government faced severe difficulties: a devastated economy, a badly damaged infrastructure (ports, roads, railways, etc.) and even a new – and still changing – world role to deal with. All of this would severely challenge politicians and officials alike, even while significant time had been spent during the war attempting to prepare for the future.

Conclusion

The most notable feature of all rhetoric concerning physical reconstruction in the period during and immediately following the war was the positive language used. Whether the discourse focused on opportunities created by German bombing or the potential for modernizing old, medieval towns and cities, there was little negativity. But of course this would not have suited either the coalition trying to keep up morale, or the parties vying for seats in an election. The words used indicated an upbeat approach, the potential for change and improvement, and the increasing tendency towards dependence on professionals in the planning and design professions. Notably lacking was a strong sense of the grave shortages to come, the difficulties of demobilization, and the rebuilding of the building labour force, as well as issues around geographical distribution of that labour.

Although British leaders seemed aware of their country's near bankruptcy, or at least its shortages, there was little tempering of the reconstruction language. Even when questioning how the rebuilding would be paid for, there was a sense of 'we'll figure it out' or an assumed reliance on government to both provide funds and to create legislation to fairly compensate for damage and frame new land use controls. In the end the views taken seem overly optimistic. In particular, the lack of a realistic approach to the practicalities of rebuilding was largely missing. It was not ignored, but certainly in hindsight wartime discussion had set blitzed cities up for a big letdown. Officials, planners, politicians and voters were not to know that the bomb sites would last for not just the first ten years after the cessation of hostilities, but for many more.

This chapter has given an introduction to the framework of reconstruction planning and the machinery created in Whitehall by the end of the war. The scale of destruction and the significance of the task of rebuilding were unprecedented in Britain. Yet there is also an overwhelming sense of positive possibility, particularly in the rebuilding of bombed cities, and a sense that these cities that had faced German bombing would receive priority for rebuilding when it eventually began.

A deeper look at the mechanisms of postwar rebuilding – of economic restrictions and materials, of legislation and the actions of central and local government – in the following chapters will tell us that much of what happened in the initial decade after the war depended on decisions of civil servants, of locally appointed or elected officials, and the relationship and interplay among them. Capital funds were not in government hands – the coffers were emptied to fight the war – but there was a huge amount of capital in the hands of private individuals and companies that had been severely restricted in their wartime investment. This study tells the story of what happened: in central planning, materials rationing, in the creation and implementation of new laws and in the cities themselves.

Chapter 3

TREASURY MANDARINS: THE APPARATUS OF POSTWAR ECONOMIC PLANNING

We should bury a number of awkward quarrelling points such as ... blitzed cities.

> – F. F. Turnbull, Chairman, IPC (1949–53)[1]

This comment, made in October 1953, stands in stark contrast to the discourse analysed in the previous chapter. Yet – as this chapter will show – even eight years after the war ended, and twelve years after most of the bombing, there was still no priority being given to the blitzed cities. It took both time and an economic crisis, or two, to push the Labour government into serious economic planning and controls. Meanwhile the wartime system of building licenses remained in place to control construction.[2] Most blitzed cities were not ready to begin construction before 1947, as they were still working out plans as well as learning the new requirements of the Town and Country Planning Act of 1944.[3] While most histories of reconstruction demonstrate an understanding of the shortages of materials and labour, and acknowledge the existence of controls, there is little published to elucidate how these problems were dealt with. Some histories note the significance of controls in restricting building in the city centres, but there is an historiographical gap around an understanding, much less an awareness, of the importance of the Investment Programmes Committee (IPC).[4]

This chapter will discuss the background of the IPC, a cabinet subcommittee charged from 1947 with assessing priorities and overseeing the control of capital investment in building, plant and machinery throughout the national economy. Though active for just over six years of the postwar period, the IPC exercised substantial control over capital investment in the United Kingdom at a crucial time politically and economically. The committee's impact on the blitzed cities meant a long period of inactivity until the first public announcement in February 1949 gave a select group of cities allocations of steel, thus signalling the start of some allowance towards reconstruction in city centres.[5] But throughout the period of controls – from 1949 to 1953 – allocations to allow rebuilding in the blitzed cities remained remarkably small. Understanding why this happened requires an examination of the origins and administration of the controls. This chapter will explain how the Cabinet mandated the IPC with responsibility for the distribution of capital investment nationally. With steel and other materials in short supply, the IPC would determine where supplies should be channelled in the best interests of the economy.

While the IPC exerted considerable influence over capital investment, in building, plant and machinery throughout the postwar period, economic historians have revealed relatively little about the committee's membership or how it worked.[6]

One of its former members, Sir Alec Cairncross, who wrote extensively on government policymaking and implementation in the postwar period, barely acknowledged the IPC's existence.[7] Similarly, Sir Edwin Plowden, who initiated the committee, says very little about its role.[8] Authors such as Cole, Broadberry and Crafts, Dow, Shonfield, Tomlinson, Toye, and Worswick and Ady all cover the workings of economic planning, policy and implementation in this period, but none of them explain the role of the IPC in significant depth, or how the controls were created and may have worked.[9] One of the earliest examinations of the postwar economy was Andrew Shonfield's *British Economic Policy since the War*. Shonfield produced a highly critical examination of the governments of 1945 and 1951, and it remains a key work, though more recently surpassed by historians such as Tomlinson, Chick and Tiratsoo.[10] Cairncross's inside knowledge is an excellent guide, but there are drawbacks to over-reliance on his information: while an insider, he is perhaps handicapped by developed opinions of both the ministers he worked with and the civil servants he worked alongside, as well as being quite close to the heart of the machinery itself. As J. C. R. Dow said in a 1987 review: 'Sir Alec may be right in suggesting that this government was singularly ill-prepared for the economic problems it was to face. But the problems were both new and large.'[11] Also reviewing Cairncross's *Years of Recovery*, Austin Robinson, a former 'Economic Adviser' who worked with Cairncross and Plowden, declared that the book failed to acknowledge a crucial aspect of economic planning in that era: the lack of steel and the necessity of rationing it – in essence the raison d'etre of the IPC.[12]

One point that doesn't come across in the economic histories, however, is the obscurity of the IPC. This chapter will argue its obscurity was one of the most important aspects to understanding the committee's role and function. Its 'hiddenness' also plays a major role in the understanding of the wider picture of postwar reconstruction. As with similar committees in this period, the Cabinet ruled that IPC documents be kept 'secret', its minutes narrowly circulated among members and a few ministers and officials who had some direct involvement. Members of Parliament and many civil servants were kept in the dark. The working of the committee and its importance to many industries – and to the economy as a whole – calls out for more investigation by historians. This chapter will provide a start. It will examine the machinery of government tasked with reconstruction, during the period when the government sought to control inflation, increase production and provide for the needs of the population. Beginning with the early postwar period of inaction – in building especially – it will also look at political leadership and how postwar politicians and officials attempted to influence the British economy. Starting with a description of the attempts to develop an economic 'infrastructure' this chapter describes how the IPC came about, what its functions were, how it operated and why it influenced rebuilding so heavily. The conflicts inherent in seeking to implement strict controls will be examined. And finally the shift into a new Churchill government from 1951 will illustrate the very strong influence of the civil service and the surprising lack of change under the Conservatives, particularly – again – in reference to rebuilding of blitzed cities.

I. *Early Postwar Period*

When elected in 1945, though surprised to be in office given the popularity of Churchill, the Labour government formed by Clement Attlee included many members with wartime experience. They clearly understood the priorities of their constituents.[13] The priority of the electorate was housing – inadequate long before the start of war, and more drastically in shortage by 1945 – yet the government understood equally the crucial role of industry.[14] British business suffered massively under a war economy with exports curtailed by circumstances as well as changing production priorities. In meeting after meeting, discussion focused on the balance of payments crisis, particularly in the dollar area. Britain had to buy too much from American suppliers, without selling enough in return to pay for it.[15] Economic management took precedence within government, though even with conflicting views among ministers and officials there was some consensus on how to manage the problem.[16] As Herbert Morrison later noted: 'All these special problems made economic planning more difficult but also, in our view, made it more necessary.'[17]

Rationing, which worked as a kind of crude demand management by choking off demand, took precedence at this stage.[18] However, production for export quickly became a top priority among government policymakers. Britain needed to build more production facilities but the materials produced, including building supplies, would also largely need to be exported rather than used domestically.[19] On top of all this, central government was near bankrupt from the cost of fighting the war.[20] The importance of proceeding cautiously can be seen in an early Cabinet conclusion: '[T]he Government should at once establish the principle that the next five years would be a period of transition in which the exercise of emergency powers by the Executive would be as necessary as it had been in war.'[21]

The incoming Labour government of 1945 was lucky to have significant wartime restrictions in place to enable control of materials and – to some extent – labour. The government saw the need to control these crucial components, in order to prevent severe cost inflation.[22] Alongside solving the balance of payments crisis, the postwar governments prioritized the prevention of inflation, which was therefore central to most of the domestic economic planning measures implemented.[23] Having been forced into savings by wartime rations and restrictions, Britons – both individuals and corporations – had money to spend, but not much to spend it on.[24] This inflationary situation of course applied to many parts of the economy, from the building industry to consumer goods and more. In the building industry, for example, should demand be allowed to dictate prices, builders would likely choose to build higher profit mansions over affordable housing, and higher end retail and office space for multiples (chain stores) over basic shops for traders.[25] This would particularly affect the bombed-out small businesses that suffered huge financial losses through destruction of both their stocks and their premises. In this vein Aneurin Bevan stated in a 1947 debate on housing: 'what we have done in two years is to deny to the building industry the right to build luxury buildings while people are needing houses'. Bevan further questioned what might happen without controls in place: 'who is going to build houses for the agricultural workers?'[26]

With severe losses throughout Britain's infrastructure and the damage or destruction of thousands of buildings, replacement costs were bound to be high and the time frame for rebuilding much slower than renewed starts in manufacturing. The government was forced to make choices based on compromises between public desire and economic possibility. Research reveals that the realities of policymaking – and prioritizing – within the Attlee government were not so much about building the welfare state by spending on housing and social services (a view expressed by historians such as Corelli Barnett), but actually to put industry and production first with housing a close second: realizing the ties of housing to the availability of workers and hence the scale of production.[27] After defence and nationalized industry, education and health followed. Clearly the greatest difficulty faced, though, was often making the crucial decisions on economic priorities.[28]

II. *Personalities and the Making of Priorities*

Although Clement Attlee remained at the head of the Labour governments throughout the 1945–51 period, the individuals involved in managing the economy changed several times so the broader sweep of economic policy was a shifting entity, even in the first few years alone.[29] Attlee's first Chancellor of the Exchequer was Hugh Dalton, who influenced policymaking in the Treasury for less than sixteen months before he was forced to resign. Sir Stafford Cripps, who had been appointed as the newly created 'Minister for Economic Affairs' lasted only two months in the position before being moved to the Exchequer with Dalton's departure.[30] When Cripps's health failed almost three years later, Hugh Gaitskell was promoted to the chancellorship, lasting until the government lost the 1951 election.

Dalton felt that there were six problems facing the Treasury at the start of his tenure: industry's reconversion including labour and expenditure issues; demobilization and other transitional problems including the avoidance of unemployment, industrial unrest and inflation; fulfilling the Labour manifesto's aim to create better social services; reducing taxes in total, while attempting to close the widening gap between rich and poor; the nationalization of industry as promised; and, crucially, correcting the economic imbalance created by the huge need for dollar imports which were important in maintaining employment and preventing starvation.[31] Chick notes that it was these physical shortages that allowed Dalton (as Chancellor) to attempt to operate under a cheap money policy.[32] But his determination to reduce excess demand was a priority in his November 1947 budget.[33] Whether Dalton had any thoughts on 'rebuilding' Britain, beyond the rebuilding of the economy, is unclear. His diary lacks any mention of physical reconstruction and it seems safe to conclude that physical rebuilding was not a personal priority during his time as Chancellor.[34] Despite this he continued the wartime reconstruction rhetoric, along with others, in Parliament.[35]

When Dalton was forced to resign in November 1947, the administrative transition to Sir Stafford Cripps's leadership as Chancellor was relatively seamless, helped by his experience at the Board of Trade (BT). Cripps was the BT president from 1945 until his appointment in September 1947 as Minister for Economic Affairs. This newly created position was meant to oversee long-term economic policy, and put Cripps in the thick of economic policymaking.[36] However, the transition brought important changes. Dalton had been a believer in Keynes' ideology of government intervention within a free market, while Cripps was – at least ideologically – more markedly socialist.[37] Though Cripps held very definite ideas about economic policy, he had no real background in economics (as a chemist turned lawyer), even though the new position gave him 'a unique concentration of authority in determining economic policy'.[38] His only previous experience in a related field had been in the coalition's Ministry of Aircraft Production where he had learned much about industry. Furthermore, Cripps's difference in outlook to Dalton's brought changes to both policymaking and the machinery of government from late 1947.[39] Cripps prioritized exports, but favoured a focus on capital investment in industry over housing and even over other more basic needs and amenities.[40] In fact he had many disagreements with Aneurin Bevan over prioritizing housing, even though it had been part of Labour's manifesto and was clearly a priority to the voters.[41] Like Dalton, Cripps made few references to reconstruction in his time as Chancellor, with no mention of any consideration of rebuilding bomb-damaged areas, much less any prioritization. Almost ironically, Cripps's constituency as an MP was Bristol East, a seat in a heavily bomb-damaged city. Though he never took up the case for Bristol or any other blitzed city in Commons debates – most likely because he sat on the Attlee cabinet – he had ample opportunity to influence, even in small part, the prioritization of blitzed cities from within the Treasury and Central Economic Planning Staff (CEPS). As will be shown, he did not.

Cripps's health deteriorated late in the first Labour term and Hugh Gaitskell replaced him as Chancellor. Gaitskell's background was well suited to the job. He had both studied and taught economics, and was well-versed in economic policy.[42] His experience at the Ministry of Fuel and Power in the fuel crisis of 1947 had highlighted his leadership skills, and in February 1950 he was made Minister of

Economic Affairs. Like his predecessors, Gaitskell does not seem to have been aware of the physical rebuilding issues.[43]

As historians have shown, the problems faced by the Exchequer throughout the immediate postwar period, and even well into the second Churchill administration, were on a massive scale: the vast difficulties of the dollar shortage, demobilization and labour shortages, a fuel crisis, a convertibility crisis and enormous inflationary pressure easily superseded notice of the relativity quiet and economically unimportant issue of (re)building city centres.[44] More broadly, over the course of this period ministers and officials also dealt with – among other issues – the sudden termination of Lend-Lease assistance from America, the military rearmament for both the Korean and 'cold' wars, the devaluation of sterling, as well as the ongoing balance of payments crisis.[45] Whitehall was focused on national interests over the less crucial, though locally emotional, issues of housing and rebuilding.

III. *The Institutional Infrastructure and Origins of the Investment Programmes Committee*

Few publications have discussed the conflicts, and potential confusion, within the administrative machinery created by Attlee in his new government.[46] Many committees and boards appear to have overlapped, creating potential conflicts. In this period a series of economic planning entities were formed, including: the new Minister for Economic Affairs (additional to the Treasury) with its Central Economic Planning Staff, as well as an Economic Section (in the Cabinet Office), a Central Statistical Office, an Economic Planning Board, Capital Issues Committee, Economic Policy Committee (EPC), Economic Advisory Council, Lord President's Committee, National Investment Council and a proposed but not instituted National Investment Board plus the aforementioned IPC – one of many subcommittees. While certainly the economy – and the planning of it – had many facets, as it still does today, in a time that predates email and other forms of easy coordination government had difficulty forming and implementing coherent policy from among so many groups. It appears that these groups had varying duties, a wide range of frequency of meetings, and for some a very limited role.[47] This new and growing form of government was a huge change from before the war, with the continued proliferation of Cabinet committees, as begun in wartime, and the increased importance of their role.[48] Already the attempted planning and control of the economy demonstrates the complexity inherent in reconstruction generally, although it was often self-imposed.

The division of economic work gave the Chancellor of the Exchequer and the Treasury continued responsibility for the budget. During the war an Economic Section had been added in the Cabinet to deal with general economic oversight and specific and short-term policy decisions.[49] Initially in the postwar government the Lord President's office had responsibility for the remaining economic committees which took a broader view.[50] But in 1947, in reaction to several crises – the fuel crisis, the convertibility crisis and the balance of payments crisis – the Cabinet created the Ministry of Economic Affairs (MEA) with Sir Stafford Cripps as its head, moving from the Board of Trade.[51] Cripps had a small staff, called the Central Economic Planning Staff (CEPS), which was directed by Chief Planning Officer Edwin Plowden. The MEA focused on broad economic issues, and a longer-term plan. It is odd, however, that Cripps was appointed 'minister for economic affairs, independent of the Treasury, and responsible for economic planning', as this seems to have removed power from the Chancellor and/or the Economic Section.[52] But all this was rendered moot: less than two months after establishment of the MEA, it was moved with Cripps to the Treasury, and the result was 'a merger of economic planning and policy with financial and budgetary matters'.[53]

Despite this broad structure for economic planning, the Labour government still struggled with managing the economy.[54] Shortages of labour and materials had become an especially pressing problem, leading the Ministry of Works to commission a report on the distribution of building materials.[55] Almost concurrently, during the convertibility crisis of August 1947, the conclusions from a Cabinet discussion of Dalton's memorandum on the ongoing balance of payments problems stated: '[T]he application of the principle that capital investment should be curtailed should be worked out by the Central Economic Planning Staff in consultation with the Departments concerned.'[56] Plowden's staff immediately took this up and set up a temporary committee on investment.

The Cabinet then approved the new IPC, which was tasked with reporting on potential controls to help solve the problems with labour and materials shortages.[57] Set up as a subcommittee of the Official Steering Committee on Economic Development, the IPC was chaired by Plowden and included representatives from key departments.[58] The new committee's brief was very similar to the wartime (and still existent) Investment Working Party, under which the control of building supplies and investment had been managed. The curtailment of capital investment, as mandated, was to be applied through allocations of capital investment – drastically limited by shifts in wartime production to munitions, armaments, aircraft and many other defence necessities.[59]

From 1945 to 1947 the Attlee government relied on exhortation of industry – a strategy that inherently lacked coordination and failed to get productivity moving.[60] In October 1947 the IPC came back to the Cabinet and ominously reported, '[H]ome investment has been planned and started on a scale well beyond our capacity to carry out at reasonable speed with the materials hitherto available.'[61] The report recommended controlling investment in various ways including applying labour ceilings in several areas, in an attempt to control manpower resources. It also suggested limiting new housing and placing restrictions on steel tonnage through sponsoring departments. The report stated that plans for 'rebuilding war-damaged city centres [should] be delayed.'[62] The Cabinet approved the report, including 'the recommendation of the Investment Programmes Committee that there should be continued supervision of the investment programme.'[63] The Treasury followed up the work of this temporary committee with the 1947 publication of a white paper, 'Capital Investment in 1948', that suggested ceilings for labour numbers in various sectors of building across the domestic economy.[64] The detail on suggested investment caps were divided into sections under two categories –'building & civil engineering' and 'plant & machinery'.[65] Blitzed cities received short shrift in the report: 'Work on new offices and other commercial buildings will be allowed only in exceptional circumstances, even though this must have the effect of delaying plans for rebuilding the centres of cities damaged during the war.'[66]

At this point the Cabinet had agreed to the continued – more formal – attempt to control capital investment, and accepted a new 'reconstituted' IPC as an official part of the already cumbersome economic planning structure.[67] The membership of the new IPC shifted noticeably from a higher-level group of ministers and top-level civil servants to mainly mid-ranking civil servants, such as undersecretaries.[68] Plowden and the Cabinet Secretary, Norman Brooke, intended this shift to create a committee of experienced civil servants without vested interests in their own departments who therefore could plan Britain's investment objectively.[69] This was explicitly stated in a Cabinet memorandum: 'The Departmental officials on the Committee have been appointed, not as representatives of their Departments, but as individuals with knowledge and experience of matters affecting the supply of investment goods and services.'[70]

The IPC began holding regular meetings in January 1948. Their remit, summarized here, was as follows: (i) To draw up general investment priorities; (ii) to approve departmental investment programmes and in the light of them to draw up national investment programmes; (iii) to consider departmental building labour ceilings; (iv) to have general oversight over all investment programmes; (v) to approve major projects for capital investment above £500,000 in value.[71] The last item gave rise to such long discussions of individual projects that two months later the Cabinet removed this task, and the focus shifted to budgeting by investment type through departments.[72]

The IPC working papers are full of discussions on the levels of investment requested by each department or ministry, with ministry representatives occasionally invited to state their department's needs at IPC meetings. Neither the IPC nor the Treasury published another white paper on investment, instead producing annual reports on allowances, issued as internal Cabinet documents marked 'secret'.[73] For this reason most ministry representatives only saw their own allowances and not the comparative data. While they certainly corresponded with each other, it is clear that colleagues shared information about departmental limits.[74] In examining economic planning decisions made by the Attlee government, the obfuscation of this part of the process was embedded in the existence of the IPC.

The membership and specific function of the IPC was unknown outside of Whitehall – and often within Whitehall, including an initial invisibility from members of Parliament.[75] Documents generated by the IPC were circulated to members and occasionally to other civil servants working on relevant issues. Cabinet members saw memoranda only when IPC members thought it necessary, otherwise decisions were made in a virtual economic cocoon. This method of policymaking had two side effects that are overlooked by many historians.[76]

First, that the decisions being made in terms of priorities and investment policy were primarily discussed and determined among civil servants, not politicians or ministers. While the Cabinet was kept informed occasionally about the investment 'programme' as a whole, they did not set the priorities. Instead officials, mainly in the Treasury, Economic Section and CEPS, set them. That is, the government allowed so-called experts to make important and far-reaching decisions.[77] Disputes were resolved occasionally between ministers – such as the Minister of Health and the Chancellor of the Exchequer on housing questions – but only when irresolvable within the committee.

Second, decisions were made which had to be justified to both Parliament and the public, but they would be 'justified' by ministers who had no say in the decision they were forced to support. While this was normal working practice in government – officials made decisions on behalf of their ministers, and ministers had to accept decisions agreed on by the Cabinet as a whole – under the IPC the decisions had far-reaching effects, particularly in the blitzed cities and other building programmes. Such decisions were approved only generally by Cabinet and not in detail. Often, the decisions had a greater effect on smaller or more controllable programmes like the blitzed cities. Additionally, the process often resulted in contemporary confusion and obfuscation among ministers and MPs, ministries and departments, as well as the public who were affected.[78] The foremost examples of this problem were found in the Ministry of Health and the Ministry of Town and Country Planning.

Neither ministry had a seat on the IPC, yet both were enormously, almost uniquely, affected by the decisions made. The Minister of Health had to answer parliamentary questions on housing numbers, while the Minister of Town and Country Planning answered for non-governmental and non-industrial sectors, including blitzed cities. It is clear from the initial correspondence on membership that officials emphasized the need to have a 'disinterested' committee, one that could make objective decisions and would not have a serious stake in the outcome.[79] In practice, the housing issues were of enough importance to be brought into Cabinet discussions, but under the Attlee administration issues regarding the blitzed cities were not brought into the Cabinet.[80] The Ministry of Town and Country Planning (MTCP) had been created first by separating planning work from the Ministry of Works, as well as shifting the technical planning staff, originally from the Ministry of Health. It fell to the MTCP then to create and manage the planning acts, then to oversee urban renewal for both blitz and blight, and later to take on the oversight for New Towns.[81] By virtue of being the local authorities' point of contact for planning and land acquisition, the MTCP became the default ministry to answer to local officials. And while many of the building types required in the city centres might have come under the purview of the Board of Trade, in this period that department was focused almost completely on export industries.[82]

The IPC attempted to oversee allocations of capital investment in buildings, infrastructure, plant and machinery from 1947 until it was dissolved in 1953. The controls for building operated through the licence system, continued from wartime, which controlled all construction starts. The Ministry of Works operated the licence system and in the initial set of controls implemented by the IPC this was done through allocating steel amounts. However, steel usage and availability varied too much and soon this control was changed to licensing based on a cost-of-building allocation. IPC members decided, amid much debate, where resources should be directed, how to prioritize nationally and – later – where cuts could be made when pressure came to bear in other areas. Coordination was difficult. Rosenberg noted: 'Planning on an exclusively national level, in other words, failed entirely to take account of the geographical location of resources and their immobility. Labour in particular was found to be extremely immobile and unresponsive to the demands of building programmes which were drawn up with only national aggregates in mind.'[83]

In an era when statistics were both created and evaluated by hand, the Committee undertook a massive amount of responsibility, particularly in attempting to enforce economic policy that would – it was hoped – help solve the balance of payments crisis. The overriding goal was to increase investment in export industries, while balancing needs for new housing and schools, the repair of infrastructure and more.[84] The gathering of background data was somewhat piecemeal and regional statistics, as well as regional economics, did not yet play a role.[85] The IPC often worked through or with various committees and subcommittees to coordinate capital investment and resource distribution, from the Materials Committee to the Headquarters Building Committee and their Priorities Sub-committee, as well as via inter-ministry correspondence with Works, Planning and Health.

This organizational complexity created further problems. For example, the Materials Committee – set up in wartime to oversee limited resources – had overlapping responsibilities with the IPC and other departments. This body had final responsibility for taking from each government department the assessment of needs, monitoring various industries for availability of materials, then suggesting allocations of materials to each department. In turn the departments – at least in the building industry – made regional allocations where officials further filtered materials to specific cities and towns. It was a complex arrangement and its administration was unwieldy.[86]

But it was not the complexity of administration or the difficulties of coordination that really affected the blitzed cities in the immediate postwar period, or even under the 1951 Churchill administration. Instead, from IPC minutes and working papers it is clear that the lack of building licence allocations to the cities and therefore the marked lack of building – where any was even allowed – were almost wholly due to the decisions of particular groups of civil servants and individuals. The decisions by the IPC were meant to channel investment into areas where they were most needed, but the effect in many places was to prevent investment. It can be clearly seen in the papers that officials in the IPC, as well as their working colleagues, gave the cities little or no priority, and when building licences were finally allocated it was only in token amounts.[87]

IV. *The IPC and Blitzed Cities: Initial Steps*

The first IPC – the temporary committee charged simply with submitting a report on capital investment – included only members from economic departments alongside officials from the Ministries of Works, Supply and Labour. Although none of the members had involvement in planning for city centre reconstruction, there was at least mention of blitzed cities in the initial report. After the introductory statement that home investment 'has been planned and started on a scale well beyond our capacity to carry out at reasonable speed with the materials hitherto available', they added that 'the prospective supplies of the more important materials for the coming year are inadequate to sustain the current actual rate of investment and meet the needs of the export and other essential home programmes'.[88] The report mentioned the rebuilding of blitzed cities only in passing, under a general heading attributed to the Ministry of Works, as the licensing department, stating the need for a reduction in office building and other commercial work: 'It will also mean delaying plans for rebuilding city centres destroyed during the war.'[89]

This was in marked contrast to the rhetoric up to 1945, as seen in Chapter 2, which had suggested rebuilding cities was a top priority. From the very first iteration of the postwar IPC, the virtual silence about the cities suggests they were already being brushed aside. When the 1947 white paper on capital investment was published using the initial IPC report as its basis, the point was reiterated, though more moderately: 'Work on new offices and other commercial buildings will be allowed only in exceptional circumstances, even though this must have the effect of delaying plans for rebuilding the centres of cities damaged during the war.'[90] Throughout the report there was constant emphasis on the need for increasing production, building and refitting factories and concern about the wider economic picture. The language of austerity suggested that any non-essential building work should be delayed.

Once the IPC became permanent the changed membership might have taken a more benevolent approach. However, membership still included mainly 'economists', with a token representative from Works, and none from the planning ministry.[91] Repeatedly in IPC meetings if the bomb-damaged cities were mentioned, it was to restate what had been said in the White Paper – that plans for rebuilding the cities would be delayed.[92] Eventually, in May of 1948, the Ministry of Works – responsible for the 'Miscellaneous Building' portion of the investment budget – circulated a memorandum to the IPC.[93] It stated: 'It is suggested that it is of the greatest importance that a start shall be made with [blitzed cities] in 1949 and that reasonably adequate allocations of steel shall be made available.'[94]

The following month the Deputy Secretary of the MTCP was invited to attend an IPC meeting. Meeting minutes show that the invitation came at the request of the Board of Trade and Ministry of Works who were concerned about the needs of the bomb-damaged cities. It was the first time since the end of the war that the planning ministry had been given the opportunity to give input on behalf of the cities.[95] Deputy Secretary Evelyn Sharp, experienced in dealing with local authorities, spoke on their behalf – reinforcing the cities' needs for *any* allocations of steel with which to make a start on reconstruction.[96] To clarify, the allocation would mean steel that could be purchased, not steel that would be given to the cities. All of the cities had been encouraged to make plans, most had submitted applications to acquire – or had started acquiring – land to build on and yet the centres remained full of bomb sites. She added, '[I]f the present restrictive policy were continued, the political repercussions might be serious.' Sharp also noted that there was some resentment among the cities, due to work being permitted in New Towns 'while the old ones remained in ruins.'[97] The meeting resulted in action items such as an inquiry by the War Damage Commission (WDC) on the extent of the damages generally in these cities and an inquiry to Coventry as to requirements for steel for city centre buildings, as an example for all provincial cities. These items were based on a conclusion which read: '[T]here should be no question of authorizing work in blitzed cities on a scale corresponding with the total damage to be made good.'[98] However, there are no papers or minutes in IPC files discussing any answers gathered from the WDC, and the rhetoric of priority seems to have simply disappeared again.[99]

An IPC stance on reconstructing blitzed cities was published in their first report issued on 16 July 1948.[100] The report contained only a small item under 'Miscellaneous Building' stating, 'The issue of license will still have to be severely restricted; but it is recommended that a very small start should be made on the rebuilding of commercial building in blitzed cities.'[101] However, it expanded the statement later:

> Shops and Office Buildings: This is the main problem and poses the question to what extent a start can be made on the enormous amount of office and other commercial building waiting to be done, particularly in the blitzed cities … work has so far been deferred almost entirely … a start should be made as soon as resources permit … Some local authorities are also becoming alarmed at the drift of customers away from the former city centres destroyed during the war … The core of the problem is undoubtedly the re-building of the city centres.
>
> The scale of the demand is, of course, immense … The Committee consider that the demand for work of this kind cannot be damped down indefinitely and therefore recommend that a start should be made … [although] only a token amount of work will be practicable. No special priority can be attached to the work.[102]

The 'priority' that was said to be due to the blitzed cities in the meeting minutes of June 1948 had essentially disappeared in the following month. This nod to the problem apparently was to pacify the Blitzed Areas Group as well as – to some extent – the MTCP and Ministry of Works.[103]

The Blitzed Areas Group of the Parliamentary Labour Party had spent several months in early 1948 pressuring the government. Deputations and letters went to the Lord President, the Chancellor of the Exchequer, the Economic Secretary and to the MTCP as well as the Board of Trade.[104] The Group insisted that all parties had made promises as had both governments, and yet the cities were being left as they had been since before 1945. They noted that very little work of any kind beyond housing and a few factories had been started, and MPs complained about the lack of coordination as well as of action.[105] Oddly, it appears there was no similar Opposition – that is, Conservative – group. As previously shown, the Group could not have been aware of the IPC's control of allocations for steel, although their complaints about coordination may have been well-founded. In November of 1948 they received a mildly encouraging reply, after much back and forth, from the Chancellor stating that a start would be allowed for city centre reconstruction in 1949. In this letter Cripps also – either erroneously or disingenuously – placed responsibility for all the coordination and allocation decisions in the hands of the MTCP.[106]

The MTCP was responsible for decisions regarding approval of licensing in city centres, that is, for non-industrial projects excluding housing, but that ministry was not responsible for issuing the licenses. However, as their primary point of contact the local authorities looked to the MTCP for assistance with obtaining building licenses.[107] The MTCP was therefore forced by circumstance to coordinate with the Ministry of Works, where the licenses originated. As shown above, the amounts budgeted by the IPC for 'Miscellaneous Building Projects' came under the Works umbrella. Yet the MTCP obviously had no say in any allocation decisions, no seat on the committee and could do nothing to get the issues onto a meeting agenda.[108] There was also ongoing disappointment with allowances for New Towns to start building, before allowing blitzed cities to rebuild.[109] All these issues came under the aegis of the planning ministry, and yet the ministry remained in the weak position it had been in since its inception: led by a non-Cabinet minister, powerless to issue building licenses, but responsible to the blitzed cities as their main point of contact.

In the House of Commons, representatives of the blitzed cities from *all* parties had increased their pressure on the government for a start to reconstruction.[110] In November 1947 Hubert Medland, Labour MP for Plymouth, complained:

> I would ask that in this respect it shall not be forgotten that we are the victims of war. We did not ask to be destroyed. There are many cities which will have their allocation of steel for factories which never had a bomb. Some of our cities have been very nearly wiped out, and we say that it is the right of those cities to come first in these priorities.[111]

It was further suggested by a Southampton MP that

> Neither the authorities who control the funds nor the Ministries who control the labour and materials have shown any desire to restore the blitzed towns to a

proper condition ... It will be agreed in every town which has been blitzed that the [government] have not given us the assistance to which the blitzed areas are entitled, in view of their having borne the brunt of the war damage.[112]

By the 1948–49 session it was increasingly obvious that the government had not given any priority to the rebuilding. Pressure from the MTCP, the Blitzed Areas Group and the questions arising in Commons finally resulted in a small allocation of steel.[113] Lewis Silkin, Minister of Town and Country Planning, presented the first allocation numbers in the House of Commons on 1 February 1949. The numbers followed the investment report suggestions, and fourteen blitzed cities were given collectively only 5,540 tons – a token amount of steel[114] (see Table 3.1). To put the amount in context, Douglas Jay, Economic Secretary to the Treasury, stated the following month in Commons that '[t]here is one major scheme in [Whitehall] which in the end, over five years, will take 13,000 tons'.[115] Building licenses still had to be secured by the cities on top of the steel allocations. In private, Jay was said to have supported the needs of the blitzed cities: he apparently told the MTCP Parliamentary Secretary that he felt the allocation was too small and that if they applied for more steel in March, 'the Treasury would support [it]'.[116]

Table 3.1 Blitzed cities (steel allocation)

House of Commons debates, February 1949	
	Tons
Bristol	390
Coventry	750
Exeter	450
Great Yarmouth, Lowestoft, Norwich	500
Kingston-upon-Hull	450
Manchester	200
Plymouth	750
Portsmouth	750
Sheffield	400
Southampton	270
South Shields	180
Swansea	75
Total	*5,165*

Note: Steel is being provided for the City of London under a separate arrangement.
Source: Announcement by Minister Silkin, as reported in HC Deb 01 February 1949, v460 c1485–6.

The small amount of steel and the relatively small number of cities selected for the allocation caused an outcry in Parliament. An adjournment debate was launched on 21 March 1949 in response to the allocation. The debate was initiated by Michael Foot (Plymouth), but many other blitzed city representatives were ready to speak. Medland (also Plymouth) had worked out that the amount of steel allocated for blitzed cities was 0.00034 (or 0.034 per cent) of the national output of 15.5 million tons of ingot steel:

We are told that the output of the country today is something like 15½ million ingot tons of steel. I had to do a little sum. I asked the Economic Secretary in a Question if he would be good enough to tell me what proportion of the total amount of steel in the country had been allocated to the blitzed cities. He answered that they did not tell people things like that. When I worked it out I found the extent of the generosity of the Government towards the blitzed cities who had been in the front line during the war. Their people knew what it was to sit up night after night and have the bombs coming down. It was not a pleasant feeling, believe me. What is the magnificent allocation, eight years after that had happened? I found that it is .00034 of the total amount of steel that is produced. That is the generosity of the Government towards the blitzed areas and the working cities. I think we deserve more consideration than that.[117]

Throughout the debates and in interdepartmental correspondence MPs and officials in the concerned departments were told by Treasury officials that the work was not a high priority and that the national economic situation took precedence over rebuilding the cities, even where cities competed for steel with undamaged areas.[118]

V. *Fighting for Priority*

The discussions over priority – or lack of – to the cities and correspondence and lobbying between ministries did not abate. In May 1949, the IPC issued a report intended to cover 1950 through 1952. Since the cities that were to receive the initial allocations of steel had not been able to immediately procure building licenses, the steel was still being taken up by the time of the report so no further allocations were given, despite the promises from the Economic Secretary.[119] Although outcry continued in Parliament, internal discussion centred around reducing or eliminating steel allocations for blitzed cities. Documents in IPC files show that the Headquarters Building Committee and the Production Committee – the highest level committee on resources below the Cabinet itself – as well as the Ministry of Works, pressed the blitzed cities' case to the IPC and were continuously rebuffed.[120] Minutes show that much time was spent debating the issue and shifting budgeted amounts away from this area. The IPC was not just making reductions but ignoring requests, and therefore not implementing some of the policy they were tasked with implementing by the EPC.[121]

Creating a further obstacle to progress in building, in October 1949 the Cabinet told the IPC to review the 1950 investment programme and make substantial reductions throughout all areas.[122] Sterling had been devalued and the economic situation therefore included increased inflationary fears. Even though only a token allowance of steel was given in 1949, further problems had caused delays to actual building. The implementation strategies of the government were unable to cope with the realities of the building industry: materials were still in severe shortage and coordination difficulties were abundant, particularly vis-a-vis manpower.[123] The 1948 Simon Report on Distribution of Building Materials had detailed how the industry worked, but not made practical suggestions for improvement, at least in the short term.[124]

The next IPC report, in November 1949, stated that the total amount allowed for 1950 for 'Miscellaneous Building' would be a 'roughly estimated' £360 million; of this the MTCP requested £5–7 million for blitzed cities.[125] The IPC had by now discovered that allocation by tonnage of steel was an ineffective method of control. No reason was given but it may have arisen from the vast differences in steel requirements between buildings of similar size (i.e., structural steel vs. reinforcing steel rods). A decision was taken to control the use of steel and other building materials through building licenses, and the limits were thenceforward set via the cost of building.[126] The MTCP had committed to a minimum value of works in the blitzed cities – which were already awaiting authorization – of only £1.7 million nationally, and so the omission of the cities seems either to be an oversight or simply too small to be shown. Considering all of the correspondence, discussions, deputations and Commons pressure on the subject of blitzed cities, it hardly seems likely to have been a simple oversight. But where the previous investment reports had contained at least a paragraph on the problem, this report included none. The MTCP files at this point show reductions by 50 per cent for projects already either licensed or awaiting licensing, while concurrent IPC minutes suggest the work should stop altogether.[127] Minister Silkin was finally frustrated enough to go above the IPC and the other departments involved and beg the EPC for allocation increases: 'I wish to emphasise with all strength at my command the grave consequences which I believe would flow from such a wholesale suspension as is proposed.'[128]

Silkin received a positive result on the EPC side, and they told the IPC that an increase should be made from within the 'Miscellaneous Building' budget. However the IPC chair, W. Strath, refused to allow the suggestion to move forward. Strath stated in a memo to Cripps and Plowden that the recommendation would mean 'an unjustifiably rapid growth in the blitzed city programme'.[129] The EPC response reiterated their original statement, adding that the Committee did not want to 'place the Government in the position of having to make public a decision to stop new work on the Blitzed Cities'.[130] Strath's successor as chair from mid-November, F. F. Turnbull, privately continued to express negative views on blitzed cities' priority through internal memos in November and December 1949. This culminated in his authorization of a long statement from a CEPS staff member on the subject.[131] Turnbull circulated the statement, in addition to other memos with claims that resources going to the blitzed cities would necessarily draw on precious needs for industry and other business relating to exports and economic recovery. To be fair, the officials concerned felt that a more detailed programme needed to be developed where needs were specifically planned for, city by city. However, IPC internal correspondence included a note that asked, re: Blitzed Cities, 'How little can we get away with in 1950?'[132]

In January 1950, Turnbull circulated a report to the IPC based on the same statements he had been making privately. The MTCP received a copy of the report and – of course – objected to the severe reductions. Their reaction stressed that the blitzed cities formed only a very small portion of the whole 'Miscellaneous Building' Programme in any case, and said they felt the programme was being singled out for poor treatment.[133] The reaction from the Economic Secretary was even stronger: 'I feel we are now getting things a little out of perspective … This is surely pushing planning to extremes.'[134] But Plowden, who suggested that this 'small item' could set poor precedents for other such items, rebuffed Jay.[135] Plowden summarized his consideration of the episode to Chancellor Cripps by stating, '[T]here is no question but that this is a form of investment which must rank low on the list and can quite well be foregone.'[136]

About the same time the MTCP's Deputy Secretary Dame Evelyn Sharp attended another IPC meeting. Sharp pleaded that anything less than an allowance of £5 million for blitzed cities' building work would be politically untenable, particularly after the promises which had been made for so many years.[137] This again is not funding to be given to the cities, merely a limit of the total building licences the cities would be allowed to have: that is, the value of the work allowed. The result, in the next IPC report, was a suggestion – but no specific allowance – for £2.5 million of licence allocations for blitzed cities, though it did make note of the MTCP's statement.[138] This amount was all of 0.6 per cent of the entire 'Miscellaneous Building' programme, which was at that time approximately 18 per cent of the whole national 'budget' (see Table 3.2 and Figure 3.1). That is, the amount was only 0.1 per cent of the entire national estimated capital expenditure of £2.3–2.4 billion. While the licence allocation amount had grown at least slightly, it was still so low that cities were being allowed to start on only one or two buildings each.[139]

In February 1950 the former Chancellor Hugh Dalton replaced Silkin at the MTCP and was now forced to fight for the licence allocations from the other side of the IPC 'fence'.[140] He wrote to the Chancellor expressing his distress about the blitzed cities situation: 'On every front – of justice, and civic pride and morale, and sheer political [practicality] – it is vital that they should be allowed to do a little more this year.'[141] Dalton seems to have had a good relationship with Stokes (Minister of Works), who apparently agreed to allow an increase for blitzed cities of £1 million in additional licences from his department's 'Miscellaneous' budget. Cripps, however, disallowed this. Dalton's reaction was to simply tell Cripps that he was 'taking £½ million on account' instead, and allocating it straightaway.[142] On 20 June the parliamentary secretary from the Ministry of Local Government and Planning (formerly MTCP) made a statement in Commons that £4 million would be allocated to the blitzed cities for 1951.[143]

At the same time, IPC correspondence shows that there was difficulty tracking much of the so-called Miscellaneous spending even within the licensed work. Muir (Ministry of Works) in his 'quick analysis' of the 'Miscellaneous' field mentions that 'some £4 million worth of work … owing to the way our records are kept gets mixed up with other office building work'.[144] Not only were the IPC officials (and Works) attempting to reduce the blitzed city licence allocations, but they were unable to say exactly how big the 'Miscellaneous' portion of the capital investment budget actually was.[145] Paradoxically, the Minister of Works issued a paper to the Production Committee in May 1950 suggesting that

Table 3.2 IPC allocation – percentage of investment planned by type

Date created	Year forecast	CIVIL							DEFENCE	Total (%)	£ mil.	Blitzed cities amount	BC%
		Industry (%)	Agri culture (%)	Fuel and power (%)	Transport etc. (%)	Housing (%)	Other incl. Health (%)	Misc (%)	All defence (%)				
Oct 1947	1948	13	3	5	15	58	6	0	1	100	[labour]	0	0.00
Jul 1948	1949	18	1	29	14	1	2	32	2	100	[steel]	5,540	0.08
Nov 1949	1950	26	4	11	15	11	5	24	4	100	1,994	2.3	0.12
Apr 1950	1951	22	3	11	15	12	6	26	4	100	2,347	3.5	0.15
Mar 1951	1952	22	4	13	14	13	6	18	10	100	2,268	–	0.00
Dec 1951	1952	18	3	12	11	14	6	28	9	100	2,653	2.5	0.09
Feb 1952	1952	19	3	12	11	14	6	28	9	100	2,709	3	0.11
Apr 1952	1953	21	2	11	13	15	4	28	7	100	3,140	4.5	0.14
Jun 1952	1954	20	3	11	13	16	4	27	6	100	3,151	6	0.19
Aug 1952	1953	20	2	11	15	15	6	23	8	100	2,839	2.5	0.09
Apr 1953	1954	20	3	11	13	15	4	27	6	100	3,173	6	0.19
Average		20	3	12	14	17	5	24	6	100	2,697	–	0.11

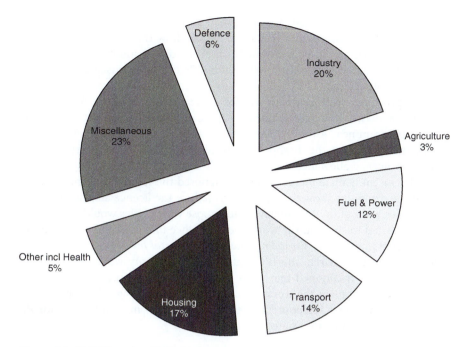

Figure 3.1 IPC Allocation 1947–54.

Table and pie chart in Figure 3.1 covering 1947–54 created from IPC (formal) reports until 1951 when reports ceased, thereafter data is from ad hoc reports.

Figures are for the next proposed full year, by percentage of total investment; these figures were not consistent throughout the reports, shifting regularly, but not drastically. Often the contents of each section changed, and every effort has been made to be consistent here with types of investment throughout.

Reports by date from: *TNA: CAB 134/437–457, 982–984.*

8 October 1947: Investment Programmes Committee Report. IPC (47) 9. Note this is by labour ceiling.
16 July 1948: Report on Capital Investment in 1949. IPC (48) 8. Note this is by tons of steel allocated.
10 November 1949: Capital Investment in 1950. IPC (49) 6 (reductions).
14 April, rev 24 April 1950: Report on Capital Investment in 1951 and 1952. IPC (50) 1, 2.
17 March 1951: Report on Capital Investment in 1951, 1952 and 1953. IPC (51) 1.
17 December 1951: Civil Investment in 1952 and 1953. C (51) 45.
8 February 1952: (Interim) Capital Investment in 1952. IPC (52) 3.
Undated (ca. April 1952). Investment in 1953 and 1954. (Not numbered) [copy 240] for 1953.
Undated (ca. June 1952). Investment in 1953 and 1954. (Not numbered) [copy 240] for 1954.
15 August 1952: Investment in 1953. IPC (52) 9 [for 1953 only].
9 April 1953: Investment in 1953 and 1954. (not numbered) showing only 1954.

building licensing be relaxed, and abolished altogether in the private sector.[146] If this were carried through, it would be curious how the (endlessly discussed) licence allocations would be controlled. All of the discussion continued to both defy wartime rhetoric and demonstrate the difficulties of consensus, including inside the civil service.

Unsurprisingly, with rearmament for Korea and the Cold War, defence spending increased very quickly during 1950, causing further reductions to non-defence programmes. Although the MLGP had circulated a paper to the IPC in December stressing the disappointment of cities where only a portion of the £4 million licence allowance was to be made available in the coming year, and asking for an immediate increase, the IPC ignored the request. In January 1951, IPC meeting minutes show that in order to reduce the licence allowances to the blitzed cities without the MLGP having to choose which cities would suffer most, it was suggested to suspend the work and announce that it was 'as a result of the defence programme'.[147] In the updated *Report on Capital Investment in 1951, 1952 and 1953* issued in March, the IPC stated that blitzed city work would stop.[148] The report oddly mentioned that while the IPC members understood the need for licence allocations in the worst hit cities, they were giving token amounts to three – Birmingham, Liverpool and Manchester – with no justification for the selection. The report further stated:

> There is an obvious case on general grounds for this work, but its economic value is small. The greater part of it consists of rebuilding shops and offices. In the circumstances which now prevail as a result of the new defence programme, we see no option but to recommend that no further work be authorised at any rate until after the end of 1953.[149]

Although the IPC made these statements about stopping work, there is no evidence that the MLGP or the Ministry of Works told any local authorities to stop, or that they did anything to halt the meagre amount of progress. However, from October 1950 the new Chancellor, Hugh Gaitskell, made a Commons statement on the position in June 1951: 'We have also considered carefully whether in the new circumstances further progress can be made with the reconstruction of blitzed towns and cities. It is clear that during the next two years it will not be possible to do much.'[150] Gaitskell further admitted that the problem was often simply in knowing how much steel would be available: '[I]t indicates the difficulty we have this year of giving the degree of precision that we should like to give to the individual investment programmes. Uncertainty about the precise output of steel is one of the difficulties I had in mind.'[151] Yet Gaitskell, like his predecessors, was still strongly under the influence of his civil servants. IPC chairman Turnbull continued to refuse requests from the Minister of Works for any increase in the 'Miscellaneous' sector.[152]

Throughout 1951 Turnbull's actions perpetuated angst among involved officials. Both Treasury and planning ministry files hold copies of a 1951 letter from Sharp to Turnbull. Apparently there had been agreements regarding allocations to blitzed cities, which had been accepted and then rescinded. Sharp is straightforward in her criticism:

> If I may say so, I do feel you have treated us rather badly over this business ... In short the agreement was gone back on. I feel exactly as though we had agreed to toss for double or quits, and it having come down double (or nearly double) you have refused to pay!
>
> I know that steel is a fresh difficulty. But it is a difficulty that confronts all investment programmes.[153]

Sharp's responsibilities were broader than just the blitzed cities, yet she understood the insignificance being attached to physical reconstruction by Turnbull and many of his colleagues. The planning ministry was continuing in the role of assisting and overseeing blitzed cities, but was unable to gain an increase in allocation priority for building licences. Wartime rhetoric had disappeared and, so far, any plans made could not be implemented.

VI. *Continuing Controversy under the New Government*

The Labour government, in a tough economic situation, was able to sell its socialist policies as both good for all and the best method of managing the struggling economy.[154] But it was not enough to keep them in power. The popularity of Labour declined through its last three years in office, proving unable to effectively administer all the controls they attempted to implement, and struggling to build enough homes to fulfil their promises.[155] It has been shown repeatedly that voter priority was housing. The Conservatives took hold of this and pushed it up their rhetorical agenda.[156] Although the new Conservative government made far-reaching promises they would have difficulty keeping, politicians, civil servants and business people in the blitzed cities might hope that such a government would encourage more rebuilding by allowing increased private investment and relaxing many controls. This proved true to an extent, yet the new government was still forced to control steel allocations and for another two years continued to use the IPC to control capital investment.[157]

In October 1951 after a Conservative government was returned, one might have expected to see significant changes in the capital investment programme. But while the Cabinet and ministers were new, the civil servants who constituted the IPC did not change, and therefore under the new government there initially was no shift in attitude towards blitzed cities. From the start, the process went on as before: the planning ministry (now Ministry of Housing and Local Government, or HLG) circulated a document to the IPC requesting larger allocations for blitzed cities, while the Chancellor, now Rab Butler, produced a subsequent Cabinet memo on 'reductions in civil investment' which stated that cuts would 'fall fairly heavily on ... work on the reconstruction of blitzed cities'.[158] Harold Macmillan, the new planning minister, then addressed a personal letter to the Chancellor, insisting that the blitzed cities needed to be allowed more building starts. As had his predecessors, Macmillan invoked issues of morale: '[The blitzed cities] bore the brunt of the attack, and have not had a very fair share of any post-war cake that has been going.'[159] As usual, this was followed by an IPC response on limits to the programme for 1952 and 1953.[160]

In Parliament, adjournment debates continued to introduce the topic of the blitzed cities' needs. Southampton MP Ralph Morley (Labour) optimistically stated: 'I hope that the new Government will show that they are willing to come quickly to the aid of our blitzed towns and cities.'[161] Throughout 1952, in debates on steel or those introduced on the reconstruction topic, members of Parliament from the bomb-damaged cities continued to press the new government for assistance, and often reiterated that it was a non-party matter.[162] In April 1952, a note was sent from Turnbull to Strath (now in the Economic Section) anticipating a coming adjournment debate, and he oddly – if not disingenuously – stated: 'The Minister of HLG has been asked a lot of questions on this subject ... His general line, I think, is quite anti-blitzed city.'[163] As if to belie the memo he had not seen, Macmillan wrote regularly to Butler from May 1952, constantly requesting specific increases for various cities. Obviously Macmillan took the cases of the cities seriously, and he proceeded to push them forward by strategically announcing decisions over the heads (so to speak) of the IPC.[164]

Macmillan also understood the dilemma he was now in as a minister, between the IPC and Parliament: 'We have therefore in effect a situation at present where the policies are formulated by bodies who are technically responsible to no-one (though in practice responsibility for their actions is taken, more or less haphazard, by different Ministers), and where the full blast of Parliamentary responsibility is directed at the application of the policy to specific industries or services.'[165] In August Macmillan wrote to Butler about impending cuts to the investment programme, acknowledging that the blitzed cities' case was not economic, but 'political and perhaps moral', a similar case to Dalton's pitch under Labour.[166] He suggested also that the situation was escalating and soon he would be unable to hide behind the various economic excuses, that there would be further adjournment debates, deputations and protests. He suggested the Cabinet be informed, and finally, that if any unpleasant announcement was to be made on the subject, the Chancellor should be the one to make it.[167] Clearly the debate was being elevated, but whether through Macmillan's instigation alone or as a response to parliamentary pressure is unknown. The response in the files shows the usual disingenuousness and digging in of heels: Turnbull wrote to Strath to suggest that it was the MHLG's fault that they were in the situation where they faced more demands from the cities: 'If the Ministry had taken more trouble to comply with previous government decisions on this they would not now be in such difficulties.'[168] In his reply to Macmillan, Butler said he would have to make any statements himself.[169]

Clearly the issue of allocations for the blitzed cities was not going to go away, but the IPC seemed to continue hoping that it would. In a document written by Turnbull and circulated as an IPC working paper, he described what he felt were effective methods for controlling investment. But on page two, he singled out the small programmes as a source of frustration: 'We should bury a number of awkward quarrelling points such as miscellaneous local government services and blitzed cities, and controversies about what could be done within these two global miscellaneous programmes would be fought out mostly in the regions.'[170] Finally, the frustration and difficulties brought Macmillan to write a short but strongly worded memo to the Cabinet. In it he adamantly pressed his colleagues for larger allocations to rebuild blitzed cities, stressing the moral issue, as well as political.[171] The memo opened with quotes from Kipling and Churchill, including: 'Of course, we must first concentrate, as we are doing, all available building labour on those parts of our cities which have suffered most.'[172]

It followed with fourteen points, brief and succinct, as to why Macmillan thought the cities deserved a larger allocation. He did not, curiously, compare the very small portion the cities were receiving to the total investment programme, or even the 'Miscellaneous' sector.[173] He did however, include a point about the importance of the votes in the blitzed cities: 'There are 68 Parliamentary seats in these cities; 40 are held by the Opposition, who will lose no opportunity to attack and embarrass the 28 Government supporters who hold the other seats.'[174]

The memorandum was met by a reply from the Chancellor. Butler continued to insist, as per his officials, that there were higher economic priorities and that the work being done in blitzed cities was sufficient, or at least was using all available labour.[175] The matter was discussed by the Cabinet on 6 November, and the conclusions show the Cabinet asking for 'greater flexibility' in the arrangements, as well as gaining support from Prime Minister Churchill: 'failure to continue and expand work on the reconstruction of blitzed cities would be open to the gravest criticism'.[176] Clearly the IPC chair did not interpret this as support, telling a colleague: 'The Prime Minister's summing up really supports both sides of the argument.'[177]

Indeed, a follow-up memo from Strath to the Chancellor suggested 'all we can do now is to see that if there are any spare building resources becoming available in the blitzed cities, these resources are not automatically seized by the Minister of Housing for blitzed city work'.[178] More correspondence ensued regarding the pending announcement to be made by Macmillan on the blitzed cities issue. In a note from Turnbull to Strath, having clearly recognized that the Prime Minister *did* in fact have views closer to Macmillan's than to the middle, he stated: 'There may however be danger that the Prime Minister whose sympathies in the Cabinet discussion were clearly on the side of rebuilding blitzed cities quickly, will not merely reject this request, but may have his attention so much drawn to the matter that he decides that the draft is not sufficiently vigorous.'[179] This was quite the turnaround from Turnbull's previous statement – demonstrating the same disingenuity that appears throughout the documents in both Treasury and HLG files. With clear ministerial support for the blitzed cities, it can be seen from Treasury files that the major impediment to progress in rebuilding was within the civil service, and particularly the Treasury.

Macmillan announced further allocations on 25 November 1952, temporarily appeasing MPs from the blitzed cities, but the battle did not end there.[180] Several

MPs pointed out that the proportion of the nation's capital investment directed at the blitzed cities was at best 0.2 per cent and at worst 0.1 per cent or less, and noted – again – that this was 'not a party matter'.[181] As Morley stated, at these rates the allocation might allow each city to build perhaps one or two new shops or offices per year, and the time to rebuild fully at such a rate would be over 130 years.[182] Macmillan, possibly from two years of frustration at fighting the Treasury, made an amusing statement in the Commons on the investment programme during a 'Blitzed Towns' debate initiated by Morley. Macmillan commented:

> As I understand, the capital investment programme was instituted immediately after the war, but it did not reach its full fruition, its peak period of beauty, until the functions of the Minister of State for Economic Affairs were combined with those of the Chancellor of the Exchequer. From that date there were brought together in the Treasury two organisations, the old Treasury financial experts and the new economic planners. It was indeed an amazing marriage. It was a fusion of those who, like the hon. Member for West Ham, North (Mr. Lewis), think that only cash matters and those who, like the planners, think that only things matter; and as we can well imagine, proceeding from the first dawn of that new era of progress which only began in the world in 1945, it pressed on rapidly.[183]

And Macmillan later continued, with further tongue-in-cheek:

> Then came 1952. Even with the Chancellor of the Exchequer having gone to the United States, I dare not tell the House what was the sum allocated under the investment programme which was compiled at the end of the year. All I can say is that £4,600,000 worth was done, and that is twice what was done two years before.[184]

Finally in 1953, when the IPC was about to be dismantled, the blitzed cities' investment allocation was increased. And even then the total amount allocated was *still not even 0.2 per cent* of the entire capital investment programme.[185] Macmillan sent one last small missive on the subject to the Chancellor on 6 July 1953. On the note it says, 'Handed to Chancellor by H. Macmillan', yet on the bottom it was clearly passed on to the 'expert', as on it was handwritten: 'Mr. Turnbull – for advice'.[186] According to memos that follow, the MHLG continued to allocate more licence amounts to cities than the IPC had approved, and continued to ask for more allocations, frustrating Treasury officials who left more peevish notes behind.[187]

According to Martin Chick, Macmillan not only pushed for the removal of restrictions on capital investment, often ignoring them, as shown, but he also led by example – inciting other ministers to ignore their departmental limits as well.[188] By 1953 the IPC had become, in many ways, ineffective. It was dissolved on 28 November 1953, after a Cabinet decision to 'change the system for controlling investment'.[189] It was soon agreed to abolish building licences as well. By the time controls on new building were relaxed almost completely in 1954, the maximum investment allowance (or licence limit) discussed for *all* blitzed cities was never more than £10 million in any one year, and never approved at more than £7 million – all to be divided among only the eighteen chosen cities on the government's 'blitzed cities' list (London was treated separately).[190] Any city affected by bombing that had been acknowledged as such but had not made the planning ministry's list of eighteen blitzed cities was simply out of luck in terms of steel allocations for retail or commercial building. The only alternative was to find some administrative work-around, perhaps finding approvals through other departments such as Works or the Board of Trade.

Conclusion

The evidence presented in this chapter provides convincing argument that the intractable mindset of the civil servants running the IPC created a major hurdle for the reconstruction of blitzed cities. Ministers relied on these officials, and refused to give the cities priority, despite the overwhelming political and moral grounds for doing so. Policy was created, but in places it was often not implemented. While, as customary, ministers (in particular the various planning ministers) answered Parliamentary questions about IPC decisions which came through their departments, though they did not control those decisions. Interestingly, Aneurin Bevan objected to the IPC's terms on precisely these grounds when Cabinet first announced them. The procedures, he declared, were 'fundamentally wrong'. Ministers should make policy decisions on the government building programme, and only their implementation should be put in the hands of the IPC. 'Unless this course is adopted', he warned, 'the major issues of policy will still have to be fought out in Cabinet after a mass of detailed work has been done.'[191] In the end, the IPC determined much of the government's investment policy generally, and certainly did so in the case of blitzed cities.[192]

Within an already overwhelmingly complex structure for economic planning, the Cabinet set up the IPC and determined that most of its members be 'objective' civil servants charged with making decisions in the best interests of the nation. But in practice the IPC officials positioned themselves as experts where many had no real expertise, and often made decisions that were apparently informed solely by their own opinions. IPC officials simply dug in to their roles and insisted on finding their own answers; they seem to have been quite closed to change, no matter what information was given them, or what party was in power. Dunleavy and Rhodes have argued that this way of operating was long entrenched in Whitehall where 'everyone knows they serve themselves by serving their departments'.[193] Alford et al. wondered about ministerial decisions: '[T]here still remains the question of how far their attitudes and actions were influenced by those on whom they relied for advice and assistance.'[194] In the case of blitzed cities, the Chancellors of the Exchequer and other ministers relied heavily on their 'expert' advisers – most of whom, unlikely to have been experts, simply treated their jobs as business-as-usual.

The large volume of unpublished evidence establishes that through several postwar governments Whitehall – except for the planning ministry – paid little heed to the rebuilding of blitzed cities.[195] Although Churchill praised the cities during the war for their fortitude, promises were made by the Coalition government that were not kept by either the Attlee or Churchill governments which followed.[196] Indeed, concern for these cities soon became a rhetorical footnote. The IPC reports show that blitzed cities ranked as one of the lowest priorities, under both postwar governments.[197] Yet ironically the blitzed cities merited much discussion, scores of meetings, long files and lengthy memos. What engaged the IPC officials seems to have been developing rationales for keeping resources for blitzed cities at a low or non-existent level. From 1948 to 1953 the cities received less than 0.1–0.2 per cent of the capital investment allocation, and the only priority they received was in being held back. While the IPC did not give priority to the blitzed cities, clearly the MTCP had been doing so. Planning legislation in 1944 and 1947, created and implemented by the planning ministry, was in part to confer this priority – at least in the physical planning sense. The following chapter will show the effect on the cities when the lack of priority from the IPC was combined with acknowledged priority within the MTCP.

Chapter 4

CENTRAL CONTROL? THE CHALLENGES OF POSTWAR PHYSICAL PLANNING

Every experiment to date has been hampered from the start by lack of wholesale legislation.

– H. Manzoni, City of Birmingham[1]

This statement from 1943 demonstrates how planners and officials of bomb-damaged cities had grown frustrated with the absence of any legal parameters within which they could proceed with postwar planning. The Ministry of Town and Country Planning (MTCP) was established in part to finally deal with this problem. From February 1943, this department created and implemented legislation for postwar land use. Although the solutions contained in the 1944 Act and the later 1947 Act were intended to resolve issues across Britain including industrial location, slum clearance, the use of rural land and more, the Acts deeply affected the blitzed cities. But, as seen in the previous chapter, many other actors and departments also impacted the rebuilding process.

Attempts to plan and reconstruct city centres were hampered by the lack of resource allocation as already shown, but equally local authorities as well as private entities had to work within the new planning laws. Alongside new legislative restrictions, planning ministry officials can be seen to have kept a very tight rein on city plans. Officials not only oversaw the plans and processed them for ministerial approval, but also chose which cities would receive building licence allocations when they became available.[2] From publications and circulars to a special series of conferences, the new ministry kept busy working on reconstruction issues in addition to its basic functions. When the Labour government came to power in 1945, Lewis Silkin arrived as minister. How the ministry under Silkin, then his successor Hugh Dalton and the following government's planning ministry under Harold Macmillan dealt with the special problems of the blitzed cities will be examined in this chapter. From the difficult relationship with the Investment Programmes Committee (IPC) to issues with local authorities and other government departments, numerous obstacles further exacerbated the problems faced by the blitzed cities in the postwar period.[3]

Though bold planning had been encouraged in wartime, none of the many plans rapidly produced in response to this exhortation were fully implemented.

This chapter will detail a number of reasons for this, particularly the complexity of issues faced during any reconstruction. It will show the context of land use planning in 1945, briefly describing precedents from before the war. Most important here will be an explanation of the legislation as it specifically affected blitzed cities. Beyond the basic legislative impacts the planning ministry was responsible for helping the cities from a practical standpoint. How this relationship played out in the years after the war, until the relaxation of restrictions on building in 1954, will be shown to have had significant effects on many cities. Planning can shape our built environment, but it is the implementation of those plans – through legal and practical means and the interplay of many actors – that produces the results we live with.

I. *Legislating for Physical Planning*

Industrialization led to enormous urban growth in nineteenth-century Britain, but the growth was essentially unregulated and cities became both broader and denser. The urban situation attracted legislative attention because the growth of slums brought an increased spread of disease, through close contact and unhealthy conditions. As a result regulatory attempts – often referred to in urban planning discussion as 'the by-laws' – were made throughout the latter half of the nineteenth century to alleviate urban problems.[4] Later land use issues included ribbon development – the growth happening along transport paths that spread from larger cities, particularly London. Agricultural and rural land was increasingly swallowed up by the need for housing; countryside began to disappear. The 1909 Housing, Town Planning, Etc. Act, the first piece of legislation to use the term 'town planning', was passed, but by the end of the First World War there was widespread recognition of the need to further improve living conditions and check the growth of industrial cities. In the war, men of all classes served the country, and the initial ideology of 'homes fit for heroes' was born: there was consensus that all those who fought the Great War deserved a decent place to live.[5]

The Ministry of Health became the government body responsible for housing and planning related issues from 1919, at a time when housing – and planning for housing – was still considered a 'health' issue.[6] Concurrently, the physical planning of communities increased and became more professional. Accordingly, this period saw the rise of education and study focused on physical planning.[7] The 1932 Town and Country Planning Act widened local authority powers through planning schemes and broadened responsibility for oversight of the new movement towards better control of land use.[8]

By the Second World War all political parties recognized the need to study problems of physical planning, and land use was addressed in various ways. The war itself – which necessitated many types of planning to carry out the aims of government particularly during the crisis of wartime – also brought forward the need to study issues of compensation, of city planning, and the related statutory problems that would be faced in the postwar period.[9] The government, as mentioned in Chapter 2, commissioned significant – if contested – studies: Barlow on the distribution of industry, Scott on land utilization in rural areas and Uthwatt on compensation and betterment.[10]

Though all three reports had important effects on planning legislation passed in wartime and immediately afterwards, the Uthwatt Report can be singled out for having the greatest influence on statutory powers as they would later be applied to the blitzed cities. Though compensation for war damage was in some respects a non-party issue, the subject of compensation and betterment, in land use generally, was politically conflict-ridden.[11] While not fully implemented in the end, the Uthwatt Report did suggest an effective nationalization of land, which would have helped resolve many of the compensation issues – issues that were a major stumbling block to effective legislation.

The final passage of the Town and Country Planning Act 1944 (hereafter 1944 Act) was fraught with difficulty. Politically divisive, it took from 1941 – when the interim findings from the Uthwatt Committee were reported – to 1944 to finally pass a piece of legislation which all parties agreed was necessary but on which very little consensus was reached on detailed regulations. As *The Times* stated: '[W]hat the [blitzed] towns need, and what their special claim on national sympathies entitles them to have, is an immediate decision which will give them some certainty in their financial arrangements.'[12] Dealing with the practical issues of bombed property was a key element of the 1944 Act. It was often called the 'Blitz and Blight' Act due to its purpose, but in the end it did set a framework for dealing with land use and land value issues of great importance. The 1944 Act set the outline that the planning ministry used to deal with bomb-damaged areas: compulsory purchase was legislated for, as were the methods of application and administration. Equally though, the 1944 Act can be seen not just as a rule-maker, but as the first positive land planning legislation, since the previous Acts in 1932 and an Interim Act in 1943 had been merely regulatory, albeit at least bringing the whole country under planning control.[13]

The MTCP was established in 1943 as the central planning authority to secure 'consistency and continuity in the framing and execution of a national policy concerning the use and development of land in England and Wales.'[14] Included in the main areas of responsibility within the new planning ministry were new administrative duties: liaising with local planning authorities, approving planning schemes, issuing interim development orders and compulsory purchase orders, as well as hearing appeals. In all cases officials did the bulk of the review work and prepared submissions for ministerial approval. This was in addition to initiating any further national planning policy and drafting legislation to oversee control of development as well as postwar planning and redevelopment of war-damaged areas.[15]

II. *Postwar Practical Issues and Further Legislation*

The 1944 'Blitz and Blight' Act set out initial guidelines to ease financial concerns about bomb-damaged properties. It had been a necessary political compromise: legislation was needed to deal with both land planning and financial issues of bomb damage, but with a Coalition government and two sides of the House disagreeing on specifics, the Act was only a shell of what it might have been. As Michael Tichelar suggests, this showed a 'failure of the coalition to reach any acceptable compromise'.[16] W. S. Morrison, the Coalition planning minister, stated three years after the Act was passed: 'When we had discussions, in 1944, on this business of the 1939 price for land, there was a great difference of opinion between the two sides – and it was not confined to party lines – when we thought the best compromise we could come to was to pin down the investor owner to the 1939 value.'[17] In practice important parts of the 1944 Act were confusing, and in some instances unworkable.[18] The most contentious aspect of the 1944 Act was the compensation basis, and Morrison also noted:

> It was quite obvious that the problem of valuation on the 1939 basis was with the passage of time becoming daily more and more fantastic and unreal. No valuer could call to his mind with any degree of certainty what the conditions were in 1939. Since 1939 everything has altered in the property market as well as in many other aspects of national life.[19]

Dissatisfaction was widespread, but especially notable within the local authorities who felt the financial provisions fell short of their needs.[20]

Further legislation was therefore needed under the new postwar government. The result of the 1945 election meant that Labour would be charged with clarifying the laws and repairing the difficulties of the initial legislative 'solutions'. Labour's land-use legislation might have been expected to fully nationalize development rights similarly to the nationalization of industries – empowering the state with both the decisions over land use and the ownership, and therefore profit, of its development. In the end, Labour passed a watered down version of land nationalization: rather than invest the state with land ownership and its profits, legislation mainly gave powers to central and local authorities to make decisions on land use, and did not fully invest the state financially.

The Labour government's Minister of Town and Country Planning Lewis Silkin was responsible for drafting the legislation that would build on the 1944 Act. A lawyer by training, with practical experience in planning matters – having chaired the London County Council's (LCC) Housing and Town Planning committees as well as having been involved with Labour Party wartime policy on the same topics – Silkin was the ideal candidate to put the new government's land planning ideology to work.[21] Based in part on the work of the Reconstruction Committee in wartime, the 1947 Town and Country Planning Act (hereafter 1947 Act) was Labour's major legislative push to bring further powers for control of land use and development into the hands of both central government and local authorities.[22] Increasing public scrutiny while putting further responsibility into the hands of 'experts', the legislation set out parameters for a new method of development control via 'planning permission'. The Act not only forced regional authorities into creating plans, but gave them the power to approve all development proposals, in more thorough detail than previously monitored by the 1932 Act.[23]

The 1947 Act was, as Silkin stated during the second reading of the bill, 'the most comprehensive and far-reaching planning measure which has ever been placed before this House ... [adding later] I believe indeed that it will be one of the most important landmarks in the social history of this country'.[24]

The 1947 Act – through new controls – put development *rights* into the hands of the state. The Uthwatt Report had laid out suggestions for compensation and betterment and the new legislation implemented many of these suggestions, though the method differed from the report's specific proposals. The 1944 Act had used prewar values as the basis for war damage payments, but payments shifted under the 1947 Act to existing land values calculations.[25] The new legislation did not change the requirements for local authorities to apply for orders – as described below – that gave it powers to acquire land. It did, however, increase control over industrial development through methods similar to building licensing, which also continued to exist.[26]

Therefore, by 1948 the MTCP had not only retained its original responsibilities but had increased them. Still the primary central government liaison with local planning authorities, and still responsible for approval of planning schemes, the MTCP now approved all Declaratory Orders (DOs) and Compulsory Purchase Orders (CPOs), Development Plans, as well as hearing all appeals. Additionally, the requirements that now faced cities after the Appointed Day (1 August 1948) were greater than the already stringent obligations they faced after the 1944 Act.

While there were exceptions, the basic land acquisition and planning requirements for each local authority were as follows:

1. To submit a DO involved an application to the MTCP. This DO would identify an outline of the areas the authority felt should be included in their redevelopment area. Back-up documentation (plans, etc.) were submitted with the DO. Submissions for DOs were made under Section 1 of the 1944 Act, to declare land that could be 'subject to compulsory purchase for dealing with war damage'.[27] The area as set out in the DOs was simply to serve as a boundary outline, indicating area(s) that would possibly be acquired by the authority in their next steps. The DO was not meant to determine an exact final outline but was rather a general guide to the area(s) legally set out for potential redevelopment. Once approved, the authority could apply to acquire land within the Order. Generally speaking, most cities applied broadly for more acreage to be included than they intended to use, in part to cover contingencies or problems that could arise with purchases, often knowing they would not be financially capable of purchasing as much land as the DO included.

2. Once the DO was approved, the authority would be able to focus more specifically on plots of land they would apply to purchase. The next step was titled the CPO and that application was to include more specific detail as to the plans of the authority for the land they were requesting. In this step, the land outlined included bomb-damaged areas, but the law allowed also for the inclusion, under Section 9, for areas of 'bad lay-out

and obsolete development (blight)'.[28] In some cases local authorities could apply directly for a CPO without a DO (Section 2(2)) where 'postponement of purchase would be prejudicial to public interest'.[29] The CPO application also had to have back-up which proved the need for the purchase of the acreage as defined by the authority. Usually, this meant the city would have already submitted a land use plan to the MTCP, though in some cases the plan would be submitted with the CPO application.

3. With an approved CPO in hand, a local authority could then take the next steps to land acquisition. The purchase price was set out by law to prevent land speculation and problems with land values, and was based on existing land use value.[30]

Although some historians have assumed there was a widespread 'land grab' of bomb-damaged property, in reality, after the passing of the 1944 Act, there was a critical stalling factor: no one could purchase bomb-damaged land and know with any certainty whether the same land would then be included in a DO (and/or a CPO) by the city.[31] Essentially the legislation put property owners on notification that they could in future be forced to sell their property to the local authority. So in practice, it would be unwise to invest in a piece of property that had every possibility of coming under a CPO and thence being acquired by the local authority at a set price. While land speculators had a chance perhaps to make a profit, there was every possibility that they could face a loss.[32]

Cities now faced several further constraints to redevelopment and reconstruction: they had to plan first and then internally agree to the plan. The 1947 Act added a requirement that every district or city council in Britain must, within three years of the Appointed Day, submit a Development Plan for its city or region.[33] The plan was to be based on a professional survey, and had to receive the approval of the MTCP. Subject to such approval, these plans were to allow the government complete central control over the growth and placement of industry and other land use. Blitzed cities were often a step ahead in this process – they had all been aware since wartime that they needed to have a plan ready to start rebuilding. The plans submitted with applications for DOs and CPOs did not have to be based on professional surveys, and statutorily the only requirement was to provide information to assist the minister in his decision. However, it was to the authority's benefit to prepare something as thorough as possible: the more professional in appearance the plans and applications, the more likely an approval. Agreeing on a plan – as will be further discussed in Chapter 5 – was a difficult hurdle for most, if not all, blitzed cities.

Beyond the laws that gave government the ability to control planning and redevelopment of all property, they were also required to levy a 100 per cent development charge should an owner, a private investor or a developer wish to build on open land, rebuild or change a property's use. This charge was intended to help government make back some of the expense of acquiring land by taxing the (perceived) increased valuation of a property, based on the intended use. Finally, all building work above a value of £10 continued to be subject to approval and issuance of a building licence from the Ministry of Works.[34] Legally this licence was the final barrier to beginning building work, because once it was granted the materials and labour were – in theory –available for the project and it could go ahead. Between the requirements for two applications to the planning ministry, city and/or regional plans, the development charge and potential legal issues with land purchase, the start to reconstruction was in no way to prove to be a quick process.

III. *Planning the Blitzed Cities: The Early Stages*

As discussed in Chapter 2, from the very start of reconstruction discussion officials and city councils in blitzed cities had begun to talk about planning for the postwar period, and some made actual plans. Those cities bombed earliest in the war were usually further ahead, but most blitzed cities absorbed the Reith ideology and made at least a start.[35] Perhaps as important as the work carried out within the cities was the start made under Reith towards examining the issues that would be faced by blitzed cities in the postwar era. Though the initial Consultative Panel looking at bomb-damaged cities did not outlast Reith's tenure,[36] when the panel was reconstituted in 1943 a more thorough investigation of the cities' issues was undertaken. The issue of priority was mentioned: 'We welcome this proposal for early planning, since we are particularly anxious that delay should be avoided once redevelopment becomes physically possible.'[37]

Demonstrating the priority then given to the issues of bombed area reconstruction, the Advisory Panel on Reconstructing Blitzed Cities chose seven example cities to visit, collect data from and then produce a report.[38] The membership of the panel included five MTCP officials and at least three outside members, including surveyors and businesspersons.[39] Teams of officials and external members were sent to the cities of Bristol, Coventry, Hull, Plymouth, Portsmouth, Southampton and Swansea.[40] The reports included a brief damage survey, the status of each city's plans and the difficulties foreseen in the cities. It also considered war damage compensation and the projected cost of reconstruction, recommending that substantial financial assistance be given for blitz reconstruction.[41]

It is clear from both the work of the Advisory Panel and additional files from the Ministries of Reconstruction, Works and the new planning ministry that there was not just a sense of impending priority for rebuilding, but an assumption that the priority would be automatically given by anyone making building licence (or steel) allocations. In fact, memos detailing how such allocations were expected to work, and how the priorities would function, can be found in a planning ministry file from 1943–45: 'Building Priorities for Blitzed Towns'.[42] Official correspondence included advance issues of coordination: 'It is very obvious, particularly from the attitude of Works, but also of Health and other Departments, that although they may be paying some lip service to the special needs of blitz, they are in fact taking no really active steps in the matter.'[43] Most noticeably, much of the correspondence refers to the priority being sought for the rebuilding: 'During the war a strictly limited number of towns have suffered from very heavy blitzing … they have a prima facie claim to priority.'[44]

The issue of priority was also brought to the Reconstruction Committee at the time, in a paper by W. S. Morrison titled 'War Cabinet, Reconstruction Committee: Priorities for Post-War Building Work'. The committee members who discussed the paper make up a list of actors later very involved in the issues of reconstruction priority – in both Labour and Conservative governments – including Lord Woolton in the chair, Attlee, Bevin, Herbert Morrison, Dalton, Cripps, Butler, Jowitt and more.[45] However the discussion was merely theoretical, and did not appear to affect the postwar realities.

By the time Labour came to power, the officials of the MTCP had a decent grasp on the sorts of problems that would be facing the authorities and their own staff, both technical and in terms of coordinating other departments, such as Transport and Health. To assist the process, in 1947, the MTCP's technical planning section published a handbook primarily written during the war. *The Redevelopment of Central Areas* gave sample plans and technical advice to help local authorities, most of which did not hire a professional or trained planner for their staff [46] (see Figure 4.1). Most used the architects, engineers or surveyors already on the city payroll rather than hire a specialist planner. The planning functions – where they even existed, before the requirement for all authorities to produce a Development Plan – were most often taken care of by either staff architects or civil engineers. But local authorities, particularly in blitzed cities, equally understood that they could best advance their cause for reconstruction by hiring either in-house professionals or external consultant planners.

In this vein a number of cities began the planning process and produced professional – and sometimes professionally published – plans for reconstruction. Examples include books that accompanied exhibitions, such as *Exeter Phoenix, A Plan for Plymouth, A Plan for the City and County of Hull, The Future of Coventry* and, of course, the *Greater London Plan*.[47] An American observer in 1947 published his perspective on Britain's physical reconstruction drive. He noted: 'Exhibits of planning charts, studies, and recommendations attract thousands in the larger cities. Documentary films, one at least that runs for more than an hour, are shown in commercial movie houses. Stories about public hearings on town plans or on the acquisition of land for larger projects are front page news in both the London and provincial papers.'[48] Such plans set a high standard, but at the same time they often 'forced' the ministry to accept a plan that had been approved by city officials and then widely circulated among – and approved by – the public. The classic example of this was at Plymouth where the plans had been in development since early in the war, were created by Professor Patrick Abercrombie, a high profile planner, and had been exhibited in Plymouth and London. Though the MTCP opposed the radical plans, they had apparently 'assumed the status of a local "Magna Carta" '.[49] It was additionally difficult for the MTCP to deny approval when ministry officials had been the ones to recommend the planners hired.[50]

Figure 4.1 Conjectural redevelopment from *Redevelopment of Central Areas*. Ministry of Town & Country Planning (London: HMSO, 1947).

IV. *Blitzed Cities in the Postwar Period*

The 1947 Act, as well as the remnants of the 1944 Act, had a heavy impact on blitzed cities. The new requirements for applications to acquire land typically involved at least two stages and any building starts were to be approved and overseen by the MTCP.[51] Partly for this reason, in the immediate postwar period the MTCP role soon included keeping very specific track of the cities' status, including monitoring readiness of plans for construction, building projects that were in the late planning stages, consequent materials requirements – particularly steel – and ongoing progress of planning and construction. With pressure being put on government by MPs and groups like the Blitzed Areas Group of the Parliamentary Labour Party, the Associated British Chambers of Commerce and Association of Municipal Corporations, the MTCP was eventually called on by the IPC to debrief economic planners on specific needs of the cities. In the interim, planning ministry internal correspondence shows that the idea to sponsor conferences for local authorities had been hatched among MTCP officials.[52]

Knowing that the new legislation would have a severe impact on cities, and that the local authority officials having to manage these new requirements would need assistance, planning ministry officials soon persuaded Minister Silkin to schedule blocks of time in autumn of 1947 when he could address the elected and appointed officials from bomb-damaged cities. Conferences were announced and arranged with local authority attendees in London during late October and early November 1947.[53] Each conference had groups of local authority representatives such as city engineers, town clerks and councillors, lasted several days and were presided over by planning ministry officials with Silkin giving a keynote speech as well as a question and answer session for each group.[54] Conferences were arranged regionally so that cities near to each other could attend together, for example, Exeter and Plymouth in the southwest.[55]

The topics covered included those suggested during the conference planning by an MTCP official:

[It] will be desirable to give Local Authorities quite a lot of general guidance on points such as the following:
(a) The use of the 1944 Act between Royal Assent and the Appointed Day;
(b) The conditions attaching to the various sections of the Act; and the policy adopted by the Ministry in dealing with Applications and Orders, illustrated by recent decisions;
(c) The type of case which should wait for the new legislation;
(d) Policy with regard to standing buildings not to be disturbed by the plan;
(e) The limitations of C.P.O.s to the land required in the next five years;
(f) Relation between plans and acquisitions;
(g) Financial aspects to be taken into account; type of financial information required by the Ministry;
(h) New Grants System.[56]

Conference transcripts clearly show that many cities were, justifiably, worried about the future. Concerns raised included the time frame in which they were to submit applications and the speed of their approval, the issue of receiving approval without being given permission to build and how priorities would then be given to various cities by MTCP officials.[57] Though still fairly positive, the MTCP was aware of issues stemming from Treasury plans, prompting Silkin to express tempered encouragement at the conferences:

I am afraid that when this series of Conferences was first arranged the prospects were rather different; we than hoped that it would be possible to proceed very speedily ... under the [1947 Act] ... Since then our economic difficulties have intervened ...

One thing is quite certain, that we must not lose the opportunity which destruction by the enemy has afforded us of rebuilding our towns and redeveloping them in a way which will make them better, healthier and more pleasant towns to live in. It would be a terrible reflection on our age if we failed to seize this opportunity.[58]

Increasingly then, the MTCP had become the primary point of contact within government for the blitzed cities: they oversaw their planning, processed their applications, negotiated changes for application and plan approval, and were the main contact for the IPC – as well as the Ministry of Works and Board of Trade – in terms of city preparedness and needs assessment.[59] From the MTCP perspective they had also become lobbyists on behalf of the blitzed cities: the MTCP provided internal governmental pressure on their behalf, while MPs and other groups – as noted here and in Chapter 3 – pressed the government through parliamentary debates and questions. In fact the MPs, groups and city officials pushed their agendas with any department they deemed appropriate, to allow starts on rebuilding.[60]

In the end, as also shown in Chapter 3, the primary obstacle to any city centre building starts was the IPC allocation system. The first meeting involving an MTCP representative giving evidence and input to the IPC was not held until June 1948.[61] At this point the MTCP was still clarifying their exact role as regards the blitzed cities, and the Deputy Secretary attending the meeting voiced this: 'the *actual* rebuilding of the blitzed cities was not, strictly speaking, the responsibility of the MTCP'.[62] Clearly, though, they were the principal liaison, as they had been the key ministry working with the cities on their postwar plans.[63] But the MTCP did not have the official ability to approve building licences for the cities; licences had to come through the Ministry of Works – although by 1950 this could only happen with 'sponsorship' from the MTCP.[64] This prompted a representative from the Board of Trade, at the same meeting, to suggest that a way needed to be found to allow some start to building work in the blitzed cities, even if only through a small general or miscellaneous allocation. The individual projects did not warrant licenses on their own but it was thought perhaps a cost of building ceiling could be provided to certain cities as a limit to start.[65]

Eventually in 1950 this idea was implemented, but in the short term no allowances were made. Correspondence between the MTCP and IPC does show that numbers for the amounts of steel needed were provided by the planning ministry as a guide to the scope of blitzed cities' building needs.[66] From about the same time, increasingly specific memos demonstrate the readiness of the IPC to allow some steel allocations. Finally on 1 February 1949 Lewis Silkin made his announcement in the House of Commons.[67] From June 1949 onwards, internal MTCP correspondence shows support for the blitzed cities from the Ministry of Works, but not at all from the IPC. Evelyn Sharp wrote:

Mr. Strath of the Investment Programmes party was our real stumbling block. He expressed a certain amount of (lukewarm) sympathy for the blitzed towns, but said that if we were to contemplate £12 million investment during 1950 (I gather this is the approximate figure if one includes London), including 40,000 or so tons of steel, it must be shown where on the programme equivalent figures were going to be saved.

This was notwithstanding that Mr. Muir said (a) that he could find the £12 million out of the £480 million allowed to M.O.W. for miscellaneous work; and (b) that there is no shortage of structural steel, which is what is involved here.

There was no room for compromise on the Committee.[68]

Sharp had been in touch with IPC officials since her first appearance at their June 1948 meeting. She was, and would further become, increasingly frustrated at the response from the committee.

The series of HLG (planning ministry) files detailing the allocations attempted and the proposed allocations by city also contain much internal correspondence.[69] Dame Evelyn often minuted her minister, giving him what might be called today a 'position' document, with an update on the status with the IPC/Treasury as well as key points to be made in meetings with those entities, as well as with Works, the Board of Trade and so on.[70] This lack of support from the IPC, as shown, continued to the end of its existence.

Even under the strictly limited amount of building licence allocations that the MTCP was able to squeeze out of the IPC on behalf of the blitzed cities, only a select group of cities received any allocations. The February 1949 announcement allowed for only fourteen cities outside of London to make a start. The list of cities was based on where planning ministry officials thought the amount of building being allowed would best be used: cities needed to be ready with either a developer or their own building plans and be thought to have available building labour as well.[71] The 1949 allocation was the only publicly announced accession to the blitzed cities for two years. No official allocations were made for 1950, and in 1951 the MTCP was, of course, still pressing the IPC for further allowances. After February 1949 the 'blitzed cities' list grew to include eighteen cities (see Table 4.1). These eighteen cities became the 'official' list of blitzed cities consistently from mid-1949 all the way through the relaxation of building licenses in 1954.[72] No evidence appears to remain in HLG files showing exactly how the cities were chosen.[73] In MTCP files numerous surveys exist showing collected statistics on bomb damage and needs for rebuilding.[74] The MTCP kept consistent records and had regular contact with city officials through the use of regional planning offices, headed by regional officers (RPOs, see Figure 4.2). Some regions had many more damaged cities than others, but all regions had at least one.[75]

It is perplexing that the list of eighteen cities ('blitzed cities' will hereafter refer to these eighteen, unless otherwise noted) did not include simply the cities with the greatest amount of damage by acreage, or even damage by square footage or housing losses. For example, it is not possible to tell why a city such as Lowestoft with a reported fifteen acres of damage was included, while Bath with fifty-five acres was not[76] (see Table 2.2). In total there are nine cities not on the MTCP's final list that had more reported damage than the bottom two, and five of these had significantly more damage (i.e., double the acreage). Cities not appearing on the list were left to obtain building sponsorship from the Board

MINISTRY OF TOWN AND COUNTRY PLANNING REGIONAL ORGANISATION

Figure 4.2 Planning regions in 1951 from Cmd. 8204, HMSO.

of Trade or Ministry of Works if they could. Nothing in the HLG files indicates that complaints were received from the overlooked cities, but the list of eighteen was very much internal to the planning ministry and not circulated outside of government. The Silkin announcement in 1949 was the only time specific cities were ever named publicly.

MTCP officials kept track of the cities directly, occasionally using the RPOs as an additional liaison. Supervision of the cities' plan status, their readiness for

Table 4.1 Blitzed city list per Ministry of Town and Country Planning

City	Region
Birmingham	9
Bristol	7
Canterbury	12
Coventry	9
Dover	12
Exeter	7
Hull	2
Liverpool	10
Lowestoft	4
Manchester	10
Norwich	4
Plymouth	7
Portsmouth	6
Sheffield	2
South Shields	1
Southampton	6
Swansea	8
Yarmouth (Great)	4

Source: TNA: HLG 71/1570, 71/2222–2230.

Table 4.2 Declaratory Orders (DOs) and Compulsory Purchase Orders (CPOs)

City	Population (1948–49)	Bombed area (acres)	Declaratory Order ALL (acres)	Comp. Purchase Order(s) ALL (acres)
Birmingham	1,096,190	60	?	1,041.07
Bristol	435,390	121	247.00	112.22
Canterbury	26,130	26	?	12.29
Coventry	251,590	160	274.00	34.05
Dover*		25	143.50	34.21
Exeter	75,680	68	75.64	104.08
Hull	294,410	136	276.17	65.07
Liverpool	792,600	208	46.26	22.14
Lowestoft*		15	?	–
Manchester	693,900	61	106.13	172.76
Norwich	118,200	78	41.10	–
Plymouth	206,110	168	415.06	238.12
Portsmouth	242,020	165	430.88	46.33
Sheffield	514,590	108	92.42	3.00
South Shields	106,820	19	13.86	2.74
Southampton	180,100	145	261.68	21.20
Swansea	158,000	42	134.00	25.98
Yarmouth (Great)	50,140	50	35.50	10.50

Sources: Cmd. 8204, Cmd. 9559. Note '?' is no data. * Dover and Lowestoft were on the eighteen cities list but not included in tables published.

building and their priorities within their plan were undertaken by central and regional ministry officials. The list of proposed allocations to each city was – like most allocations from the IPC – done by building value after 1949, rather than by steel tonnage allowed.[77] Relationships with city officials were often strained where the local authorities felt they were not receiving enough allocations, and placed blame on the planning ministry. More frequently, they complained of the slowness of progress by the planning ministry, a complaint which was only partially justified.[78] As we have seen, though MTCP officials were possibly overwhelmed with work, the fact that they had to await decisions by the IPC – and often the Headquarters Building Committee (HQBC) and Priorities Sub-Committee as well – was obscured from local officials.

The MTCP was tasked with processing a significant amount of paperwork from the initial passing of the 1944 Act and more so under the changes from the 1947 Act. Officials processed DOs, CPOs and reviewed Development Plans, in addition to the oversight of New Towns and coordination with other ministries on industrial locations, roadways, housing and more. Blitzed cities seemed to command some priority – at least within the planning ministry – for perceived moral reasons, though, of course, they also presented the ministry with much of its workload. Coordination proved difficult though, and files show increasing frustration with the Ministry of Works, who in early 1950 agreed that the blitzed cities should have an increased allocation out of their 'miscellaneous' capital investment budget, but then rescinded this and suggested cutting it to zero. Internal communication shows how MTCP officials argued the position, and pressed for priority.[79] MTCP officials also kept track of outside opinion, and many of the files detailing blitzed city work from 1949 to 1952 contain a number of national press clippings.[80]

Officials in the planning ministry spent a great deal of time making decisions on acreage and specific outlines when approving the applications. But the outcomes – from the local authority perspective – could vary greatly. Cities with huge amounts of bomb damage often had smaller DOs and CPOs approved than one might expect, while at the same time small cities with relatively smaller areas of damage could see comparatively vast acreage in their approvals. Examples include Exeter with a very large DO compared with its size and bomb damage, Liverpool with a smaller DO proportionally and Birmingham with the largest DO of any city, but most of it for blight rather than blitz (see Table 4.2).

In the end, the list of approved DOs and CPOs makes for interesting reading. While it might have been logical to assume that approvals would be proportional to the damage sustained – and the MTCP had collected these statistics from all the planning regions by the end of the war[81] – the actual totals varied enormously.[82] Clearly the planning ministry made decisions based on the actual plans submitted, the readiness of each city and professional quality of their plans, as well as the supporting arguments made. The HLG file series held at the National Archives includes thousands of pages of documentation on the DO and CPO applications from this period. While TNA records do not include 100 per cent of the files created in the period, or even 50 per cent, the selection that survives demonstrates a good breadth of the range of issues encountered between city officials and the planning ministry.[83]

Yet another problem beyond the allocation issues seems to have been the interaction of central and local officials.[84] The planning ministry had constant contact with the local authorities, including both city clerks and councils as well as private interests represented on local reconstruction committees, so they were very aware of the increasing frustration from lack of building progress. The correspondence and memoranda found in the HLG files indicates that very few local authorities had a good relationship with planning ministry officials.[85] For the most part tension seemed to originate in a few places: the city officials were slow to provide a final plan; the planning ministry insisted on overriding the city plans with their preferences for layouts and so on; the goals of the cities and the ministry officials could be at odds; and external issues involving other ministries (i.e., Ministry of Transport for roadways and rail) could interfere with final approvals.

The following chapter will detail specific examples at Hull, Exeter and Liverpool, but it should be noted that a number of local authorities did become aware that they needed to develop a good relationship with MTCP officials. Some also reduced the size of their DO and CPO applications when they – probably correctly – decided that the likelihood of approval would be much higher if they applied for lower acreages.[86] Probably the most frequent issue between the central and local authorities, though, was the finalized plan for the city centres. Local authorities planned as they saw fit for their area, but often found themselves at cross-purposes with MTCP 'experts' as will be shown in the next chapter.[87]

Where city officials were slow with their plans, this appears usually to have been due to internal disagreement within the cities. Property owners, traders, large and small businesses, residents and city planners frequently had competing visions for the postwar reconstructions. These problems kept many cities from submission of plans as well as DO and CPO applications. Ministry files show the central government perspective on these problems, clearly frustrating for MTCP officials, slowing their ability to process approvals but also affecting the ministry's ability to provide the IPC or Ministry of Works with the building requirements of the cities. These problems, as they applied to specific cities, will be discussed thoroughly in the next chapter.

It is equally clear from documents preserved in the National Archives that the perspective within the planning ministry reflected a sense that since ministry officials were theoretically a body of professional planning 'experts', they felt their opinions and decisions on how the city layouts should proceed were the most important – in many cases overriding the preferences or decisions of the local authorities.[88] This created more tension and further delays. The goals of the MTCP with regard to specific cities were often unclear. From surviving documents, however, it is clear that planning officials were focused frequently on the circulation within the cities, but it is unclear from the files themselves whether these opinions or disagreements were based on a particular planning theory. Quite often they appear to be simply based on the opinion of the lead official in correspondence with the city officials. In any case, the plans brought forward by most cities were based on local knowledge and – more importantly – the local compromise, or consensus. Finding that the planning ministry had different ideas about the goal for a city plan posed many difficulties.[89]

All plans required some coordination with other ministries for implementation, and this frequently set up yet another barrier for rebuilding. The Ministry of Health was responsible for issues relating to housing (until 1951) and additionally had jurisdiction over water mains, sewers and drainage. The Ministry of Transport provided grants for road building and so had jurisdiction over final roadways designs. Conflicts could arise on either front based on the planned infrastructure, particularly where cities had 'planned boldly' – attempting to make significant changes to city centre layouts. Problems also arose from conflicts with privately controlled infrastructure such as docks and railways. For example, new plans could be dependent on coercing firms such as the London and Northeast Railway (LNER) into agreeing plans and moving railways.[90]

Further affecting the outcome of the requests to the IPC were the ministerial relationships between the Treasury or Chancellor of the Exchequer and the Minister of Town and Country Planning, as shown in Chapter 3. While Lewis Silkin was fairly dynamic in drafting legislation for the 1947 Act, when it came to pushing other ministers or cabinet members to assist with problems like the blitzed cities, he seems to have remained mostly silent.[91] Silkin's rhetoric, in particular at the 1947 conferences, shows that at least early on he accepted the IPC excuses of economic priority. When Silkin lost his seat at the 1950 general election – due to its being removed by the boundary commission, rather than an electoral loss – Attlee appointed Hugh Dalton, former Chancellor, to replace him. This was an ironic choice from the perspective of the blitzed cities, since Dalton had been the final word in not allowing any initial allocations for the cities – now he was forced to argue on their behalf to receive and increase them.[92]

Dalton left little in the files to show any prioritization of the Blitz reconstruction issues. However, his diary entries are clear on his priorities: first, housing; second, New Towns; third, national parks.[93] There is no mention of reconstruction, but he does mention his staff. Sharp had clearly developed a good working relationship with her ministers and Dalton said of her when he was reorganizing the ministry to take on housing, 'I shall need Evelyn Sharp – the best man I've got – more than ever.'[94]

But Dalton did not have to fight the planning fight for very long. His tenure lasted only twelve months before Labour lost power at the general election held in autumn 1951. When the new Conservative government took office very little changed initially with regard to allocations for blitzed cities. Yet within the planning ministry – now called 'Housing and Local Government' but retaining the planning functions – a new and dynamic leader brought several changes to the department, eventually affecting blitzed cities more profoundly. Harold Macmillan headed the new ministry for three years and oversaw the majority of actual starts to postwar reconstruction. Under Macmillan adjustments were made to the 1947 Act; removal of the development charge was the most significant. For the blitzed cities though, Macmillan's greatest strength was his advocacy of their cause. As shown in the previous chapter, he was the first minister to take the issue to Cabinet, and the first to examine the possible impact on votes. Macmillan was the first minister to deliberately ignore the instructions of the Chancellor of the Exchequer and, probably in his eyes, as well as in the eyes of many of his officials, was therefore first to 'do the right thing' on behalf of the cities.

Though his clear priority was to build houses – after all the Conservative campaign had included great promises towards solving the housing issues – Macmillan still found time to advocate for other problems he saw as important.[95] After being debriefed and having an early immersion into the problems of blitzed cities, he increasingly pushed forward the agenda for the needs of the cities. Although his diary looked back at the period from October 1952 as a 'new storm' which he felt was a 'by-product of the capital investment dogma', Macmillan had been pressing the issue internally since the start of his administration. Correspondence with the Chancellor, Rab Butler, was regular and consistently requested larger allocations for the blitzed cities. Macmillan clearly realized that fighting the officials' battle with the IPC was not having much effect. As he said publicly to local authority representatives in 1952: 'All too often I have to tell you that I cannot let you do this or that because there is a "capital investment programme" which does not provide for all you want to do. This is exasperating for you; and, also, if you will believe me, for me.'[96]

As planning minister, Macmillan made a far greater impact on the plight of the blitzed cities than his predecessors. During his tenure there was increasing pressure coming through Parliament to speed up reconstruction, and the first public line of defence had to be taken by Macmillan. Internally Macmillan had been pushing, even though as he admitted in his diary: 'it was becoming known that the sum available [for the blitzed cities' allocation] was likely to be severely reduced. How severely even the cities did not fully realize.'[97] As shown in Chapter 3, Macmillan fought the blitzed cities' battle with the IPC and Treasury (or Chancellor) much more forcefully and vociferously than his predecessors. More than his predecessors Macmillan could be called successful – from the cities' perspective – not only for overriding some of the Chancellor's decisions, but for managing to secure large increases in allocations, even if they were still a very small percentage of the 'Miscellaneous' building allocation budget.

Conclusion

In terms of government's postwar relations with blitzed cities there were constant conflicts in the planning ministry between achieving urgent objectives and being logical and comprehensive in planning, building and development.[98] At the same time the planning ministry was still searching for, and creating, its role while dealing with the Whitehall bureaucracy. The role of officials in the planning ministries cannot be understated, and here too Cullingworth concurs that the greatest influences on outcomes in planning often came more from the civil servants than from the politicians, even while also agreeing with Dame

Evelyn Sharp that the policies made 'depended more on political than technical objectives'.[99] Still, he also notes that the ministry often set 'impossible goals', while still managing to get the work done eventually, as well as transforming the machinery of planning in Britain.[100] This chapter has emphasized the decisive role of officials in the planning ministry, who wielded a great deal of power, impacting the physical outcome of planning and rebuilding. Additionally it has demonstrated that the blitzed cities had to work their way through both new legislative requirements and through the webs of Whitehall, a daunting task indeed.

It is critical to note that the most important conclusion gleaned from this research was the overwhelming complexity of issues that affected the work to rebuild the cities. From legislative complications and requirements to old and new constraints of bureaucracy and the additional weight of the personal interactions and conflicts, the plans alone do not tell a complete story about Britain's built environment in the postwar era. Additionally, the very clear priority accorded to the issues of rebuilding in wartime stayed with planning officials, and were often recognized by official colleagues in other ministries, but they were ignored by economic planners and decision-makers.[101] The following chapter will show that even given the numerous difficulties generated by *central* government, these problems might have played only a small part in the issues faced by the cities. Local issues were abundant and often intractable.

Chapter 5

LOCAL CONSTRAINTS: THE CITIES OF HULL, EXETER AND LIVERPOOL

Are we going to make this necessary rebuilding an opportunity for real replanning, for creating in Britain more of the delights and advantages that urban living can provide?
> – RIBA's *Rebuilding Britain* exhibition publication, 1943

Blitzed cities certainly presented opportunities for applying modernist visions to new plans and new spaces in Britain. But what plans did the cities make? And within the constraints presented in the previous chapters, how did they cope with the difficulties of economic and legislative barriers? This chapter will illuminate the various actions taken within central government, how these affected blitzed cities, and additionally show the diversity of uniquely local issues faced by councils and officials within each city. While central government struggled with national economic issues, so too did the blitzed cities struggle with local issues. The loss of business in the city centres was a crucial blow, but greater still was the revenue loss from tax rates that were uncollectable: buildings destroyed left no reason for payment, and evacuated or bombed out homeowners represented further losses. Additionally, rents were generally uncollectable on destroyed, empty or badly damaged properties. However, equally crucial to obstruction of progress in some cities were the issues created by attempts to make plans for the future. From property owners unwilling to give up locations or freeholds to disagreement over changes to roadway layouts and usage zones, the lack of consensus in most bomb-damaged cities was palpable. All cities eventually had to decide who would create a plan – an external consultant or in-house official – as well as be sure the plan was agreed on – at the least by the city council or concerned officials.

As seen in Chapter 4, city officials also needed to prepare submissions for land acquisition, including plans for development, under the planning acts of 1944 and 1947. Most cities had understood the rhetoric of the 1940–45 period as encouraging bold plans and felt assured that they would receive priority in the postwar phase for rebuilding. It took many years before local authorities and city councillors became aware of the abandonment of such promises.

During the war every city had developed a separate rapport with central government, particularly in the planning ministry. Communication had been established regarding future plans with all bomb-damaged cities, not just those chosen for test case investigations.[1] For better or worse these relationships would also affect the outcome of local plans, applications and proposals in the postwar period. The cities chosen for this chapter – Hull, Exeter and Liverpool – each had a unique relationship with Whitehall, but all also had unique problems to resolve within their reconstruction plans and implementation.

Hull was the closest city to Germany and received a large portion of the bombing outside London. The city had nationally important industry as well as one of the busiest ports in Britain. Further, Hull had serious congestion issues and a lack of consensus about the future of the city. It also had one of the poorest local authorities in the country, and suffered most from the loss of rates. Exeter is a distinct example of a non-industrial city targeted for its historic value and beauty. Its city centre was one of the most devastated in the Blitz, suffering the loss of proportionally more of its shopping area than any other city. And while more consensus about future plans existed in Exeter than in Hull, the disagreements with various ministries overseeing aspects of the plan caused great difficulties.

Liverpool was the largest city outside London to have suffered extensive blitz damage. In fact, by acreage, Liverpool suffered more than any other city.[2] Although Liverpool officials had to have been aware of the need to plan, they were the slowest of the three cities to submit plans under the 1944 Act, in part due to the slowness of the city council's committee on reconstruction issues. The relationships developed with Whitehall were much less fraught than other cities' interactions, but Liverpool's representatives frustrated the planning ministry with their lack of preparation. Here plans were far less ambitious than in other cities, and postwar rebuilding was a more organic process – even if the results were similar. Together these cities provide excellent and varied examples of the interplay of local and national government and of the myriad of potential problems faced by cities in the postwar period. The variety of city size, the political make-up of both councils and MPs, and the different problems faced in the three cities make them ideal cases for investigating postwar progress.

I. *Kingston-upon-Hull*

Founded officially by Edward I in 1293, Hull is rarely called by its full and formal name; it is usually abbreviated into simply the name of the river whose banks it straddles.[3] Established for its location at the confluence of the River Hull and the River Humber, the city sits on the north side of the deepest channel of water on the Humber, creating an ideal port that grew in size alongside the growth of ships themselves over many centuries. A centre for international trade and fishing, Hull has long been a nationally important place for commerce.[4] Its shipping tonnage increased from 109,000 in 1775, to 3,250,000 in 1891, then to a peak of 7,500,000 in 1923. Industries that grew around shipping included railways and other transport, milling from timber imports, paint and chemicals, and engineering.[5]

Like other British cities in the nineteenth century, Hull's growth was mainly uncontrolled, and the mix of industry with housing and shopping was also unregulated and unplanned. The railways came to Hull to distribute both fish and imports, but were simply laid out as the rail companies saw fit and were able to obtain land, mainly at ground level and frequently passing across roadways. By the Second World War, the city centre of Hull was not only busy but very congested. Road traffic – including public transport such as buses – fought rail traffic, and industrial sites too close to shopping and other commerce further exacerbated central congestion.[6]

An easy target due to its proximity to Germany, between 1940 and 1945 there were 823 warnings and 86 major raids on the city (see Figure 5.1). The heaviest raids came in the spring and summer of 1941.[7] The total damage, spread over 136 acres of Hull, was said to be as follows:[8]

- 1,100 shops (17+ per cent of prewar hereditaments),
- over 600,000 square feet warehouses (public and private),
- over 2 million square feet industrial building,
- 25 pubs (plus 6 severely damaged),
- 25 churches (plus 9 badly damaged),
- 6 cinemas, 1 theatre,

Figure 5.1 Bomb damage in Hull. Image: Alamy.

- several city institutions, including 12 schools destroyed totally and 26 damaged,
- City Hall and several other city buildings badly damaged,
- 5,305 houses totally destroyed,
- 3,021 houses badly damaged, many more partially damaged: only 5,700 (6 per cent) of 92,600 were unscathed.

The loss of life was not as high in Hull as in other similarly bombed cities, with 1,100 killed and about the same number injured in total.[9] Hull possibly suffered more raids than other cities due to its location: bombers targeting Liverpool or Sheffield that were forced to turn back due to poor weather would simply have re-targeted Hull, as it was en route.[10] Locally, morale was also affected not just by the raids but by the subsequent lack of publicity as well because officials kept blitz locations quiet so as not to give the Germans information, particularly regarding their success.[11]

While wartime bombing clearly pushed the issue of planning to the forefront, Hull officials had seen the need long before the war began. Planning in Hull had started well before 1939, with two schemes already approved under the 1932 Town Planning Act and two further plans awaiting approval at the outbreak of war.[12] During the war the governing body of the city, Hull Corporation, sent a deputation to Whitehall to discuss the future of the city and investigate what government assistance might be forthcoming. The attendees were not named in the records of the meeting but they authored a full, possibly verbatim, report of the visit on 5 June 1942.[13] The report shows that the relationship with Whitehall at the time was quite good, with positive reactions from both Lord Portal and Sir William Jowitt described in the transcript.[14] Two reports had been sent earlier to Whitehall, in March 1940 and February 1942, both of which – according to the meeting report – were also appreciated by Portal and Jowitt.[15] As the government was about to publish reports on the issues being discussed, the deputation was told that the conversation would be confidential.

The deputation members were assured that Whitehall was aware of the enormity of the future reconstruction in Hull: Col. Sir A. Lambert Ward told them that 'the damage done in Hull was out of all proportion to the size of the City, compared with the rest of the country'.[16] They were assured too that legislation would soon be passed to deal with the issues of land acquisition and costs. There was additional agreement among the attendees, including the ministers, that a central planning authority was necessary to assist and guide cities in their reconstruction plans. Further demonstrating the positive relationship being developed with Hull officials, Lord Portal was reported to have said that 'he wished Hull would go round and tell everybody that, as people did not look at it in the same way as Hull were doing, in his opinion there must be some central authority'.[17] Hull's Town Clerk then wondered whether, in the meantime, the city could be in touch with any government department in order to get started with planning. He hoped there could be one department involved, rather than several. Jowitt replied that although there was not yet legislation to deal with the issues being faced, nothing should prevent Hull 'working out and getting on with their plans and proposals forth-with, so that, in due course, they could be put before the appropriate Government department'.[18] Lord Portal then suggested that should they have great difficulties in planning before the war's end, they should come back to his ministry with their problems.

In closing the deputation wondered about the hiring of an 'expert' for planning. They were told unequivocally that they should hire an expert planner, with Jowitt adding that 'the LCC, Southampton and Plymouth had done it'.[19] The Hull group was not given a specific suggestion, but was told the Hull Corporation should decide for itself. The report stated that the deputation concluded with the intention to: hire an expert planner, begin planning immediately, open discussions with the local county council, submit plans as completed to the planning ministry with a request to pressure the Treasury for assistance. It also authorized further contact between the expert planner and Lord Portal without Corporation approval 'in case of any difficulties'.[20]

In Hull it appears that, somewhat unusually, not only were the City Council and officials concerned with planning, but individuals and non-governmental organizations also took it on themselves to investigate local issues and make their own plans and recommendations.[21] The best known, and largest, of these was the survey headed by Max Lock from 1939. Lock had received a Leverhulme research grant for a complete survey of Hull, its industry, business, transport, housing and more – all the major assessments thought necessary for a comprehensive future plan.[22] Lock left his position as head of the Hull School of Architecture to complete the work. The survey was completed with employees paid under the grant and with informational assistance from certain town officials and from the planning ministry, though neither officially sanctioned it.[23] Still, it was a useful document to both when it was published in 1943. Lock's report ran to ten very detailed sections, including surveys of geographical and physical conditions, the utilization of land, transport, housing, shopping and social services. It concluded with recommendations for the future planning of Hull.

Even before the official publication of Lock's work, city officials had taken note of both the encouragement from Whitehall and the popularity of small local planning exhibitions. Based on the deputation of 1942 Hull officials hired Sir Patrick Abercrombie, a leading town planner who was also on the board of the Housing Centre, the group sponsoring Lock's work. He was engaged for the work in partnership with the famous architect Sir Edwin Lutyens, and they were encouraged by local officials to create a plan befitting the status of the city – considering its importance in trade, industry and shipping.[24] From the start, however, there was clearly no consensus in Hull on how bold such a plan should be. The City Council at the time was divided, though a majority was held by an anti-Labour group, which seems to have been mainly Conservative though not aligned specifically with that party. The group, known as the Municipal Affairs Group (or MAG), had agreed with the Labour opposition that a plan should be made and an expert hired, but it would soon find that the Abercrombie suggestions were rather bolder than they had expected.

In July 1943, W. S. Morrison, Minister of Town and Country Planning, opened an exhibition of the Lock survey in London.[25] Morrison was encouraging and enthusiastic about the potential for the Abercrombie and Lutyens plan, with the Lock survey as its base.[26] But such enthusiasm within Hull soon waned. By November 1944 the council had received an initial proposal from Abercrombie (Lutyens had passed away in January 1944). The plans apparently included building bridges to relocate all railway crossings over roadways; creating a new main railway station; separating central area usage into zones such as civic (city hall, library, etc.), commercial and residential; as well as relocating the main shopping area entirely and adding more open public spaces.[27] While officials agreed to hold an exhibition of the early proposals, the radical nature of the plans alarmed members of MAG and the local press.[28] Opposition to such bold – even utopian – ideas would only increase as the end of war approached and planning legislation, especially the 1944 Act, began to have a local impact.[29]

The Lord Mayor, during the June 1942 visit to Portal and Jowitt, is reported to have 'intimated that he thought it would be a disaster if the re-planning of big cities was left entirely to local authorities, as it was bound to result in certain interests creating difficulties'.[30] The comment was prescient: from 1945 well into the 1950s divergent interests in the city of Hull made constant protests about the Corporation's plans. From hearings to lawsuits and from propaganda to editorials, opposition was fierce and constant. Many, but not all, of the issues local to Hull are described below.

As mentioned in the previous chapter, an Advisory Panel on the Redevelopment of City Centres was convened by the Ministry of Town and Country Planning (MTCP) in September 1943. The seven cities chosen included Hull, and the Panel visited in October 1943. Before their visit, the Panel had preliminary notes set out for each of the cities. In the note on Hull the Panel stated: 'The LNER own most of the river frontage appropriate for industrial development but are not willing to cooperate with the planning authority'.[31] While the Panel's report was not intended to approve or disapprove of any planning already taking place, it did gather information about potential plans and potential problems. This was the only initial issue of which a note was made. In practice the difficulty over the railways and their dock connections became a much greater hurdle for the local authority and the planners.

Files in local archives show that reconstruction in Hull was dominated by issues caused by prewar layout and subsequent damage to the docks and the railways. While it had been noted that the London and North East Railway (LNER) was uncooperative as early as 1943, the issues worsened throughout the immediate postwar period. Discussion took place within the city, between the MTCP and the Ministry of (War) Transport and between these entities and the LNER (later the nationalized British Rail), but very little seems to have been resolved even by 1954.[32] In May 1945 Abercrombie met with transport ministry and LNER representatives to 'informally discuss' the level crossing situation and the ongoing traffic problems caused by these crossings.[33] Hull traffic had for many years been hostage to both the trains which came through to the centre and those en route to the docks.[34] The following March a meeting between the LNER and the Hull Inc. Chamber of Commerce and Shipping (HICCS) centred around rail congestion in the streets and the economics of changing the rail routes to the docks. It was agreed that no ideal solution could be found which would not cost the city a great deal, or cause a huge loss of revenue to industry.[35]

Later talks also took place concerning the redevelopment of the bomb-damaged docks. These talks were complicated by the fact that not only did the LNER – a substantial dock owner – need to agree to plans with the industry using the docks, but the fishing industry in Hull decided to opt out of negotiations. Future reconstruction plans then excluded the fish trade at St Andrew's Dock from proposed upgrades or changes.[36] The fish trade it seemed, like other traders throughout the city of Hull, wanted neither change nor displacement.

In addition to the local dock and rail problems, the City Corporation was under pressure from the MAG and various traders, so the City Engineer was asked to prepare an alternative to the Abercrombie plan. This was completed in early 1945, not long before the Abercrombie plan was officially published.[37] Ministry officials also made regular visits from early in 1945, though they never seemed to be able to affect the planning process to their satisfaction. Even when compromises were attempted, results seemed elusive, and one official voiced what appeared to be collective ministry concern: 'to my mind the situation is most disquieting'.[38] The lack of agreement on plans prompted many internal MTCP meetings to discuss the problems. Decisions on whether to 'dockise' (deepen and develop) the River Hull were debated, stalling some industrial reconstruction and repair, as well as holding up a plan for industrial location: 'trade revival is hampered by the inability of industrial organizations to formulate plans for reconstruction or expansion'.[39]

The Corporation prevaricated, wavered and changed their minds. Although archival evidence does not indicate why, the biggest issue seems to have been worry about potential opposition to the plans.[40] For example, in a letter regarding an upcoming visit to discuss areas for potential Declaratory Orders (DOs) or Compulsory Purchase Orders (CPOs) the Town Clerk, Bullock, added a handwritten note: 'I also wish to raise the question of transferring the two [illegible] schemes affecting certain parts of the city back to the "interim" stage'.[41] Becoming impatient, the primary Whitehall planning official dealing with Hull (H. Gatliff) finally told officials that they needed to at least move along with clearing bomb damage, even if their plans were not yet final: 'I am sure that the future life of the city will be seriously prejudiced unless a number of the conspicuous blitzed buildings are either repaired or … cleared entirely'.[42] Shortly after this exchange, Gatliff visited Hull and noted repeatedly how desolate he found it; at the same time Gatliff visited Bullock, and they agreed Abercrombie was 'too ambitious'[43] (see Figure 5.2). In fact, this was a mild comment compared to his follow-up back at the MTCP. An internal memo makes clear a concern about what appears to be an imminent attack on Abercrombie and his competence. The note quotes Gatliff as having said about the Hull plan, '[W]e have got to be prepared to overthrow most of it somehow at once'.[44]

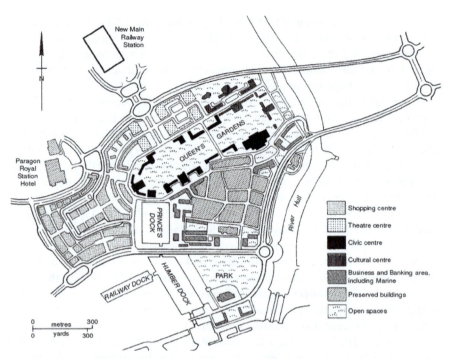

Figure 5.2 Plan for Hull: Abercrombie plan. From *A Plan for the City & County of Kingston Upon Hull* (Hull, A. Brown & Sons, 1945).

At a local election in 1945, Hull returned a predominantly Labour council by fifty seats to thirty-four.[45] Labour members of the council took this as a mandate for the Abercrombie plan and pushed ahead with the proposals in 1946. These included a major shift in the location of the shopping centre; the movement and containment of industry to particular areas outside the centre; and a radical change to the road system in the city centre.[46] Hull officials also went ahead with preparations for a 3,000-acre DO application under Section 1 of the 1944 Act. In public they stated that the intent was to make the central area of Hull 'the property of the people', but officials likely worried about the potential success of such an application, given how quickly they retreated.[47]

The Corporation faced opposition not just from MAG but from the LNER, the Ministry of (War) Transport and a growing group involving the Chamber of Trade, the local property owners' association and more. Opponents – particularly MAG, the Chamber of Trade and the property owners – objected to the overreaching size of the DO. Many opponents assumed incorrectly that a DO would mean purchase of all land outlined, but in practice the city would not have been able to do this. The MTCP would not have been likely to approve such a large DO, and would have reduced it. Additionally the city were going to need CPOs to follow, and these would necessarily cover smaller and more specific areas.[48] However, the biggest constraint would simply have been financial. Under no circumstances would

Hull – a city that suffered heavily in the war from lost rates – be able to purchase, or obtain loans to purchase, anywhere near 3,000 acres. In fact, it was unlikely that the Corporation could have purchased even a portion of the land needed to implement the Abercrombie plan. Only the coercion or cooperation of freeholders in the city centre could have made the plan's implementation possible, and that was unlikely to happen in a city with vocal vested interests. This was common to most blitzed cities, but especially in those with 'bolder' plans such as Plymouth, Coventry and Bristol.[49]

In November 1946 council minutes show that a Reconstruction Coordinating (Special) Committee (RCSC) had noted the success of the Abercrombie plan, mentioning both sales of the plan itself and the large number of attendees at the local exhibition earlier that year.[50] The exhibit was attended by the Minister of Town and Country Planning, Lewis Silkin, who was subsequently effusive about the Abercrombie plan.[51] In early 1947 the Chamber of Trade began requesting information on future plans from the Corporation.[52] While the Chamber group was clearly intending to pressure city officials, minutes show that the Corporation intended to 'be frank and public about their intentions'.[53] Officials made clear their intent to develop on a leasehold basis after acquiring land through the MTCP regulations, and that the DO and CPO applications would be made public. Protests would be heard, and they welcomed these being brought to the council through the Chamber of Trade as 'a locus'.[54]

Though the MTCP showed support for the Abercrombie plan, this did not stop the opponents of the Corporation from stepping up their efforts against it. A coalition of the Chamber of Trade, MAG, the Retailers' Advisory Committee and the Hull & District Property Owners' Protection Association decided to hire their own planner, W. R. Davidge, and exhibit a new plan of their own.[55] By July of 1947 the Town Clerk was prompted to write to the MTCP and request a conference, essentially to use the MTCP as arbiter.[56] The solicitors for the Chamber of Trade group also wrote to the planning ministry, pressing their points and agreeing to the proposed conference.[57] In August the conference was held in Hull, with five attendees from the MTCP, eight from the Hull Corporation and twelve from the Chamber of Trade group.[58] It was agreed that the major point of disagreement lay in the roadway designs that would necessitate the acquisition of a number of freeholds, affecting many businesses in the city centre. In an apparently amicable resolution it was then decided that the City Engineer would draw up a modified road plan, and present it to the Chamber and the MTCP, after approval from Abercrombie.[59] While this was completed, the issue of the location of the new shopping area – still planned by the Corporation to relocate to a completely different area – did not go away.[60]

By October 1947, with the Town Planning Committee of the Corporation reiterating their intent to apply for a comprehensive central area in the DO, the Chamber of Trade group stepped up its action once again.[61] Council minutes show only that applications for four DOs were resolved to be submitted in December 1947.[62] These applications had been massively reduced, with the main central area application at only 228 acres.[63] This did not stop protests: according to minutes of one hearing on the DOs, 577 objections were lodged against the proposals.[64] Propaganda from the Property Owners' group demonstrated a somewhat paranoid view of the Corporation's intentions:

> The Orders, if granted, are to be immediately followed by Compulsory Purchase Orders to enable the Corporation to purchase at the earliest possible date the whole of the vacant land within those areas. Subsequent Compulsory Purchase Orders will follow from time to time to acquire the whole of the remaining properties or any portion of the remaining properties ... If these Orders are granted the Corporation will have the power to acquire all existing freehold interests in these areas, and impose their own terms on the present owners and occupiers on a leasehold basis.[65]

Clearly the council was attempting to clarify their intent when they 'approved and adopted' the following statement of policy in June 1948:

> In the first instance it should be made perfectly clear that the Corporation do not intend to embark upon a policy of capricious acquisition of properties or the disturbance of owners and occupiers.
> The Corporation will only seek to acquire compulsorily properties which it is necessary to acquire in order to secure satisfactory, regular, comprehensive and properly staged development in accordance with planning requirements. There will be no disturbance for disturbance sake.[66]

The statement continues to reassure constituents that it is not intended to pull down buildings that are sound, instead 'every endeavour will be made to fit such a building into the detailed plan'.[67]

Again, the Chamber of Trade continued to press its own agenda, with a further exhibit containing updated plans by Davidge. Propaganda issued by the Chamber group still blasted the Corporation: 'The Hull and District Chamber of Trade, realising the disturbing and expensive implications of the Corporation's recent proposals for the Redevelopment of the Central Area of Hull, have prepared an alternative plan for the consideration of Ratepayers and interested persons.'[68] Furthermore the Chamber stated that the Corporation's proposals 'show that reason and common sense in matters of planning have been ignored' and that MTCP recommendations 'have not been adopted'. They invited the public to judge for themselves at the exhibition, concluding, 'THIS MATTER IS VITAL'.[69]

In any case the MTCP sided with the Corporation on almost all of the central area application, approving 212 acres and disallowing only 16.[70] However, this too was followed by further protest and more hearings once the CPOs were submitted immediately following the DOs.[71] Local authority files contain volumes of correspondence regarding specific sites and protests from freehold traders and homeowners.[72] At almost exactly the same time as the DO approval came through, the first steel allocations were announced in the House of Commons.[73] Hull received 450 tons, which was a small amount in absolute terms but represented 8 per cent of the total allocation, a large sum nationally. In theory the allocation was to have gone to the local authorities' sponsored building scheme(s) but since none of the land had yet been acquired, it took some intervention from the MTCP to get an initial project off the ground.[74] Because the CPOs were only just then being prepared, the allocation was divided between three small freehold projects. Still awaiting a start was Hammond's department store, in a key location opposite Paragon Station – the main railway hub. Hammond's had faced difficult negotiations with the Corporation over keeping their site.[75]

Many other businesses insisted on keeping their original sites or freeholds, and protests continued against the CPOs, with two property owners taking legal action. One was an industrial site, the other was a lawsuit filed against the Corporation by Montague Burton.[76] Owners of Montague Burton, the national chain of men's clothiers, felt their property should be exempted from the CPO. The Hull Corporation won their case, and received costs, but by the time much of this was resolved after an appeal it had further slowed the progress of the Corporation's modified plans, with the MTCP awaiting the outcome of the court's decision on the issue to finalize the CPOs.[77]

Another problem for the Corporation in terms of the city centre's redevelopment turned out to be an almost exactly converse issue to the protests over land acquisition: a section of the 1947 Act required that local authorities must purchase war-damaged land in places where the owner had been refused an application to reinstate the property, if the property owner applied.[78] So in a kind of reverse compulsory purchase, the Corporation was legislated into acquiring land it might not want, including land outside the boundaries of the DO. According to one city official, this was a significant problem in Hull, and was 'proving some embarrassment to the Corporation'.[79] The official also noted that the MTCP had issued a circular stating that authorities should not purchase land that could not be used within two to three years, and in many cases this then conflicted with the law.[80]

Considering the evidence in MTCP files, local news and Hull Corporation archival material, it is clear that while there were many barriers to reconstruction, Hull city councillors and officials were at various times indecisive, obstinate and constantly divided over final plans for rebuilding the city centre.[81] According to local news and MTCP files, the chairman of the Town Planning Committee, Councillor Body, was repeatedly insistent on using as much of the Abercrombie plan as possible.[82] Disputes over the plan, mainly with the Chamber of Trade group, continued to slow progress, and attempts were made regularly to resolve the issues using the MTCP as the arbiter.[83] Ministry officials also continued to press Hull to hire a full-time planning officer, as it was clear the City Engineer had neither the time nor ability. 'The Council is still living in the hope that buildings will rise from the Abercrombie plan (one might almost say from the ashes), while the City Engineer sits on the sidelines.'[84] The Ministry of Transport (MOT) proved to be a further stumbling block, requiring a traffic survey before any approval of planned road layouts.[85]

By the time of the London conferences for blitzed areas in October and November 1947, MTCP correspondence with Hull officials had warmed slightly, with improved relations and attitudes on the ministry end – even if the Chamber of Trade group was still causing problems.[86] When ministry planner Vince wrote to Bullock on 8 October 1947, he actually congratulated him on finally having got the Corporation to agree on 'a reasonable proposal'.[87] In fact by the following summer MTCP officials were sounding positive about Hull, even sending filmmakers to use the city as an example of blitzed city reconstruction.[88]

By the end of 1948 MTCP officials had begun collecting information about projects that might be ready for steel in blitzed city centres, with the first steel allocation pending. Files show both that MTCP officials assisted Hull in receiving a share of the first allocation, and that – internally at least – they understood they needed to be more careful with the Chamber of Trade and their solicitors, who were felt to be attempting to 'play off the Ministry against the Council'.[89] In early 1949 after successful completion of the DO application city officials began asking the MTCP for further assistance. With CPOs as the next step, Hull representatives hoped to get through the process as smoothly as possible. Planning technique notes show some very detailed issues about the updated preliminary plans, but by this point the remaining objections were not strong enough to initiate further negotiations or meetings. In fact at the end of March the MTCP and MOT agreed to specific road proposals that were key to the city's plans.[90]

Slowly the Hull Corporation had started to come into line with planning ministry expectations. Certainly the MTCP were pleased when they were asked to meet with Bullock in July 1949, because he intended to introduce Hull's new Town Planning Officer, a Mr Coates.[91] However, it took some time before Mr Coates was able to make an impact on city centre plans. Opponents continued to complain, and the local press published their views – 'Here is the national problem in a nutshell' – describing issues with promoting and reinstating industry in Hull. As illustrative of the problems in Hull the *Daily Mail* claimed that a local fish company could not expand their business because the final zoning outlines were not yet set – for instance, between industry and shopping – claiming the plans were still just 'idealistic dreams'.[92] This seems to have prompted a response from the Corporation, or at least from the new planning officer, as they released a plan for 'The New Hull' to the *Hull & Yorkshire Times* on 4 March 1950.[93]

A further small allocation was made in 1950, not publicly announced, and Hull was allowed £50,000 under the new allocation scheme of maximum allowed building licences by cost of work rather than by tonnage of steel. But without a final approved plan yet in place, negotiations continued between Hull officials, the MTCP and the various traders hoping to make a start to building.[94] City officials pressed the ministry – as did most blitzed cities – for larger allocations, claiming they were ready to start £500,000 of work in 1950. The MTCP Deputy Secretary, Sharp, assured officials that the £50,000 allowance was only 'an interim allocation', and that they hoped to do more for the cities as decisions about 1951–52 came online.[95] When Hull contended they had both developers ready to build and labourers ready to work, the ministry suggested that commitments to developers could be made, assuring the authority representatives that work would be able to go ahead soon.

Documents show that the new planning officer, Coates, spent a great deal of time negotiating not only a compromise, but a workable solution for the shopping area – which had been the major ongoing point of contention in the city. He concluded in a note to the MTCP that the best solution was to leave a good portion of the current shopping area in its same location[96] (see Figure 5.3). This apparently satisfied all parties with the exception of the Town Planning Chairman, Councillor Body. MTCP internal correspondence reveals that Body was said to have been a major impediment, having insisted since the start of the planning process that a few of the major shops (department stores) in Hull must move location.[97] While the Regional Planning Officer (RPO), Tetlow, thought that Body's later proposals were more practical than Abercrombie's, Body continued to upset the Chamber of Trade.[98] Coates however, did not approve of Councillor Body's suggestions, and was able to push through what were likely more practical solutions. Tetlow opined regarding the original Abercrombie plan: 'I think it only fair to them to say that they have sought professional advice at a very high level only to be lead into wild schemes incapable of fruition.'[99]

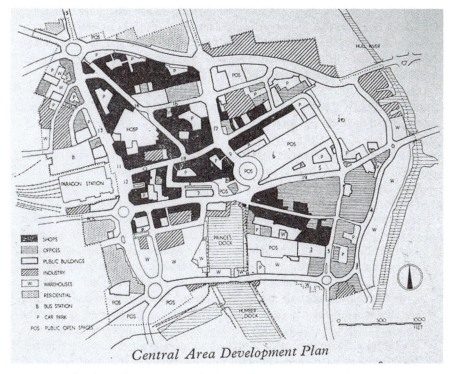

Figure 5.3 Plan for Hull: City Engineer's plan. *Architect's Journal*, 2 July 1953.

On the date of submission for all local authority Development Plans, Hull Corporation took no chances with the post and delivered their plan in person to the ministry offices in London.[100] Only days before, however, the local and national press ran stories on the probable reduction of allocations by Gaitskell, the new Chancellor of the Exchequer.[101] Still, as shown in Chapters 3 and 4, this did not always prevent cities from going ahead with work, particularly with construction already begun. Hull had to appeal for extra allocations in December 1951 when it turned out they had stated not the cost of works for 1951 allocations, but only the portion of cost of works expected for 1951 (in that year alone).[102]

When building allocations were finally announced for 1953, Hull received an even larger share than the original allocation, with 9 per cent of the national total for blitzed cities.[103] But – again as seen in Chapters 3 and 4 – the total allocations still meant that city centres were being allowed only a few buildings a year in new construction. In a debate on 'Blitzed Towns' in March 1953, when MPs from many blitzed cities were still pressing the government for more priority and larger allocations, an MP outside of Hull added some humour to the debate:

[Mr. Buckle] told the 'Hull Daily Mail' yesterday: 'We feel that Hull's allocation is very disappointing and hopelessly inadequate. We feel bitter that we have not been given a fair chance when we have the labour and the materials. We shall expect our Members of Parliament to stamp on Mr. Macmillan's doorstep.' I should imagine that, if the hon. and gallant Member for Hull, Central (Captain Hewitson) has done much stamping on the Minister's doorstep, there cannot be much doorstep left. The quotation goes on: 'We shall stamp ourselves, if he will let us. May be, we shall stamp if he does not let us.'[104]

Humour aside, a Conservative MP for Hull, Richard Law (Hull, Haltemprice), summarized the local situation of the past nine years:

As well as being non-party, this is the kind of debate in which one may properly put forward the case of one's own constituency. I do so all the more readily since what Hull endured during the war was not generally recognised at the time … Hull endured [air raids] with great patience and fortitude but nobody outside the city knew that it had had anything to bear at all, because, for security reasons, it was not permissible to mention the name of Hull … There is, however, one great gap in Hull … I refer to the shopping centre and business centre, which was almost completely destroyed and which Hull has scarcely begun to replace.

This has been a great inconvenience to the people of Hull; it has represented a considerable loss of trade to the city; more important perhaps than anything else, it has represented a great loss of rateable value, because the area in the centre of Hull, which was completely wiped out, was probably the richest area in rateable value in the city. It is difficult to make exact calculations but, as a result of the virtual obliteration of the shopping centre of Hull, I believe that an additional charge of about £200,000 per annum falls on the rates.[105]

Law blamed the 'Socialist' council rather than the 'last government' for prevention of progress.[106] However, support for the Corporation was added from George Lindgren who had been Parliamentary Secretary to the MTCP until 1951, 'It is only fair to say that certain sections of the business community of Hull were not as co-operative as they might have been. There was a clash between the two, and whenever there is a clash, all the faults are not on one side.'[107]

Clearly the City of Hull as a whole faced numerous problems in local attempts at postwar reconstruction. City Council members – or at least a few very vocal or powerful members – insisted on supporting the Abercrombie plan for many years, against the wishes of an apparent majority of traders and shopkeepers. The city officials responsible for liaising with the planning ministry did not always provide timely information, though they were at least always civil. Worse though, the planning officials in the ministry took a dim view of the drastic plans even while being forced to wait on the sidelines as the various factions battled for their city centre preferences. Additionally the railway company, even after nationalization, was unwilling to help alleviate traffic problems in the city centre.[108] Overall we have seen that the greatest barriers to rebuilding were related to property ownership: freeholders did not want to sell or move, railway companies did not want to pay to move their lines or re-route them, while homeowners had issues with the proposed new zoning.[109]

The example of Hull demonstrates clearly the overwhelming complexity in preparing and implementing reconstruction in blitzed cities. Taken with the previous chapters detailing economic constraints and planning requirements, the local issues – of many shapes and sizes – explain why the Abercrombie plans were not only controversial, but in practical terms also impossible to implement. Although Abercrombie himself considered that this was 'probably the best report he had been connected with', 'no other wartime plan was so ignored or apparently ineffective'.[110] But Hull was not alone in the mixture of problems it faced. Further examples in Exeter and Liverpool will display even more local constraints.

II. *Exeter*

When Exeter was bombed in the first of the so-called Baedeker raids of 1942, in retaliation for the Allied attack on Lübeck, much of the centre of the city was destroyed. The rebuilding efforts, however, proceeded slowly. Not only did the city centre feel like a gaping hole for ten years or more, but many comments were subsequently made regarding the result of the rebuilding in both the local and national press. Comments ranged from 'handsome, up-to-date new shops' to 'architectural compromise' to 'bland'.[111]

The originally Roman city of Exeter was attacked by air on three occasions in 1942. The first raids in April were relatively minor, but the third raid was devastating to this small city. When compared to the bombing of Würzburg or Dresden by the Allies, Exeter seems to have come through fairly intact, yet compared with other such cities in Britain it suffered severe damage. Most bombed, or blitzed, cities in Britain were targeted as centres of industry, shipping or military installations. Yet a city such as Exeter was simply a local shopping area, a cathedral city and a tourist destination. It is likely Hitler himself ordered what became known as the 'Baedeker' raids, named for the German tour book series, the *Baedeker* guides. The term described the raids on beautiful and historic British cities such as Bath, Canterbury, Norwich and Exeter.[112] As Thomas Sharp, Exeter's planner, noted: 'Exeter had paid a heavy price for being classified as one of the most beautiful places in England.'[113]

Though in the early and more minor raids German planes were said to have missed their targets, the major raid on 3–4 May 1942 dropped seventy-five tons of bombs and destroyed:

- 37 acres of central Exeter,
- 400 shops,
- 150 office buildings,
- 50 warehouses,
- 26 pubs and clubs,
- 4 churches (plus 2 severely damaged),
- 3 cinemas,
- several city institutions (e.g., library),
- 1,500 houses,
- 2,700 houses badly damaged,
- 16,000 houses partially damaged.

The loss of life totalled 81 in April 1942 and 161 in May 1942, in addition to 582 injuries reported.[114]

Though these numbers do not compare with the damage done in Greater London, the impact upon a small regional shopping centre was significant. While the loss of shops and other premises was devastating, so was the loss of much of Exeter's historic core. Most damaging for the city government was the loss of rates from the destroyed premises.[115] According to a post-blitz survey carried out by the Board of Trade, Exeter lost a total of £158,778 through the damage to business and trade premises.[116]

Almost immediately following the raids, Exeter officials set to work clearing the bomb sites (see Figure 5.4). This necessity was not free to the city; labour had to be paid, as on any construction or demolition project.[117] In addition to the loss of rate revenue and the clearing costs, there was significant damage to all statutory undertakings, and the clean-up and repair of these became yet another cost to bear. Clearly Exeter was among a large number of cities bombed in the Blitz, and its residents and city officials were aware that many others in Britain suffered the same or worse inconvenience and expense, particularly in London.[118] Therefore it is not surprising that little mention of appeal or application for government assistance seems to have been made until almost a year had passed.[119] Issues such as the loss of rates were first noted by the Exeter's Finance Committee in a report to the City Council dated 13 April 1943. The report stated the Committee's

Figure 5.4 Exeter, bomb damage: the cathedral from beyond the High Street, 1945. *Exeter Express & Echo.*

frustration at the refusal of the government to provide any assistance towards the loss of rate revenue.[120] However, the deputation had been sent to the Ministry of Health, apparently asking for general financial assistance in reconstruction. It is odd that the group did not visit an entity relating to finance such as the Treasury or the War Damage Commission, or even the planning ministry. Other cities pursuing the issue of lost rate revenues appear to have waited until after the war.[121]

By January 1943 officials fortuitously realized that with the pending introduction of new planning legislation – the 1944 Act – they would need to have a plan in place for rebuilding the city after the war and that a head start might help their success. The City Council created a Re-planning and Reconstruction Committee, and it recorded a visit from W. Morrison, Minister of Town and Country Planning in September 1943.[122] He urged the appointment of a consultant to advise on the replanning of the city. A short list of planners was made, interviews were conducted and Thomas Sharp – a reputable planner who was at that time employed in a project for the planning ministry – was selected and officially appointed in October 1943.[123] Sharp had authored a book called *Town Planning*, which sold a quarter of a million copies, and had also consulted for the cathedral city of Durham during the war.[124] The City Council contracted with Sharp for a general plan 'which they could work with' and asked that his plan be thorough but not too detailed.[125] He was given a fairly extended time period for completion, with a plan expected in approximately twelve months.

In the interim, the primary focus of the City Council turned, unsurprisingly due to the national housing shortage, to housing and accommodating bombed out families. Councillors closely followed any government plans for assistance: for example, minutes dated in September 1944 noted the Ministry of Health's possible offer of prefabricated houses. After the City Council's fruitless visit to Whitehall in April 1943, the matter of financial assistance appears to have been dropped until near the end of the war. In February and September of 1945 the City Council decided to try again and sent a second and third deputation, again without success.[126]

In October 1945 J. C. Maude, Exeter's new Conservative MP, made his maiden speech in a Commons housing shortage debate. He asked when the government would be returning to their owners both housing and offices – many of which had been requisitioned for wartime – because the housing shortage was particularly severe in blitzed cities.[127] In any case, no definite answer or assistance was forthcoming. In Whitehall – though Exeter officials probably could not have known this – the moves towards planning for reconstruction were mainly through liaisons and surveys with much larger blitzed cities such as Hull or Plymouth. As mentioned in the previous chapter, the Advisory Panel on Reconstruction chose seven examples, all much larger and more heavily bombed in absolute terms – though not proportionally – than Exeter. Blitzed cities were an emotional issue, but the government paid attention only to big cities.

Also in 1945 bombed out businesspeople in Exeter organized themselves into a 'Blitzed Traders Association' to press for action from the City Council and collectively keep abreast of any potential news or developments in finding new premises, obtaining temporary shops and applying for relief from the Board of Trade.[128] Most of the traders faced great financial difficulties, since temporary shops were not available or even erected until at least 1947.[129] According to former City Engineering department employee Norman Venning, the traders had signs erected: '[T]here were displayed on the various bombed sites notice-boards indicating the name of the firm that formerly stood there and, if they were trading elsewhere, their new address.'[130]

Beyond attempts to procure temporary shops, City Council and officials continued with both the finalization and approval of the plan by Thomas Sharp, and prepared to submit an application under the 1944 legislation for a DO to cover the bomb-damaged acreage in the city centre plus land they hoped to redevelop. Although past his contracted time frame Sharp was not satisfied that he had completed the plan when the Exeter City Council insisted that he appear and present a report in March 1945.[131] The Council was impatient and clashed to some extent with Sharp's perfectionism. The City Council was also apparently eager to show Whitehall they were ready to get started. The plan was exhibited to the public from 27 December 1945, opened officially by Lewis Silkin, the new Minister of Town and Country Planning.[132] Its central elements were a northern route for a large by-pass road, widening of several major shopping streets including the High Street, new intersections to include a major roundabout at the largest and a new pedestrian shopping area to be created cutting across old

Figure 5.5 The cathedral view from Thomas Sharp's *Exeter Phoenix*. London: Architectural Press, 1946.

narrow streets and oriented to have a view to Exeter Cathedral[133] (see Figures 5.5 and 5.6).

Demonstrating the fact that Exeter was among the first of the blitzed cities to publish such a plan, and possibly because they had used Sharp – a prominent planner who during his work for Exeter was elected President of the Town Planning Institute – or perhaps at Sharp's instigation, the Exeter exhibit was followed by a further exhibition in London. It opened in March 1946 to coincide with the full colour publication of Sharp's plan in book form, entitled *Exeter Phoenix*.[134] Though generally well-received, particularly nationally, objections surfaced in the local press. Sharp's plan was considered radical but not controversial in principle, yet the reaction of the local MP summed up a very practical perspective that city

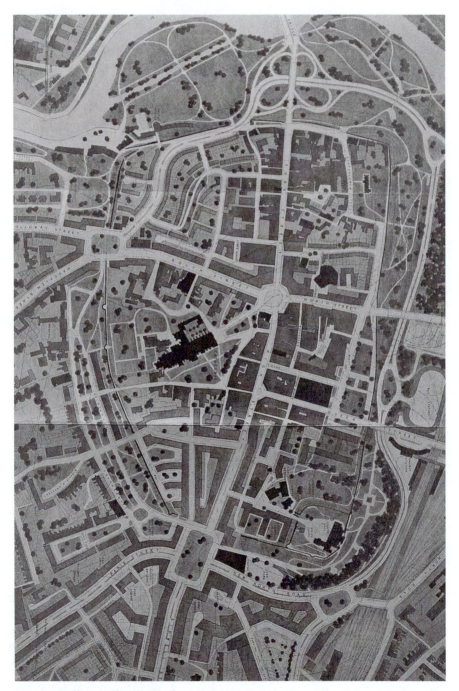

Figure 5.6 Thomas Sharp's plan from *Exeter Phoenix*.

officials did not express. He was quoted in the papers as saying that he liked the plans but queried who would pay for all the work:

'It is a beautiful plan that will make the city lovely, but who is going to pay for it?' asked Mr. J.C. Maude, K.C., M.P. for the city, at the Exeter Insurance Institute lunch yesterday.

That has never been explained. I am not in any sense trying to put the brake on the progress of the scheme, but how is it to be paid for? Will the burden be put on the rates or is the money to be provided by the Government?[135]

This question had not yet been seriously considered by the City Council either. As stated by the Council and in a few local summaries by involved parties, the Council only intended to make use of Sharp's plan 'in broad outline', even while it had been prepared in detail.[136]

With a plan 'approved' (by the MTCP) at least verbally in place, Exeter's first and only DO was approved by the MTCP in December 1946. It is remarkable that the order approved covered 75.64 acres of central Exeter whereas it was documented by the Ministry that the war-damaged area totalled only about 37 acres.[137] That the government was willing to double the size of the bombed area and allow Exeter to potentially acquire so much land in the city centre was unprecedented for a non-industrial city. It would also prove to be one of the only such approvals by the MTCP, who soon suggested to local authorities that DOs be made smaller, and that land acquisition should only include property that could reasonably be expected to see construction within two to five years.[138] There were few larger DO approvals proportionally; only cities such as Bristol, Coventry and Plymouth received more acreage but these cities were much larger in both population and bomb damage (see Table 4.2). Exeter likely received the approval because they applied so early. Most cities would prove to be two years or so behind them, and faced very different circumstances economically, as shown in the previous chapters.[139] However, as broad as the DO approval was, the application for CPOs would prove more difficult for Exeter officials. Filing of CPOs would set up acquisition of the land to be redeveloped and enable control of when and where and how the city centre would be rebuilt. Once it became clear how much land the City Council might potentially control, there were strenuous objections from many of the blitzed traders, as well as from property owners and local voters.[140]

Well aware that City officials would likely seek to redevelop the central shopping area at the lowest cost to themselves while attempting to make a profit on the subsequent ground rents and to increase prewar rate revenues, local traders feared they would be squeezed out of their old locations by 'multiples' (national chain stores) who would pay higher rents. Several sources state that Exeter's High Street was one of the highest valued sites in the southwest before the war, and at the least was a very desirable location – serving not just the city but a large portion of the population of the rural southwest of England.[141] After a public inquiry in 1946 to consider the objections of the traders, and further discussion with the Ministry, the first CPO was approved for 65 acres in August of 1947. Of this CPO

60 acres was for the High Street area alone.[142] Proportional to the size of its bomb damage and to the DO total, Exeter would later prove to have received one of the largest CPO allowances in the country (see Figure 5.7). Under Section 2(1) for war damage acquisition, Exeter received 13 acres more in a single order than any other city. Only Plymouth came close, when calculating the total of their six CPOs, though only three were in their city centre and totalled 35.25 acres, compared with Exeter's 65.5.[143]

Exeter City Council had in fact worked diligently to pursue replanning and rebuilding of the city centre, and in 1946 had created a new department for planning with a new 'Chief Planning Officer', Harold Gayton. Despite this, many factors continued to hold up any serious start on the full clean-up of blitzed sites – or any actual building work. Physically, by 1945, few bomb sites were cleared, and it was still another four years before any new building commenced.[144] To combat the problem of the postwar labour shortage, the City Council apparently approached the local Prison Governor to request the use of convict labour for site clearance. The request was granted.[145]

Another major task before full clearance and before any road rebuilding was the necessity to coordinate all of the statutory undertakings.[146] City officials had to establish where new roads were to be laid out, and if they intended to follow all or part of Sharp's traffic plan. Further, they needed agreement from the MTCP on the plans, in addition to agreement from the Ministries of Health (for sewers) and Transport (for roads). But planning officials in Whitehall appear in archival files to have been less than cooperative; even claiming internally that Exeter had 'no programme for reconstruction'.[147] They also claimed that city officials ignored their advice and input, later commenting on 'Exeter's general disregard of this Ministry'.[148] There is no evidence for the specific reasons behind this hostility, though it might have been a personality clash with the very vocal and strong-willed town clerk (discussed further in the next chapter). However, cities such as Hull appear with a similar tone in internal planning ministry files. Ministry officials seem to have insisted on being the primary experts and expected the cities to acquiesce to their suggestions and expertise.[149]

Of all the complexities involved in securing both approvals and allocations, the roadway designs proved to be the biggest stumbling block for Exeter officials. On 13 March 1946 the local newspapers reported that the City Council had approved the Sharp plan on the recommendation of its Re-planning Committee, but – again – only 'in broad outline'.[150] A final modified version of Sharp's plan was not actually adopted until September 1947.[151] Major changes were made to the plan as the City Council were clear they never intended to utilize it in full. Very likely the Council and Committees went forward with Sharp's plan as a tool to secure approvals from Whitehall.[152] Local authority officials soon found, however, that a delay in materials allocations would greatly slow rebuilding efforts, in addition to the further approvals needed from Whitehall.

In applying to the Ministry of Transport for approval and financial assistance on road rebuilding, the city was told it would have to carry out a traffic census before approvals would be considered.[153] Both the City Council minutes as well

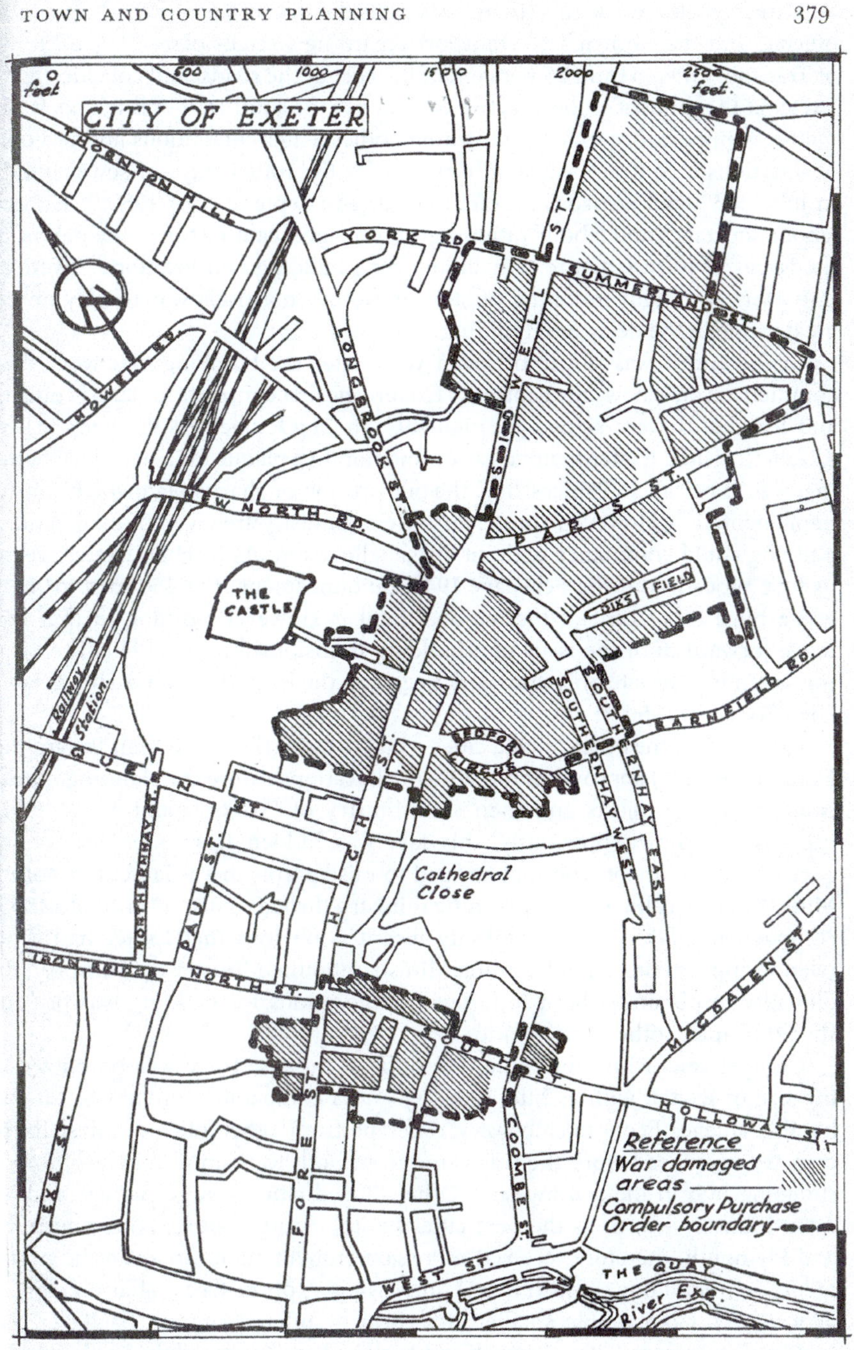

Figure 5.7 Exeter showing bomb damage and CPO outlines. *Town and Country Planning*, vol 26 (1958). Courtesy Town & Country Planning Association.

as Ministry files show that there was considerable disagreement between city officials and the Ministry of Transport regarding Exeter's plans.[154] The Ministry of Transport was to fund 75 per cent of the cost of the roads, and considering that Exeter at the time sat at the effective entrance to the southwest of England, it was a matter of importance to both governing bodies. After contentious and prolonged negotiations a contract was finally signed for the initial stage of sewer building in July 1949, with a roads contract following in September of 1950.[155] Although labour shortages and labour rationing were a significant factor in the delays, and the issues of infrastructure – including road building and locations – were also important, the tight rationing of steel and other materials was to play an even greater role in the delay of rebuilding.

In the end it was not until seven years after the bombing that work finally commenced on a 'new' city centre for Exeter. The first contracts for land acquisition and leaseholds were signed in 1948–49. On 21 October 1949 (then) Princess Elizabeth visited Exeter to unveil a commemorative plaque for a new development that was to be called 'Princesshay', the one portion of Sharp's plan which was fully implemented.[156] However, these starts were almost purely ceremonial, since no building could commence without a steel allocation. As in Hull, Exeter received its first allocation in the February 1949 announcement. The 450 tons for Exeter was a huge 8 per cent of the national total.[157] However, nothing further could move forward until the issue of a building license in October 1949. The licence was given for one site only and work began on the Pearl Assurance House, on the High Street, in 1950.[158]

Exeter – like the other blitzed cities – had to await the Investment Programmes Committee (IPC) approval of investment allocations before the planning ministry could sponsor projects and then the Ministry of Works would issue building licences. As shown previously, this fact was hidden from members of local government, many of whom continued to raise points in Parliament to both the Ministries of Health and the planning ministry throughout 1949 and into 1953.[159] Although in both Ministry and city files it is obvious that Exeter had a poor relationship with both the Planning Ministry and the Ministry of Transport, their difficulty in obtaining both funding and allocations for building was of course shared by many other blitzed cities.

Comparisons with other cities are difficult because there was no blitzed city the size of Exeter, with as little industry and a comparable amount of extensive bomb damage. Economically very different from other blitzed cities, Exeter's primary revenues before the war came from both tourism and its position as a shopping hub in the southwest.[160] Other blitzed cities – larger in size and with more industry – such as the port cities Bristol, Southampton, Portsmouth, Hull and Plymouth, therefore received more government attention given the postwar focus on rebuilding industry and increasing exports (see Table 3.2 for IPC allocations). Comparable smaller cities which suffered similar 'Baedeker' raids such as Canterbury, Bath, Norwich and York had not sustained the level of damage to their centres as Exeter and therefore were not as highly prioritized nationally. If the size of the bombed area in Exeter is compared with other cities based on population, the damage ranks in the middle, though much higher than any other 'Baedeker' city (see Table 4.2). The size of Exeter's DO was small compared with the larger port or industrialized cities, but very large compared to their damaged acreage. In their CPOs Exeter obtained far more land proportionally and even literally than several worse-hit cities such as Bristol, Coventry or Southampton.[161]

An alternative comparison is in the amount of IPC investment allocation. In the five years that allocations were made to the 'blitzed cities' (1949–53) Exeter received more than twice the allocation of Canterbury, and more funding in some years than Bristol or Hull.[162] Investment allocation reports show only the allocation directed to each city for rebuilding *outside* of government building, building for industry or for housing, health or education, so it is perhaps unsurprising the small, non-industrial Exeter ranks highly compared to other cities. Yet cities such as Coventry and Birmingham had both central shopping as well as larger outlying areas to be rebuilt, and did not receive substantially more building licence allocations, though both had more industry. Exeter officials were ready with their officially submitted plans very early, and it appears they put more pressure on the government than some other blitzed cities.[163] This preparedness and pressure certainly paid off, but rebuilding was still slow and due to the IPC holding back allocations for building work, even given Exeter's head start allowed only a few new buildings per year. However, by the time the licence allocations to blitzed cities were starting to be increased and allowed more than just a minor amount of construction, Exeter still received allowances (i.e., permission) to build as much new work as in cities such as Birmingham and Manchester.[164]

However, as shown in Chapter 3, until 1951 the IPC made almost no allocations beyond industry, the basics of housing and buildings for public services. Also, 'Baedeker blitz' cities had no recourse to the allocations received for industry or housing allocations on the scale of larger cities. Therefore cities that had been shopping centres for their county or for a large local area had to make do with temporary shops and offices – if they were even able to acquire the materials to construct them – until they could rebuild the holes in their cores. An additional issue for cities related to the tardy rate of allocation was the cost. In fact, it was the Exeter Town Clerk C. J. Newman who – while attending the 1947 MTCP London conference – pointed out to Minister Silkin that once each city completed their CPO and purchased the land the 'clock will run against them'. Since they would be paying loan charges without assurance about when they would be able to begin building, they would pay out with no time frame towards recouping the cost and the loss of rates.[165]

Clearly the blitzed cities were caught between loss of rates and the inability to recoup them. In Exeter from 1949, when the smallest of starts was made, until 1953, when the Conservative government relaxed key controls – removal of the 100 per cent 'development charge' and relaxation of allocations for building licensing – construction proceeded at a slow pace. Even though by late 1950 some starts had been made on buildings in the city centre, this covered only about five to ten acres of the nearly sixty in the central shopping area which was to be redeveloped. Though only thirty-seven acres were said to have been destroyed, the

CPO essentially allowed the City Council to purchase and pull down any building in the sixty-acre area for redevelopment.

Investment allocations picked up slightly the next year and by 1952, ten years from the Blitz, much of the north side of the High Street had been rebuilt.[166] Still, the southern portions of the city centre were very slow in getting underway. Roadways and statutory undertakings in the very core near the High Street were completed but the further construction of the inner by-pass road did not start until 1954.[167] Exeter's appearance from 1942 to 1950 was that of a large bomb site, followed by a transformation to a huge construction zone. But the experience of many other blitzed cities is similar, and rebuilding continued slowly for all of them, even into the 1960s and 1970s.

Yet the City of Exeter faced a few further problems of its own. City government in the postwar era has been repeatedly criticized by historians, journalists and Exeter citizens.[168] City officials' priorities were questioned, and official interests often clashed with perceived public interest. The disenfranchisement of local businesses, the destruction of historic buildings and poor relationships with both consultants and national government indicate few positives to working with or in this city. Certainly the city officials' efforts to bring Exeter to the attention of national government and secure both funding and allocation were thorough and, though irritating to those they pressed, constituents had to applaud their efforts. But forming difficult relationships with public servants in Whitehall probably often hurt the city's cause, rather than helped it.

The difficulties Sharp had in dealing with Exeter officials are mentioned in both the Sharp archives and in the National Archives. A letter to Sharp goes so far as to say 'what sons of bitches that Exeter City Council is composed of'.[169] This tone is exemplified in the situation shown in both City Council minutes and the local press: for example, officials attempted to negotiate and fix ground rents for the blitzed traders on new sites before the traders were told how much War Damage Commission compensation they would receive for their old sites. Additionally, several sources strongly criticized many aspects of the way certain officials carried out their duties.[170]

The local press was critical and while their attacks were not often directed at specific Councillors or city officials, they did take up the cause of local businesspeople, particularly the displaced traders who had been bombed out. At issue were both the attempts by the city to redevelop the shopping areas without consultation or priority given to the old businesses and the slowness of providing temporary shops to keep traders' businesses running until they could acquire new space. Former City Engineer John Brierley claimed that the city had done all it could to recognize the best interests of the business owners but the traders obviously did not see it this way.[171] From the time of the Blitz in May 1942 to the actual provision of temporary shops the wait was five years for some, and a further year or two for most.[172]

Further upsetting many residents and shopkeepers, city officials made a constant effort to plan for increased rateable value in the city centre. The effect of this policy was that redevelopment preference went to national chain retailers.

Some businesses, such as Marks and Spencer and Lloyds Bank, were already established and disputed the sites the city tried to give them when they were not offered a chance to reoccupy their old sites.[173] The report by City Planner Gayton, submitted with the Development Plan (under the new 1947 Act) in 1950, shows an increase in the city centre of 34 per cent in floor space for offices alone.[174] Writing in *The Municipal Journal* in August 1953, the City Treasurer stated that 'the rebuilding of the blitzed areas will be largely self supporting and will more than restore the rateable value lost in 1942'.[175]

Another stumbling block the city created for itself emerged in the by-pass road issue. While the Council allowed Sharp to submit a plan for a northern by-pass and approved it in outline form, officials did not think it was feasible, nor did the Ministry of Transport. Both parties felt a southern by-pass was necessary but could not agree on the route. The crossing over the Ex river was an issue, as there was only one bridge to flow all cars over in 1945, and anyone planning for the future realized they would need to accommodate much greater numbers of vehicles, even if they underestimated the actual scope.[176]

The eventual abandonment of many elements in the Sharp plan had long-term consequences when Exeter failed to resolve traffic issues until the inner by-pass was completed in the 1960s.[177] Though his plans could be controversial, his success in the City of Durham showed that Sharp had a good grasp of traffic resolutions. Not quite comparable in size to Exeter but still an historic cathedral city, Sharp had completed the Durham plan almost immediately prior to the Exeter plan.[178] Durham implemented the major part of Sharp's traffic plan and as a result kept their historic core intact.

Local historians have argued that Exeter lost much of its history and beauty with the unprecedented number of historic buildings removed from the city core.[179] Many writers speak with regret of the losses suffered at the hands of the City Council. Not only were individual buildings of historic interest pulled down for redevelopment, but whole areas of historic interest were removed as well. Examples include Bedford Circus as well as Dix's Fields, which suffered severe damage but when inspected by the Ministry of Works was recommended for preservation.[180] Even where historic buildings were left with intact facades, in Exeter they were removed rather than adapted for reuse (see Figure 5.8). City officials in Exeter appear to have been concerned first and foremost with replacing lost rateable value, and did not worry much over whether buildings were historic or not.[181]

According to the local newspaper, Exeter City Council was also at fault for acquiring such a large amount of unblitzed land in order to carry out their development plans.[182] It was claimed that this went against the spirit of the 1944 legislation, yet the Ministry approved the seventy-five acres for Exeter's Declaratory Order, at twice the size of the amount of city centre land damaged in the Blitz. The MTCP seemed, at that early stage, to be following the wartime instructions of Lord Reith, and Silkin's earliest comments on the 'great potential' for improving blitzed cities.[183] Approval of a CPO the size of Exeter's suggests that MTCP officials – at least in 1947 – still imagined wholesale central redevelopment in blitzed cities.

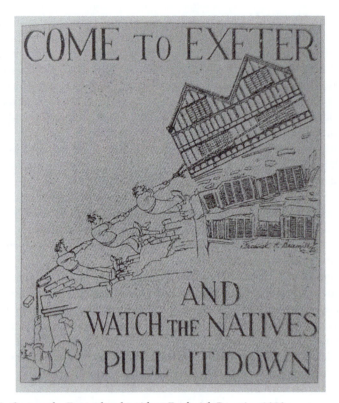

Figure 5.8 Cartoon by Exeter local resident Frederick Beamiss, 1959.

However, final responsibility sat with the City Council and city officials, because it is clear that Exeter could have retained more of its historic core, and city officials could have regulated the rebuilding to be more pleasing to the eye.

In the *Oxford Companion to British History*, Exeter's entry simply states: 'Since 1942 it has suffered grievously from both air raids and insipid post-war redevelopment.'[184] If it is 'insipid' – and with regard to the redeveloped and widened High Street arguably little disagreement can be registered on this point – why is this so? National policy and macroeconomics critically affected the outcome because governments were forced to put industry first, and the economic situation encouraged stripped-down or frugal building techniques. It is certainly worth asking whether local government was responsible for the failure to preserve history and the result that is today's modern High Street, and it is certain the policies implemented to affect the greatest possible financial benefit to the city played the most significant role in the outcome. Additionally, correspondence shows that Exeter's government was both pushy and difficult for Whitehall to deal with, which exacerbated many of their internal problems.

Like Hull, Exeter further demonstrates the extremely difficult position of a blitzed city in the postwar period. Like Hull, there were many opponents to widespread redevelopment and implementation of modernist plans. But Exeter had started early, and it has been shown that officials benefited from this early action by achieving large DO and CPO approvals. However, it also allowed officials to go ahead faster than many other cities, building big, cheap and quickly. But the war, the postwar economic situation and two successive governments must share responsibility as well for the lack of investment and the pace of rebuilding, which made the officials impatient to recover both physically and financially from the devastating effects of the German bombing raids. Unlike Exeter, the final example, Liverpool, was much slower off the mark – at least from the view of the planning ministry.

III. *Liverpool*

The City of Liverpool provides an excellent juxtaposition to the examples given while exploring the experiences of Hull and Exeter. Bigger than both, but equally with a form more planned in nature than the others, it has both a long tradition as a port, and a long tradition of physical planning. Founded by a charter under King John in 1207, the city was an early example of a settlement of freemen, and was not simply built – as many feudal places were – to the plans or designs of a controlling lord.[185] As a free city the history of cooperation in Liverpool is therefore lengthy. The original 'H' layout of six streets was a much more modern grid-like layout than in most medieval towns. As the city grew, and before 'town planning' existed (see Chapter 4), Victorian Liverpool was planned through civic design of grand buildings and street widening projects.[186] The city had one of the first railway stations in Britain at the end of the first major line to/from Manchester.[187] Liverpool's tremendous growth, as well as its status as a world port and migration hub, created typical urban problems – especially in terms of housing.[188] The drive to improve conditions led to drives for slum clearance in the late nineteenth and early twentieth centuries. But by the First World War Liverpool could claim to be a hub of town planning: the School of Architecture had the oldest department of civic design founded in 1909, and the new journal *Town Planning Review* was being published out of the school.[189]

Due to its importance in the war effort, especially its prominence as a port, Liverpool was bombed probably more than any city outside London. Its damage estimates by the MTCP were higher in acreage than any other provincial city.[190] But unlike other blitzed cities, Liverpool did not suffer from concentrated bomb damage in its centre. The city centre of Liverpool had more single buildings and small blocks of buildings lost than cities where there were proportionally large areas of destruction: 'with one or two exceptions the war damage is widely spread and interspersed between standing buildings'.[191] And, while other blitzed cities were literally making plans, Liverpool was busy trying to solve a severe housing shortage. The problems of overcrowding had prompted a prewar regional study, completed and published in wartime, *The Merseyside Plan* (1944).[192] Clearly the destruction from bombings compounded this issue.

A prime target for any attack on the shipping industry, and a major import site, the City of Liverpool suffered raids from August 1940 with the heaviest raids coming in the first week of May 1941 and the last in January 1942.[193] By the end of the attacks almost 700 aircraft had dropped nearly 900 tons of high explosives and well over 100,000 incendiaries. The total damage, estimated at 208 acres spread over some 1,500 acres, was said to be as follows[194] (see Figure 5.9):

- 258 factories,
- 91 acres of dock storage space,
- 726 business premises or offices,
- 684 commercial properties,
- 4,400 houses
- 16,400 houses seriously damaged,
- 45,500 houses slightly damaged.

Approximately 51,000 people had been made homeless in Liverpool and another 25,000 in nearby Bootle where it was estimated only 15 per cent of the local housing stock remained. Casualties numbered 2,736 killed in Liverpool, and over 4,000 in Merseyside in total, plus 3,500 seriously injured.[195]

Planning in Liverpool had been actively carried out since the powers given by the 1909 Act for housing, through the city's 'Health Committee', and from 1932 the same group had been actively working on town planning schemes, under the

Figure 5.9 Bomb damage in Liverpool. Getty images.

supervision of the City Engineer and City Architect.[196] By the start of the war, plans were apparently underway for the improvement of roads in the central area and the ongoing battle for housing provision – in addition to cooperation on the Merseyside regional plan mentioned above. The plan for the central area of Liverpool, as it existed in late 1941, was presented by Alderman Alfred Shennan at an annual meeting of the Merseyside Civic Society.[197] Though a prominent member of the City Council and a local architect, Shennan claimed to be making the presentation 'as an interested citizen' rather than a political leader. In outlining the plan he stressed that 'I am not going to propound some grandiose scheme which could be carried out only by first laying waste the present city and starting afresh. The plans for such a scheme might look very pretty on paper but they would quickly meet with the reception they deserve'.[198] The plan involved only a new layout for a proposed inner ring road, but was slightly more drastic perhaps than the Alderman's rhetoric suggested due to the fairly major changes in the roadway design (see Figure 5.10).

Most notably, the address given by Shennan also noted that cooperation on planning in Liverpool was already part of the planning process. Unlike other cities whose councils and officials made plans and then presented them to the citizens and business-people, Liverpool invited 'representations' from 'interested parties'. The list given included private developers at the start, and was followed by eleven groups comprising both internal committees and external bodies such as the railway companies, the docks board, the School of Civic Design and others.[199] The City Council followed this presentation by formally acknowledging the need to study postwar city centre issues in February 1942, founding a committee to advise on plans and implementation. Notably, the committee name did not use the word 'reconstruction' in its title like most other cities.[200] The Post-War Redevelopment Advisory (Special) Committee (hereafter PWRASC) met in wartime beginning in September 1942. The intention stated by Alderman Shennan in December 1941 to work with local groups of institutions, owners, traders and more was spelled out clearly again in a January 1944 meeting of the committee established to deal with postwar issues. The minutes list groups that the committee intended to involve in decision-making, stating that such inclusion was 'with a view to ensuring the closest co-operation with independent bodies which may be directly or indirectly concerned in any scheme of civic replanning'.[201] So, from wartime the city – clearly experienced in matters of civic design and change – involved the groups that would be impacted most by plans made and changes sought. In contrast to other blitzed cities that did not extend inclusion in planning to outside groups, this cooperative effort would set up Liverpool councillors and officials for a generally smoother implementation of plans in the postwar period.

The PWRASC seems to have had an odd hiatus in the immediate postwar period – according to City Council records the group met only once in 1946 even after multiple admonishments from the Council.[202] At their meeting in March 1946, the PWRASC members approved a report produced by the City Engineer with the City Architect's cooperation; it was approved by the City Council in April and published in June of that year.[203] The plan shows a greatly modified inner

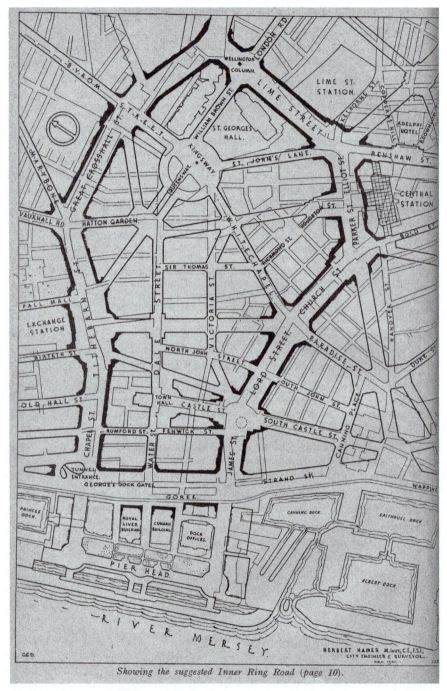

Showing the suggested Inner Ring Road (page 10).

Figure 5.10 Liverpool: inner ring road plan, 1941. Courtesy of Liverpool City Council, Planning Department.

ring road, still wide but cutting across or removing less of the larger roads (see Figure 5.11). While the road plan was less drastic than the 1941 version, the plans also proposed applying for a DO of over 1,500 acres. Theoretically, city officials wanted to be able to plan freely within these boundaries, but made it clear they did not intend to redevelop the entire area, which included areas also designated as 'blight'.[204] Again, officials reiterated their intent to work with local institutions and business and so on: 'The Council are very conscious that without the co-operation of all sections of the community no scheme of redevelopment can be brought to fruition'.[205] This was confirmed by resolution at a City Council meeting 'with a view to ensuring the closest cooperation of independent bodies'.[206]

Soon after the publication of the newest plan in June 1946 council and committee minutes show that there was some fear – erroneously – that the impending passage of the new Town and Country Planning Act (1947) would rescind 'the greater part' of the provisions of the 1944 Act and therefore DO applications had to be rushed and received at the MTCP before this happened.[207] There is no explanation in the council minutes, although later minutes suggest the MTCP did tell city officials they should hurry to apply before the new Act.[208] None of the other cities examined here, appear to have made similar assumptions. The City Council also then took the decision to enormously reduce the size of the DO application, from 1,500 acres to 45.45 acres.[209] At the same time, the Council issued instructions to the City Engineer & City Architect to 'prepare a [new] Reconstruction Scheme'. The DO application was not rushed much, in any case, and in January 1948 the exact size of the application approved was 46.26 acres.[210] This January meeting appears to have been lengthy and contained much discussion of the city centre area. It was agreed at the meeting that the preference in land acquisition, after ministry approval of the DO, would be for larger blocks of land, that is, several buildings in size, on which the leasehold could be sold to private companies, large multiple shops or development companies who would build out the whole as a cohesive development. Additionally, there was discussion of the need to 'ensure harmony' in the new buildings, but without 'monotony'. The committee resolved its intention to therefore create rules for future development to control architectural character as well as type of materials to be used.[211]

Up to this point, although city centre, and particularly shopping, areas had not begun reconstruction – and in any case the City Council was not ready to begin, having no specific plans in place – many reconstruction projects had begun in Liverpool. The docks had been undergoing repair, and certain factory or export-related works were already under sponsorship for rebuilding and repair from the Board of Trade.[212] So, while slow, and having a number of outside factors to consider, the progress of Liverpool was in some ways quicker than many cities, particularly since much of the allowed reconstruction work was near the city centre, in the docks and near the docks.

The DO for Liverpool under Section 1 was approved at the full 46.26 acres in January 1949, coming into effect on 4 February. The City Council moved that the redevelopment committee should 'proceed with all possible speed ... with the object of securing the necessary licenses and allocation of steel and other

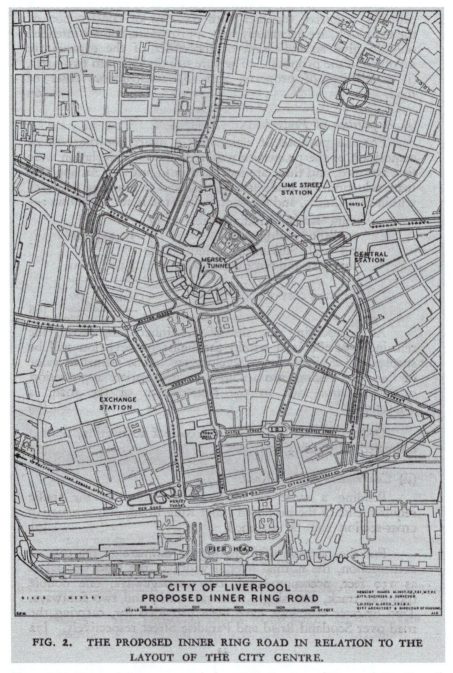

FIG. 2. THE PROPOSED INNER RING ROAD IN RELATION TO THE
LAYOUT OF THE CITY CENTRE.

Figure 5.11 Liverpool: inner ring road plan, 1946. Courtesy of Liverpool City Council, Planning Department.

building materials'.[213] The DO had not passed without objections, however. Of the 48 originally filed with the MTCP, after some withdrawals, the ministry heard eighteen.[214] Most objections came from freeholders simply not wanting their property compulsorily acquired, with others feeling that their 'site [was] not requisite for the purpose of dealing satisfactorily with the extensive war damage in the area'.[215] PWRSC (the "Advisory" was dropped somewhere after 1947) minutes show the feeling of the committee members as to the objections: '[T]his type of objection amounts to disagreement with the principle of redeveloping the designated area as a whole, and strikes at the very root of the application'.[216] Such issues show simply that Liverpool – like other cities – had to deal with property owners who did not wish to give up their sites, even if destroyed or damaged.

The PWRSC resolved immediately to move forward with more definite plans for acquisition of properties and the necessary CPOs.[217] They were, however, tempered by the notice from the MTCP in March 1948, stating that 'local authorities will be expected to limit their expenditure on the purchase of land to those needs which can be shown to be both essential and immediate'.[218] It went further, the committee noted, and stated that land acquisition should be limited to sites on which clearing work and statutory undertaking could be begun at once, adding that it might be two or three years before labour and materials restrictions would be relaxed. Still, the City Engineer felt it likely that it would be possible to go ahead with the redevelopment of three city centre sites: a large site on Church Street, a proposed temporary post office (the main post office having been destroyed) and a third site just outside the proposed inner ring road.[219]

The City Council also took action on these issues, renaming the redevelopment committee and altering its terms of reference in March 1949. The committee had dropped the 'Advisory' from its title and gained more powers to negotiate on behalf of the City Council, rather than simply advise.[220] The City Council followed this change with an instruction to the PWRSC to develop more concrete proposals for the CPOs proposed.[221] Yet the Council clearly was aware that the work involved would be more than the current staff could manage, and concurrently created a new 'town planning' branch of city government. Council minutes show a list of new employees including an assistant planning officer alongside the City Engineer, who functioned as Town Planning Officer, and second assistant as well as twenty-four additional staff.[222] Applications for CPOs for housing projects had been approved by the MTCP, but the application for the central area would involve a more definite plan and negotiation with the landowners.

The PWRSC soon discovered the difficulty of negotiating to acquire sites, to procure definite developers or companies to build, and at the same time felt they were getting the short end of the MTCP's treatment, having received no allocations to allow for city centre work in 1949. Ministry files show that planning ministry officials did not feel that Liverpool was prepared to begin work on the redevelopment of the city centre, and were probably correct.[223] The redevelopment committee heard and approved the City Engineer and City Architect's joint report that covered several key issues regarding the impending work: first, they suggested that the key site at Lord Street bordering the inner ring road should be the next priority for redevelopment; second, that 'in light of experience gained since the first proposals for postwar redevelopment were prepared' the future proposals should incorporate existing street lines, 'rather than attempt to impose a new street pattern'.[224] The reason given was, unsurprisingly, the reduction of cost – a savings in both the headache of negotiating to purchase sites as well as a savings in laying out new services (i.e., drainage, etc.). Further, the city officials recommended a new layout that would provide increased open spaces, and increased car parking.

Finally, and perhaps most importantly, they noted that rather than attempt to acquire land within the DO by compulsory acquisition, 'the opportunity should first be afforded to all owners to sell their land by agreement to the Corporation, compulsory purchase orders to be made only for the outstanding interests then remaining'.[225] The reason given was that if the property had already been determined to be able to receive a cost of works payment under the War Damage Act 1941, then a CPO 'would destroy this benefit, to the financial disadvantage both of the owner and the Corporation', whereas purchase by agreement was not subject to the same disadvantage.[226] It is especially interesting to note that other cities do not seem to have either shared this view, or taken note of the details, and it is curious why this was so. Either the other cities did not understand the laws in the same way, or the payments for war damage were possibly higher than in Liverpool. After all a district valuer, who differed by region, determined the payments. Potentially too, the other cities did not want to take the time and patience needed for such negotiations. Liverpool generally seems to have been more concerned with costs while Hull and Exeter seemed more concerned with executing their plans. For the reason noted above, Liverpool Corporation did not apply for many CPOs, beyond housing, as they found it better for all parties to simply negotiate a purchase agreement on land they needed to acquire to carry through the redevelopment plans.[227]

While this action did assist the City Council to acquire much of the land in the central shopping area without significant problems, it did not apply to all land. A CPO had been applied for to acquire property owned by the very large firm of men's clothiers, Montague Burton.[228] Burton objected to the CPO (oddly on a purely legal point) and filed against the Corporation in court on 14 October 1949.[229] This was the same firm that had objected in Hull and taken that city corporation to court as well. The court found no legal grounds for objection to the CPO and awarded costs to the Liverpool Corporation.[230] Burton filed an appeal in January but that too was lost.[231] Throughout, it appeared that the City Council's policy of acquisition by agreement was successful, with the few problems – such as Burton – also going in the Council's favour.

By 1950 the PWRSC – and possibly the City Council – appear to have been concerned with the slowness of rebuilding and the appearance of the city centre. As they first discussed in September 1949, one issue that was continually raised in the PWRSC minutes related to open spaces. City officials (the engineer and architect) continued to press for acquisition of land for open space in the city centre and lobbied for speed as well. They claimed that 'the psychological effect of the laying out of this open space would justify its carrying out immediately, and prove to the public that the Corporation actively wish to encourage redevelopment'.[232] They suggested an application for a CPO under section 38(1), which would enable the Corporation to temporarily redevelop the site themselves, as open space.[233] Additionally, from April 1950 they proposed to install 'showcases' on empty blitzed sites.[234] These showcases were proposed to be placed on empty bomb sites then in use as car parks.[235] It was suggested to erect a strip of 'garden' with some seating and the – presumably ugly – land at the rear would be hidden from view by screens. Furthermore, 'a certain amount of revenue could be obtained by permitting the display of suitable advertisements on the screens'.[236] An added impetus was the upcoming 1951 Festival of Britain, when Liverpool would host events, activities and exhibitions, and city officials clearly hoped to clean up as much of the unkempt bomb sites as possible.[237] By October city officials reported poor progress with coercing empty site owners to assist with some form of beautification, and so made clear their intent to use the War Damaged Sites Act 1949, which was passed to prevent sites becoming hazardous, or even ugly.[238]

City Council minutes show some impatience with progress on several fronts, but particularly with the attempt to redevelop the Lord Street site, suggesting that the PWRSC invite the Merseyside Civic Society's traders group to consult.[239] Input from local businesses seems to have helped determine the policy of the city on this and similar developments. Such input also appears to have prompted the City Engineer to suggest that no new roadways be planned for the city centre, and that an amended inner ring road was in progress, as the prior plan 'would have seriously affected the business and commercial development in the area'.[240] This may have been a beneficial plan to local property owners, but it slowed progress on the relief of traffic congestion in the centre, with both the City Council and the PWRSC discussing the problem at meetings from October 1950 through 1951, including surveys on car parking being drawn up to help plan for some relief.[241] No roadway solution was agreed, although the PWRSC agreed to make additional car parking a responsibility of developers/owners of new shops.

Also in 1950, after pressure on the MTCP from Liverpool officials, and political pressure in the House of Commons from Liverpool MPs, Liverpool received its first allocation for city centre work through the MTCP.[242] Of a total allocation determined at £4 million for 1951, Liverpool received a £100,000 building licence allowance.[243] This greatly upset the committee and officials, since comparatively (by city size) they felt Liverpool deserved a larger share of the allocation.[244] To be fair, however, the MTCP had clearly stated they would only approve sponsoring of licenses for work ready to begin, and Liverpool had reported £95,000 worth of work was ready.[245] In the end, the PWRSC had difficulty in distributing the licences, when it was found the work was indeed not all in hand.[246] Happily, one of the buildings to receive the go-ahead under this allocation had burnt down from an incendiary bomb fire, but the steel frame could be kept in place. In another case, however, an allocation set to be used in 1951 was not needed, when the shop receiving the allocation, a food purveyor, received a license instead sponsored by the Ministry of Food.[247] This miscommunication, or perhaps attempt by the business to pursue all potential sponsoring opportunities, only points further to the complexity in administering a centrally sponsored building programme in this postwar period.

At the same time, as licensing allocations shifted within the city, the difficulties of tracking building work so exactly were clearly shown.[248] For this reason the planning ministry allocations were – and had to be – moving targets. While it was always possible to say with some specificity what the cost of a building would be, or even to competently estimate the value of the amount of work to be completed, the vagaries of labour and particularly delivery of materials as well as availability caused the building programmes everywhere to force flexibility into the system of control. Certainly the city receiving the allocations – that is, Liverpool – intended to exhaust the allowance, and hoped to build or rebuild as quickly as possible. But the reality of shortages in this period of construction hampered many efforts.

By 1951 the City Engineer and City Architect, with their staff and the PWRSC, were also attempting to complete the required Development Plan, due in December. Although the area had received approval for the *Merseyside Plan*, which was completed with the cooperation of the wartime MTCP, there were several issues to overcome before the new plan could be satisfactorily completed. The issue of housing had not been resolved, and even though the housing functions were now situated with the planning minister at the Ministry of Local Government and Planning, there were negotiations ongoing. The subject of the discussions involved the continued problem of overspill. Liverpool could not fit all the housing needs within its boundaries, but needed to agree in principle for overspill sites with adjacent planning authorities. Both Bootle and Lancashire County Council continued to cause delays for the completion of the Liverpool plan.[249] Within the city issues with traffic and parking continued, and committee minutes contain several substantial reports on the car park issue.[250]

The Development Plan was submitted eventually, but the acute housing shortage issues continued to plague the City Council and officials for many years to come.[251] The City Council minutes for all of 1952 through 1954 show only housing issues in relation to the PWRSC.[252] While other cities sent frequent deputations to ministries in Whitehall, chasing bigger allocations for rebuilding their centres, Liverpool's officials focused more on visits to other countries to study their housing solutions.[253] The focus on housing indicates that this was still the primary focus of the City Council, and most likely the focus of the citizens as well. This may well have contributed to the swing of the council majority from Conservative to Labour in 1955, the first Labour council ever elected in Liverpool.[254]

However, the minutes of the PWRSC itself contain continuous correspondence and discussion notes about the development of the retail shops in the central area. Even *The Times* in London ran a short piece about the slowness of reconstruction progress, lamenting – on Liverpool's behalf perhaps? – the very small portion of the allocation and how little impact it made on the vastness of work yet to be started.[255]

By 1953 the allocation had grown to £300,000 for the cost of work allowed, which was now approximately 7 per cent of the national (blitzed cities) total. Still, only five projects could receive licenses out of this amount: a project by

Littlewoods, three smaller shop developments at scattered sites in the centre and the largest chunk of allocation was to go to the first phase of rebuilding of the Corn Exchange.[256]

City officials and councillors would continue to press various ministries for increases to building allowances for Liverpool city centre. Not only did they pursue increases through the planning ministry (now called Housing and Local Government, hereafter MHLG), but they must have also become aware that the Ministry of Works controlled a far greater amount of licensing powers than that run through the 'Blitzed Cities Scheme' under the MHLG. Officials initiated discussions with Works to propose further projects being licensed directly through that ministry, and were hopeful of the results.[257] At the same time decisions were made as to the priority of projects awaiting starts in the city centre, so that if licenses were made available, or if originally planned allocations came under other sponsorship – that is, Food again – there were companies ready to take on the licenses if offered.[258]

Also in 1953, although there were clearly still numerous empty bomb sites in the central shopping area, nearby plans had been put in motion and construction soon started on one of the large open space schemes that the City Engineer and City Architect had promoted to the PWRSC.[259] Coronation Gardens was only partially completed by the time of Elizabeth II's festivities, but did reach completion soon after and provided a large open space in the city centre in the 1950s and 1960s.[260]

In November of 1953, as shown in Chapter 4, the building license allocation scheme that had run through the IPC and then various departments was abandoned, with all licenses now to be applied for directly to the Ministry of Works. The effect of the change meant that the city no longer had to decide which projects to put forward for sponsorship, and the MHLG no longer had to ration out allocations to the blitzed cities. Licensing stayed, for the time being, but rationing of licenses was finally ended. What this meant for Liverpool was an almost immediate increase in the amount of city centre construction, and lessening of the workload and headache on the city officials in the planning department.[261] While still approving schemes, officials could prioritize without having to exclude building projects, allowing more simultaneous construction work.

The results of Liverpool's redevelopment up to 1954 were published in a broad special supplement of the *Liverpool Daily Post* on 23 June 1954. 'The New Face of Liverpool' was subtitled 'City of Bright Prospects' and the sketch plan proposal for the city centre was splashed across the front page.[262] The supplement had sections on 'How Liverpool is meeting the challenge of the blitz', 'Restoring the stores', 'Do you know your new Liverpool?' and others on housing, the docks, the university and even 'Planning for the helicopter age'.[263] The opening page statement from the Lord Mayor acknowledged: 'until this year the severe restrictions on capital expenditure for redevelopment made progress slow and unsatisfactory'.[264] An article by Alderman Shennan described the process of redevelopment through the period of restriction, and detailed the decisions made by the PWRSC and the City Council as they had affected progress – that is, the decision not to allow temporary shops in the centre.[265] Shennan additionally made the case for the construction of multistorey car parks to come, when temporary car parks on blitzed sites were lost as rebuilding continued. But he also made it clear that there was not some great finished product towards which the City Council was working: 'When we speak of the changing face of Liverpool, we are speaking of a continuous process.'[266]

This comment seems to point to a change in policy from the suggestion of the City Architect in 1942, Keay, who had said in the radio programme 'Making Plans' that he felt it was very important that the redevelopment of Liverpool not be 'patchy' and rebuild only bomb sites, but such cities should be planned 'on the large scale ... and always keep in mind your master plan.'[267] Then again, the City Council had – on advice of their officials and for financial reasons – eventually stated that they did not intend to make huge sweeping changes, at least not in the heart of the city centre. Although the city administration eventually did have a full-time planning department, there was no pure planner hired to oversee their functions, instead keeping the City Engineer and City Architect at the helm. Alfred Shennan, a local architect, who surely had much involvement with the outcomes, ran the PWRSC but he was not a planner by training in any case. No consultant planner was engaged, as many other large and small cities had done, and such an option seems not to have been introduced. Equally, only small exhibitions were mounted, and no publications beyond the few in-house brochures and booklets, and the 1944 *Merseyside Plan*.

Docks and industry were rebuilt with priority from the Labour and Conservative governments, and sponsorship of most of the work would have been through the Board of Trade and the Ministry of Works. Housing construction too was prioritized through the Ministry of Health and then the planning ministry. The City Architect, Ronald Bradbury, claimed in 1954 that 21,000 postwar homes had been built – 'an achievement unequalled by any city of comparable size.'[268] From city archives and central government archives it also seems as though the city officials maintained good relations with Whitehall, something other cities also did not always manage. But here, too, Liverpool does not appear to have had dominant personalities; as involved as Alderman Shennan surely was, his 'voice' does not appear to dominate council records, and his statements seem reasonable and cooperative unlike his peers in Hull.[269]

Conclusion

Although historians of reconstruction planning have often examined the cities in light of political influences, and have often politicized the planning issues, this chapter and its predecessors have shown that personalities often had substantial impact on the planning and reconstruction process. While Exeter City Council had a Conservative majority they tended to plan comprehensively, acquired large portions of city centre land and did not make cooperative gestures to local business. Liverpool, meanwhile, also Conservative until 1955, planned less comprehensively and was very keen to cooperate with local business. Hull's council was fairly split, though it shifted from a more Conservative to a Labour majority after 1945, and had always planned boldly, with councillors digging in against local business opposition and rarely making efforts to work with them. These examples show that the personalities of the actors involved can be at least as influential as local politics. Roy Hattersley's comment on his experience, albeit in the 1960s, is apropos: 'In those days ... local government offered a pleasure which Whitehall and Westminster could never provide. It was possible to watch ideas turn into reality.'[270] Planning laws were oriented towards state ownership, in theory, but it varied from city to city how much of the opportunity to acquire land was actually taken. The three cities in this chapter alone illustrate how hugely varied the approaches were – in terms of redevelopment, modernization, expansion or simply problem-solving.

From strong personalities on city councils and in local authority offices, from obstinate or difficult individuals to those who were cooperative and amenable, the stories detailed within the blitzed cities vary greatly. But the complexity of issues is dominated mainly by property ownership: from owner-occupier traders to large multiple firms and department stores, to public transport and even utilities, most of the obstacles to implementing postwar plans came from those who either did not want to be displaced, or inconvenienced, to those who saw the changes as a loss, whether financially or personally. The interplay of relations – even where the players did not know each other or of the existence of the other – was also crucial. The web of negotiations between the Treasury, IPC, planning ministry, transport and housing ministries and more were all part of the nuanced and complex picture that is an overlooked aspect of the postwar period, particularly around reconstruction. Still, the final negotiations were those with the developers, freeholders, leaseholders and others who would privately – or in cooperation with local authorities – complete the process and build the city centre buildings. The following chapter will show how the last of these negotiations played out in the provincial blitzed cities.

Chapter 6

POSTWAR REBUILDING: HOPEFUL PLANS, DIFFERENT REALITIES

It is true that not only the planners but the Government itself had
promised, if not a new heaven at least a new earth, at the end of the war.
– Professor William Holford[1]

While Chapter 2 documented the very positive wartime rhetoric of hope and
promises made, the subsequent three chapters have shown how the positive tone
disappeared. From the end of hostilities in 1945 blitzed cities faced seemingly
endless obstacles to reconstruction, in particular to the implementation of new
city centre plans. This chapter, however, examines the steps taken in Hull, Exeter
and Liverpool to finally begin implementing plans, or at least to begin replacing
lost commercial square footage in the city centres. Though the period after 1945
is often seen as the high point of social democracy, in that it witnessed the vast
growth of the British welfare state, if we turn to the landscape of British cities we
get a very different picture. Here postwar economic history plays out in modernist
developments – developments built within the construct of a new 'socialist'
government, but with very 'capitalist' origins.

In addition to all the government restrictions and the vagaries of local interests
and politics, local authorities had to rely very heavily on private investment in
order to physically construct new buildings in blitzed city centres. But how did this
physically translate into the built product? In this chapter the rebuilding of each
of the cities investigated in the previous chapter will illustrate how development
and construction evolved as the plans, the Declaratory Orders (DOs) and the
Compulsory Purchase Orders (CPOs) fell into place. The physical results of all the
legislation, the allocations, the objections, the legal actions, the negotiations and
the numerous policy actors were the new city centres of the 1950s. As this chapter
will demonstrate, although 'planning' was seen as broadly necessary for all cities in
the postwar period, it in no way determined the final outcomes within the rebuilt
centres of the blitzed cities. This chapter will examine examples of negotiations
and partnerships created by these cities, demonstrating the key role of private
investment. It therefore looks beyond previous scholarship where the planning
process has been closely examined, but where the narratives also stop short of
explaining how most of the rebuilding was carried out, or of evaluating the results.

To be fair, most work on city centre reconstruction has been clearly focused on 'replanning' rather than actual 'rebuilding'; indeed several scholars have given a sense of the complexity and the constraints that this book seeks to investigate in greater depth.[2]

After examining the specific examples and the role of developers, as well as their interactions with city officials, this chapter will also summarize the constraints of cost, coordination and the multiple government restrictions on building as they affected reconstruction. We will then see how these constraints were embodied in examples of the final building designs: in the materials used and the final layouts. Rounding off this discussion is a brief look into public perceptions of early reconstruction efforts, using a number of different reactions to the new provincial city centres – reactions to the plans as implemented and to the architecture as built.

I. *The Role of Private Investment in Hull, Exeter and Liverpool*

The juxtaposition of Labour's new planning laws with a market economy predicated how the reconstruction was paid for, and in some ways even how its appearance was determined. Along these lines, a fascinating story was told by a contemporary journalist named Oliver Marriott. In *The Property Boom* Marriott described the emergence of a particular kind of property development company in the late 1940s and early 1950s.[3] The book helped explain a number of circumstances, or the origins of what became the practical solution to the high cost of rebuilding. In one telling example Marriott detailed how two enterprising young war veterans – Louis Freedman and Fred Maynard – formed a property company. In 1949 the company won its first bid to develop shops in an estate of new council houses in Bristol.[4] They were backed substantially by Harold (later Lord) Samuel, a London property owner and former estate agent who would soon branch into rebuilding in the capital.[5] Samuel had purchased a very small investment trust involving a few London properties in 1944. He had turned the business into enough of a success to back Freedman when he started a company called Ravensfield Properties in 1946. Soon after, Freedman met and forged a partnership with Maynard.

After securing the work in Bristol, Freedman and Maynard noticed that blitzed cities were likely to have plentiful commercial development opportunities. Their next venture was to persuade Plymouth City Council to allow them to secure the leasehold on a prime city centre site.[6] The Plymouth site was taken at a fixed ground rent for a specific term and Freedman and Maynard – now trading as Ravenseft Ltd. – proceeded to develop forty-one shops at their own expense. According to Marriott, Plymouth's reason for taking on such inexperienced developers was that no one else wanted to build the scheme, and financially Plymouth took little risk.[7] Continuing to expand these potential business opportunities Freedman and Maynard pitched successfully to various blitzed cities, particularly after they had one or two contracts signed and could use the work to advertise their services to other cities.[8]

Between 1945, when most cities needing to rebuild war damage were preparing early plans, and 1950, when the cities had just begun to piece together actual building projects, a trend started in which cities – including London – found private investors to build on publicly owned land. Some of the larger 'developers' were companies such as Woolworths, Marks and Spencer, Prudential Assurance and Pearl Assurance.[9] But the first of the purely commercial and speculative developers to chase business in the city centres was Ravenseft. By 1950 they acquired the right to develop buildings on Princesshay, the new street in Exeter[10] (see Figure 6.1). Soon after, Ravenseft added Coventry, Hull, Swansea and more.[11]

The capitalist economy, combined with the state as landowner, created a reconstruction solution where both sides would benefit financially. According to *The Times*'s 'Business Diary', Ravenseft developments had grown from 1946 'over the next 17 years ... into new shops in over 400 developments in 150 towns in Britain'.[12] This small postwar development company grew quickly and was bought out in 1955 by one of its original investors, Lord Samuel, who absorbed it into his investment trust – Land Securities (LSIT) – a corporation that became one of Britain's biggest landlords.[13] Samuel retained Ravenseft in

Figure 6.1 Aerial view of Exeter, Princesshay, under construction, 1953. Image: Britain from the Air (Historic England).

name as LSIT's provincial commercial development wing, and left Freedman and Maynard in charge.[14] It continued to grow and pursue more provincial development.[15]

However, not all cities welcomed large areas of development or redevelopment. In the larger city of Hull, as shown in the previous chapter, many freeholders dug in and tried to retain their prewar locations. Hull had more widespread damage than Exeter, however, and more local – and vocal – opposition. The city did eventually obtain a CPO for the central area, beyond a number of industrial sites, but only for 11 acres out of over 200 in the central area DO.[16] After 1951 two portions of the area were developed concurrently: a large property of shops and offices called The Queen's House was developed by Ravenseft from 1952[17]; the other commercial property, across a wide shopping street from the Ravenseft site, was built by a collaboration of the Hull Corporation, local shop owners and property-owners turned investors (see Figure 6.2). This team, called Triangle Development Trust (for the shape of the site), was at the time an unusual partnership of public and private development, put together to rebuild a block of commercial property without CPOs being necessary.[18] Additionally, the Corporation developed a number of sites, comprising temporary shops for bombed-out traders who had not found new accommodations.[19] Most of these shops were near the main railway station, and were part of the modified city plan's shopping area (see Figure 6.3). Hull's prewar shopping area had also contained a much larger number of department

Figure 6.2 Queen's House and the Triangle Trust buildings, Hull. Author photo, 2011.

Figure 6.3 Temporary shops in Ferensway, Hull, ca. 1948. Courtesy of Hull History Centre.

stores and other large shops than many other cities; most of these rebuilt even if they were re-sited.[20]

Unfortunately for Hull, the slowness of reconstruction in industry, the docks and the city centre apparently drove people from the city, with the population dropping from 318,000 in 1939 to 296,600 in 1950.[21] Although the City Council claimed in 1958 that the extent of war damage was no longer noticeable, as of 2017 many bomb sites are still used as commercial car parks in the city centre and have never been redeveloped.[22] Other sites do actually contain 1950s buildings that now sit empty and almost derelict, such as the Edwin Davis department store. The temporary shops, built on Ferensway in 1947 and 1948, remained until the 1960s and 1970s, and some were still in place even into 2012, presumably because the City could not find a developer for the site(s) (see Figure 6.4). Still, despite the problems with reconstruction in Hull generally, the City Council could claim in 1958 that 700,000 square feet of shopping floor space had been built, with an additional 300,000 in progress and 240,000 new square feet of office accommodation completed as well. It was also claimed that more than £5.5 million had been spent on building in the central area and another £900,000 on new civic buildings.[23]

In contrast with many other blitzed cities, Liverpool did not use any CPOs, as seen in Chapter 5. There the local authority worked diligently to accommodate

Figure 6.4 Temporary shops in Ferensway, Hull, 2011. Author photo.

owners as well as negotiating with new developers to work on the sites the City Council had bought from groups of small business owners. The first – and the only substantial – sites to be developed by 1954 were those in the main shopping area on Church Street and Lord Street.[24] This was the same street, changing its name as it crossed Paradise Street. Redevelopment of the sites did not go forward very quickly. Liverpool was not, in the planning ministry's opinion, ready to build by February 1949 when the first steel allocation was announced and so the city received nothing. In fact by 1949 the Corporation still needed to identify tenants for these sites.[25] Generally, the local authority's first obligation was legal: they had to negotiate with the former tenants, who would then agree to retain their sites under the approved planning scheme as submitted with any DO or CPO application, or businesses would have to be re-sited. If business owners agreed to stay they would undertake a new lease and then build a new building. Alternately they could work with a developer if they could be persuaded to build, as long as the developer allowed former occupants to remain at the same location should they desire to stay.

In 1949, while still in negotiations with various firms for the Lord Street site, the Liverpool City Architect prepared suggestions for the scheme. They even drew elevations and a 'sketch model' of the proposed development, which were then circulated to the potential tenants.[26] It is unclear from committee or council minutes whether this helped or hindered the final negotiations, but it was likely the latter, since no definite developer/leasehold tenant was found in the following year. The empty site and ongoing negotiations brought excuses from the Post-War Reconstruction Special Committee (PWRSC) – the 'high cost of building [is] worrying developers' – and prompted the City Council to recommend erecting temporary shops on the site. City officials, who felt that temporary shops would not likely be removed in a timely fashion, adamantly opposed this.[27] Throughout 1950 negotiations continued for both the Church Street and Lord Street sites, considered key developments and of great importance to the shopping area by the PWRSC and officials.[28] Two companies were the final contenders for the prime site at Church Street: Littlewood's Mail Order stores and Ravenscroft Properties Ltd, who were Ravenseft under a different name, the same developer as worked with Exeter and Hull.[29] Eventually Littlewood's was selected and agreed tentatively to terms of the leasehold. The terms continued to fluctuate over the next two years, due to a changing economic situation as well as the ability – or inability – of the city to allow, through their building allocations, a start to construction.[30]

Liverpool's Littlewood's development provides another example of the ways in which city officials were able to avoid some of the hurdles introduced in the new planning legislation. As mentioned above, acquiring land without a CPO was financially beneficial for both the city and the owner: offering savings in both cost and time of public inquiry. The land was determined by officials to be eligible for Section 83 of the 1947 Act: that is, if the City Council could agree purchase terms with existing owners without using a CPO – or with a CPO as long as the authority acquires the land – and then lease the land to a company to develop lettable spaces or for their own use, then the site was not subject to a development charge. The City Council would then pay a nominal sum to the betterment fund, which could then be rolled into the lease terms – so that effectively charges were avoided on all sides.[31]

By 1952 the Littlewood's development was still stalled and meeting minutes detail many concerns about the project.[32] City officials did manage to obtain an interesting agreement with Littlewood's: once the shops were completed the owner would occupy a portion but would let the rest of the ground floor. That floor was to be retail only and would not include any of the football pools or betting shops for which Littlewood's was well known.[33] Further stalling development however, and despite having drawn out his requirements before agreeing the lease terms, the City Architect claimed to have some problems with the owner's building design details when they were submitted. However, PWRSC minutes also show he appreciated that modifications would probably be made when the larger scale details for construction were drawn up. While it appears the city probably made the process even slower by insisting on design changes, they did finally allow the project to go ahead and gave Littlewood's about a third of the city's building license allocation for 1953[34] (see Figure 6.5). By the following year the sites on Lord Street were still in the process of being acquired, so a large part of that section of the shopping area remained empty. There was still no developer in place by October 1953 for the south side of the street even though the site had been discussed, and negotiations had been continuous, since the start of redevelopment planning.

Figure 6.5 Littlewood's building on Church Street, Liverpool, 2011. Author photo.

Additionally, PWRSC minutes show that once again the City Architect was told to prepare a 'suggested elevation' of the proposed frontages, 'for the guidance of prospective developers'; the development was to be 'no less than four upper floors', as well as the usual ground floor retail space.[35]

The planning ministry had made note of a similar situation in Exeter: 'it rather struck me from the sketches which Rowe produced … that his attitude to developers is perhaps more rigid than is desirable, and may partly account for the difficulties in coming to terms.'[36] It is highly likely that this applied to many more blitzed cities than just Exeter and Liverpool. A 1967 property development brochure directed at attracting development partnerships with local authorities also supports this suggestion. Arndale Property Trust, established in 1950, had grown into one of the largest city centre commercial developers, but they stated very clearly on the opening page of their brochure: 'It should be recognized at the outset that a successful and profitable scheme for the Developer automatically means benefit to an Authority. It is therefore vital from the Authority's point of view that it should not prejudice the development by making its "terms" too onerous.'[37] Despite the attempts to control building design by city officials, and although Liverpool suffered more bomb damage than the other cities, officials there made fewer attempts to drastically change the city fabric; this was despite the opportunities available through DOs and CPOs. Several planning histories have suggested that radical plans were due to Labour councils, and often imply that

Conservative councils sought less change.[38] This may have been true for Liverpool, with a Conservative council throughout the postwar period, but Exeter's council was Conservative and pursued more drastic changes than this idea of a party divide would suggest. It seems more likely that cost was a bigger barrier in Liverpool, while Exeter was greedier in terms of making up, and even increasing, lost rateable value.

II. *Examining the Constraints of Cost, Coordination and Restrictive Government*

As shown here and in the past several chapters, the reconstruction – or redevelopment – of blitzed cities took place amid an exceptionally complex set of issues. Numerous factors contributed to the product of rebuilding, which was always in flux, and in any case cannot be said to be a completed project in the sense of having made plans and implemented them. Through the examples examined here, as well as absorbing information in planning ministry files about other cities, a picture emerges around the many significant factors affecting the built environment in the rebuilding of bombed cities. Constraints ranged from the many external factors that city officials could not control – particularly the restrictions on capital investment in buildings, to the intransigence of local business owners and landowners, from costs combined with the loss of rates to difficulties agreeing DOs and CPOs, sites and plans. And among all of it was the subsequent reliance on private enterprise to bear the expense and effort of construction.[39] Not only had the cities suffered large losses in terms of rate income, they were forced to spend local funds on making plans, acquiring land and – where possible – developing the land themselves.[40] This was in addition to any local expenditure to develop new public housing, re-siting of industry and rebuilding or re-siting of roads and other public works.[41]

Unsurprisingly, complaints in Parliament became more frequent with many MPs stating their concerns, backed by a good deal of evidence.[42] Regardless, little financial assistance was available to the blitzed cities beyond that for public housing. The only grants made available to assist the cities in redevelopment or implementation of plans were those for loan charges on cost of land acquisition and clearing.[43] Up to March 1954 this had included grants of £876,000 for almost £36 million of land acquisition over 730 acres nationally; the grant applied only until the land was developed, that is, the rates were recovered. Complaints in 1947 about the loss of rateable value (RV), which demonstrated that only one blitzed city received assistance, grew in scale as cities awaited building allowances and were refused permission to build more, thereby handicapping their ability to recover rates[44] (see Table 6.1).

The Labour government had continued a long-running scheme of grants (until 1948 termed 'block grants') that were meant to assist cities that had low rate income and were unable to provide basic local services. However, in practice, the terms of the grants favoured the very poorest councils around the country, which

Table 6.1 Rateable value and Exchequer grants

City	Population (1948–49)	Bombed area (acres)	Total rateable value (1938)	Total rateable value (1948–49)	RV increase or decrease	Est. damage to trade (per Board of Trade) in £	Exchequer equalization grants under Section 2 (1948–49)	Exchequer equalization grants under Section 2 (1949–50)	Exchequer equalization grants under Section 2 (1950–51)	Exchequer equalization grants under Section 13 (no date)	Grant totals by city
Birmingham	1,096,190	60	7,199,226	7,245,591		unknown	816,014	928,634	1,103,777	347,049	3,195,474
Bristol	435,390	121	3,331,637	3,365,328	33,691	464,280	–	–	–	115,626	115,626
Canterbury	26,130	26	231,927	222,219	(9,708)	21,552	–	–	–	5,875	5,875
Coventry	251,590	160	1,474,600	1,629,433	154,833	315,260	188,065	174,534	131,376	52,419	546,394
Dover*		25	–			unknown	–	–	–	–	–
Exeter	75,680	68	683,172	686,409	3,237	158,778	–	–	–	17,525	17,525
Hull	294,410	136	1,776,328	1,703,164	(73,164)	548,376	498,957	573,040	598,351	124,384	1,794,732
Liverpool	792,600	208	6,769,194	6,311,237	(457,957)	409,085	–	–	–	388,340	388,340
Lowestoft* (Great)		15	–	–		4,112	–	–	–	–	–
Manchester	693,900	61	6,662,119	6,269,991	(392,128)	unknown	–	–	–	255,741	255,741
Norwich	118,200	78	758,311	808,366	50,055	88,275	53,661	36,799	36,993	44,118	171,571
Plymouth	206,110	168	1,758,459	1,655,278	(103,181)	401,837	–	–	–	55,977	55,977
Portsmouth	242,020	165	1,888,366	1,776,837	(111,529)	unknown	–	–	–	62,593	62,593
Sheffield	514,590	108	3,265,164	3,264,960	(204)	367,188	485,996	510,620	487,340	192,133	1,676,089
South Shields	106,820	19	548,752	575,316	26,564	unknown	172,816	198,928	209,467	54,363	635,574
Southampton	180,100	145	1,580,327	1,474,158	(106,169)	370,607	–	–	–	45,642	45,642
Swansea	158,000	42	1,068,573	991,160	(77,413)	unknown	158,013	164,954	187,843	69,461	580,271
Yarmouth (Great)	50,140	50	346,811	331,030	(15,781)	unknown	38,331	33,854	30,197	19,907	122,289

Sources: Cmd 8204, Cmd 9559 (HMSO).

Note: *denotes cities not included in Cmd 9559, therefore some data is missing. [also see table 4.2].

meant that almost no assistance was provided to blitzed cities until 1948.[45] The Local Government Act of 1948 changed the grant system, but in debates on the bill it was clear the blitzed cities were gaining no special treatment. Thomas Lewis, Labour MP for Southampton, argued:

> It is the question of the blitzed areas. I want to ask the Minister why he has not put in a short Clause dealing with that matter, which is still a very pressing one. All the Ministries – not merely the Ministry of Health – have treated the blitzed areas in a disgraceful fashion. That may seem to be strong language, but I feel strongly about it, as do some of my hon. Friends who represent other blitzed areas. Neither the authorities who control the funds nor the Ministries who control the labour and materials have shown any desire to restore the blitzed towns to a proper condition … I maintain that the relief which it is proposed to grant under this Bill is not sufficient to enable blitzed areas to put themselves on to a proper footing.[46]

Even then, after the Local Government Act increased such assistance with new 'Exchequer Equalisation Grants', the scheme did not provide any special assistance to blitzed cities – grants were available to all. This eventually instigated further debates. In 1951, Ralph Morley, Labour MP for Southampton, stated: 'I wish to draw attention to the necessity for securing continued financial assistance from the central Exchequer to compensate blitzed towns for the great loss of rateable value which they have suffered as a result of enemy action during the late war, a loss which subsequent building and reconstruction has by no means restored.'[47] He continued angrily: 'We suggest that there is a very strong case for a continuation of the Exchequer grant to the other heavily blitzed towns. [Blitzed cities have] gained no advantage at all from the rate equalisation formula … We in the blitzed towns are the orphans of the storm, and we feel that we are the neglected orphans of the storm.'[48] Morley was supported by several MPs from both major parties, though perhaps Lucy Middleton (Labour, Plymouth) summed up the problems best. Middleton pointed out that the problems were not simply the burden of lost rates, but the heavier public housing burden in blitzed areas, plus schools and other public buildings needing replacement combined with the inability to gain back rates from normally profitable city centre commercial property.[49] It is easy to see then, why – without further financial assistance from central government – city councils grew increasingly desperate to replace the lost rates. Partly in order to cut costs Liverpool negotiated for land acquisition rather than put together and apply for CPOs, or even attempt to implement a grand plan.[50] In cities such as Hull and Exeter, where grand plans *were* made, only portions were implemented, if for many different reasons. As Alderman Shennan of Liverpool said, as much as the city would have liked to acquire and redevelop the forty-six acres within their DO, 'the effect on its finances would be severe'.[51] Cities thus often decided not to proceed with developing the sites themselves, even if acquired under the planning acts; instead, they launched partnerships with private companies as has been discussed. By 1950 most cities had bomb sites that were about ten years old, many in the most valuable areas of the centre rate-wise, and it is no surprise that city officials and councils became increasingly impatient to redevelop.

Of course, many constraints further slowed reconstruction progress. All of the cities examined here, and it is almost certain the same applies to all other blitzed cities, encountered problems with property owners who did not wish to move, have their land acquired or otherwise undergo forced changes.[52] Such difficulties were highlighted by the legal action taken by the owners and traders to protect what they saw as their right not to acquiesce to the intentions of the local authority. Hull and Liverpool had to await both divisional court and appeals court decisions, while Plymouth faced similar obstacles as well as a final opinion of the High Court.[53] Beyond the court battles were the objections, sometimes numbering in the hundreds, fought in hearings for both DO applications and CPOs by almost every city.[54] Many traders, owners, national firms and others with vested interests did not want change, even if for collective 'improvement'.

Adding to the complexity of these problems were the numerous factors external to each city that further prevented comprehensive implementation of plans: the railway companies' frequent refusal to cooperate, the Ministry of Transport's oversight of roadway design and power to override other decisions, the priorities set by the Board of Trade or the Ministry of Health on industrial development and housing, and constant further input and opinions from officials representing all these Whitehall departments.[55] The problem of dealing with so many government entities did not go unnoticed, and the Labour MP for Plymouth, Hubert Medland, noted:

> In order to rebuild the city, which is no small job, it is necessary to work in the closest co-operation with the Government Department responsible for rebuilding, the Ministry of Town and Country Planning. But what do we find in trying to rebuild the city? We have to deal not only with that Ministry, we have far too many Ministries to attend and to make representations to in this respect. I submit to the Parliamentary Secretary that he should inform his principals and the Ministries generally that if we are ever to rebuild Britain, and rebuild it quickly, we shall have to deal with one responsible Department.[56]

However, the cities were subject in particular to the power of the planning ministry; the design, implementation and priority of building projects as well as DOs, CPOs, development plans and more were all scrutinized for ministerial approval by officials in the Ministry of Town and Country Planning (MTCP) and its successors.

Arguably most significant was the lack of priority and subsequent slowness of reconstruction forced on the cities by the involvement of the IPC. Though the Ministry of Works might well have simply swept much of the allocation to blitzed cities into the large 'miscellaneous' figure, as shown in Chapter 3, from 1948 it was decided to both seek the input of the planning ministry – who argued for priority to the cities – and to restrict the allocations to the cities. The consequence of the IPC's involvement and restrictions was a radical slowdown of reconstruction, but this also made cities all the more eager to find other solutions – including quick fixes. Some of the work in city centres was therefore licensed through the Board of Trade, if a case could be argued successfully for trade/export importance, or occasionally through the Ministry of Works – particularly in the case of public work (i.e., town halls, libraries, etc.). In many cases the frustration of the wait and the severe need to speed up the reinstatement of more traders and their shops meant choosing to build temporary shops when approvals and licenses could be found. These were key installations to help the city bring back business and rates, although some city officials feared the sites would then be difficult to redevelop later – often justifiably, as seen in the example of Hull's shops on Ferensway.

In the end, the problems of slowness and obstruction created a great dependence on developers, as investors and builders, to rebuild the blitzed city centres.[57] Local authorities were financially unable to do much beyond acquiring the land, and – as shown – even then there were difficulties. Most city councils therefore preferred to negotiate leaseholds with private firms for the land they had acquired. Traditionally the lessees would have been large multiple stores, insurance firms or estate agents, and most would plan to let out some or all of the building constructed.[58] Although the majority of deals were expected to be with these sorts of owner-occupiers, as they were in prewar development, very quickly a different kind of specialist – and speculative – commercial property developer, such as Ravenseft, came to the fore of reconstruction work in the blitzed cities.[59] Alderman Shennan of Liverpool noted in 1954 that local achievements in postwar redevelopment 'have been brought about by a combination of municipal and private enterprise.'[60] This rise in collaboration between local authorities and private developers came to be seen as *de rigeur* by the 1960s. The 1967 Arndale Properties brochure, created as general promotional material for local authorities, acknowledged the origins of this partnership: 'Post War development of central urban areas really started with building on blitzed land. This was invariably related to the availability of sites owned by the Authority and could rarely be described as comprehensive.'[61] And it further stated: 'The primary function of the Company is the redevelopment of central areas in towns and cities. Whilst most of these schemes are today planned on comprehensive lines ... it is usual ... to carry out these projects in some form of partnership with the Local Authority.'[62]

III. *Designing the New City Centre Buildings*

Once the financial hurdles were surmounted and the developers or owner-builders for various city centre sites in place, the last step was to erect buildings. These buildings were not the result of the city and/or developer – be it either a private owner-occupier or a property company – simply hiring an architect to draw what they all agreed on and then hiring a contractor to build it. Many further factors then came into play, as they still do, in determining the final scale and appearance of the postwar redevelopments. First the appearance of the building could be significantly dependent on the site itself, particularly if surrounded by other buildings. The new building had to fit the site, and the local authority – since the 1947 Act – had the ability to control the look of the façade (hereafter the building 'elevation'), at a minimum, before permission to build was given, though there were no laws at this time governing building design or appearance. While the developers may not have had fixed ideas about the building materials or specific design intent, the city officials and/or councillors often had definite preconceived ideas about what they wanted built.[63]

Thus, second, city officials often governed – if not dictated – the exact appearance, controlling architectural details and materials. This has already been shown in the case of Liverpool's Lord Street development, in which the City Architect was charged with producing elevations for potential developers, giving them specific ideas about what would be expected architecturally. Similarly at Exeter the planner Sharp provided schematic elevations and perspectives, and the eventual development did look remarkably similar to his suggestions.[64] Marriott quoted Freedman of Ravenseft claiming, 'Aesthetically we had virtually no control. The local authorities always dictated.' He then gives a very specific example of the application of design control: 'In one city we got so fed up about the details of the architecture being messed about by officials that we said to our architect: "Go down to – with a blank sheet of paper and ask that damned City Architect to draw on it exactly what he wants." '[65] The ability of the city officials to closely control the designs stemmed from the 1947 Act and the 1948 General Development Order which followed.[66] As the planning ministry stated in a section on the 'External Appearance of Buildings' in its 1955 report: 'The initiative in preparing "well-mannered" designs for building must rest with the developer and his architect, and a general improvement in the standard of design can only come about as a result of an improvement in public taste and an awareness of the possibilities of good design.'[67] Additionally, design in cities was apparently heavily influenced by the 1947 MTCP publication, *The Redevelopment of Central Areas*, previously discussed in Chapter 4. Further, control of appearance could also be partially invested in the transport ministry. In the postwar period this was a key issue since there was an increasingly car-centred approach to planning and design, with streets made wider, and an increased importance of provision for parking.[68]

Third, the primary builders in the blitzed cities were increasingly property developers such as Ravenseft, whose motives for building were more often driven by potential profit over aesthetic concerns.[69] Owner-occupiers generally showed careful concern about their building's appearance but the developers were more interested in lettable space.[70] To be fair, many city officials probably had complementary motives, given their desire to make up huge losses in rateable income caused by the wartime damage. Professor William Holford worked for the MTCP in the war and after, before he resumed teaching. Many years later at the 1966 Guildhall seminars Holford spoke of the lack of 'individual achievement and distinction' in the architecture of postwar reconstruction:

> The other factor, which I think we underestimated in 1947, was the growth in importance of the property developer, rather than the owner-occupier, as the main rebuilding agent. I think that it cannot really be denied that, with few

exceptions, owner-occupiers and their architects had cared about the design of their buildings, even though the design might have been extravagant or pretentious or dull; whereas in the post-war speculative office blocks design was only incidental to the procedure of getting consents and approvals and licenses, and borrowing the money to pay construction costs; it was not an integral part of the building process, still less the creative idea behind it.

. . .

No wonder that Osbert Lancaster complained – as he did again in a recent letter to me – '... the fact that there is, or is alleged to be, a plan behind it all, will simply be used as a weapon with which to beat off unwanted criticism.' This is sad and – I'm afraid – justified criticism of post-war reconstruction.[71]

Rationing – particularly of steel – further impacted appearance because shortages forced the use of other materials such as reinforced concrete. In fact, the Ministry of Housing and Local Government (MHLG) actively encouraged the use of reinforced concrete over structural steel. Speaking in the House of Commons during 1952, the Conservative parliamentary secretary, Ernest Marples, stated:

At the moment, however, the restricting factor is not capital investment but steel. As I have said before, I hope that the blitzed cities will plan their forward programme as far ahead as they can, using the minimum quantities of steel, using reinforcing rods and reinforced concrete in place of structural steel, thereby halving the amount of steel for a given building, or using high tensile wire or pre-stressed concrete in place of the heavier steel sections. I hope that the blitzed cities will proceed on those lines.[72]

An MHLG official reiterated this in a later letter to officials of blitzed cities: 'wherever possible reinforced concrete or load-bearing walls should be used in preference to steel frames'.[73] Postwar materials shortages must have strongly affected building design. Oddly, however, there is a marked lack of discussion of the issues of materials shortages, or even innovations, in the architectural press. One rare example is the transcript of an RIBA meeting of the 'Architectural Science Board' in 1947, then published in its journal: 'Substitute Materials and their Influence on Design'.[74] While not strictly applicable to blitzed city centres, the Ministry of Works' Building Research Station (BRS) had existed since the 1920s and certainly carried out extensive research into alternate materials. The BRS may not have been strictly applied to private development, but its work probably filtered into the architectural profession influencing materials usage to some degree. The BRS provided input, advice and solutions to public architects, particularly for housing-related solutions but for schools and other building types as well.[75] Generally speaking, there was not just an effort to save steel, enforced by the shortages and rationing, but there was in this period, according to Peter Hall, an 'enthusiasm for technology'.[76]

Finally, one of the key influences on building appearance was the rise in popularity of the modernist style of architecture. This modernism had originally developed in Europe and spread to Britain in the 1930s. After the war the new style continued to flourish within the architectural profession, though this time in its own particularly British form.[77] In urban areas this modernism was composed of straight lines: a box-like style with a smooth facade, though often embellished with sparse neo-classical details. The taste for modernism was prevalent among architects and planners, who certainly espoused the clean lines and new materials, but local authorities – who controlled much of the appearance of 1940s and 1950s city centre building – enthusiastically adopted it as well.[78] Much of the development was a modern version of a neo-Georgian style (see Figure 6.3). This stripped-down style blended well with concrete and glass, sometimes also built – or faced – in more traditional brick.[79] Archival records such as city council minutes and municipal journals for local authorities show an overriding sense of the embracing of modernity and a wish to be seen as a forward-thinking city not stuck in the past.[80]

Interestingly, reconstruction in Europe often eschewed modernism for more faithful reconstructions.[81] A number of Polish and German cities, however, paid much attention to the past by rebuilding in a thoroughly historic idiom, re-creating versions – if not some exact copies – of what had been destroyed by Allied bombing. Minister Silkin visited Poland and called the reconstruction of Warsaw 'an almost superhuman task'.[82] But archival research shows no evidence of Britons discussing the potential to rebuild a bombed city 'as it was', despite several continental examples. The best known of these is Warsaw, where the historic core of the city was rebuilt in its prewar form – slightly modified – and is now a UNESCO World Heritage site.[83] A 2010 television programme on Germany visited Dresden and on viewing the 'historic' city, compared it to Britain: 'It seems strange to us, but this is what Germany feels it needs to do. It has to claim back that artistic heritage lost during the war by building the old anew ... In comparison, Coventry has hardly had the same five-star restorative treatment.'[84] While there were certainly contemporary complaints about pulling down individual historic buildings, none of the archival material yields any discussion of rebuilding any part of a city or single historic street as it had been.[85] In fact, the planner Thomas Sharp is cited as having stood firmly against rebuilding on old lines in Exeter, calling it a 'dreadful mistake', although he stated that a city's 'character' should be preserved.[86] In Great Yarmouth, there was similar disagreement and then destruction.[87] One exception was found though at Liverpool, where the City Council helped a few firms rebuild nearly the same design as existed on their prewar sites, but in all cases substantial portions of the buildings remained, and the decision not to demolish and build new was due to the slowness of approvals and the fact that steel allocations for 'repair' were easier to procure.[88]

This lack of concern for historic value, for a general sense of what might be good, have 'character' and therefore might be saved does not reflect the intense pressure for preservation which – though not new – did not truly take off until more than ten years after reconstruction hit its peak.[89] There were a few notable campaigners for historic preservation, such as John Betjeman, but until the later 1960s such discussion was confined to the sidelines.[90] Unusually, while perhaps German and Polish officials foresaw the potential for tourism in 'historic' towns, local authorities and city councils in Britain did not seem to see any importance in this prospective value.[91] This was later noted by numerous geographers, cultural historians and others as a great loss for Britain, and was usually blamed on reconstruction planning: 'the main wave of postwar central redevelopment in British towns and cities ... damage[d] irreparably a major part of that country's townscape heritage'.[92] In the blitzed cities – with some exclusions such as Bath, Canterbury and York, where most historic buildings had survived the 'Baedeker' raids – the lack of attention to character and particularly potential tourism meant a great revenue loss to the redeveloped cities when 'heritage' took off in the 1970s.[93] However, from the poor urban conditions of the prewar period, and incomplete efforts at interwar slum clearance, to the rising use of modernist forms and concerns for 'modernization' and car-friendly urban spaces, it is not surprising that there was little nostalgia for exact reconstruction in the 1940s and 1950s[94] (see Figure 6.6).

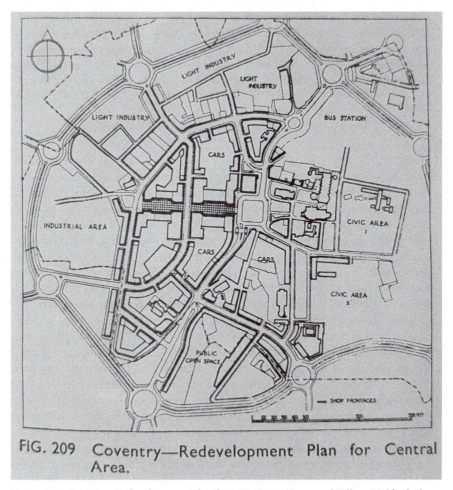

FIG. 209   Coventry—Redevelopment Plan for Central Area.

Figure 6.6 Coventry Redevelopment Plan from *Design in Town and Village*. Holford, Sharp & Gibberd (London: HMSO, 1953).

But if city officials, city councils, developers and architects were not paying attention to 'heritage', they were paying attention to other contemporary demands, worth restating in the words of John Pendlebury:

> Many historic cities that had slowly evolved over hundreds of years commissioned plans that if implemented would have entailed relatively rapid large-scale urban transformation ... the root cause was a crisis in responding to the pressures of the modern world that had been building up for some time, in particular the impact of the motor car ... Major changes to urban form were considered to be inevitable.[95]

Clearly this drive for modernization took over – at least in the ideologies of those responsible for making the reconstruction(s) happen – and instead of the historic sense of place found in much of Britain, replaced it with the 'mid-twentieth-century sense of a modern planned economy and society, expressing a landscape which it was hoped would further a post-war social democratic consensus of [stability]'.[96] How Britain saw itself in the late 1940s and 1950s, and how it would see itself ten or twenty years on, were very different phenomena indeed.[97]

IV. *Public Reception of Postwar Development*

From 1952 to 1953 *The Architects' Journal* ran a series called 'The Rebuilding of Bombed Cities'. Over the course of sixteen months there were nine reviews of cities.[98] The criteria for the selection of the nine is unclear – some had arguably had done the most building, some had attempted to implement radical modern plans, but not all were gauged a success. As the journal's editor, D. Rigby Childs, said in his summary piece: '[With] the new permanent buildings one gets the impression that only too frequently the architects have been overwhelmed by frustrations of all kinds, allied with problems of finance, leading to a building which is, at best, humdrum and lifeless.'[99] Most of the pieces were authored by the editor, D. Rigby Childs, and were as much critical as congratulatory. Most of the criticism, however, was focused on aspects of the cities that were not part of any reconstruction efforts, but often part of previous Victorian growth. For example, Childs was scathing about the views encountered on entering Liverpool, but complimentary of much recent architecture there.[100] Yet in a few cities such as Plymouth, Exeter, Bristol and Coventry the focus was mainly on city centre work. Very few of the buildings reviewed could be – even then – considered innovative, but many registered praise with the architectural critic(s). On the plans themselves Childs and series co-author Boyne were mainly appreciative.[101]

In local news there was little criticism, and though some of the praise may have stemmed from relief that there were finally buildings going up, generally the modern shops and offices were seen in positive terms. Exeter's Princesshay was called 'a most attractive precinct', with the general reconstruction progress headlined 'The New Exeter Arises in All Its Glory'.[102] And though pulled down in 2004 and replaced with theoretically 'bigger and better' shops, the original redevelopment at Princesshay was said, in 1958, to be a 'pleasure' to shop in, and it was claimed that the new buildings in the centre retained the 'old intimacy', also touting the 'human scale' of the new shopping areas.[103] In Hull the *Yorkshire Post* ran a big spread in September 1954 headlined 'A new city centre is rising from the bombed sites of Hull'.[104] In Liverpool the press gave a glowing review of a parking garage! '[A]ttractive premises', 'a clean, light building designed on modern lines', it said.[105] Reconstruction progress was also promoted in the *Journal of the Town Planning Institute*.[106] Other positive press included a note in *The Times*, mentioning Hull's destruction, and noting that Hull was 'proud' of its postwar progress.[107] Nationally, *The Times* also commended reconstruction around the country: Coventry in 1952 had constructed a portion of their plan and it was said to be 'a solid achievement ... offering a satisfying foretaste of what they expect their city to become'.[108]

Generally, the contemporary perspective on city centre reconstruction was one of success.[109] But criticism came soon, initially through texts such as Ian Nairn's *Outrage*, and today, many city centres are said to have bland high streets.[110] Critics mention the 'clumsy redevelopment of historic town centres', or worse the 'barbarism of postwar planning'.[111] Much postwar building is – and has been for many years – criticized and even reviled.[112] Sunand Prasad, a recent president of the Royal Institute of British Architects (RIBA), made note of the contemporary attitude towards such building: 'We can perhaps lay some of the blame for our distrust of modernism at the feet of postwar architecture and planning'.[113] He later continued: 'In rebuilding ... generally well-intentioned politicians chose the instantly understandable, easily bureaucratized, and apparently cheap solutions proffered by town planners and architects', adding that 'words and phrases like "concrete monstrosity" and of course Prince Charles' 'carbuncle' would have had far less resonance in popular opinion if postwar building design had not let us down on such a terrible scale'.[114] But such an attitude is purely or even naively visual, as well as being highly subjective. It simply does not take into account the realities of the situation in which these buildings were created.[115]

Certainly there were further factors – even more complexity – in the final design products that formed city centre buildings not mentioned here in detail.[116] Among these were the regional availability of materials in addition to the general shortages, issues encountered during construction such as site problems, technological or logistics issues and the vagaries of the various building contractors or builders – who sometimes determined that an architect's detail would not work and insisted on changes. As the architect and author Edward Hollis stated: '[T]he reality is, builders make buildings. It's completely cooperative, like an orchestra producing a symphony'.[117] All this was summed up by Childs in the *Architects' Journal*: 'One feels too often the architects have been the victims of forces outside their control: planning and administrative machinery steadily grinding on its way, the weight of financial interests, and the high cost of building'.[118]

Another post-1945 change took place in the field of architecture when many architects moved into public practice or direct employment in industry, given that most of the building allocations were going to public sector work and to industry-related building such as factories and warehouses.[119] Housing and schools saw innovation and creativity in postwar designs, whereas commercial – or what we would call today 'retail' – architecture was considered mundane, simply built to maximize square footage and create rentable space for profit.[120] It may indeed bear investigating whether this move towards taking public sector jobs affected *who* designed commercial or retail spaces, and whether anything can be found to support potential differences in design quality. Certainly after 1954 more architects were engaged on private developments, and the building boom from the relaxation of licensing possibly then created more aesthetic competition – or at least attention to appearance. However, developers in blitzed cities often knew in advance who their tenants would be – a number were forced to re-accommodate the traders who had lost their sites (by law) – and so they had no reason to create a building to 'sell' to anyone.[121]

By the mid-1950s the building boom generated by the relaxation of licensing and the abolition of capital investment allocation was underway, even though the cost of building had continually increased. Eventually the boom generated more interest in preservation as a reaction against destruction, as well as changes in planning law. But the bulk of city centre building and development was still

Figure 6.7 Aerial view of Coronation Gardens, Liverpool, 1953. Image: Britain from the Air (Historic England).

left to private interests.[122] City centres continued rebuilding – mainly through private investment – well into the 1970s, and the partnerships continue. In 2000 a small invitational conference was hosted by a group of private developers which reviewed postwar successes in development partnerships and promoted further collaboration.[123] Today those private interests are once again reaping massive benefits from postwar investments, as well as those initiated in the 1950s boom and after.[124] Shopping centres of the 1950s and 1960s are being pulled down or given facelifts, and most strikingly the retail (lettable) square footage is often vastly increased – creating larger profits for the developer and substantial increases in rate income for the cities.[125] A premier example can be found in Liverpool, where the 'Liverpool One' development, taking up over forty acres of the city centre, has replaced many 1950s shops and bomb site car parks, but also sadly the 'centrepiece' of the original redevelopment, Coronation Gardens (see Figures 6.7 and 6.8).

The most prolific and noticeable example of this new profitable regeneration of 1950s development has to be found in the portfolio of Land Securities. Today LSIT is the largest commercial property company in Britain;[126] they have pulled down many of the shops built by Ravenseft in the 1950s and replaced them with contemporary, and very large, new developments. Examples include: Bristol's Cabot Circus, Exeter's Princesshay, Canterbury's Whitefriars and London's One

Figure 6.8 Liverpool One, 2011. Author photo.

New Change[127] (see Figures 6.9–6.11). The Land Securities company history claims that Ravenseft 'was a pioneer of the post-war regeneration of Britain's shopping centres, rebuilding blitzed cities such as Hull, Exeter, Plymouth, Bristol and Coventry'.[128] While there is some exaggeration in this statement, it should probably also give the founders credit for landing the future Land Securities in a pile of profit – the largest holdings according to the Land Securities website are in provincial cities, with Bristol ranking number three.[129]

The detail in relationships between councils and developers and their attitudes to each other in this period are almost always obscured within the archives. Possibly developers were seen as a 'necessary evil'. Certainly city archives seem to have very little correspondence from this time. Private developers' archives are notoriously difficult to access, and some may be non-existent. This dynamic has been addressed to some extent but could still provide fruitful for future researchers.[130]

Without the profit motive, and risk takers such as Freedman and Maynard, city centre reconstruction in blitzed cities would have been slower still. While hampered by the restriction of building licenses for almost nine years after the war, the cities had more problems to manage than just allocations from Whitehall. Many people, from local authorities to MPs, were vocal about the restrictions with debates and deputations continuing into the early 1950s to try to get more licenses out of the responsible ministries. But the actual building – the new architecture in the city centres – did not depend on the planners, or even the city officials alone, but on many additional factors.

Figure 6.9 Princesshay, Exeter, 1979. Courtesy of David Cornforth, Exeter Memories.

Figure 6.10 Exeter's new Princesshay, 2007. Author photo.

While the blame rhetoric still persists, some of those denigrating 1940s and 1950s architects and planners do occasionally show some appreciation for external factors. Former RIBA president Sunand Prasad, as quoted above, clearly blamed architects but he also added:

> [There was] certainly a deal of naïve utopianism in the planning and architecture of the postwar decades, and maybe that period *can* be described as a gigantic and failed experiment driven by idealism ... But it's not idealism – laudable or foolish or otherwise – that shapes modern cities, it's their political economy.

With the benefit of hindsight, we can see that for *all* the good intentions our confidence in professional knowledge was much greater than our real understanding of how it would all work ... In the second half of the 20th century, we thought we were replacing trial and error with science.[131]

Such awareness should serve to shift the discourse closer to something less distorted by visual response and closer to an acknowledgement of facts that surely had a profound effect on postwar developments. All of the plans and many of the buildings could be considered experimental. There was, for example, no certain knowledge of how a concrete building would age.[132] There was no knowledge of whether a plan such as Abercrombie's Plymouth or Hull would work successfully, even if implemented. In fact, in Plymouth the separation of uses advocated by the plan proved to be unsuccessful in large part, creating spaces that were too

Figure 6.11 Land Securities redevelopment, One New Change, London, 2010. Author photo.

segregated. The shopping area was – and remains – empty after the stores shut in the evening; the civic centre, which has no theatre or auditorium, did and does not mesh with the rest of the city and it, too, is deserted at night.[133] As Jeremy Gould noted in 2007: 'The insistence of single use within the shopping centre was and is damaging and it is extraordinary that this theoretical idea that has so much influence on a city's character persisted for so long.'[134] In Coventry perceived failures were sometimes more profound: 'The Coventry scheme seems to have failed simultaneously in several ways: it was grounded on assumptions about the city's growth and the social behaviour of its residents that were not reliable, it buried a past that still had psychological value to local communities, and it imposed a highly integrated urban aesthetic that owed more to fashion than to pragmatism.'[135] However, *blaming* the planners is blaming someone who could not have known the outcome. And blaming architects does not take into account the myriad of issues faced between drawing board and completion, plus the materials shortages, much less the whims of clients and local authorities.[136] While historians are not assigning blame generally, critics still do.[137] What they crucially overlook is the strong belief in 1940s and 1950s Britain that planners were experts and this technocratic knowledge was somehow 'right'. More importantly, they fail to acknowledge the postwar political economy and consequently the connected factors that played into the designs of city centre reconstruction.[138]

Some evidence of early postwar rebuilding still remains in the case study cities. Most recently, places like Exeter have earned poor press notices for its High Street blandness.[139] Like many regional shopping centres, Exeter is a mix of a few very old buildings with a large number of 1950s 'neo-Georgian' buildings. Certainly on Exeter High Street, however, there is a lack of variation in size and texture that the old city centre had. Perhaps as testimony to the lack of appreciation for the rebuilding efforts of the 1950s, the flagship 'Princesshay' development by Ravenseft Properties was pulled down in 2004. It has been replaced by a bigger, newer and more modern shopping centre with hugely increased floor space that brings higher rates to the City and rents to the developer.[140]

In Liverpool today the city centre retains some of its postwar redevelopment: the facades of Church Street remain mostly untouched, with much of Lord Street similarly unaltered. But new and very large development has occurred around it in the past few years. Like Exeter – but on a much larger scale – the city centre of Liverpool now has a mega-development, Liverpool One, opened in 2008.[141] Gone is the old park created on a bomb site, Coronation Gardens, which was meant to be the centrepiece of the redevelopment south of Lord Street, as well as one of several 'green little oases of peace and beauty'.[142] But the city centre remains vibrant with barely any evidence or recognition of the Blitz outside of the occasional memorial parade.[143]

While the end result in Hull meant that both compromise and financial considerations prevented any single plan being fully implemented, the city may be the better for such 'problems'. As a BBC reporter said in a programme about the blitz and rebuilding of Hull, there is now 'gratitude for the slowness of rebuilding' and the fact that without the implementation of a drastically different, and modernist plan, many historic buildings were therefore saved.[144] Abercrombie was not, however, forgotten. In 1971 a local folk singer wrote a song about the plan: 'It was like magic, a dream, such a fascinating scheme, yes that was the Abercrombie plan.'[145]

Conclusion

Even without much 'planning' experience, the Attlee government, local authorities and design professionals in the postwar period simply thought that what expertise they could bring to bear would prove to reveal the best course of action, and the nation would indeed progress and improve (see Figure 6.12). An honest belief in the expertise of planners, but also in their 'humanist' intentions was noted by Holford in a 1961 article in *The Times*: 'Town planning, civic design and a humanist approach to layout and landscape have combined to produce some characteristic British developments since the war.' Holford adds, 'A temporary exhibition that summed them up was that on the South Bank of the Thames for the Festival of Britain in 1951.'[146]

The Festival of Britain was indeed the quintessential concrete realization of the possibilities of the early 1950s, not least because it too – like the city centres – was restricted in the use of steel and designs were modified to accommodate materials shortages.[147] This 'ideal' development of British design from top to bottom with modern street furniture and contemporary architecture, the latest materials and an air of newness, the Festival was set to inspire British cities, and tourists, and impress with postwar progress.[148] Impressively, too, not a single complaint can be

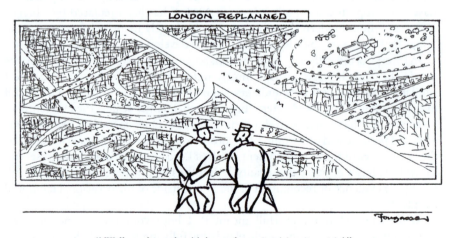

" Well, anyhow, there'd be no harm in giving it a trial."

Figure 6.12 Fougasse cartoon, *Punch*, 11 August 1943.

found from blitzed city representatives – in local or national archives – that the Festival buildings were using steel they 'ought' to have. If the cities were frustrated at the building up of a fantasy on the South Bank, they did not publicize it. Perhaps they took inspiration from the same clean-slate approach many cities hoped to take in their new plans.

Many plans were made which treated the cities as *tabula rasa* – particularly in Hull, Coventry and Plymouth – though the rhetoric of wartime was tempered by realities such as the economy, the legislative hurdles and local financial constraints. Seen – and later legislated – as a necessity, planning still did not determine the final outcomes within the blitzed city centres. As shown here the role of private investment was a more significant determinant of the physical results. Still, anyone investing in new building had to manage to get past negotiations, legislation, license allocations, objections, legal action and even individuals with personal agendas for their own cities. What was built in the end reflected all these variables, as well as the aesthetics of the postwar period. Visual appearance was also driven by the purpose of the buildings, reflecting commercial values. In fact, a fascinating potential investigation could look into the rise of consumerism as reflected in 1950s city centre architecture.[149]

In the end it was not only planning that shaped the blitzed city centres. The postwar economy and lack of steel changed and challenged the building industry, but equally crucial – if not more so – were the opinions and decisions of civil servants and local authorities, the necessity of using private developers and the myriad of external factors faced by all the actors involved. Modern visions translated into somewhat less desirable realities: but then planning does not create reality.

CONCLUSION: REBUILDING BLITZED CITY CENTRES, DESPITE PLANNING

Planners in this country have always been the bravest, the boldest, the most resolute of social reformers. Otherwise they could not have achieved the astonishing results of the past 50 years.

– Harold Macmillan, 1953[1]

Macmillan's compliment about planners was directed at members of the Town and Country Planning Association, and though perhaps meant to flatter, contrasts remarkably with the quotation by a later Conservative Prime Minister, Margaret Thatcher, who in 1987 claimed that planners had 'cut the heart out of our cities'.[2] The thirty-five years in between represents a deeply telling and transformative period: in the 1940s and 1950s the idea of 'planning' generally was still in ascendancy, at least as it regarded the physical environment. Government ministers and officials in Whitehall espoused the prewar ideals of modern planning which local authorities also took up, whereas by the late 1980s planners' wisdom was being questioned and as a group they were receiving most of the blame for urban problems. This latter short-sighted view did not and does not consider the context in which the planners of the 1940s and 1950s worked, nor does it appreciate their efforts to modernize and improve postwar cities. As Gold argues, '[T]he pre-occupation with identifying culprits and with constructing simplistic chains of cause-and-effect [has] distorted understanding of processes of urban change.'[3] The built environment of the 1950s – and by extension probably also the 1960s, 1970s and 1980s – needs to be read with greater depth and context.

Although the study of planning is important for an understanding of Britain's built environment, the examples discussed here – of postwar plans and rebuilding in blitzed cities – demonstrate why planning rarely determines the final outcome. Many structural factors external to the planning process itself affected the rebuilding of blitzed cities, and these cities faced even more difficulties than existing scholarship has yet revealed. In particular, the postwar economic constraints had enormous impact: from the national situation which prompted the control of capital investment, to the role of the Investment Programmes Committee (IPC) in severely limiting investment in blitzed cities and then on to the local problems of lost rate revenue, land acquisition and development costs. Further constraints included new planning laws and requirements that placed an increased workload on the local authorities and forced them to seek approval from planning ministry officials before implementing any plans. These local authorities spent many years from the initial bombing raids to the final development negotiations investing time and money in outcomes of which they felt confident, but which were – as shown – influenced by the complexity of even more local factors, from individuals to businesses to infrastructure.

We have also seen how the wartime rhetoric of positive planning carried an assumption that central government would logistically and financially assist the cities in the rebuilding process. In the end, quite the reverse occurred: the central government hampered the process at least as much as it helped, and a minimal – if not miniscule – amount of financial assistance was given to blitzed cities. The role of private investment has also been shown to have significant impact on the rebuilding of the cities – logistically, financially and visually. The physical results of reconstruction reflect the necessity of involving private developers and other large companies, even though planning legislation had been created to enable local authorities to redevelop their own cities. The discourse of blame still seen today is directed at architects and planners, but overlooks the economic constraints, the involvement of many different actors and the very different ideology of the postwar era.

I. *The Ideology and the Reality of Rebuilding*

The ideology of postwar planning had clear roots in the rhetoric of wartime reconstruction.[4] This book has examined the period in question beginning in wartime by looking at the rhetoric of reconstruction and the reconstruction machinery as a whole, to explain postwar hopes and expectations. Chapter 2 looked at the wide variety of media – from printed material to radio, film and exhibitions – that very clearly promoted positive visions for postwar Britain. The plans made reflected the spirit of 'opportunity' that bombing was said to provide. City leaders were encouraged from early in the war to plan boldly and were given to expect assistance with these plans, legally, administratively and financially. While there was plenty of positive rhetoric, we've seen how the machinery of planning was messy, confused and even incompetent. And the policy goals for reconstruction were contested.

The third chapter demonstrated the disappearance of any priority for rebuilding bombed cities within the economic planning structure developed in Whitehall. The Investment Programmes Committee was a result of the instigation of machinery for economic controls, but the IPC barely recognized the need for city centre reconstruction. When the issue was later acknowledged in committee meetings and reports, officials – in particular the two consecutive chairmen from 1948 to 1953, Strath and Turnbull – continued to refuse planning ministry requests for increases to building licence allocations for the cities, heavily restricting the amount of city centre building until 1954 when the committee had been disbanded and licensing relaxed.

Statistics from IPC reports support the impression gleaned from correspondence and related meeting minutes – of which there exists a surprising volume – and show that blitzed cities were one of the lowest priorities under both postwar governments. Yet until Harold Macmillan's appointment as minister there seems to have been general acceptance among local authorities and most planning ministry officials that the reasons given for the lack of priority were somehow 'fair' and certainly explicable. Additionally, except for Macmillan in Cabinet, only the bombed cities' MPs pushed the moral point that blitzed cities had suffered and were not receiving the priority they had been promised. Complaints mainly focused on the very small amount of building allowed and the lack of financial assistance forthcoming from the government.[5] As late as March 1953, Percy Morris (Labour MP for Swansea) lamented these facts in a debate on rebuilding blitzed cities:

> None can deny that the blitzed areas are severely handicapped through no fault of their own, and we are engaged in an unequal struggle with towns and cities that were fortunate enough to escape some of the worst penalties of the last war. We suggest that we are entitled to priority in respect of capital expenditure and a greater supply of steel. The devastation of our towns was a national calamity, and if it is not accepted as a national responsibility we should at least be given every facility to expedite the work of reconstruction.[6]

It could not be argued that blitzed cities deserved more priority on purely economic grounds, and not even Macmillan made such a suggestion. Instead, it was argued, the cities deserved some priority based on moral grounds at least, if not also on political grounds – as Macmillan also argued. The Conservative party stood to gain support from the forty of sixty-eight seats in heavily bombed areas that were held by Labour in 1952.[7] The paucity of building licence allocation given to the blitzed cities – always a fraction of 1 per cent of overall investment planned and rarely more than 1 per cent of 'miscellaneous' building investment allowed – seems astonishingly low given their size and needs, particularly considering the large amount of work in the miscellaneous category that was unquantifiable and far outweighed the amounts allowed in blitzed cities. An investigation of economic planning as it affected blitzed cities has not previously been undertaken and the point made is critical: the priority assumed – if not promised – to the postwar reconstruction of blitzed cities ceased to exist when the Attlee government implemented economic planning and controls, and this continued under Churchill's 1951 Conservative government.

Chapter 4 examined the planning ministry, alongside the legislative changes affecting blitzed cities. Most important in terms of reconstruction were the 1944 and 1947 Acts, whose impacts were delivered through the large number of new administrative requirements enforced on local authorities. Although the cities were suffering financially from the bombing, not least in terms of lost rate revenue, they faced a number of new costs, from creation of plans to the preparation of planning and land-use applications. Planning ministry officials, far more sympathetic to the blitzed cities than the Treasury or IPC, attempted to oversee and sometimes facilitate all local planning. In some cases the assistance was seen to be useful, such as the 1947 autumn conferences for provincial cities. But in many cases the ministry insisted on the speedy preparation of plans at the same time as the lack of building licensing was restricting the ability of authorities to build anything. At times officials could be obstructive, requiring plan changes or additional information or meetings, which slowed the progress of approvals. As Exeter's Town Clerk brought to attention at one of the planning conferences, the encouragement to apply for orders to acquire land also set in motion the 'clock running against [them]', because the city would be paying for land on which they were not allowed to build.[8] The worst – and possibly most frequent – kind of Whitehall obstruction arose from the poor coordination and disagreements about priorities among ministries. This was especially true between the planning ministry and the Ministry of Transport.

In fact, both contemporary comments and more recent histories assume that somehow since capital investment was controlled, it was also coordinated, in terms of reconstruction at least. But in reality, as shown by the IPC's categorization of capital investment (Table 3.1) these aspects of reconstruction were treated separately, and at the national level not coordinated city-by-city, even within a ministry such as Housing and Local Government. The building licence allocation system outlined allowances for building by type – 'housing', 'factories', 'warehouses', 'defence' and so on. Therefore local authorities' assumptions about licence allocations for rebuilding cities as a coordinated entity were usually erroneous. The planning ministry considered the various building types as a whole within the city plans, but outside of their administration, coordination of licensing was rare.

Even within the cities there was some assumption of central cohesion in investment allowances, because officials were unaware of the logistics of capital investment control – they knew (eventually) only of its existence.[9] Historians too often make the same assumption about the reasons for restrictions and the coordination of reconstruction.[10] In reality, however, all decisions were completely separated. Views of ideal city plans may have even encouraged or sustained this compartmentalization, since uses in city centres were segregated as well. Rather than thoughts of the coordinated whole, government planners and private planners sought to solve perceived urban and economic issues with segregated instead of integrated solutions. Additionally, the rhetoric to plan boldly, which continued past the end of the war, was then hampered by increasing restrictions on capital investment. The planning ministry scaled back earlier suggestions, with new advice to reduce the size of planned acquisitions due to economic constraints.[11] If previous work on reconstruction planning has acknowledged Whitehall's official interventions, it has rarely discussed in any depth the difficulties imposed by new legislation, and has not uncovered the relationship of the planning ministry to the machinery for prioritizing building licence allocations – as embodied, for instance, by the IPC and Ministry of Works.[12] This book elucidates the importance of these plural interactions for the first time.

The case studies of Hull, Exeter and Liverpool have been provided to tease out specific local issues, and the interplay of central and local government. Chapters 5 and 6 have shown that many specific problems within the cities themselves presented further barriers to rebuilding. Overwhelmingly property-owners, and the groups representing them, significantly hindered planning implementation, land acquisition and proposed changes in road patterns or land-use. Physical issues of space and access also existed in many cities, whether it was a river crossing in Exeter or numerous level railroad crossings in Hull – or simply the scattered nature of bomb destruction in Liverpool leaving many owners in place and wanting to remain. All these kinds of situations affected plans as well as relations with other entities, and they even divided local opinion on reconstruction planning. Although some consensus existed at the national level on the need for planning and comprehensive local development, these case studies show that internally the cities lacked consensus about what 'improvements' would look like; all cities encountered resistance to change, if in varying amounts. Generally central government officials perceived large cities to be in need of many improvements in layout, transport and more, but locally little agreement emerged as to specifics and the extent of improvement needed. Although prior histories of reconstruction planning have acknowledged many local issues, they have not done so within both the national economic *and* land planning framework necessary to build the local story. Here we have seen that local issues were as disruptive to progress – if not more so – than national restrictions and legislative requirements.

Finally, the rebuilding that did eventually take place was less coordinated and more piecemeal than wartime and early postwar planners assumed it would be. Postwar cities were indeed not the 'product of imposing utopian visions'.[13] Plymouth – and to a lesser extent Coventry – were exceptional in implementing large portions of the plans made and agreed upon by city officials, councillors and Whitehall. The example cities of Hull, Exeter and Liverpool were shown to have negotiated sites, designs and final building plans with a number of private entities, including new firms led by Ravenseft, who saw the potential for making deals with blitzed cities and created an emerging public–private partnership for urban commercial development. Final designs, however, clearly reflected manifold compromises, not merely external constraints. Shortages of building materials, particularly steel, encouraged the use of concrete and other modern materials such as aluminium. Profit motives came first for developers looking solely at the return on their investment: creating as much lettable floor space as possible, for the best price possible.[14] At the same time, city officials were motivated to approve designs based on size for rateable value and the speed of potential construction to bring rate revenue back as soon as possible after a wait of over ten years since bombing left piles of city centre rubble.

Critics may be justified in saying that city centre commercial buildings of this period are often bland and lack architectural interest, but at the same time research here has shown that no discussion took place in postwar Britain about rebuilding bombed city areas either near or exactly as they had been, much less any substantial discussion of issues such as 'heritage' and potential tourism. The values intrinsic to a contemporary perspective on our built environment are not the same as those held in the postwar period by planners or officials or even citizens. However, historians of British postwar reconstruction have very rarely recognized this point which needs further examination. Professor William Holford, speaking to the Civic Trust in 1960 on the subject of 'Rebuilding City Centres', reflected one aspect of wartime values that was perhaps lost in the rush to rebuild and replenish city coffers: 'We must therefore find something to enable the public interest to secure some form of betterment in order to do those things which are commercially unprofitable and which are socially extremely desirable.'[15] The wartime consensus of serving the greater good disappeared in part amid the reality of constrictions upon rebuilding.[16]

II. *Rebuilding Blitzed City Centres: Addressing the Wider Picture*

Complexity underlies the whole of the narrative of postwar reconstruction: an understanding of the outcomes requires comprehension of economic and political processes, alongside local and individual factors.[17] This study contributes to knowledge of the postwar period and the machinery of government in general. Choices made by both elected and appointed officials were based in some way on the priorities of each decision-maker. The investigations described in the previous chapters therefore tell us a great deal about priority-making. Within Whitehall, themes can be seen of self-protection, gathering of power, attempting to exercise influence as well as cases of simple stubbornness or narrow-mindedness. That is, Treasury officials created a protectionist bubble of power: F. F. Turnbull, in particular, repeatedly pushed his own agenda when deciding not to prioritize building licence allocations for blitzed cities. Ignoring the political and moral arguments from outside ministries, and sometimes his own ministers, Turnbull formed an opinion and then stuck to it, justifying decisions solely on a very broad background of economic policy. Similarly, planning ministry officials insisted on maintaining superiority over local authorities, particularly in the smaller cities, and exercising their fairly new role as 'experts' – even if their advice on planning was untested, as most such planning on this new scale was. The heightened level of central authority control was new to the cities, but it was clear that planning mandarins insisted on the acknowledgement by local authorities of their weight and influence.

Hence, the work here has exposed priority-setting on a national level, as well as on a local level, to be at least as individual as it was collective – possibly more so nationally given the low level of institutional capacity in Whitehall.[18] On the micro level, priorities reflected attention to financial issues, but also a resistance to change. Business-owners prioritized profit, but also resisted relocation particularly where a site had been the premises for generations of a family business. Additionally, citizens resisted further upheaval in road-building and other construction after the disruption of war. City officials and councillors, however, prioritized replacing lost rateable value in the near term, both through city centre reconstruction – and even expansion of prewar commercial square footage – and new housing provision.[19] Some leaders such as Hull's Body or Exeter's Newman also pushed their own priorities for grand planning schemes. Though the archives do not suggest why, it may well be that they hoped to leave a permanent legacy in their cities.

We have also seen here that officials in a number of roles, particularly at the centre in Whitehall, could exert a momentous impact on outcomes. Turnbull as IPC chair was a prime example: he was not only given control of a committee that made significant decisions, but evidence shows that somehow all questions about blitzed cities came back to him, without senior ministers taking responsibility themselves for consideration of the issues. Within the planning ministry impacts can be seen from the many officials assigned to various cities and regions who approved, disproved or forced changes to city plans. At the ministerial level, Harold Macmillan made the greatest individual impact on building programmes, forcing not only IPC increases in building licence allocations for his programmes, but – as shown in Chapter 3 – probably helping bring on the end of the IPC itself. Macmillan also had great individual impact because he was an example of the rare minister who pushed back against the policies he had to answer for in Parliament: policies that sometimes were made by other departments, or by individuals outside of the elected government. The fact that a number of departments had to answer for IPC decisions – over which they had little to no control – resulted in Macmillan's protests. He had seen and heard the numerous debates about blitzed city priority in the House of Commons, debates that IPC members often ignored, even if they knew that they had taken place.[20] Finally, a dynamic minister like Macmillan was also likely to be following a personal agenda. Macmillan wanted success in his Housing and Local Government role, and he pressed economic planners hard to achieve this.[21] Conversely, Silkin, Attlee's first minister in charge of these issues, appears to have had no interest in his own political advance, and so did not make great efforts to push his departmental agenda as he might have done. Silkin's priorities seem to have been broadly to create some impact in all areas of town and country planning.

The still-wider picture is provided by an exploration of the economic and political issues that centred upon physical planning and demonstrated the political priorities of government leadership. In the immediate postwar Cabinet discussions, as well as more general economic discussion, Attlee and all of his Chancellors of the Exchequer focused not just on the dollar area balance of payments, as repeatedly shown, but on Britain's prominence via its previously powerful currency.[22] A constant insistence on the maintenance of Britain's world role, particularly as the Cold War escalated, overrode a good deal of economic discussion, as well as Cabinet discussion. The tendency to focus on global status diminished some of the discussions on the domestic agenda, sweeping them aside for civil servants to act (or not act) upon.[23]

The narrative of the blitzed cities also provides insights for the world at large. The Second World War was a great physical disaster, and the subsequent widespread reconstruction holds many lessons for disaster recovery, not least of which is that rebuilding is inevitably a slow process.[24] A great deal of patience is required, and the economic situation is key. After disaster plans are made for recovery: the successful implementation of the plans depends on consensus as well as cooperation, both of which are difficult to achieve. In postwar Britain the deals struck were intrinsically political, making choices, choosing priorities – processes that reflected contending visions of the future.[25] It has been said: 'The greatest achievement of the human brain is its ability to ... think about the future.'[26] Planning is thinking about the future, and can lead to great achievements, but these are dependent on the implementation of the plans. Planning has been very thoroughly studied, but the wider context of that planning and particularly its implementation have not been studied thoroughly enough.

III. *Lessons and Questions from a Study of Blitzed Cities*

What might this research lead to for future scholars? On one hand this work uncovers a wealth of information about the IPC and points to the need for further investigation of both its role and the interaction between central and local government in the 1940s and 1950s. The committee had a very strong impact on an admittedly small programme, and its potential impact on other areas of the postwar economy should be examined.[27] More work can be done to discover if the IPC further affected other programmes, and where those impacts might carry through today.

The work here also provides key information about the workings of postwar Whitehall, demonstrating the importance of individuals to policymaking and implementation. Throughout Treasury, Cabinet and planning ministry files, volumes of correspondence and minutes have shed light on decisions made – often by individuals instead of ministers or committees. Hundreds of thousands of documents may reveal further examples of personalities and crucial decision-making. Additionally, an investigation of the impact of persons not seen to be in positions of power would contribute to existing work on the civil service. Rodney Lowe's official history of the civil service points the way to many avenues of exploration in this area.[28] Further, we have seen how quickly political priorities can change. The dramatic shift from wartime suggestions of hopeful rebuilding and acknowledgement of the suffering of citizens in blitzed cities was set aside almost immediately at the end of war, and national economic needs were put first, at the expense of rebuilding. This filtered through to the planning ministry and impacted how they dealt with applications for land acquisition, telling cities to drastically reduce the size of applications and therefore the ability to really plan comprehensively.

The city case studies here contribute specifically to postwar British historiography by showing the significance of local issues, even while central government controls remain contemporaneously important. Indeed, local issues exert equal, and sometimes more, influence on outcomes. Many of the authors writing on reconstruction planning such as Larkham, Pendlebury, and Essex and

Brayshay are very thorough on local histories in this respect. It is vital to look at local factors when examining national policy impacts, and historians can do still more work in this area.

Historians and critics see the past from their own perspective, too often overlooking the context and the contemporary perspective of the period they are examining – particularly in the realm of the built environment. In a collective sense the impacts investigated here help us to improve our understanding of the built world. The emphasis of the analysis has been on the complexity and context of the postwar situation, but this complexity applies to any period. There is no simple cause and effect, no planner laying out roads and buildings followed by a contractor putting it in place. As geographer Mark Llewellyn has noted, 'The built environment is shaped and given meaning through the active and embodied practices by which it is produced, appropriated and inhabited.'[29] Infinite historical threads exist that can help explain the exact shape of our built environment, and therefore both blame and praise should not be confined – if apportioned at all – to particular actors and individual acts. This book set out to examine archival evidence for explanations of the results of rebuilding in postwar Britain, and at a basic level why cities look the way they do. The answers lie in the priorities created and the values espoused, and by the intent and interactions not just of architects and planners, but a number of other and less famous actors: postwar governments, officials, local authorities, businesspeople and citizens as well.

APPENDICES

Appendix I

White Papers on Balance of Payments, 1947–55

Treasury and Central Statistical Office. *Cmd. 7324 United Kingdom. Balance of Payments, 1946 and 1947*. London: HMSO, 1947.

Treasury and Central Statistical Office. *Cmd. 7520 United Kingdom. Balance of Payments, 1946 to 1948*. London: HMSO, 1948.

Treasury and Central Statistical Office. *Cmd. 7648 United Kingdom. Balance of Payments 1946 to 1948 (No. 2)*. London: HMSO, 1948.

Treasury and Central Statistical Office. *Cmd. 7793 United Kingdom. Balance of Payments 1946 to 1949*. London: HMSO, 1948.

Treasury and Central Statistical Office. *Cmd. 7928 United Kingdom. Balance of Payments 1946 to 1949 (No. 2)*, 1950.

Treasury and Central Statistical Office. *Cmd. 8065 United Kingdom. Balance of Payments 1946 to 1950*, 1950.

Treasury and Central Statistical Office. *Cmd. 8201 United Kingdom. Balance of Payments 1946 to 1950 (No. 2)*, 1950.

Treasury and Central Statistical Office. *Cmd. 8379 United Kingdom. Balance of Payments 1948 to 1951*. London: HMSO, 1950.

Treasury and Central Statistical Office. *Cmd. 8505 United Kingdom. Balance of Payments 1948 to 1951 (No. 2)*, 1951.

Treasury and Central Statistical Office. *Cmd. 8666 United Kingdom. Balance of Payments 1949–1952*, 1951.

Treasury and Central Statistical Office. *Cmd. 8808 United Kingdom. Balance of Payments 1949 to 1952 (No. 2)*, 1952.

Treasury and Central Statistical Office. *Cmd. 8976 United Kingdom. Balance of Payments 1946 to 1953*, 1952.

Treasury and Central Statistical Office. *Cmd. 9119 United Kingdom. Balance of Payments 1946 to 1953 (No. 2)*, 1953.

Treasury and Central Statistical Office. *Cmd. 9291 United Kingdom. Balance of Payments 1946 to 1954*, 1953.

Treasury and Central Statistical Office. *Cmd. 9430 United Kingdom. Balance of Payments 1946 to 1954 (No. 2)*, 1954.

Treasury and Central Statistical Office. *Cmd. 9585 United Kingdom. Balance of Payments 1946 to 1955*, 1955.

Treasury and Central Statistical Office. *Cmd. 9731 United Kingdom. Balance of Payments 1946 to 1955 (No. 2)*, 1955.

Treasury and Central Statistical Office. *Cmd. 9871 United Kingdom. Balance of Payments 1946 to 1956*, 1955.

Appendix II

THIS DOCUMENT IS THE PROPERTY OF HER BRITANNIC MAJESTY'S GOVERNMENT

Printed for the Cabinet. October 1952

Copy No.

CONFIDENTIAL
C. (52) 350
20th October, 1952

CABINET

INVESTMENT IN 1953: RECONSTRUCTION OF BLITZED CITY CENTRES

Memorandum by the Minister of Housing and Local Government

It's 'Tommy this, an' Tommy that,' an'
　'chuck 'im out, the brute';
But it's 'Saviour of 'is country,' when
　the guns begin to shoot!
　　　　　　(R. Kipling.)

'Of course, we must first concentrate, as we are doing,
all available building labour on those parts of our
cities which have suffered most . . .'
　　　　　(Mr. Churchill, Central Hall,
　　　　　　Westminster, 15th March 1945.)

1. This is the story of the blitzed cities.

2. Excluding London, there are 18 which suffered severe and concentrated war damage. Since 1949 successive Ministers for Planning have contrived to get an 'investment allocation' to enable some reconstruction to be done in these 18 cities.

3. Work has been carried out each year to the following value: –

　　　1949 and 1950: £2.3 million.

　　　1951: £3.5 million.

　　　1952: £4.5 million (estimated).

4. This work is almost entirely financed by private developers, and consists mainly of shops to replace those destroyed in the central shopping areas. Encouraged by promises made during the war, the Local Authorities bought the devastated land in order to provide convenient plots for rebuilding. As soon as building is allowed, rents and rates are paid to the Authority. At the moment the

Authorities are incurring heavy expenditure (by way of loan charges) on idle land; so is the Exchequer, which pays a high rate of grant.

5. The Chancellor of the Exchequer does not feel able, however, to allocate more than £2.5 million in 1953 to reconstruction. Completion of works in progress will take up to £2 million in 1953 and £700,000 in 1954. Therefore there will be only £½ million to allocate (among 18 cities) to new work in 1953.

6. The rebuilding programmes are already running down. With only £½ million to pump in, most of them will come to a complete stop early next year.

7. I have got to announce the allocation; Local Authorities and their Members are already clamouring for it. When it is known, there will be a bitter outcry and much agitation – questions, adjournment motions, deputations and press campaign.

8. There are 68 Parliamentary seats in these cities; 40 are held by the Opposition, who will lose no opportunity to attack and embarrass the 28 Government supporters who hold the other seats.

9. Up to now we have been able to blame the steel shortage; this, people can understand. But that cock won't fight much longer. Everyone knows we can use reinforced concrete or, in some cases, load-bearing walls. Besides a lot of jobs either do not require new steel or require very little because the firms have it already in hand from salvage or from stock.

10. Nor can we argue that labour freed from blitz reconstruction can be diverted to other more important work, except in a heavily over-loaded area like Coventry. It is admitted that in most of the eighteen cities the building labour for a modest reconstruction programme can be provided without interfering with other building programmes. In certain cities, such as Plymouth there is no other building work in need of labour. Housing cannot absorb them all. So the men drift out of the building industry, or go on the dole.

11. The best way out would be to authorise 'in principle' the starting of new work in 1953 to the value of further £2 million; i.e., a total 'programme' for the year of £4.5 million. But *where* any project was to be, and *when* it was to start, would be settled by the Minister of Works, through the machinery of the Regional Building Committee (representing all Ministries concerned). The Committee would only allow new work where it would not interfere with the progress of defence projects, industry, housing, schools; they would have special regard to the labour situation in each locality.

12. If we do this we can meet the local outcry even if the starting dates have to be put off from month to month.

13. In view of all the promises made to the blitzed cities I think we must recognise that there is a moral as well as a material problem. There is also a political problem.

14. I must point out that most of these developers are still willing to spend their own money. They ask for no subvention, subsidy, or assistance; indeed they are prepared to reduce the burden of public expenditure. If we put them off too long, we may put them off altogether.

H. M.

Ministry of Housing and Local Government, S.W.1,
20th October, 1952.
(TNA: CAB 129/55 [C(52)350, 20 October 1952])

Appendix III

52 Charles Street,
Berkeley Square, W.1.

8th July, 1952.

City Engineer & Surveyor's Office,
Municipal Buildings,
Liverpool 2.

Dear Sirs,

52/78 Lord Street, Liverpool.

I refer to the meeting which took place in your office on April 8th between the write and Representatives of the owners of 52/56 and 72/78 Lord Street, Liverpool. As we pointed out at that meeting, we are very anxious indeed to develop this site. You may remember that we had considerable discussions with your Department in May 1950 in regard to the Church Street site subsequently taken over by Messrs. Littlewoods.

This Company is probably the most active shop development Company in the United Kingdom today. We have recently completed very substantial developments in Hull, Plymouth, Swansee, and Exeter and have extensive building operations in progress on further sites in Hull, Plymouth, Swansee, Canterbury, Wakefield, Exeter and Great Yarmouth. Apart from this work, which has a capital value of well over 2,000,000, we are shortly to commence further schemes in Sunderland, Billingham on Toes and Sheffield and have additional sites in Hull, Plymouth, Swansee, Exeter, and Sheffield which will commence as soon as steel can be made available and the Government authorize capital expenditures.

A study of the above lists will show that we shall eventually have large capital sums invested in the majority of the blitzed cities. Frankly, we are proud of the national character of our investments and are anxious to extend our holdings to such an important City as Liverpool.

As a result of a great deal of consideration in regard to the particular problems appertaining to the re-development of numbers 52–78 Lord Street, I wish to put forward the following proposals for the formal consideration of your Council.

(1) (i)   These various interests should be acquired by your Council and that my Company should be granted a Building Agreement followed by a 99 years lease.

(ii)   From our past experiences of negotiations with other Cities and Corporations, we appreciate that you cannot consider a considerable capital expenditure without an immediate return. We would, therefore, be prepared to commence the payment of the full ground rent from the date of the exchange of the Building Agreement, irrespective of whether or not a Building Licence was issued.

(2) (i) It would be our intention to develop the site with shops, show rooms and staff rooms over and we would develop, as far as possible, to the exact requirements of particular traders. You will, of course, appreciate that these requirements may vary as to the frontages and also depth of the upper floors, but we envisage a development along the lines of the plans which are enclosed with this letter.

(ii) We are not quite certain as to the effect of Section 19 (vi) of the 1944 Act on this particular site, but we would be prepared to offer accommodation to any person or Company affected by this Section.

(3) (i) The elevational treatment has been very carefully considered and we have borne in mind the necessity for an imposing building and one which would match in height the existing buildings. We are also sending with this letter a perspective of the building we envisage and we think you will agree that it adequately typifies the importance of the Lord Street area.

If the above proposals are acceptable to your Council, we shall be only too pleased to give you any assurances you may need as to the financial ability of this Company to carry through the proposed scheme. We would be quite willing to place you in touch with our Bankers and Accountants and give you any financial guarantees you may require.

I shall be pleased to receive your acknowledgement of this letter together with plans and perspective and will be glad if you will let me know when you anticipate the proposals contained therein will receive the consideration of your Council.

Yours faithfully,
for and on behalf of

RAVENSEFT PROPERTIES LIMITED.
(sgd) F. Maynard.
Director.

If the Committee approve, in principle, the scheme submitted by Ravenseft Properties Limited, the City Engineer and Surveyor requests authority to discuss the project with the Ministry of Housing and Local Government, and in the event of the Ministry's approval being given, to negotiate for the acquisition of the land and buildings involved, and subsequently terms of a Building Agreement and lease of the area to Ravenseft Properties Limited.

Appendix IV

Blitz Reconstruction in House of Commons Debates (including written answers).

Note: This list is not exhaustive, but includes most primary discussions on the topic of blitzed city centres.

Building Materials HC Deb 25 March 1946

Housing HC Deb 30 July 1946

Acquisition of Land HC Deb 01 August 1946

Town and Country Planning Bill HC Deb 29 January 1947, 20 May 1947

Betting Duty (Dog Totes and Football Pools) [*sic*] HC Deb 12 November 1947

Local Government Bill HC Deb 18 November 1947

Temporary Shops, Plymouth HC Deb 16 September 1948

Blitzed Cities (Steel Allocation) HC Deb 27 January 1949

Blitzed Areas (Steel Allocation) HC Deb 21 March 1949

War Damages Sites Bill HC Deb 08 November 1949

Blitzed Cities (Reconstruction) HC Deb 11 May 1950

Bombed Cities (Reconstruction) HC Deb 16 May 1950

Bombed Cities (Reconstruction Programmes) HC Deb 20 June 1950

Bombed Cities (Reconstruction Programmes) HC Deb 04 July 1950

War Damage (Late Claims) HC Deb 11 July 1950

Building Work (Business Premises) HC Deb 18 September 1950

Town and Country Planning Bill HC Deb 23 January 1951

Blitzed Cities (Building Licences) HC Deb 20 March 1951

Capital Investment Programme (Government Policy) HC Deb 21 June 1951

Blitzed City Centres (Reconstruction) HC Deb 03 July 1951

Bomb-Damaged Cities (Reconstruction) HC Deb 20 November 1951

War Damaged Areas (Assistance) HC Deb 05 December 1951

Steel Supplies HC Deb 19 February 1952

Blitzed Cities (Reconstruction) HC Deb 25 February 1952

Blitzed Areas (Reconstruction) HC Deb 10 April 1952

Reconstruction Work, Plymouth HC Deb 06 May 1952

Bombed Cities (Reconstruction) HC Deb 14 October 1952

Bombed Cities (Reconstruction Programme, 1953) HC Deb 18 November 1952

Bombed Cities (Reconstruction) [includes new allocations] HC Deb 25 November 1952

Capital Investment (Bombed Cities) HC Deb 01 December 1952

Blitzed Cities (Reconstruction) HC Deb 04 December 1952

Blitzed Towns HC Deb 02 March 1953

[No substantial debate in 1954 dealing with blitzed cities.]

Bomb-damaged Towns (Subsidies) HC Deb 13 December 1955

NOTES

Preface: In Spite of Planning

1 J. R. Gold, 'In Spite of Planning', *Journal of Urban History* 28 (May 2000): 551 (author's emphasis).

1 Introduction: A Blessing in Disguise, or an Opportunity Squandered?

1 M. Lock, 'Civic Diagnosis: A Blitzed City Analysed' (Hull Regional Survey), Published by the Housing Centre, London, July 1943 (exhibition brochure, pages unnumbered, but taken from first page). See also notes in section on Hull later in this chapter.
2 Charles, Prince of Wales, speech at Mansion House, London, 1 December 1987. Accessed on 22 November 2015: http://www.princeofwales.gov.uk/media/speeches/speech-hrh-the-prince-of-wales-the-corporation-of-london-planning-and-communication.
3 For example: J. B. Morrell, *The City of Our Dreams* (London, 1940, rev. ed. 1955); F. H. Rushford, *City Beautiful: A Vision of Durham* (Durham, 1944); T. Sharp, *Exeter Phoenix: A Plan for Rebuilding* (London, 1946); J. P. Watson, P. Abercrombie et al., *A Plan for Plymouth* (Plymouth, 1943). See also P. Larkham and K. Lilley, *Planning the 'City of Tomorrow': British Reconstruction Planning, 1939–1952: An Annotated Bibliography* (Pickering, 2001).
4 See R. Overy, *The Bombing War* (London, 2013); Mark Clapson and Peter Larkham (eds), *The Blitz and Its Legacy* (London, 2013); Juliet Gardiner, *The Blitz: The British under Attack* (London, 2010).
5 See N. Tiratsoo, *Reconstruction, Affluence and Labour Politics: Coventry 1945–1960* (London, 1990); also J. and C. Gould, *Coventry: The Making of a Modern City 1939–1973* (Swindon, 2014).
6 House of Lords Debates 'Post-War Reconstruction', HL Deb, 17 July 1941, vol. 119, cc844-80 (879). See also J. Hasegawa, *Replanning the Blitzed City Centre: A Comparative Study of Bristol, Coventry and Southampton 1941–50* (Buckingham, 1992), 49.
7 See, for example: J. Düwel and N. Gutschow (eds), *A Blessing in Disguise: War and Town Planning in Europe, 1940–45* (Berlin, 2013).
8 Winston Churchill, Broadcast to the Nation, BBC Radio, 21 March 1943, BL Sound Archive T 5499.
9 TNA: HLG 88/10 Ministry of Town and Country Planning: Advisory Panel on Reconstruction of City Centres, Draft report by H. Wells, 31 May 1943.
10 H. Perkin, *The Rise of Professional Society: England since 1880* (London, 1990). On training and the planning profession, see S. Ward, *Planning and Urban Change* (London, 2004; original edition, 1994).

11 J. Lubbock, *The Tyranny of Taste: The Politics of Architecture and Design in Britain 1550–1960* (London, 1995); and R. Hewison, *The Heritage Industry: Britain in a Climate of Decline* (London, 1987).

12 P. J. Larkham, 'Disasters: Recovery, Re-planning, Reconstruction, and Resilience', in C. Hein (ed.), *The Routledge Handbook of Planning History* (Abingdon, 2018); J. Diefendorf, 'Reconstructing Devastated Cities: Europe after World War II and New Orleans after Katrina', *Journal of Urban Design* 14:3 (2009): 377–97.

13 One of the earliest publications was based on a conference in 1987 led by Jeffry Diefendorf. The resulting publication marks a take-off point for most subsequent studies of the topic: J. Diefendorf (ed.), *Rebuilding Europe's Bombed Cities* (Basingstoke, 1990).

14 Most recently: P. J. Larkham, J. Pendlebury and E. Ertem (eds), *Alternative Visions of Postwar Reconstruction* (Abingdon, 2014); Clapson and Larkham, *The Blitz & Its Legacy*; J. Bold, P. J. Larkham and R. Pickard (eds), *Authentic Reconstruction: Authenticity, Architecture and the Built Heritage* (London, 2017). As previously noted: Hasegawa, *Replanning*. Also, Tiratsoo, *Reconstruction*; S. Essex, and M. Brayshay, 'Boldness Diminished? The Post-War Battle to Replan a Bomb-Damaged Provincial City'. *Urban History* 35:3 (2008): 437–61; J. Hasegawa, 'The Reconstruction of Portsmouth in the 1940s', *Contemporary British History* 14 (2000): 45–62; S. Essex and M. Brayshay, in 'Vision, Vested Interest and Pragmatism: Who Re-made Britain's Blitzed Cities?', *Planning Perspectives* 22:4 (2007): 417–41; Larkham, Pendlebury and Ertem, *Alternative Visions of Postwar Reconstruction*; Clapson and Larkham, *The Blitz & Its Legacy*.

15 A selection includes: J. Tomlinson, *Managing the Economy, Managing the People* (Oxford, 2017), and *Democratic Socialism and Economic Policy: The Attlee Years* (Cambridge, 1997); *British Macroeconomic Policy since 1940* (London, 1985) and his many journal articles; M. Chick, *Industrial Policy in Britain, 1945–1951: Economic Planning, Nationalisation and the Labour Governments* (Cambridge, 1998); S. Broadberry and N. Crafts, 'British Economic Policy and Industrial Performance in the Early Post-War Period'. *Business History* 38:4 (1996): 65–91; J. C. R. Dow, *The Management of the British Economy 1945–60* (Cambridge, 1964); A. Shonfield, *British Economic Policy since the War* (Harmondsworth, 1959); R. Toye, *The Labour Party and the Planned Economy, 1931–1951* (Woodbridge, 2003); G. D. N. Worswick and P. H. Ady (eds), *The British Economy, 1945–1950* (Oxford, 1952); N. Tiratsoo, *The Attlee Years* (London, 1991).

The ongoing debate on conflict versus consensus in the postwar period is also useful in this context. See: B. Pimlott, D. Kavanagh and P. Morris, 'Is the "Postwar Consensus" a Myth?' *Contemporary Record* (later *Contemporary British History*) 2:6 (1989): 12–15; P. Addison, 'Consensus Revisited', *TCBH* 4:1 (1993): 91–4; J. Tomlinson, 'After Decline?' *Contemporary British History* 23:3 (2009): 395–406; his 'Thrice Denied: "Declinism" as a Recurrent Theme in British History in the Long Twentieth Century'. *Twentieth Century British History (hereafter TCBH)* 20:2 (2009): 227–51; idem, chapter 10 'Economic Decline in Post-War Britain', in H. Jones and P. Addison, *A Companion to Contemporary Britain, 1939–2000* (Oxford, 2005).

16 See H. Meller, *Towns, Plans and Society in Modern Britain* (Cambridge, 1997); A. Ravetz, *Remaking Cities: Contradictions of the Recent Urban Environment* (London, 1980).

17   See O. Marriott, *The Property Boom* (London, 1967); P. Ambrose and B. Colenutt, *The Property Machine* (Harmondsworth, 1975); J. Rose, *The Dynamics of Urban Property Development* (London, 1985); P. Scott, *Property Masters: A History of the British Commercial Property Sector* (Abingdon, 2013).

18   A few key examples are: N. Bullock, *Building the Post-War World: Modern Architecture and Reconstruction in Britain* (London, 2002); J. R. Gold, *The Experience of Modernism: Modern Architects & the Future City 1928–53* (London, 1997); and J. R. Gold, *The Practice of Modernism: Modern Architects and Urban Transformation, 1954–72* (London, 2007); P. Hall, *Cities of Tomorrow: An Intellectual History of Urban Planning and Design in the Twentieth Century* (Oxford, 1988); also L. Esher, *A Broken Wave: The Rebuilding of England 1940–1980* (London, 1981); N. Pevsner, *Pioneers of Modern Design from William Morris to Walter Gropius* (London, 1991).

19   For a start a key essay is G. Cherry, chapter 14, 'Reconstruction: Its Place in Planning History', from J. M. Diefendorf (ed.), *Rebuilding*. See also: P. Johnson-Marshall, *Rebuilding Cities* (Edinburgh, 1966); J. B. Cullingworth and G. E. Cherry, *Environmental Planning, 1939–1969. Vol. 1: Reconstruction and Land-Use Planning 1939–47* (London, 1975); Ward *Planning and Urban Change*; N. Taylor, *Urban Planning Theory since 1945* (London, 1998). P. Hall, *Cities of Tomorrow*, and his *Urban and Regional Planning*, 3rd edn (London, 1992); P. Larkham and J. Nasr (eds), *The Rebuilding of British Cities: Exploring the Post-Second World War Reconstruction*, Working Paper, School of Planning and Housing (UCE, 2004). Larkham's co-authored, annotated bibliography of reconstruction publications is particularly useful for the historian of planning. Larkham and Lilley, *Planning the 'City of Tomorrow'*.

20   P. Mandler, 'New Towns for Old: The Fate of the Town Centre', in B. Conekin, F. Mort and C. Waters (eds), *Moments of Modernity: Reconstructing Britain 1945–1964* (London, 1999).

21   Ibid., 227.

22   In a similar vein, but more focused on the evidence in a social and cultural context, is David Matless's *Landscape and Englishness* (London, 1998). Matless explores many similar themes about what, in the postwar period, has contributed to the built – and unbuilt – world around us. In Matless's intended sense 'landscape' refers to the whole of the environment around us, not specifically to green areas of trees and grass, and so on.

23   H. Meller, 'From Dyos to Daunton', *Urban History* 28 (2001): 269–77. Also S. Ewen, *What Is Urban History?* (Cambridge, 2016); and E. Baigent, 'Typologies of Urban History', *Journal of Urban History* 28 (1999): 536–42. Baigent also cites some still informative early views of urban history from H. J. Dyos, Editorial, *Urban History Yearbook* 1 (1974): 2–6.

24   J. B. Jackson, *Discovering the Vernacular Landscape* (New Haven, 1984).

25   Chick, *Industrial Policy*, especially chapters 2 and 3.

26   N. Tiratsoo 'Labour and the Reconstruction of Hull, 1945–51', in *The Attlee Years*.

27   See C. Flinn, 'Exeter Phoenix, Politics and the Rebuilding of a Blitzed City', in *Southern History* 30 (2008): 104–27; also A. While and M. Tait, 'Exeter and the Question of Thomas Sharp's Physical Legacy', *Planning Perspectives* 24:1 (2009).

28   Fortuitously, a new book on interwar Liverpool has just been published: C. Wildman, *Urban Redevelopment and Modernity in Liverpool and Manchester, 1918–1939* (London, 2017).

29 C. Behan McCullagh, 'Bias in Historical Description, Interpretation, and Explanation', *History and Theory* 39:1 (2000): 39–66; R. Lowe, 'Plumbing New Depths: Contemporary Historians and the Public Record Office', *TCBH* 8:2 (1997): 239–65; B. Brivati, J. Buxton et al. *The Contemporary History Handbook* (Manchester, 1996).
30 J. R. Gold, 'In Spite of Planning', 551 (author's emphasis).

2 Considering Reconstruction, 1940–45

1 T. Sharp, 'Building Britain: 1941: Words for Pictures Perhaps a Film Script', *The Town Planning Review* 23:3 (1952): 203–10.
2 Such ideology runs throughout the contemporary rhetoric of postwar planning. This is discussed in much recent work, a good example of which is J. Pendlebury, 'Planning the Historic City: Reconstruction Plans in the United Kingdom in the 1940s', *The Town Planning Review* 74:4 (2003): 371–93.
3 For example, in American history 'reconstruction' is capitalized and refers to the era that followed the Civil War of 1861–65. Initially in Europe it meant the period of political reorganization after the First World War.
4 Cabinet discussions of 'reconstruction' included a wide range of topics such as the Beveridge report and other proposed social service changes. See TNA: CAB series 65, 66 and 67. For histories using the term generally, see, for example, A. Millward, *The Reconstruction of Western Europe 1945–51* (London, 1984); and D. Ellwood, *Rebuilding Europe: Western Europe, America and Postwar Reconstruction* (Harlow, 1992).
5 See P. Addison, *The Road to 1945: British Politics and the Second World War* (London, 1994), pp. 126ff. Also D. Ritschel, *The Politics of Planning: The Debate on Economic Planning in Britain in the 1930s* (Oxford, 1997); Toye, *The Labour Party*.
6 The origins of this ministry (in a smaller reconstruction secretariat) are discussed later in this chapter. The file series for it are in TNA: CAB 117 and 124.
7 Churchill battled against setting up formal administrative machinery for 'reconstruction', believing that the war effort was of utmost importance and such discussion would detract from such effort. See discussion on the creation of reconstruction machinery later in this chapter. Also see R. Lowe, 'The Second World War, Consensus and the Foundation of the Welfare State', *Twentieth Century British History* 1:2 (1990), 158; and Addison, *Road to 1945*, 126.
8 For 'reconstruction' as a 'sensibility', see Matless, *Landscape*.
9 A more extensive bibliography of physical reconstruction publications is too large for this space, but a very thorough review of post–Second World War reconstruction publications is found in: Larkham and Lilley, *Planning the 'City of Tomorrow'*. For a similar discussion from a geographical perspective, see Matless, *Landscape*, chapter 5, 'Landscapes of War', subheader 'Plans in Wartime', 189–200.
10 That is, Halford J. Mackinder, 'The Round World and the Winning of the Peace', *Foreign Affairs* 21:4 (1943): 595–605.
11 Again see Larkham and Lilley, *Planning the 'City of Tomorrow'* for examples. See also V. Holman, *Print for Victory: Book Publishing in Britain 1939–1945* (London, 2008), particularly chapter 4, which includes sections on both social and physical reconstruction.

12 *Picture Post* was owned by Edward Hulton 'a radical liberal' (Bullock, *Building*, 20n 20).

13 *Picture Post*, Plan for Britain, 4 January 1941. Fry; other authors included J. B. Priestley, Elizabeth Denby, A. D. K. Owen and more. See also online book *A History of Picture Post*, http://www.lacrossehistory.org/literature/AlltheBest(2010).pdf. Not covered here but given some mention in Matless's *Landscape* are the additional visions of the future Britain as seen through advertisements, for example, Pears Soap in 1941 on the back cover of *Geographical Magazine*; see chapter 5.

14 Examples include *News Chronicle*'s 1943 special edition 'Rebuilding Britain', also 'Replanning the Towns', *The Manchester Guardian*, 25 July 1941; 'Blitzed Cities: Control of Rebuilding Views of Lord Mayors', *The Observer*, 31 May 1942; a lengthy list by Charles Reilly (architect and planner) including 'How Can We Plan a New and Beautiful Britain?' *Telegraph and Independent*, 16 December 1940, is found in the appendices of P. Richmond, *Marketing Modernisms: The Architecture and Influence of Charles Reilly* (Liverpool, 2001).

15 G. and E. McAllister, *Town and Country Planning* (1941) and *Homes, Towns and Countryside* (1945); M. Bondfield, *Our Towns: A Close Up* (1943); C. Purdom, *Britain's Cities Tomorrow: Notes for Everyman on a Great Theme* (1942); J. B. Morrell, *The City of Our Dreams* (1940); B. Townroe, *The Building of a New Britain* (1941). Also see Larkham and Lilley, *Planning the 'City of Tomorrow'*.

16 LSE: BLPES archive holds many such pamphlets, and books, mainly in HD7 series. For the Co-operative Permanent Building Society, see HD7/32. There are many further examples including 'Handbooks for Discussion Groups', an extensive series published for 'the Association for Education in Citizenship by The English Universities Press Ltd.'. A group called the Individualist Bookshop had a pamphlet series called 'Post War Questions' which included titles such as 'Reconstruction of Bombed Buildings' by B. S. Townroe (1941).

17 For example, Puffin books published *The Building of London* by Margaret and Alexander Potter in 1946, with sections on planning and rebuilding.

18 Town and Country Planning Association (TCPA), *Rebuilding Britain* (series) (London, 1941). This was distributed by the Ministry of Information. A second series was published in 1943 based on the Nuffield Social Survey of Reconstruction. Authors included F. J. Osborn, Lewis Mumford and Seebohm Rowntree.

19 *Planning for Reconstruction*, Architectural Press (Cheam, 1943); Institution of Municipal and County Engineers, 'Post-war Planning and Reconstruction' (1942); and in *Architectural Review* 'Rebuilding Britain' 93 (1943), 'Towards a New Britain' (same issue), and 'Destruction and Reconstruction' 90 (1941). Other series included *Architectural Review* 'Reconstruction Supplement' (monthly from June 1941).

20 Royal Institute of British Architects, *Rebuilding Britain* (London, 1943), 63.

21 Army Bureau of Current Affairs (ABCA), 'Town Planning', no. 27, 26 September 1942.

22 ABCA, 'Social Security', no. 45, 5 June 1943, 39. (They did not acknowledge the quotation as Churchill's.) See also ABCA no. 56, 20 November 1943, 'Building the Post-war Home' and no. 75, 12 August 1944, 'After the Blitz Is Over?'.

23 Laura Beers points out that Butler and Churchill both held this view. According to R. A. Butler's memoirs: 'The forces vote, in particular, had been virtually won over by the leftwing influence of the Army Bureau of Current Affairs', and 'The title of this article alludes to the famous series of ABCA posters, "Your Britain: Fight for it Now", which Churchill regarded as thinly veiled Labour propaganda.' L. Beers, 'Labour's Britain, Fight for It Now!' *The Historical Journal* 52:03 (2009): 670.

24　See, for example, BOD CPA: PUB 57/2. 'Looking Ahead' published by the Central Committee on Post-War Reconstruction of the National Conservative and Unionist Party, pamphlets on housing issued in March 1944 and January 1945 also include discussions on town planning and rebuilding. Also PUB 57/1 Assorted Conservative Party Pamphlets, Conservative Women's Reform Group, 'When Peace Comes: A National Programme from the Standpoint of Women' (1945). LSE-BLPES: HD7/472 Labour Party *Housing and Planning after the War: The Labour Party's Postwar Policy* (London, 1943). Labour Party Archive (LPA) Research Dept (RDR) series has minutes from the wartime Housing and Town Planning Committee as well as a Central Committee on Reconstruction Problems; see appendices.

25　TCPA, *Replanning Britain* (series) (London, 1941); also E. F. Towndrow (ed.), *Replanning Britain* (London, 1941). *Report of the Oxford Conference of the Town and Country Planning Association, 1941* Also Holman, *Print for Victory*, 203.

26　Larkham and Lilley emphasize in their text the volume of plans and publications, see *Planning the 'City of Tomorrow'*, 6–7. (Though some in their list were published after the war.) Also see P. Larkham, 'The Place of Urban Conservation in the UK Reconstruction Plans of 1942–1952', *Planning Perspectives* 18 (2003): 295–324.

27　G. D. H. Cole, *Building and Planning* (London, 1945). Cole saw proposals for control of land use as a restrictive force: 'Control of land-use is in itself negative: it is a matter of prohibitions and restrictions on what may be done – not a matter of doing anything positive, but only one of providing a framework of order within which things must be done, if they are done at all.' He added, '[T]he futility of expecting from the Coalition Government any measures capable of serving as a reasonable foundation for post-war housing and development policy.' Clearly Cole's perspective was perhaps more realistic than Sharp's, a 'whole shining world is possible', 64–5. See also Cole's chapter VII 'Post-War Demand for Buildings' (other than houses), esp. section IV 181 ff. Sharp, 'Building Britain'; see note 1. To be fair, Cole was not the only non-positive voice; see 'The way to lose the peace: political exploitation of the reconstruction programme' pamphlet by the National Federation of Property Owners (London, 1942) in LSE-BLPES: D(4)/658. Also G. D. H. Cole and A. Bevan et al., *Plan for Britain: A Collection of Essays* prepared for the Fabian Society (London, 1943).

28　Morrell, *The City of Our Dreams*; Rushford, *City Beautiful*; Sharp, *Exeter Phoenix*; J. P. Watson and P. Abercrombie et al., *A Plan for Plymouth* (Plymouth, 1943). See also Larkham and Lilley, *Planning the 'City of Tomorrow'* and P. Larkham, 'Remaking Cities: Images, Control, and Postwar Replanning in the United Kingdom', *Environment and Planning B: Planning and Design* 24 (1997): 741–59.

29　See above regarding Oxford and Durham. Additionally, see wartime 'letters of suggestion' sent to various ministries but eventually collected by the planning ministry. TNA: HLG 71/619 'Post-War Reconstruction Miscellaneous Suggestions, Memoranda, etc. Dated 1941–43'. Includes letters with suggestions to Lord Reith at the Ministry of Works and Buildings, and later to Morrison, Minister at the newly named Ministry of Town and Country Planning; also notes addressed to the technical planner Mr. Vincent (MTCP, previously at Health), to the Ministry of Health (responsible for housing) and to Greenwood the prior Minister (without portfolio), with responsibility for reconstruction planning priorities.

30　Larkham and Lilley, *Planning the 'City of Tomorrow'* lists over 200 plans and admits that there are likely more to add.

31 P. Larkham and K. Lilley 'Plans, Planners and City Images: Place Promotion and Civic Boosterism in British Reconstruction Planning', *Urban History* 30:2 (2003): 183–205.

32 Exhibitions were also increasingly aimed at, and reached, the working classes – not just upper and middle. An extensive history of promoting science and industry goes back to the Mechanics Institute. For more on exhibition history, see K. Luckhurst, *The Story of Exhibitions* (London, 1951) Also see R. Freestone and M. Amati (eds), *Exhibitions and the Development of Modern Planning Culture* (Farnham, 2014); P. Greenhalgh, *Ephemeral Vistas: The Expositions Universelles, Great Exhibitions and World's Fairs, 1851–1939* (Manchester, 1988).

33 P. J. Larkham and K. D. Lilley, 'Exhibiting the City: Planning Ideas and Public Involvement in Wartime and Early Post-war Britain', *Town Planning Review* 83 (2012): 647–68; also K. Lilley and P. Larkham, *Exhibiting Planning: Communication and Public Involvement in British Post-war Reconstruction* (Working paper, Birmingham, 2007).

34 The Festival of Britain is of course the premier postwar example; see M. Banham, et al., *A Tonic to the Nation: The Festival of Britain 1951* (London, 1976).

35 M. Amati and R. Freestone 'All of London's a Stage: The 1943 County of London Plan Exhibition', *Urban History*, July 2015, 1–18.

36 See Lilley and Larkham, 'Exhibiting the City' and *Exhibiting*. (Note that the first exhibit was before the Coventry blitz.)

37 *Express and Echo*, 8 March 1946, also *News Chronicle*, 7 March 1946.

38 Lilley and Larkham, *Exhibiting*. The paper also covers reconstruction publications relating to the exhibitions, their structure and content, discussion of visitors and a list of public figures who opened them – in addition to useful data about the numbers and locations. Similar but updated work is found in their paper 'Exhibiting the City'.

39 Matless, *Landscape*, 189–98 and 202–15.

40 Ibid., especially 208–11.

41 Greenhalgh, *Ephemeral Vistas*, 170.

42 Lilley and Larkham, *Exhibiting*, p. iii and 26–7. Also see S. Cowan, 'The People's Peace: The Myth of Wartime Unity and Public Consent for Town Planning', in Clapson and Larkham, *The Blitz and Its Legacy*, 73–85.

43 Betjeman gave broadcast talks on and off throughout the war. See, for example, Steven Games' introduction to John Betjeman, *Trains and Buttered Toast*, ed. Stephen Games (London, 2006). Priestly, however, only gave his 'Postscripts' from June to October 1940. Judith Cook wrote that he gave a 'reminder to listeners of what had happened to the men of the First World War who had returned from the trenches only to be faced with unemployment and poverty, and demand[ed] that it did not happen again. A critical minority, led by the MP Brendan Bracken and a section of the media, demanded that the broadcasts be stopped on political grounds; although letters were running 300:1 in Priestley's favour, the BBC dropped him'. J. Cook, 'Priestley, John Boynton (1894–1984)', *Oxford DNB* (Oxford, 2004). Priestley's broadcasts are available in book form with the same title: J. B. Priestley, *Postscripts* (London, 1940). Also see Siân Nicholas, ' "Sly Demagogues" and Wartime Radio: J. B. Priestley and the BBC', *TCBH* 6:3 (1995): 247–66.

44 Nicholas, 'Sly Demagogues', 256. She adds: 'Graham Greene (who detested Priestley's plays) praised him in similar terms in the Spectator, "people need to be told that they are fighting for something more than survival".'

45 Ibid.

46 Betjeman, *Trains*, 'Coming Home, or England Revisited', 25 February 1943, 137–8. 'If it were some efficient ant heap … then how could we love it as we do?'

47 Ibid. See also his views on speculative house-builders (from May 1937, 69–71, 76). Betjeman eventually became a strong and influential advocate for architectural preservation. See Bevis Hillier, *John Betjeman: New Fame, New Love* (London, 2004), especially chapter 21 'One Air in the Forties' and chapter 23 'A Preservationist in the Making'. In 1949 Betjeman appeared with the planner Thomas Sharp, 'his old friend', to debate opposite sides of a preservation issue (390). There are also general comments on his architectural views in Games' Introduction. See also M. Tewdwr-Jones, ' "Oh, the planners did their best": The Planning Films of John Betjeman", *Planning Perspectives*, 20:4 (2005): 389–41.

48 Nicholas, 'Sly Demagogues'. F. J. Osborn (ed.), *Making Plans. Based on the B.B.C. Series of Discussions* (London, 1943), also quoted in Hasegawa, *Replanning*, 6.

49 Osborn had edited the TCPA's *Rebuilding Britain* series and published another edited series annually called *The Planner's Yearbook* (London, 1942 through 1946).

50 Holford was professor of architecture at Liverpool but in wartime had been appointed senior research officer in the Ministry of Works and Planning (later Town and Country Planning). M. Miller, 'Holford, William Graham, Baron Holford (1907–1975)', *Oxford DNB* (Oxford, 2004).

51 Physical planning was considered necessary generally, but the methods of application were heavily debated. See Chapter 4.

52 Osborn, *Making Plans*, Introduction, 5.

53 Perhaps the biggest issue was the conflict between public planning and private ownership (an issue than would never go away, in any case); see especially the Talk on 'Ownership of Land', *Making Plans*, 63ff.

54 Osborn in Introduction: 'Actually, when I read the Talks over carefully, I was surprised to find how little we disagreed on the main issues of planning', 5.

55 Keay in talk on 'The Reconstruction of the Old Town', in Osborn, *Making Plans*, 37.

56 Manzoni, in 'Any Planning Questions?', in Osborn, *Making Plans*, 73. For coverage of similar issues in Europe and other countries, see Düwel and Gutschow, *A Blessing in Disguise*.

57 Lord Balfour of Burleigh quoting Winston Churchill from 1 October 1942 in 'Foreword', in Osborn, *Making Plans*, no page number. See also Ian McLaine, *Ministry of Morale: Home Front Morale and the Ministry of Information in World War II* (London, 1979).

58 Winston Churchill, Broadcast to the Nation, BBC Radio, 21 March 1943. BL Sound Archive T 5499 Note the use of the word 'immediate'.

59 The most thorough study is Toby Haggith, unpublished PhD thesis, 'Castles in the Air: British Film and the Reconstruction of the Built Environment, 1939–51', University of Warwick, 1998. Another two studies are very valuable, looking at the films in connection with planning and the promotion of planners and of the profession: J. R. Gold and S. V. Ward, 'Of Plans and Planners: Documentary Film and the Urban Future, 1935–52', in D. Clarke, *Cinematic City* (London, 1997), 59–82; and Gold and Ward, ' "We're Going to Get It Right This Time": Cinematic Representations of Urban Planning and the British New Towns 1939–51', in S. Aitken and L. Zonn (eds), *Place, Power, Situation and Spectacle: The Geography of Film* (Lanham, MD, 1994), 229–58.

60 Gold and Ward, 'We're Going to Get It Right', 231 and 253.

61 Haggith, 'Castles in the Air', 85.

62 *New Towns for Old*, 1942, dir. J. Eldridge, Strand Film Productions for the Ministry of Information (MOI).

63 *When We Build Again*, 1943, dir. R. Bond, Strand Film for Cadbury Brothers. See also (book) *When We Build Again*, introduction by Lord Cadbury, Bournville Village Trust (London, 1941) and Gold and Ward, 'We're Going to Get It Right', 241.

64 *A City Reborn*, 1945, dir. J. Eldridge, Gryphon Films with Verity Films, for MOI.

65 Ibid.

66 'Town and Country Planning', 1946, dir. Unknown, Army Bureau of Current Affairs Magazine series, Army Kinematograph Services for the War Office. Quoted in Gold and Ward, 'We're Going to Get It Right', 241.

67 *The Way We Live*, 1946, dir. J. Craigie, Two Cities for Rank.

68 Ibid. Foot's comment turns out to be prescient, and – as will be seen in later chapters – he continued to fight a battle for support of the blitzed cities after he entered Parliament in 1945.

69 *Proud City*, 1945 (release 1946), dir. R. Keene, Greenpark Productions for MOI; *The People and the Plan*, 1945, dir. F. Sainsbury, Realist for MOI; P. Abercrombie and J. Forshaw, *County of London: Plan Prepared for the LCC* (London, 1943).

70 *They Came to a City*, 1945, dir. B. Dearden, prod. S. Cole (Ealing Distribution); the play was revived May 2011 for the stage in London: http://www.guardian.co.uk/stage/2011/may/09/they-came-to-a-city-review.

71 *Land of Promise*, 1946, dir. P. Rotha, Films of Fact Ltd. Quotation from Haggith, 'Castles in the Air', 193.

72 Oddly even more true in the 1951 election. See H. Jones, ' "This is Magnificent!": 300,000 Houses a Year and the Tory Revival after 1945', *Contemporary British History* 14:1 (2000): 99–121.

73 Laura Beers describes a Labour Party poster aimed to appeal to women: 'The poster underscores the extent to which the issue of housing was conceived in gendered terms during the 1945 campaign, as well as the centrality of the issue [for Labour].' Beers, 'Labour's Britain', 688. In fact Beers shows that the heaviest pamphlet distribution was on the topic of housing and physical planning.

74 Of course the question to ask of the apparent omission is 'why?'. The answer could not be determined from the files, but perhaps in the reality of the impending postwar demobilization housing was (correctly) seen as a top priority, matched only by employment concerns. (All candidates' leaflets in each archive were examined.) Only two minor exceptions were found, W. S. Morrison and a Liberal candidate.

75 BOD-CPA: 'Looking Ahead' series and 'When Peace Comes'; Lord Woolton, 'The Adventure of Reconstruction' (London, 1945).

76 Italics original. G. Orwell, *The Lion and the Unicorn* (Harmondsworth, 1941; 1982 edn), 106.

77 J. Betjeman, *English Cities and Small Towns* (London, 1943), 42.

78 For ideas about the increase in nostalgia and saving British heritage, see the article by Frances Spaulding, including this quotation from the architect Clough Williams-Ellis: ' "Recording Britain" drew fresh attention to Britain's architectural heritage, its state of decline and its vulnerability to enemy attack. This reappraisal of the past had implications for the present and the future: it highlighted national character and showed what Britain was fighting for.' F. Spaulding, 'Art in Dark Times', *History Today* 9:9 (September 2009): 19–22. *Recording Britain* was a four-volume series on historic architecture (London, 1946–49).

79 For the popular preference of houses over flats, see C. Langhamer, 'The Meanings of Home in Postwar Britain', *Journal of Contemporary History* (special issue, 'Domestic Dreamworlds: Notions of Home in Post-1945 Europe') 40:2 (April 2005): 341–62, especially 346. Also see S. Cowan, 'The People's Peace: The Myth of Wartime Unity and Public Consent for Town Planning', in Clapson and Larkham (eds), *The Blitz and Its Legacy*, 73–86.

80 See J. Sheehan, *Where Have All the Soldiers Gone?* (New York, 2008), 144; P. Thane, 'Family Life and "Normality" in Postwar British Culture', in R. Bessel (ed.), *Life After Death* (Cambridge, 2003).

81 For postwar issues after 1918, see, for example, S. Ward, *The Geography of Interwar Britain: The State and Uneven Development* (London, 1988).

82 For various permutations of reconstruction committees and ministries, see TNA files series CAB 87, 117 and 124.

83 The committee actually recommended the establishment of a secretariat for reconstruction, which Churchill did not think worthwhile and originally prevented its formation. See TNA: CAB 21/1584.

84 I. McIntyre, 'Reith, John Charles Walsham, First Baron Reith (1889–1971)', *Oxford DNB* (Oxford, 2004). Reith was elected to the House of Commons for Southampton in January 1940.

85 HC Debs, 24 October 1940, vol. 365, col. 1150–2 (Attlee describes the new Minister's duties).

86 TNA: CAB 67/8/121 [WP(G) (40) 321]; also see CAB 21/1583.

87 Ibid., para 7.

88 TNA: CAB 21/1583, Bridges to H. Wilson, Treasury, 9 December 1940.

89 TNA: CAB 21/1583, Reith to Bridges, 10 December 1940. Note that while Bridges played a role throughout, organizationally, his biographer perhaps overstates his importance here: 'At the same time Bridges was heavily involved with detailed planning for the reconstruction period after the war: he designed the organization to do this and chose the officials for it.' However, correspondence in the committee documents clearly shows that while Bridges attempted to choose the committee members, he was overridden by Churchill, who came close to scolding him for overstepping his authority after Churchill had clearly stated who he wanted to receive the few appointments. R. Chapman, 'Bridges, Edward Ettingdene, First Baron Bridges (1892–1969)', *Oxford DNB* (Oxford, 2004). See also CAB 21/1583 correspondence, 30 December 1940–4 January 1941, Churchill with Bridges.

90 TNA: CAB 21/1583 PM's minute, 30 December 1940, See Table 2.1 for a list of Ministers and their roles.

91 TNA: CAB 21/1583, Churchill to Bridges, 4 January 1941. Churchill appears to have had little use for Greenwood, who he was stuck with in the Coalition, and gave him this position to move him out of the way. For more on Churchill's reluctance to consider discussing reconstruction – in many forms, but particularly economic and social – see Lowe, 'Consensus', 158, and also Addison, *Road to 1945*, 126.

92 HC Deb, 22 January 1941, vol. 368, col. 264.

93 TNA: CAB 161/2, 55 also CAB 67/9/24.

94 Ibid. However, Reith did not give any kind of time frame in his memo.

95 W. Reith, *The Reith Diaries* (London, 1975), 272–3.

96 Ibid., 93.

97 Files on the committee origins and so on can be found under TNA series HLG 86.

98 Reith had only held the planning function for eleven days. 'Reith', *DNB entry*.

99   See TNA series CAB 117, on reconstruction ministry.

100 See TNA CAB 161 series Cabinet Committee books. The Committee on Reconstruction Problems absorbed the functions of the Committee on Economic Aspects of Reconstruction Problems, which was then dissolved.

101 B. Pimlott (ed.), *The Second World War Diary of Hugh Dalton* (London, 1986), 668.

102 T. Legg and M. Legg, 'Jowitt, William Allen, Earl Jowitt (1885–1957)', *Oxford DNB* (Oxford, 2004).

103 '[T]he dual arrangement of two major ministerial committees, under different chairpersons, dealing with reconstruction problems, continued until the office of the Minister of Reconstruction was created on 12 November 1943.' TNA catalog CAB 117.

104 J. Harris, *William Beveridge* (Oxford, 1997), 415, on publicity and copies sold.

105 Documents authored for War Cabinet by 'W.A.J.': TNA: CAB 66/35/27, 'Post-War Reconstruction – Quarterly Survey', First W(43) 127 dated 26 March 1943; CAB 66/39/16 Second W(43) 316, dated 16 July 1943; CAB 66/42/20, Third W(43) 470 dated 15 October 1943. There seems to be no Fourth Quarter Survey after Jowitt's duties were split with Woolton on creation of the new ministry in November 1943. For more on the setup of the ministry and discussion of economic priorities, see CAB 117/20.

106 TNA: CAB 66/42/17 [WP(43) 467], 19 October 1943; also see CAB 65/36/12 [WM (43) 144], 21 October 1943.

107 TNA: CAB 66/42/15 [WP(43) 465], 20 October 1943. See also CAB 65/36/12 as above (caps original).

108 M. Kandiah, 'Marquis, Frederick James, First Earl of Woolton (1883–1964)', *Oxford DNB* (Oxford, 2004).

109 TNA: CAB 124 series description.

110 Ibid. Jowitt did retain both his title and a special responsibility for the Beveridge Plan, and on October 1944 was appointed to a new position as 'Minister of National Insurance'. See Jowitt, *Oxford DNB* entry.

111 TNA: CAB 66/43 [WP(43) 541]; see also TNA: CAB 124. In the Caretaker government Woolton was appointed Lord President of the Council, although he retained his responsibility for reconstruction policy. The former committees were reworked into one single body called the 'Reconstruction Committee', which was to handle 'under the war cabinet all questions of reconstruction on the Home Front'.

112 See TNA: CAB 124. Dates of the Office were November 1943–May 1945.

113 Ward, *Planning and Urban Change*, 29–30, 43. J. B. Cullingworth, *Environmental Planning, 1939–1969. Vol. 1: Reconstruction 1939–47* (London, 1975). A lengthier description of legislative developments is found in Chapter 4.

114 Cmd. 6155 Report of the Royal Commission on the Distribution of Industrial Population (Barlow Report) (London, 1940).

115 See Cmd. 8204, 'Town and Country Planning 1943–51' (London, 1951).

116 G. Gibbon, *Reconstruction and Town and Country Planning, with an Examination of the Uthwatt and Scott Reports* (London, 1943).

117 Ward, *Planning and Urban Change*, 82–4.

118 See TNA catalog for file series HLG 86 and CAB 87/21, HLG 86/3 through 86/20, particularly 86/5 and 86/8. Also set up in 1941 was the Nuffield College Social Reconstruction Survey which mainly examined social and economic issues, but did

so at local and national levels. See HLG 82 series, also D. Ritschel, 'The Making of Consensus: The Nuffield College Conferences During the Second World War', *TCBH* 6:3 (1995): 267–301.

119 Ibid. See also Hasegawa, *Replanning*, 8–9.

120 Ibid.

121 House of Lords Debates 'Post-War Reconstruction', HL Deb, 17 July 1941, vol. 119, cc844-80 (879). See also Hasegawa, *Replanning*, 49.

122 Under Lord Portal's direction the Ministry of Works and Planning initiated a programme for the design of prefabricated houses to help relieve housing shortages, a version of which became known as the 'Portal house'. Through the publicity surrounding these houses, Lord Portal became known more for the house than for his work in planning. Portal left government in late 1944 when it was decided his ministerial role should originate in the House of Commons. See J. V. Sheffield, 'Portal, Wyndham Raymond, Viscount Portal (1885–1949)', rev. Robert Brown, *Oxford DNB* (Oxford, 2004).

123 See Table 2.1 for a list of these ministers and the ministries they served.

124 For persons, responsibilities, titles and dates, please refer to the list in "Persons and Affiliations" on page x.

125 See TNA series description for HLG series files. (Primary responsibility for policy in connection with industrial location remained with the Board of Trade and for housing with the Ministry of Health.)

126 Ibid. See Chapter 4 for a thorough discussion of MTCP responsibilities.

127 J. Ramsden, 'Morrison, William Shepherd, first Viscount Dunrossil (1893–1961)', *Oxford DNB* (Oxford, 2004). According to this entry, Morrison confessed to Hugh Dalton in November 1943 that he was 'having rows all round just now' (Pimlott, *War Diary*, 663).

128 TNA: HLG 88/8. See also Hasegawa, *Replanning*, 13–16.

129 TNA: HLG 88/8.

130 TNA: HLG 88/9 and 88/15. See also notes in HLG 88/10–13. See Chapter 4 for more on the Panel.

131 Ministry of Town and Country Planning, *The Redevelopment of Central Areas* (London, 1947).

132 Although many of these later raids caused proportionally worse damage as they were often on smaller cities.

133 P. Scott, 'The Evolution of Britain's Urban Built Environment', in M. Daunton, *The Cambridge Urban History of Britain. Vol. III 1840–1950* (Cambridge 2000), 517.

134 Ministry of Reconstruction, Cmd. 6609. *Housing* (London, 1945), para 34. There was no differentiation here between houses that could be repaired and houses that would have to be pulled down.

135 TNA CAB 65/53 [CM (45) 7], dated 11 June 1945, 47.

136 HC Debs, 1 November 1944, vol. 404, cc813 WA. This statement would prove to be wildly optimistic.

137 TNA: HLG 71/601 and 602, dates are mainly in September 1947.

138 TNA: HLG 71/601 and 71/602. Note this figure has been adjusted to account for only blitz damage in Birmingham, whose regional officer reported blitz and blight together. See also Cmd. 8204, appendices.

139 TNA: HLG 71/596. Letters requesting information dated in February 1945, answers mainly March 1945. Note that cities often gave differently calculated answers to what was requested.

140 D. Rigby Childs, 'A Comparison of Progress in Rebuilding Bombed Cities', *Architects'*
     Journal (8 July 1954): 41–52.
141 For further discussion of this dilemma, see N. Rosenberg, *Economic Planning in the*
     British Building Industry, 1945–49 (Philadelphia 1960), chapter 1.
142 For priorities, see Jones, 'This Is Magnificent!', 99–121; and G. O'Hara, 'Social
     Democratic Space: The Politics of Building in "Golden Age" Britain, c.1950–1973',
     arq: Architectural Research Quarterly 10:3–4 (2006): 285. These references include
     notes on Mass-Observation surveys about public priorities.
143 Chapter 3 discusses this more fully.
144 See, for example, discussion in HC Deb, 18 November 1947, vol. 444, cc988-1101,
     esp. col. 1095, debate 'Local Government Bill'.
145 Rosenberg, *Economics*, Chapter 1 'The Aftermath of War'.

3 Treasury Mandarins: The Apparatus of Postwar Economic Planning

1 TNA: CAB 134/983 [IPC WP(53) 50, 11 October 1953] 'Methods of Controlling
   Investment, Note by the Chairman', item 5, 2.
2 Building licences were issued by the Ministry of Works for any work over £10
   in value, increased to £100 for houses (July 1948) and £1,000 for industrial and
   commercial activities (November 1948, but lowered to £500 in February 1953).
   N. Rosenberg, 'Government Economic Controls in the British Building Industry,
   1945–9', *The Canadian Journal of Economics and Political Science* 24:3 (1958): 347;
   A. Cairncross, *Years of Recovery* (London, 1985), 455.
3 Hereafter 1944 Act. Also see Chapter 4.
4 Despite its profound impact on the building industry, the IPC is not mentioned in
   Christopher Powell's *The British Building Industry since 1800: An Economic History*
   (London, 1996 ed.); see his chapters 7–8 for this period.
5 See J. Hasegawa, 'The Rise and Fall of Radical Reconstruction in 1940s Britain',
   Twentieth Century British History 10:2 (1999): 152; and Tiratsoo, *Reconstruction*, 42
   and 109. Announcement in HC Deb, 1 February 1949, vol. 460, c1485-86.
6 Of any published information, the most thorough is found in Chick, *Industrial*
   Policy.
7 Cairncross, *Years*; and with N. Watts *The Economic Section* (London, 1989).
8 E. Plowden, *An Industrialist in the Treasury: The Post-war Years* (London, 1989).
9 G. D. H. Cole, *The Post-war Condition of Britain* (London, 1956); S. Broadberry and
   N. Crafts, 'British Economic Policy and Industrial Performance in the Early Post-
   War Period', *Business History* 38:4 (1996): 65–91; J. C. R. Dow, *The Management of*
   the British Economy, 1945–60 (Cambridge, 1964); A. Shonfield, *British Economic*
   Policy since the War (Harmondsworth, 1959); J. Tomlinson, *British Macroeconomic*
   Policy since 1940 (London, 1985); and *Democratic Socialism and Economic Policy: The*
   Attlee Years (Cambridge, 1997) and his many journal articles since; Toye, *The Labour*
   Party; Worswick and Ady, *The British Economy*, 212ff. Also: Tiratsoo, *The Attlee*
   Years. Further informing the economic history here are K. Thorpe, ' "Statistical
   Floodlighting"? The Unpublished Economic Surveys 1946–47', *Contemporary British*
   History 11:4 (1997): 86–111; N. Tiratsoo and J. Tomlinson, *Industrial Efficiency and*
   State Intervention, 1939–51 (London, 1993) and their *The Conservatives and Industrial*
   Efficiency, 1951–1964 (London, 1998); N. Tiratsoo, *From Blitz to Blair* (London, 1997).

10 Shonfield, *British Economic Policy*. The later work obviously benefits from greater availability of documentation as well as perhaps more objective views.

11 J. C. R. Dow, 'Review: Cairncross, Alec. Years of Recovery', *Journal of Economic Literature* 25:3 (1987): 1327–9.

12 E. A. G. Robinson 'The Economic Problems of the Transition from War to Peace: 1945–49: Reviewing: Alec Cairncross, Years of Recovery: British Economic Policy 1945–51', *Cambridge Journal of Economics* 10:2 (1986): 165–85. Robinson also wrote about the problems of economic historians. As they gain chronological distance from their research topic, they have the opportunity to draw from a wider range of statistics: 'To understand the decisions made it is more relevant to know what we *then* believed to be the position' than to know what the position actually was (this author's emphasis; 184). Martin Chick has produced the broadest and most comprehensively on aspects of the IPC. Chick detailed the work of the IPC in relation to industry, while Jim Tomlinson has published on numerous aspects of policy and implementation in the Attlee governments. See Chick, *Industrial Policy*; Tomlinson, *Democratic Socialism*; J. Tomlinson, *The Politics of Decline: Understanding Post-war Britain* (London, 2000); J. Tomlinson, 'Managing the Economy, Managing the People: Britain circa 1931–1970', *Economic History Review* 58 (2005): 555–85; J. Tomlinson and B. Clift, 'The Labour Party and the Capitalist Firm, c.1950–1970', *Historical Journal* (September 2004).

13 Historians argue that Labour won the election based on being able to convey this understanding. See S. Fielding, 'What Did the People Want: The Meaning of the 1945 General Election', *Historical Journal* 35 (1992): 623ff. Also D. Tanner, P. Thane et al. *Labour's First Century* (Cambridge, 2000). Also see Beers on the use of media by Labour in the 1945 election: Beers 'Labour's Britain', 667–95. See chapter 2 on election materials which touted the importance of house-building after the war.

14 T. Tsubaki, 'Planners and the Public: British Opinion on Housing during the Second World War', *Contemporary British History* 14:1 (2000): 81.

15 J. Tomlinson, 'Balanced Accounts? Constructing the Balance of Payments Problem in Post-war Britain', *The English Historical Review* CXXIV:509 (2009): 863–84; also Cairncross, *Recovery*, 73–5; Worswick and Ady, *The British Economy*, 212ff. From 1946 a series of white papers were issued regularly regarding the balance of payments; see, for example, Cmd. 7324–9871 (1946–56). See Appendix I for a list of these white papers up to 1955.

16 The white paper on Employment Policy (Cmd. 6527) issued in 1944 can be said to have 'affirmed the responsibility of the Government for employment and economic well-being', showing some consensus (widely debated since). H. Morrison, *Government and Parliament: A Survey from the Inside* (London, 1960), 288.

17 Ibid., 289. Lord President during the Attlee government, Herbert Morrison, wrote about the postwar damage to trade, industry, infrastructure and so on.

18 Chick, *Industrial Policy*, 4.

19 For primary source discussion of issues with building materials particularly, see Investment Programme Committee Capital Investment Reports in TNA: CAB 134/437 [IPC (47)9], 134/439 [IPC Report 1949], 134/440 [IPC Report 1950], 134/442 [IPC Report 1951], 134/982 [IPC Reports 1952 and 1953]. On materials allocation, see Dow, *Management*, 159–60.

20 TNA: CAB 167/11 'Cost of War' (in *Long Term Planning*, 1964); A. Milward, *The Economic Effects of Two World Wars on Britain*, 2nd edn (London, 1984); also Cairncross, *Years*, 3–16.

21 CAB 128/1 [CM (45) 23, 16 August 1945, Conclusions, 44].

22 Although they did not immediately attempt to implement or continue many controls, as the postwar atmosphere was 'expansive and unfavourable to checking investment'. TNA: CAB 139/209, P. Vinter, 'Note on Investment Programmes (Revised)', dated 14 July 1950, 2 It was also considered burdensome to continue administering very strict controls, although it was later found that controls were still needed. See also Morrison, *Government*, chapter 13 'Economic Planning and Controls', 286–310, especially the section 'Prolongation of War-Time Controls', 294–7.

23 Cairncross, *Recovery*, 12–15.

24 See N. Rosenberg, 'Government Controls', esp. 346. See also P. Addison, *Now the War Is Over: A Social History of Britain 1945–51* (London, 1995), chapter 2.

25 Rosenberg, 'Government Controls'; also Rosenberg, *Economic Planning*, 14–15.

26 HC Deb, 28 July 1947, vol. 441, c80–85.

27 C. Barnett, *The Lost Victory* (London, 1995). For an excellent refutation of the Barnett version of postwar history, see J. Tomlinson 'Correlli Barnett's History: The Case of Marshall Aid', *TCBH* 8:2 (1997): 222–38 (see Tables 3.1 and 3.2 and notes).

28 'The problem was to settle the allocations and priorities within the limits of the practicable, in such a way that the public interest as a whole would be met to the greatest possible extent.' Morrison, *Government*, 289.

29 See List of Persons: Leadership and Roles in the Treasury, page x.

30 P. Clarke and R. Toye, 'Cripps, Sir (Richard) Stafford (1889–1952)', *Oxford Dictionary of National Biography (DNB)* (Oxford, 2004).

31 B. Pimlott, 'Dalton (Edward) Hugh Neale, Baron Dalton (1887–1962)', *Oxford DNB* (Oxford, 2004); See also B. Pimlott, *Hugh Dalton* (London, 1985).

32 Chick, *Industrial Policy*, 4.

33 Ibid., 11.

34 Pimlott, *Dalton*. Ironically Dalton later became planning minister in 1950 and had to fight the Treasury/Exchequer/IPC for more allowances for blitzed cities. See later in this chapter and the next. For an example of his attitude to physical rebuilding, see TNA: CAB 128/10 [CM(47) 68, 1 August 1947].

35 In a Commons debate on Land Acquisition in 1946, Dalton stated: 'The Government have already given indications – and I repeat them now – that they would desire to go even further in assisting those places which stood up under enemy fire more than the rest of the country.' HC Deb, 1 August 1946, vol. 426, c1323. He continued: 'Do not make too much argument on what is a relatively small detail in a large picture. We will consider sympathetically claims from the blitzed areas wherever they may be.' His concern for the blitzed cities did grow when he later became Minister of Local Government and Planning (see later in chapter).

36 Cripps retained both titles. (The MEA is explained in the next section.) P. Clarke, *The Cripps Version: The Life of Stafford Cripps* (London, 2002), Part 6; also Morrison *Government*, 299–300.

37 Ibid. Also Pimlott, *Dalton*.

38 Clarke, 'Cripps'.

39 Clarke, *Cripps*, 493–512.

40 Ibid.

41 See, for example, Cabinet discussions in TNA: CAB 195/5 [CM (47) 81, 20 October 1947, item 4, 325], also CAB 195/7 [CM (50) 10, 13 March 1950, item 1] for a vociferous insistence on housing cuts.

42 B. Brivati, 'Gaitskell, Hugh Todd Naylor (1906–1963)', *Oxford DNB* (Oxford, 2004).

43 H. Gaitskell and P. Williams. *The Diary of Hugh Gaitskell, 1945–1956* (London, 1983). No mention is made of reconstruction, rebuilding, town and country planning and so on (Though of course the diary is an edited version.)

44 See notes 8, 12 and 15.

45 See Cairncross, *Recovery*, chapter 1; Addison, *War*, chapter 2.

46 A significant exception, rarely cited because it is written as a handbook for records in the PRO, is Alford, Lowe and Rollings, *Economic Planning 1943–1951: A Guide to Documents in the Public Record Office* (London, 1992).

47 Nor did the leadership chosen have a great deal of economic expertise. Dalton and Gaitskell were trained economists (admittedly a fairly new field of study), but Cripps was a chemist turned lawyer turned politician, and the civil servants working within the various departments on economic policy had similarly mixed backgrounds. The notable exception is Sir Edwin Plowden.

48 According to Simon James, there were 461 ministerial and official committees under Attlee, and governance shifted noticeably in this period from Cabinet government to a 'Cabinet system'. S. James, *British Cabinet Government* (London, 1999), 2–3.

49 Also added to assist the Cabinet, and which outlasted the Economic Section, was the Central Statistical Office. See R. K. Mosley, *The Story of the Cabinet Office* (London, 1969), 66. According to Cabinet Secretary Edward Bridges, the Economic Section was 'charged with presenting a coordinated and objective picture of the economy as a whole, and the economic aspects of projected Government policies'. Mosley (66) quoting from Bridges. There is more on the CSO in Alford et al., chapter 8, 'Central Statistical Office', Introduction, in *Economic Planning 1943–1951*, 270. For a full history of the Economic Section, see Cairncross and Watts, *The Economic Section*.

50 Apparently the chief economic planning officer was appointed to work in the Lord President's office, before it moved to Cripps's new office and then subsequently the Treasury. See Morrison, *Government*, 299. Morrison claims that the primary task of the CEPS was 'the creation of a long-term plan for the use of the nation's resources, but its functions gradually widened' (299–300). The creation of the Central Economic Planning Staff (CEPS) and the associated Economic Planning Board (EPB), both under Edwin Plowden, was announced in March 1947. He moved to the Treasury with Cripps but remained – in title – separate from it. See P. Jay, 'Plowden, Edwin Noel Auguste, Baron Plowden (1907–2001)', *Oxford DNB* (Oxford, 2004).

51 See M. Chick 'Economic Planning, Managerial Decision-Making and the Role of Fixed Capital Investment in the Economic Recovery of the United Kingdom, 1945–1955', unpublished PhD thesis, London School of Economics, 1986, 14–17. Also Chick, *Industrial Policy*, 7. Additionally, the Lord President, Morrison, had been very ill.

52 Clarke, 'Cripps'.

53 Morrison notes that when Cripps became Chancellor and brought the CEPS staff (and Plowden) to the Treasury, it removed responsibility entirely from the Lord President's office, though Morrison describes this as a positive move. *Government*, 300. See also Alford et al., *Economic Planning 1943–1951*, 8–11.

54 See M. Daunton, *Wealth and Welfare: An Economic and Social History of Britain, 1851–1951* (Oxford, 2007), chapter 17, esp. 593–602. Also Tomlinson, *Democratic Socialism*, chapter 11.

55 Report commissioned July 1946. Ministry of Works and Viscount Simon, *Distribution of Building Materials and Components: Report of the Committee of Enquiry Appointed*

by the Minister of Works (London, 1948). The number of building licences issued apparently outweighed available labour and materials: see Dow, *Management*, 150–1.

56   TNA: CAB 128/10 [CM (47) 68, 1 August 1947, 195; also CM (47) 69, 5 August 1947, 205]. The Dalton memo was CP (47) 221 (found in CAB 129/20). A note by an IPC member in CAB 139/209 makes clear the decision to control investment more carefully was taken 'in the aftermath of the convertibility crisis'. P. Vinter, 'Note on Investment Programmes (Revised)', dated 14 July 1950, 2. Interestingly, an earlier letter from Bridges to Plowden dated 24 July 1947 suggests setting up such a committee. This may be how the suggestion landed in the Cabinet discussion, but the specifics appear untraceable. TNA: T 229/208 Bridges to Plowden, 24 July 47.

57   TNA: CAB 129/20 [CP (47) 231, 13 August 1947]. For more on the Cabinet structure, particularly committees, see S. James, 'The Cabinet System since 1945: Fragmentation and Integration', *Parliamentary Affairs* 47:4 (1994): 613–29.

58   Ibid. Treasury, Ministry of Works, Ministry of Supply, Ministry of Labour, Board of Trade, Economic Section, Central Statistical Office and Central Economic Planning Staff, with secretaries supplied one each from the Treasury and CEPS. See TNA: CAB 134/437; also CAB 161/3, March 1948, [Cabinet] Committee Organization, 22.

59   In fact the Cabinet secretary's note stated that the 'relation of the Committee to the Investment Working Party … will be considered later'. TNA: CAB 129/20 [CP (47) 231, 13 August 1947].

60   See Chick, 'Economic Planning', 9–17. Cairncross, *Years*, 309, for 'targets' set by Cripps at BT. More recently, Jim Tomlinson on attempts to push productivity: *Managing the Economy*, especially chapter 7 'Productivity'.

61   TNA: CAB 129/21 [CP (47) 284, 16 October 1947, 1] of report. For conclusions on the discussion, see CAB 128/10 [CM (47) 81, 20 October 1947]; also see Cabinet secretary's notebooks CAB 195/5 [CM (47) 81, same date] for disagreements on housing targets being set as well. The report also recommended a continuing structure for control of investment.

62   Ibid., 13 (Works, Appendix 11), also 29.

63   TNA: CAB 128/10 [CM (47) 81, 20 October 1947, 65].

64   Cmd. 7268 *Capital Investment in 1948* (London, 1947).

65   It is from this white paper that historians possibly have held the impression that capital investment was to be controlled via labour, when in fact the future reports of the IPC (as will be shown) were not published, and used suggested caps of steel in 1948, and thenceforward investment caps determined by production or building cost.

66   Cmd. 7268, item 86, 23.

67   TNA: CAB 129/22 [CP (47) 322, 5 December 1947]. The permanent committee was then listed with its new membership in the Cabinet committee books found in CAB 161 (the initial listing in CAB 161/3 is dated March 1948). For detailed information on the IPC, see CAB 21/2976: IPC: Machinery for Supervision and Control (1947–53). See also Chick, *Industrial Policy* and 'Economic Planning'.

68   IPC membership remained at this level for the rest of its existence. Membership analysed using *The British Imperial Calendar and Civil Service List* (London: HMSO, 1945, 1948, 1949, 1950, 1951).

69   TNA: CAB 130/27, Meeting minutes, 31 October 1947 and 5 November 1947; see also CAB 134/438 (especially IPC (48)5, 19 March 1948). Also see CAB 21/2975 'Investment Programmes Committee: Composition and Terms of Reference'.

70   TNA: CAB 129/22 [CP (47) 322, 5 December 1947], Cabinet Memorandum. Strath from the Central Economic Planning Staff, R. L. Hall from the Economic Section of

the Cabinet Office, A. K. Cairncross (then) from the Board of Trade, L. B. Hutchison from the Ministry of Supply, and E. F. Muir from the Ministry of Works. Additionally there were two secretaries: F. R. P. Vinter from the Treasury, and J. L. Croome from the Central Economic Planning Staff. Annual membership lists are also found in TNA: CAB 161 series (1–8 for 1945–56).

71 List shortened for clarity. Full remit at TNA: CAB 161/3, March 1948 [Cabinet] Committee Organization, 22. Includes reference for authorization of the committee as 'CM (47) 81 Conclusions and CP (47) 322'. Notably, the Ministry of Health – the ministry then responsible for public housing – was not represented, nor was the Ministry of Town and Country Planning, responsible for all non-governmental and non-industrial building approvals (but not licences).

72 TNA: CAB 21/2975 [IPC (48) 4, 20 March 1948], 'Change to the Committee's Terms of Reference'. Also CAB 161/4, May 1949.

73 See the files series in TNA: CAB 134/437–457 and 982–984 for minutes and reports of the IPC.

74 See, for example, correspondence between MTCP and Works in TNA: HLG 71/2222 and 2223 on War Damage Reconstruction. Also see note 86 on materials committee.

75 IPC papers were not released through the Public Records Office until 1978, though most were released later in the 1980s.

76 Specialist political scientists are an exception, for example, P. Dunleavy and R. Rhodes, 'Core Executive Studies in Britain', *Public Administration* 68:1 (1990): 3–28.

77 Not all 'economists' working in the Treasury, Economic Section or CEPS were trained as economists (in any case a relatively new subject at Oxbridge). Many were career civil servants, classically educated, who had ended up in these roles through connections to ministers or by chance. For example, several chairmen of the IPC had classics degrees, worked in departments as diverse as the India Office, the Air Ministry and Supply, and virtually no real economic or business training, yet were charged with making decisions on national economic priorities. See A. W. Coats, 'Economists in Government – an Historical and Comparative Perspective', *Economic Papers: A Journal of Applied Economics and Policy* 7:2 (1988): 89–102.

78 The lack of published information available contributes to the obscurity of the IPC and its absence from economic histories. Additionally, if former members such as Cairncross, or economists involved such as Dow, did not include (or downplayed the role of) the IPC in their histories of postwar economic policy, it makes sense that historians have possibly accepted this as proof of its relative lack of importance. In addition, domestic issues have long been passed over historically for bigger macroeconomic discussions, as well as explorations of monetary policy (sterling and its ups and downs) and a focus on balance of payments issues. The problems generated by obfuscation of the decision-making process will be demonstrated as more detail is discussed on the issues of allocating to the blitzed cities below. For a brief overview of the IPC, see also Rosenberg, *Economic Planning*, 80–1. Also Chick, 'Economic Planning'.

79 See TNA: CAB 21/2975 as well as CAB 134/437–438 for discussions.

80 See, for example, the discussion on 20 October 1947 in CM (47) 81 found in TNA: CAB 128/10 and 195/5. The Minister of Town and Country Planning was not a Cabinet position.

81 Ward, *Planning and Urban Change*, 85–6, 93.

82 The Board of Trade (BT) did actually inadvertently announce a start for blitzed cities when pushed in an adjournment debate regarding Temporary Shops on 16 September

1948. See HC Deb, 16 September 1948, vol. 456, c369-378. The BT was responsible for approving industrial projects, as well as many other businesses.

83 Rosenberg, 'Government Controls', 351. For problems of coordination, see also Rosenberg, *Economic Planning*, 32.

84 IPC files are in two series: TNA: CAB 134/437–457 and 134/982–984.

85 See note by IPC Secretary P. Vinter in TNA: CAB 139/209, 5 para 15. For more on regional statistics as they developed in the 1960s, see G. O'Hara, 'A Journey without Maps: The Regional Policies of the 1964–70 British Labour Government', *Regional Studies* 39:9 (2005): 1183–95.

86 The Materials Committee (renamed Materials Allocation Committee in 1950) file series in TNA is CAB 134/475–487 (the TNA web catalogue entry for CAB 134/485 explains the name change). See especially CAB 134/485 and CAB 134/1006 for more on coordination. For inter-ministry correspondence, see, for example, TNA: HLG 71/2222 and 2223 on War-Damage Reconstruction, and files throughout the series HLG 102/260 to 271, especially 267.

87 Note that the initial allocations were allowances of steel, but thereafter allocations were done via caps of costs, through building licences. This will be explained further in the next section.

88 TNA: CAB 129/21 [CP (47) 284, 16 October 1947, Report of the Investment Programmes Committee, 248].

89 Ibid., 29.

90 Cmd. 7268 'Capital Investment in 1948', 23, para 86. While blitzed cities received passing mention, New Towns were given a section of the report.

91 Note that the term 'planning ministry' is used throughout because over the period from 1940 to 1954 the ministry responsible for planning changed name or location five times. The term is used to refer to whichever ministry was responsible for planning at the time, be it Works and Planning, or the MTCP, or Local Government and Planning, or Housing and Local Government. In each case those entities were responsible for the physical planning functions of central government.

92 See IPC series of meeting minutes in TNA: CAB 134/437–457 for the period up to the change of government in 1951.

93 The Ministry of Works may have been responding in part to some Parliamentary pressure from November 1947 where the plight of blitzed cities had been brought up vociferously in two debates on 12 and 18 November. See HC Deb, 12 November 1947, vol. 444, c483ff and HC Deb, 18 November 1947, vol. 444, c046ff.

94 TNA: CAB 134/447 [IPC (WP) (48) 82, 6 May 1948, item 5]. It further suggested '25,000 tons [of steel] would be required to make any impression on the problem'.

95 TNA: CAB 134/438 [IPC (48)38, 9 June 1948, 1–3]. It will be shown in the next chapter more fully that the MTCP was a key point of contact – they had been dealing with numerous city officials and representatives since wartime.

96 Sharp had been many years in the Ministry of Health working on housing and after a wartime placement in the Treasury (ironically) had returned to Health and then sent to the MTCP. She had a reputation for working well with regional offices and officials. (Miss Sharp was appointed DBE later that year, so will appear again as 'Dame Evelyn Sharp'.) See Kevin Theakston, 'Sharp, Evelyn Adelaide, Baroness Sharp (1903–1985)', *Oxford DNB* (Oxford, 2004).

97 TNA: CAB 134/438 [IPC (48)38, 9 June 1948, 1–3].

98 Ibid.

99 Ibid. The answer for Coventry, however, did appear in the IPC report in July.

100 TNA: CAB 134/439 'Report on Capital Investment in 1949' [IPC (48) 8, 16 July 1948]. The permanent IPC would issue a number of semi-annual reports over the next five years.

101 Ibid., 12. Sharp had written to the IPC after her attendance at the meeting with the Coventry answer and a suggestion to allocate 10,000 tons of steel for the blitzed cities. TNA: T229/520, Sharp to Strath, 12 June 1948.

102 Ibid., 82.

103 See correspondence in TNA: T229/520 and memoranda around these dates from Works in CAB 134/448.

104 See correspondence in TNA: T229/520 commencing December 1947 (Proper to Trend) and through November 1948. The pressure seems to have produced results.

105 Ibid.

106 TNA: CAB 129/520 and HLG 71/2222, Cripps to Jones, 25 November 1948. The MTCP margin notes on the letter next to the outlining of MTCP duties says 'this is incorrect'.

107 See TNA: CAB 134/438 [IPC (48)38, 9 June 1948, 1–3]. Meeting minutes, E. Sharp (MTCP) states that the ministry is not, strictly speaking, responsible for the actual rebuilding of the blitzed cities, but that they are assisting with planning and acquisition of land, which has 'led the local authorities to expect assistance from them'.

108 After the invitation by the IPC to the June 1948 meeting, an MTCP representative did not appear again until 1950.

109 Again, see minutes from 9 June 1948. See also TNA: HLG 102/262 HQBC circulated papers, 1947–48. At the same meeting there was additional discussion on the need to increase allowances for office buildings in larger cities with export businesses, and it was argued that this work could be crucial to the export drive, but was being overlooked, in both London and larger provincial cities such as Liverpool.

110 HC Debates: see Hansard website. From the passage of the 1947 Act to January 1949 at least six Commons discussions centred on these issues, but many more instances exist over the same period where blitzed cities were brought up in conjunction with similar or overlapping issues.

111 HC Deb, 12 November 1947, vol. 444, c484, Medland, Plymouth Drake.

112 HC Deb, 18 November 1947, vol. 444, c1046, Thomas Lewis, Labour, Southampton.

113 Per note 81 above, Board of Trade did actually inadvertently announce a start for blitzed cities when pushed in an adjournment debate regarding Temporary Shops on 16 September 1948. HC Deb, 16 September 1948, vol. 456, c369-378.

114 HC Deb, 1 February 1949, vol. 460, c1485-86. MTCP officials had argued for 25,000 tons (note 93), then 10,000 (note 100) and then 7,700 tons (see TNA: HLG 71/2222). Oddly, after the announcement was made, and though it was already public knowledge – by virtue of the cities themselves each being told what their allocation would be before the Parliamentary announcement – the Treasury sent a note to the MTCP stating that they had violated a rule about disclosing allocations of raw materials. Mitchell (Treasury) to Williams (MTCP), 4 February 1949, TNA: HLG 71/2222. Follow-up correspondence indicates the MTCP protested that they could not have known about this 'rule'.

115 HC Deb, 21 March 1949, vol. 460, c173. This government building was said to cost £1.3 million, an amount that totals more than most blitzed cities' combined allocations over the period of its construction. See also TNA: HLG 102/262.

116 TNA: HLG 71/2222, Memo, Jones to Sharp, 4 February 1949.

117 HC Deb, 21 March 1949, vol. 463, c161-2 (debate 157–174). See also TNA: CAB 134/439, 'Report on Capital Investment in 1949' IPC (48) 8, 94, para 496, and the Supplementary Report at IPC (48) 9. Others calculate it was a similar portion of approximately 11.5 million tons allocated; see Hasegawa, 'Rise and Fall', 152.

118 See correspondence throughout the sets of 'blitzed cities' files in both the Treasury and the planning ministry: TNA: T 229/520–521 and HLG 71/2222–2230. Also see Hansard for a list of debates and related discussions in the House of Commons.

119 TNA: CAB 134/440 'Report on Capital Investment in 1950–1952' IPC (49) 3, 12 May 1949, item 354.

120 See documents in TNA: T 229/520 especially July–September and November 1949.

121 TNA: T 229/520, [EPC (49) 139, Memorandum, 17 November 1949] and [EPC (49) 46th meeting, 22 November 1949]. Minutes state that savings on allocations, per the Chancellor of the Exchequer, 'should be secured by means … which would not place the Government in the position of having to make public' bad news on the blitzed cities. At the time, out of 130k tons of steel for Works' line item 'Misc': 3,000 tons was put to universities while 2,000 tons was earmarked for blitzed cities after many arguments about allocation specifics.

122 TNA: CAB 128/16 [CM (49) 61st Conclusions, 21 October 1949].

123 See Rosenberg, *Economic Planning*, chapter VI, blames the problem more on manpower, as does his article 'Government Controls'.

124 Min Works and Simon, *Distribution of Building Materials and Components* (op cit).

125 TNA: CAB 134/440, 'Capital Investment in 1950', IPC (49) 6, 10 November 1949. The report also states that items which could be 'specifically controlled' totalled only £125 mil., leaving £235 mil. of uncontrolled investment as a target. The total capital investment budget was over £2 billion.

126 TNA: CAB 134/438 [IPC (48) 64 on 14 September 1948] and [IPC (48) 65 on 21 September 1948], also CAB 134/448 [IPC (WP) (48) 173, 23 September 1948]. The change to an allowed amount based on value of building caused some confusion in relation to blitzed cities. The allocation amounts were henceforward the allowed cost of building, *not* grants made to the cities to pay for the cost of rebuilding. See, for example, HC Deb, 18 November 1952, vol. 507, c50-1W, and *The Times*, 'Grants to Bombed Cities', 5 August 1950, 4.

127 TNA: HLG 71/2223. In IPC (49) 66th meeting, 26 October 1949, the minutes state that 'except for existing commitments the blitzed city scheme would have to be abandoned'.

128 TNA: T 229/520, '1950 Programmes for Blitzed Cities' Memorandum by the Minister of Town and Country Planning. EPC (49) 139, 17 November 1949.

129 TNA: T 229/520, Strath to Cripps, via Plowden, 21 November 1949.

130 TNA: T 229/520 [EPC (49) 46th meeting, 22 November 1949, Conclusion 4].

131 TNA: T 229/520, C. D. Smith to Turnbull, 13 December 1949. See also inter alia this file, November to end December 1949.

132 TNA: T 229/520, PV (likely Vinter) to Turnbull, 13 December 1949. The Ministry of Transport added their objections via the EPC, as they were expected to carry roadway items for blitzed cities in their allocations.

133 TNA: T 229/520, Walsh (MTCP) to Turnbull, 4 January 1950. Turnbull later says to a colleague: 'It passes my comprehension how anything in the report can be regarded as singling out these schemes for specially unfavourable treatment.' Turnbull to Hodges, 4 January 1950, same file.

134 TNA: T 229/520, Jay to Cripps, 13 January 1950.

135 TNA: T 229/520, Plowden to Jay, 16 January 1950.

136 TNA: T 229/520, Plowden to Cripps, 9 March 1950. Note that an IPC report in April 1949 had also stated that in the Miscellaneous Building field 'it is impossible for us to make recommendations which could be effectively enforced *except for very small areas*' (author's emphasis). TNA: CAB 134/452 [IPC (WP) (49)72, 25 April 1949, 2].

137 See TNA: CAB 134/441 [IPC (50) 16th meeting, 7 February 1950, item 3]. Two days before this meeting the Ministry of Works had circulated a statement to the IPC on 'Miscellaneous Licensed Building' that stated, '[T]here must be a stop laid upon additional approvals of new blitzed city ... rebuilding schemes.' TNA: CAB 134/453 [IPC (WP)(50) 47, 9 February 1950, item 5, 1].

138 TNA: CAB 134/441 [IPC (50) 2, 24 April 1950], *Capital Investment for 1951 and 1952*.

139 Ibid. By comparison, university allowances were increased from £2.5 to £5 million and spending by the defence ministries was allowed to grow from £22.5 to £40 million. Note that defence spending increased drastically due to the build-up around the Korean and Cold Wars, at the (budgeted) expense of other programmes.

140 The ministry was soon renamed Local Government and Planning (LGP), also taking over housing from the Ministry of Health.

141 TNA: T 229/520, Dalton to Cripps, 25 April 1950. Also 6 April 1950, handwritten. Dalton notes, 'I am very much troubled over the blitzed cities', something he clearly was not as Chancellor, indicating that – like many ministers – he intended to make the most of his position, and hoped to make an impact.

142 TNA: T 229/520, Dalton to Cripps, 25 April 1950. Stokes later wrote to Cripps stating that 'there is absolutely nothing to come out of the miscellaneous programme which can be used for blitzed cities, except the million which I offered you ... and which you refused'. Stokes to Cripps, 18 May 1950, same file.

143 HC Deb, 20 June 1950, vol. 476, c103W (the record says MTCP, though this had changed).

144 TNA: T 229/670, Muir to Turnbull, 24 March 1950. Further attempts to quantify the 'Miscellaneous' field are found in this file, with similar dates.

145 In the DNB entry for W. Strath, Cairncross noted that a problem within the IPC was that 'no one could say with confidence whether the total level of investment in Britain was rising or falling'. While this was true about the level of investment, the concern of the IPC was actually to know how much building labour and particularly materials were available for various 'programmes', rather than to control the *total* investment picture. However they themselves seemed to mix this objective frequently. A. Cairncross, 'Strath, Sir William (1906–1975)', *Oxford DNB* (Oxford, 2004).

146 TNA: T 229/670 [PC (50) 42], see Jay to Cripps on his reaction ('I am shocked'), 23 May 1950.

147 TNA: CAB 134/442 [IPC (51) 3rd (revised), 23 January 1951, 6, item 5]. At the same time discussions took place as to whether the Board of Trade might sponsor work up to £4–5 million nationally, to include hotels, insurance companies and any office buildings which could demonstrate a national benefit from an exemption to the capital investment embargo. See IPC minutes 1951, inter alia. 'Miscellaneous Building Works' was still being budgeted at anywhere from £100 to £400 million.

148 TNA: CAB 134/442 [IPC (51) 1, 17 March 1951], *Report on Capital Investment in 1951, 1952 and 1953*, 5, item xvi (c).

149 Ibid., 30, item 100 (also 25, item 76). At the same time Turnbull issued a long internal statement again suggesting blitzed cities should not receive any more allocations; see CAB 139/209, Turnbull to Redfern, 15 May 1951. They go on to admit that the planning ministry had stated this could force the government to give financial assistance to a number of cities by an extension of grants that had expired a year previously. However, these grants had only been available to a few cities with the greatest need: those who could prove that they were unable to provide basic services. Eight of the blitzed cities received these grants from 1948 to 1951. See Cmd. 9559, *Report of the Ministry of Housing and Local Government for the Period 1950/51 to 1954* (London, 1955).

150 HC Deb, 21 June 1951, vol. 489, c714.

151 Ibid., c719.

152 TNA: T 229/670, Turnbull to Shaw, 28 May 1950, and Turnbull memo to file, 29 May 1950.

153 TNA: T 229/520, Sharp to Turnbull, 23 August 1951.

154 See Cairncross, *Recovery*, chapter 1; Addison, *War*, chapter 2. For contemporary criticism of economic policies, see Shonfield, *British Economic Policy*, esp. 30–3.

155 Labour completed only 50,000 houses in 1946 and 115,000 in 1947, and by 1950 the government had failed to reach targets set at 240,000 per year. See Cmd. 6609, *Housing* (London, 1945).

156 The Tory's 1951 electoral target was 300,000 new houses per year, even though the total output of public housing for the interwar years had only averaged 50,000 per year. See Jones, 'This is Magnificent!', 102. Jones also discusses the almost accidental setting of this target in the Conservative election campaign of 1945. Numbers given by N. Rosenberg are even lower: Rosenberg, 'Government Controls', 348, however, he excludes houses built to replace war-damaged houses. See also O'Hara, 'Social Democratic Space', 285.

157 Cairncross, *Recovery*, chapter 17. Direct controls on steel, removed in 1950, were reinstated from February 1952 to May 1953, 338–9.

158 TNA: CAB 134/457 [IPC (WP) (51) 58, 26 November 1951], Allocation for Blitzed Cities, Note by Ministry of Housing and Local Government; CAB 129/48 [C (51) 52, 18 December 1951], Reductions in Civil Investment in 1952. Also see T 229/521.

159 Macmillan to Butler, 1 January 1952, TNA: T 229/521. It is worth noting that Butler and Macmillan had a long history of 'political football'; see Ian Gilmour, 'Butler, Richard Austen [Rab], Baron Butler of Saffron Walden (1902–1982)', *Oxford DNB* (Oxford, 2004); also see Pimlott, *Butler* and HLG 71/2227 and 2229.

160 TNA: CAB 134/983 [IPC (WP) (52) 30, 26 February 1952], Allocations for … Blitzed Cities, Note by the Joint Secretaries.

161 HC Deb, 5 December 1951, vol. 494, c2491.

162 See Hansard website for relevant HC debates. Much was precipitated by Butler's statement on 29 January 1952 about the severe shortage of building steel, and his comment, '[T]he programmes for rebuilding the blitzed cities, I am very sorry to say, will have to be further delayed.' HC Deb, 29 January 1952, vol. 495, c57.

163 TNA: T 229/521, Turnbull to Strath, 4 April 1952. Turnbull also suggested that Macmillan should be answering to Parliament regarding the allocation decisions, even though he was not meant to be making them, as it was the IPC's role.

164 See, for example, TNA: T 229/521, Macmillan to Butler, 22 May, 5 June, 25 June and 16 July 1952. Just as regularly the letters were passed to Turnbull, who memo'd Plowden about restrictions, even mentioning the attempt to avoid a 'head on

collision' with Macmillan; Turnbull to Plowden, 29 May 1952, same file (and others). One internal reaction to Turnbull noted: 'I doubt if it is worth struggling further with the Ministry of Housing on these small marginal amounts.' GB Blaker to Turnbull, 23 July 1952, same file.

165 BOD-MPP: Macmillan, Dep c. 291 Correspondence 1951–55, fol. 504–505.
166 TNA: T 229/521, Macmillan to Butler, 22 August 1952.
167 Ibid.
168 TNA: T 229/521, Turnbull to Strath, 28 August 1952. The follow-up memo by Strath to Butler restated the usual position, and claimed that 'constitutionally' the responsibility for speaking on the matter rested with Macmillan. Butler replied by hand that he would write and speak to Macmillan, though 'rather less curt' in manner. Strath to Butler, 29 August 1952, same file, handwritten response. A further memo appears from GB Blaker to Turnbull, restating the position that it was the MHLG's own fault for disregarding the government. 23 September 1952, same file.
169 TNA: T 229/521, Butler to Macmillan, 9 September 1952.
170 TNA: CAB 134/983 IPC WP (53) 50, dated 11 October 1953, 'Methods of Controlling Investment, Note by the Chairman', item 5, 2.
171 TNA: CAB 129/55 [C(52)350, 20 October 1952]. A copy is in Appendix II.
172 Ibid. 'Mr. Churchill, Central Hall, Westminster, 15th March 1945'.
173 TNA: CAB 129/55 [C(52)350, 20 October 1952].
174 Ibid.
175 TNA: CAB 129/56 [C(52) 385, 3 November 1952]. An exchange of letters about the impending memo appear in a Treasury file, with the Butler drafts being written by the usual officials. See TNA: T 229/521. A reply came also from the Minister of Works, who generally supported Macmillan, albeit moderately. [C(52) 390, 4 November 1952].
176 TNA: CAB 128/25 [CC (52) 93rd conclusions, 6 November 1952].
177 TNA: T 229/521, Turnbull to Strath, Henley, 8 November 1952.
178 Ibid., Strath to Butler, 11 November 1952.
179 Ibid., Turnbull to Strath, 17 November 1952. For the whole set of papers relating to the issue at this time, see also HLG 71/2229.
180 HC Deb, 25 November 1952, vol. 508, c35-6W; also 2 March 1953, vol. 512, c104.
181 HC Deb, 4 December 1952, vol. 508, c1906-16, esp. 1908 and 1911.
182 HC Deb, 4 December 1952, vol. 508, c1906-13. The prior year Morley had estimated fifty years; see HC Deb, 5 December 1951, vol. 494, c2490.
183 HC Deb, 2 March 1953, vol. 512, c99 (debate in c42-109).
184 Ibid., c104.
185 TNA: CAB 134/982 [IPC (53) 2, 9 April 1953], Investment in 1953 and 1954. Blitzed cities were raised to £6 million. The total programme was £3,173 million. See Table 3.1.
186 TNA: T 229/521 Macmillan to Butler, 6 July 1953.
187 See TNA: T 229/521 esp. May–September 1953. Interestingly the same Treasury file then includes letters from MPs and from outside lobbyists complaining about the 'inadequate' allocations for rebuilding, for example, a letter from the Association of British Chambers of Commerce dated 17 June 1953.
188 Chick, *Industrial Policy*, 206–7.
189 TNA: CAB 134/982 [IPC (53) 3, 28 November 1953], Note by the Secretary of the Cabinet.

190 Discussed at further length in chapter 4, this list was created by the Ministry of Town and Country Planning; see TNA: HLG 71/1571, for details of the Ministry's work relating to the 'blitzed cities programme'.

191 TNA: CAB 21/2975, Bevan to Attlee, 19 August 1947. An early concern had also been raised not by a fellow minister but by a senior official. A letter from Sir Godfrey Ince (Ministry of Labour) to Brook protests that the IPC will be making decisions without the involvement of the departments who the decisions most affect; ibid., Ince to Brook, 8 December 1947.

192 Attlee had told Bevan this would not be the case, that the IPC would provide the information to ministers to make policy decisions, but it seems not to have worked this way, and the IPC often was simply told by Cabinet to make cuts, but left to decide where the cuts went. See CAB 21/2975, Attlee to Bevan, 23 August 1947.

193 Dunleavy and Rhodes, 'Core Executive Studies', 11, whose argument quotes H. Heclo and A. Wildavsky, *The Private Government of Public Money: Community and Policy inside British Politics* (London, 1977, 2nd edn), 369–71.

194 Alford et al., *Economic Planning 1943-1951*, 12.

195 With the exception of a recent article by C. Flinn, ' "The City of Our Dreams"? The Political and Economic Realities of Rebuilding Britain's Blitzed Cities, 1945-54', *TCBH* 23:2 (2011): 221–45.

196 'Ever since the blitz of 1940–41, the people living in the blitzed towns have been led to believe that after this war their towns would be replanned and redeveloped in such a way as to make them better and more beautiful and healthier places to live in … The Prime Minister has taken a hand, and in his usual picturesque language has talked about the new towns rising phoenix-like from the ruins of the old.' Lewis Silkin (MP, Peckham) in HC Deb, 12 July 1944, vol. 401, c1749-50. See also TNA CAB 66/42/17 para 5, and Quarterly Reports by the Ministry of Reconstruction, particularly TNA CAB 66/35/27 para 22.

197 See Table 3.1.

4 Central Control? The Challenges of Postwar Physical Planning

1 Manzoni, *Making Plans*, 40.

2 Though the allocations were at first done by tonnage of steel. They were never, however, allocations of funding, only allowances to begin building.

3 Chapter 5 looks at several cities in depth as examples.

4 Y. Rydin, *Urban and Environmental Planning in the UK* (Basingstoke, 1998), 13–16; Ward, *Planning and Urban Change*, 2–7, 9–27. Also see J. B. Cullingworth, *Town and Country Planning in the UK* (London, 14th edn 2006); A. Sutcliffe, *British Town Planning: The Formative Years* (Leicester, 1981).

5 See M. Swenarton, *Homes Fit for Heroes: The Politics and Architecture of Early State Housing in Britain* (London, 1981). At roughly the same time, the word 'planner' begins to be used to describe a professional, and the Town Planning Institute was founded as well. Ward, *Planning and Urban Change*, 32. Also G. Cherry, *The Evolution of British Town Planning: A History of Town Planning in the United Kingdom During the 20th Century and of the Royal Town Planning Institute, 1914-74* (Leighton Buzzard, 1974).

6 See Hall, *Cities of Tomorrow*, 74–6.

7   Ward, *Planning and Urban Change*, 32–3. Also J. Pendlebury and S. Davoudi in 'Centenary Paper: The Evolution of Planning as an Academic Discipline', *Town Planning Review* 81:6 (2010): 613–46.

8   For a thorough discussion of planning and the TCP Acts, see Cmd. 8204, *Town & Country Planning 1945–51* (London, 1951) particularly chapter I. Also see Rydin, *Urban and Environmental Planning*, 19–23.

9   For 1940s planning specifically, see J. Pendlebury, 'Planning the Historic City: Reconstruction Plans in the United Kingdom in the 1940s', *Town Planning Review* 74 (2003): 371–93.

10 Ward, *Planning and Urban Change*, inter alia; Ward calls the reaction to the three reports a 'test case of the government's commitment to building a better world after the war.' 84. Also see Cmd 8204, 5–8, and Cullingworth, *Environmental*, 53–73.

11 Ward, *Planning and Urban Change*, 83–4. For a contemporary account of issues, see Morris Finer, 'The War Damage Act, 1941', *The Modern Law Review* 5:1 (July 1941): 54–63.

12 *The Times*, 4 October 1944, 5, Issue 49969, col. C. See also 25 October 1944, 5, Issue 49981, col. B: 'to delay further the legislative remedy for the war-damaged areas is a choice which cannot seriously be made'.

13 See J. V. Punter, 'A History of Aesthetic Controls', *Town Planning Review* 58:4 (1986): 351–77; Ward, *Planning and Urban Change*, 86–7.

14 See TNA red books describing the HLG file series, also the TNA website headings for the HLG series. It is also noted here that '[p]rimary responsibility for policy in connection with industrial location remained with the Board of Trade and for housing with the Ministry of Health'.

15 Ibid. Also see Cullingworth, *Environmental*. Though the 1947 Act reduced the number of planning authorities from over 1,400 to 145, the MTCP, beyond its minister and top officials, had only about 230 staff to manage all the applications and paperwork. See Cmd. 8204, 16, 20.

16 Tichelar, 'The Conflict over Property Rights during the Second World War: The Labour Party's Abandonment of Land Nationalization', *Twentieth Century British History* 14:2 (2003): 167. See also J. Lubbock, '1947 and All That: Why Has the Act Lasted So Long?' in Iain Boyd Whyte (ed.), *Man-Made Future: Planning, Education, and Design in Mid-20th Century Britain* (London, 2007), 1–15.

17 HC Deb, 12 May 1947, vol. 437, c1231 (in the series of debates on the new Town & Country Planning Act 1947, 12–14 May 1947).

18 For problems, see TNA: HLG 101/225 T&CP Act 1944 Pt 2: Compensation re Acquisition of Land, dated June 1945–May 1948. Also HC Deb, 13 May 1947, vol. 437, cc1413-35 (esp. 1416); and Cmd. 8204, 9–15.

19 HC Deb, 12 May 1947, vol. 437, c1179.

20 Hasegawa, 'Rise and Fall', 147. See also Cmd. 8204, 40–1, on the MTCP view of repairing defects of the 1944 Act.

21 R. Weight, 'Silkin, Lewis, First Baron Silkin (1889–1972)', *Oxford DNB* (Oxford, 2004); also Ward, *Planning and Urban Change*, 93.

22 See Cullingworth, *Environmental Planning*, 59.

23 D. Heap, *An Outline of Planning Law*, 7th edn (London, 1978), 12–14; also Ward, *Planning and Urban Change*, 99–101.

24 HC Deb, 432, 29 January 1947, 947 (2nd reading T&CP Act); HC Deb, 437, 20 May 1947, 2197 (3rd reading). For the continued importance of the 1947 Act, see also The Town and Country Planning Association, *Your Place & Mine, Reinventing*

Planning: The Report of the TCPA Inquiry into the future of planning (London, 1999),
6. For the aesthetic impact of the 1947 Act, see J. Lubbock, '1947 and All That'. Also
see J. B. Cullingworth, *British Planning: 50 Years of Urban and Regional Planning*
(Linton, 1999).

25 Heap and Ward as note 23.

26 The 1947 Act also strengthened controls over historic buildings, introducing the
listing system, though controls were not yet legislated to the extent seen today. See
Ward, *Planning and Urban Change*, 101.

27 The 1947 Act retained these sections under the Tenth Schedule. See R. Doble, 4
and Cmd. 8204: *Town & Country Planning 1945-51*, 40–5, 181. Also see Ministry
of Town and Country Planning. Cmd. 7006 *Town and Country Planning Act,
1947: Explanatory Memorandum* (HMSO, 1947) and Central Office of Information.
Town and Country Planning: The 1947 Act: 144 Questions and Answers
(HMSO, 1949).

28 Bad layout mainly referred to slums, that is, unliveable, unhealthy neighbourhoods.
See Cmd. 8204, 188.

29 Section 2(2) was intended to assist local authorities who had been slow to plan or to
agree internally on plans and so had not submitted a DO in a timely manner. There
was also a Section 10 for 'Land bought for miscellaneous purposes', Cmd. 8204,
185, 188. Also see R. L. Doble, *A Guide to the Town and Country Planning Act, 1947*
(Current Law Guide No 2) (London, 1947), 1–5.

30 See Cmd. 8204, 40–5.

31 See, for example, the statement that developers were 'busy buying up bombed
plots', in N. Tiratsoo, J. Hasegawa, T. Mason and T. Matsumura, *Urban
Reconstruction in Britain and Japan, 1945-1955: Dreams, Plans and Realities*
(Luton, 2002), 9.

32 No specific archival evidence on this point was found, beyond allusions in *The Times*,
although House of Commons debates on the 1944 Act often implied such issues. See,
for example, *The Times*, 4 October 1944, 5, Issue 49969, col. C; and 25 October 1944,
5, Issue 49981, col. B.

33 Many local authorities could not meet this deadline and applied for extensions.
See, for example, the next chapter re: Liverpool. Cmd. 9559 *Report of the Ministry
of Housing and Local Government* shows that 126 of 148 were extended; see 61 &
Appendix VI.

34 The Ministry of Works, as well as the Board of Trade, liaised with the MTCP on
licenses for buildings in blitzed city centres. This is covered further below.

35 Coventry had been planning to make changes to their city plans since before the war;
see Tiratsoo, *Reconstruction, Affluence*.

36 See Chapter 2: this was after the Ministry of Works and Building, then Works and
Planning, had shifted their planning functions into the MTCP.

37 TNA: HLG 88/8, Overton? [illegible] BT to Whiskard MTCP, 15 April 1943.

38 For terms of reference, see Chapter 2; for an example of the preparation and visits and
so on, see TNA: HLG 79/259 on Hull.

39 Hasegawa, *Replanning*, 139, 39.

40 TNA: HLG 88/8-13, 15. See also Hasegawa, *Replanning*, 13–16.

41 TNA: HLG 88/8-13, esp. HLG 88/10.

42 TNA: HLG 71/914, dated 1943–45.

43 Ibid., Neal to Pepler, 22 January 1945.

44 Ibid., Wells to Pepler, 5 February 1945.

45 Both W. S. Morrison and the MTCP official Neal discussed the priority as being crucial in the first two to five years immediately following the war. TNA: HLG 71/914, paper dated 25 January 1945 [R (45) 17].

46 MTCP, *The Redevelopment of Central Areas* (London, 1947). Larkham and Lilley claim this was substantially complete early in the war; see *Planning the 'City of Tomorrow'*, 7.

47 See Larkham and Lilley, *Planning the 'City of Tomorrow'*, 12–20.

48 C. Woodbury, 'Britain Begins to Rebuild Her Cities', *The American Political Science Review* 41:5 (1947): 901–20. From this perspective, the impetus of reconstruction rhetoric, begun in wartime, lasted into the peace.

49 Essex and Brayshay, 'Boldness', 451–2. For the success of Coventry's exhibitions, see P. Hubbard, L. Faire and K. Lilley, 'Contesting the Modern City: Reconstruction and Everyday Life in Post-War Coventry', *Planning Perspectives* 18:4 (2003): 384.

50 At Plymouth, George Pepler is said to have recommended Abercrombie (Essex and Brayshay, 'Boldness'); at Exeter, Morrison encouraged the appointment of a consultant and they hired Sharp who was then engaged on a project with the MTCP; at Hull, officials were told by Jowitt and Portal that they needed an eminent planner, and the city was already being surveyed by Lock who was a Housing Centre colleague of Abercrombie's. Internal correspondence also shows the MTCP feared having to approve Hull's Abercrombie plan as a public exhibition went ahead, TNA: HLG 79/261, 23 November 1944, Gatliff to RPO Region 2.

51 MTCP officials, as shown in Chapter 3, approved blitzed cities' building work but were unable to issue the building licences, as will be further discussed here.

52 See in TNA: T 229/520, 521 and HLG 71/2222 and 2227.

53 See TNA: HLG 71/601 and 602: War-Damaged and Reconstruction Areas: Minister's meeting with Local Administrations, October and November 1947 (2 part file).

54 Ibid. The MTCP invited four officials from each authority, but almost every authority brought seven or eight attendees.

55 Ibid.

56 TNA: HLG 71/601, Walsh to Secretary, 29 July 1947.

57 Ibid. Full transcripts of Silkin's talk as well as the full Q&A sessions that followed are saved in HLG files 71/601 and 602 and 71/34. Concerns varied from city to city and conference to conference.

58 TNA: HLG 71/601, transcript of conference, 6 November 1947.

59 Examples of relations with cities include TNA: HLG 79/259–262 for Hull, 79/307–313 for Liverpool and HLG 71/1284 for Exeter. Also see MTCP issued documents such as Circular 39 (London: HMSO, 1948).

60 Correspondence in both T229/521-521 and various HLG files show constant mentions of visits and deputations and ministries referring groups and officials and so on back to other departments.

61 See TNA: CAB 134/438 [IPC (48)38, 9 June 1948, 1–3].

62 Ibid., 1 (author's emphasis).

63 The planning ministry had evolved out of other ministries; so it was essentially new, and therefore still working out what its exact role was to be.

64 See in TNA: HLG 71/1571–1572, 2223–2230.

65 TNA: CAB 134/438 [IPC (48)38, 9 June 1948, 1–3]. Bowen (BT) added that he did not mean to include the City of London in this group as it 'presented a special problem'. See also Bowen memo in T 229/520 dated 18 June 1948.

66 TNA: T 229/520, Sharp to Bavin (Cabinet Office), 12 June 1948.

67 See Chapter 3, note 113.

68 TNA: HLG 71/2222, Sharp to Walsh, 27 July 1949.
69 The primary file series, which include MTCP and MLGP files, though labelled HLG, are in TNA: HLG 71/1570–1572 and 71/2222–2230.
70 Ibid. For an excellent example of a position paper, see: Sharp to Silkin, 16 May 1950 and 17 May 1950 in HLG 71/2224.
71 See TNA: HLG 71/2222 and 2224. 'In working out these allocations … it was necessary to see [they] went to places that could spend it.' Walsh to Sharp, 2 May 1950, in HLG 71/2224. See also the MTCP/HQBC file HLG 102/271 which details the internal work of investigation into blitzed cities' requirements and so on.
72 The same list is found, always in the same order – by region numbers – throughout many HLG files, as well as in IPC files.
73 There is one document hinting only that lists included cities ready to start building, TNA: HLG 71/2222, Sharp to Bowen (BT), 27 September 1948. References to 'the list' of blitzed cities can be found in the wartime files examining cities beyond those chosen for the special Advisory Panel investigation. See TNA: HLG 71/1245.
74 See especially TNA: HLG 71/601, 602.
75 The regions appear to be the same as civil defence regions (i.e., on bomb census maps found in TNA: HO 193).
76 A few areas not included on the list of eighteen, such as Birkinhead, Salford and Wallasey, may have been lumped together with their 'parent' cities, that is, Liverpool and Manchester. Of course there were more than the twenty-one cities listed with war damage, and other files in the HLG series do have more survey information, particularly from wartime. Possibly, the Public Record Office did not keep the files with details of the choices.
77 This can cause some confusion, when it is thought that the 'allocations' of hundreds of thousands of pounds might be allowances given to the city in grant money, but as shown the only grants given were towards interest payments on land purchases. See, for example, Northern Ireland Ministry of Health to Wood, MTCP, 4 September 1950, in TNA: HLG 71/2224.
78 Local authority officials often assumed that allocations were not forthcoming because the MTCP was not allowing them. This, of course, was incorrect. For disgruntled cities such as Bristol and Southampton, see the city chapters in Hasegawa, *Replanning*.
79 See especially TNA: HLG 71/2223 letters and memos in March 1950.
80 For example, see TNA: HLG 71/2224 (and others in the series).
81 TNA: HLG 71/601 and 602 contain statistics collected by the MTCP. These are shown in Table 4.2.
82 See Table 4.2.
83 See, for example, files for applications for Liverpool in HLG: 79/310–313. The application files are not organized in a series (although the reconstruction of blitzed cities files are); see note 68 and HLG 102/271.
84 See P. J. Larkham, 'Hostages to History? The Surprising Survival of Critical Comments about British Planning and Planners c. 1942–1955', *Planning Perspectives* 26:3 (July 2011): 487–91.
85 The only documentation found in any ministry files or in Attlee's papers relating to blitzed cities was correspondence in 1947 with Silkin. Attlee wrote to ask about complaints he was receiving from Labour groups in Bristol about their perceived (or real?) poor treatment by MTCP officials. TNA: HLG 71/633, Attlee to Silkin, 1 August 1947. Also see Larkham, 'Hostages', 487–91.

86   For example, in TNA: HLG 71/34 and 71/601, including reductions by Hull, Liverpool and Birmingham.

87   See also Hasegawa, *Replanning*, chapters 4–6.

88   See Larkham, 'Hostages', which mentions 'the apparent sense of superiority of the Ministry over all other actors' (490). In TNA files there is extensive documentation on specific cities, including internal MTCP correspondence about such issues, for example, TNA: HLG 71/1284 on Exeter. Often the patronizing or superior remarks came from the Planning Technique group.

89   See the following chapter. Also see examples in Hasegawa, *Replanning* (Bristol, Coventry and Southampton).

90   An example of this is provided in Chapter 5 which discusses the issues faced in Hull, where the extensive network of railways created traffic problems from large numbers of level crossings. But the onus was then on a private company to pay for the new layouts, which of course was a huge barrier to the plans. Nationalization of the railways did not change this situation.

91   An exception was his intervention, in November 1949, through the Economic Policy Committee (hierarchically above the IPC). This was initiated, however, by his officials. TNA: HLG 102/263 '1950 Programme for Blitzed Cities', 17 November 1949.

92   Changes were as follows: The Ministry of Local Government and Planning was formed in January 1951 by the merger of the Ministry of Town and Country Planning with the housing, local government and environmental health divisions of the Ministry of Health. From November 1951, following the election of a Conservative government, the title of the department was changed to Ministry of Housing and Local Government. The 'new' department retained all the functions of the Ministry of Local Government and Planning. TNA website, HLG series header.

93   B. Pimlott, *Diaries of Hugh Dalton* (London, 1985), 516, 25 March 1951.

94   LSE-PEP: Dalton MSS, 2/9 Papers of 1950–51. Dalton to Attlee (draft), 23 December 1950 (fol. 118).

95   See Jones, 'This Is Magnificent!'. Also H. Macmillan, *Tides of Fortune, 1945–1955* (London, 1969).

96   BOD-MSS; Macmillan Dep c. 731 (Speeches, MHLG), Speech at Association of Municipal Corporations. Folkestone 18 September 1952 (fol. 332–3).

97   Macmillan, *Tides*, 414.

98   Cullingworth, *Environmental*, 87, describes a similar issue, clearly ongoing. Also Larkham, 'Hostages'.

99   Cullingworth, *Environmental*, xii–xiii.

100 Ibid.

101 See TNA: HLG 71/914 for priorities and throughout files HLG 71/2222–2230, and 1571–72.

5   Local Constraints: The Cities of Hull, Exeter and Liverpool

1   See Chapters 2 and 4 for test case panels in wartime. Also see TNA: HLG 71/596 War Damaged and Reconstruction Areas: Shops Factories and Commercial Buildings, Information on War Damage (dated 1945) and HLG 71/1245 War Damaged Towns (Non-Panel) Special Investigation (dated November 1943–January 1945).

2 For more information and detail on provincial raids in general, see J. Gardiner, *Wartime: Britain 1939–1945* (London, 2005), 350–435.

3 G. Wilkinson, *Hull* (Salisbury, 2006), 10. Originally 'Kingstown-upon-Hull'.

4 For a brief history of Hull, see: Hull History Centre (HHC) L711: City Council of Kingston-upon-Hull (HCC), *Planning in Action: An Account of the Aims and Achievements in Kingston-upon-Hull* (undated) c. 1958–59, 9–11.

5 Ibid. See also G. Jackson, *Hull in the Eighteenth Century: A Study in Economic and Social History* (Oxford, 1972); and E. Gillett and K. A. MacMahon, *A History of Hull* (Hull, 1989).

6 See HCC, *Planning in Action*.

7 D. Atkinson in *Hull: Culture, History, Place* (Liverpool, 2017), 245–7. Also P. Graystone, *The Blitz on Hull, 1940–45* (York, 1991).

8 HHC: C TPG 4, 'Central Area Plan', 29 August 1950, from file 'Kingston upon Hull Scheme General', original ref: 102.24.1, 1–2. (The file appears to be a damage and reconstruction survey completed to comply with a request from the MTCP, and answers questions as found in files such as TNA: HLG 79/259.)

9 This could be due to Hull docks and industry being the primary targets, which also would have been emptier during night raids than during daytime. See Tables 2.2 and 4.2 for statistics.

10 Graystone, *Blitz on Hull*. Probably for similar reasons Hull also has the dubious distinction of being the last place in Britain to receive German bombs before the war ended.

11 Ibid. Also see *The Times*, 8 October 1952, 3, Issue 52437, col. D: 'The cloak of secrecy veiled from public knowledge the measure of war devastation suffered by [Hull]'.

12 HHC Town Clerk's Office 'Memorandum on the effect of the war upon the city and its future planning and reconstruction', February 1942. (Also found in TNA: HLG 79/259.)

13 HHC: L.711 A, Hull Corporation; Parliamentary and General Purposes Committee, 'Post-war re-planning and reconstruction/report of deputation who interviewed Lord Portal and Sir William Jowitt in London on the 5th June 1942'. 6 pages. The notes show that the Lord Mayor and three Hull MPs were part of the deputation.

14 Lord Portal was then [as in text above these are uppercase Minister etc] minister of works and planning, Jowitt was to become the minister of reconstruction. For their exact roles, see Table 2.1.

15 Certainly the report submitted in February 1942 is the same as cited in note 12, above, the Town Clerk's 'Memorandum on the effect …'. This and a report dated March 1940 are found in TNA: HLG 79/259.

16 HHC: L.711 A, 'Post-war re-planning … report of deputation' (no page numbers).

17 Ibid.

18 Ibid.

19 Ibid.

20 Ibid.

21 'Civic Diagnosis'. Printed by the Housing Centre, but also printed in the *Architects' Journal* as 'Hull Regional Survey', 29 July 1943, and partially printed in a journal called *World Review*, July 1943. (Copies in HHC and TNA: HLG 79/259.)

22 The Leverhulme funding was supplemented by the Housing Centre of London, the subsequent publisher is named as the Housing Centre, 'Civic Diagnosis'.

23 Tiratsoo 'Labour and the Reconstruction of Hull, 1945–51', 126–9.

24 P. Jones, '" … A Fairer and Nobler City" – Lutyens and Abercrombie's Plan for the City of Hull 1945', *Planning Perspectives* 13:3 (1998): 301–16.

25 'Civic Diagnosis', front cover.

26 See excerpt from speech given on 14 July 1943 in the *Architects' Journal*, 'Civic Diagnosis', 29 July 1943, 13.

27 See documents in TNA: HLG 79/261, Hull C.B. Replanning General, dated 1944–48.

28 See Tiratsoo, 'Hull', 128–30.

29 A new book on Hull has an excellent summary of the war and utopianism of the new plans: D. Atkinson, 'Trauma, Resilience and Utopianism in Second World War Hull', in McDonaugh et al. (eds), *Hull: Culture, History, Place* (Liverpool, 2017), 239–69.

30 HHC: L.711 A, 'Post-war re-planning … report of deputation'.

31 TNA: HLG 79/259 'Advisory Panel on Redevelopment of City Centres: Short Notes on the Seven Cities' (preliminary to visits), dated 25 May 1943, 2.

32 See especially notes and a draft letter to the town clerk of Hull from the MTCP, dated 13 February 1946 in TNA: HLG 79/262 (Hull C.B. Replanning & Reconstruction, Railways Level Crossings). HHC: L388.1, Traffic volumes and traffic delays at the principal level crossings, dated March 1954. Also in 1954 the *Hull & Yorkshire Times* published an extensive article on the problems with the level crossings, 'No easy answer to the bugbear of the gates', *HYT*, 5 July 1954. Note that the Ministry of War Transport dropped 'War' from its name in July 1945.

33 HHC: DPD/14/DH/530/1, Dock Reconstruction/Engineers Post war reconstruction. Notes on meeting 25 May 1945. HLG files show meetings may also have happened in 1944 (TNA: HLG 79/261).

34 Discussed in Section 5 of Lock's 'Civic Diagnosis'. The number of level crossings in the centre was between eleven and thirteen (sources vary).

35 HHC: DPD/14/DH/530/1, Dock Reconstruction/Engineers Post war reconstruction. Meeting minutes dated 14 March 1946.

36 HHC: DPD/14/DH/530/2, Dock Reconstruction/Engineers Post war reconstruction. Minutes of LNER Board of Directors Meeting, 29 November 1946. For further negotiations and meetings, see also the third file in the same series: DPD/14/DH/530/3. There is no explanation in the files for the exact reason why the fish trade (who owned their docks) opted out of dock redevelopment discussions.

37 E. Lutyens and P. Abercrombie, *A Plan for the City & County of Kingston upon Hull* (London, 1945). City engineer's plan can be found in TNA: HLG 79/261 (undated but 1945 per correspondence).

38 TNA: HLG 79/261, Cameron to Gatliff, 4 June 1945.

39 TNA: HLG 79/261. 'Discussion of Hull CB', meeting minutes, 12 June 1945. Decisions on the river plans also held up sewer rebuilding, affecting housing.

40 Interestingly, in the file above (12 June 1945) MTCP officials worry about whether *they* will be blamed for the delays due to the lack of approval from the MTCP and MOT on roadway and level crossing issues.

41 TNA: HLG 79/261, Bullock, Town Clerk to Gatliff, 11 October 1945. The response on 12 October 1945 suggested it would be detrimental to Hull's planning.

42 TNA: HLG 79/261, Gatliff to Bullock, 17 November 1945.

43 Ibid. Gatliff concludes: 'there is a sense of desolation, frustration and depression'. Gatliff notes on Hull visit, 5 December 1945. As also noted by Tiratsoo, the comments by this official seem quite prejudiced against Hull. See 'Hull', 141.

44 Ibid., Hill to Gatliff, 21 December 1945. Asked if he thought the problem was technical or financial, Gatliff replied (in a handwritten note on the page) that neither

was the bigger issue, but that implementation would take too long and Hull would likely lose a large amount of the trade and industry they should be attracting.

45 Tiratsoo, 'Hull', 126.

46 For a detailed political analysis, see ibid., 131–4.

47 *Hull Daily Mail (HDM)*, 22 July 1946. As will be shown, the DO application was later drastically reduced in size. There is no documented evidence for the reasons the Corporation did this.

48 See, for example, the appendices in Cmd. 8204. Plymouth was a notable exception, having managed to comprehensively redevelop an extremely large central area, though much of the credit goes to the temerity of Lord Astor. See Essex and Brayshay, 'Boldness' and Table 4.2 (DOs and CPOs).

49 See Essex and Brayshay, 'Boldness' and 'Vision'; and Hasegawa, *Replanning*, esp. chapter 6 on Bristol.

50 HHC: Kingston-upon-Hull Municipal Corporation. Minutes of the Council (hereafter HMC Council Minutes), 1946–47, RCSC, 25 November 1946. (Ibid., 28 January 1946, the exhibit took place 19 February–9 March 1946.)

51 Tiratsoo, 'Hull', 132. Also see MTCP notes in TNA: HLG 79/269. 'Kingston Upon Hull: Case History', 5. The notes show that in February 1946, on his first visit, Silkin had suggested submission of a DO covering as large an area as possible, which would then be 'considered sympathetically'. This clearly did not align with the (later) outlook of his officials.

52 HHC: HMC Council Minutes, 1946–47, vol. 1, 6 February 1947, 56–8.

53 Ibid.

54 Ibid.

55 Davidge was also responsible for plans in Chester, Wallasey, Croydon, Swindon and more; see Larkham and Lilley, *Planning the 'City of Tomorrow'*.

56 The letter claimed this was to avoid 1944 Act procedural steps, which would cost time and money. TNA: HLG 79/268. Bullock (Town Clerk) to Secretary, MTCP, 4 July 1947. See also HMC Minutes of Committees, Town Planning Committee, 1946–47, vol. 6.

57 TNA: HLG 79/268. Payne and Payne to MTCP, 5 July 1947.

58 Ibid., conference minutes, 12 August 1947.

59 Ibid.

60 MTCP files include one full file on this subject alone. See TNA: HLG 79/268 Hull C.B. Redevelopment Proposals: Location of Shopping Area. Oddly, MTCP notes dated July 1947 in the general replanning file show that a technical planning meeting was held at which the Town Planning Committee chair (Body) had presented a new tentative plan, which all agreed was a preferable scheme, but nothing seems to have come of this. Stephenson to Walsh, 17 July 1947 in HLG 79/261.

61 See correspondence throughout HLG 79/268 with the solicitors for the group constantly contacting MTCP officials over their continued grievances. (No correspondence indicates that the MTCP ever told the group that they would deal with Hull Corporation alone, although legally they could have made such a statement.)

62 HHC: HMC, Council Minutes, 4 December 1947, 33–8. Per *Hull and Yorkshire Times* (*HYT*), 19 December 1949, they were submitted on 23 December 1947.

63 Details of this application, that is, portion of area destroyed totally, partly destroyed area, area of roadways or open space and so on are found in HHC: C TPG 5, Orders/ Proceedings, 'In the matter of applications for Declaratory Orders', 1 June 1948.

Only twenty-six acres was undamaged, and kept in the application as part of the redevelopment plan.

64 Ibid., 3.

65 HHC: L.711 CC *Replanning Kingston upon Hull*, Hull and District Property Owners' Protection Association (HDPOPA), no date but 1947–48. The planning ministry had a file on this group as well: TNA: HLG 79/270, dated 1948.

66 HHC: HMC, Council Minutes, 1947–49, vol. 1, 3 June 1948, 99–100.

67 Ibid.

68 HHC: U DDMM/x1/9/51 Pamphlet. Replanning of Central Hull. Issued by Chamber of Trade (no date but 1949).

69 Ibid. (caps are original).

70 See Cmd. 8204, Appendix IV, 181. Approval date 22 February 1949. It may be worth noting that Hull had received approvals from 1946 to 1948 for a number of CPOs under Section 2(2) but all for industrial and housing areas (approximately fifty-three acres total). HLG files also show that Hull had agreed in advance for some areas to be included in the application but they were excluded by the MTCP upon approval; see HLG 79/261, Gatliff to Vince, no date (but October 1947).

71 HHC: C DBRI/6/6 Confirmation of CPO, 3 February 1949. Also HMC: Council Minutes 1947–49, vol. 1, 162, 3 February 1949.

72 See HHC: C TPG/2 Development Plan 1948–50 for various files including DOs and CPOs; objections are contained in a book for the purpose, listed by site address. Also see summaries in, especially, HMC, Committee Minutes, 1946–47, vol. 6, Town Planning Committee, inter alia.

73 HC Deb, 1 February 1949, vol. 460 cc1485-6; also see Chapters 3 and 4.

74 TNA: HLG 79/260, Tetlow to Vince, 25 January 1949.

75 Hammond's negotiations had included allowing some footprint modification for road widening on Ferensway at the rail station. The store's history and this episode in particular is found in John Markham, *Hammond's of Hull* (Beverley, 2004), especially chapter 'The Battle to Rebuild'. See also stories in the *Yorkshire Post (YP)*, 2 February 1950 and *Hull Daily Mail (HDM)*, 6 February 1950.

76 See *HYT*, 19 December 1949.

77 Ibid. and *YP*, 2 February 1950.

78 See Cmd. 8204, 35–6 and 45, for more on Section 19 and details of the 1947 Act.

79 HHC: TP Box 8498B Reconstruction in Hull. 'Reconstruction of War Damaged Areas', Notes on a speech given to the Town Planning Institute, no author, no date (but 1948), 21.

80 Circular 39, 'Limitations on Land Acquisitions for Planning Purposes during Present Period of Restrictions', 16 March 1948.

81 See also H. Jackson, 'Problems of Planning and Reconstruction in Kingston-upon-Hull', *Journal of the Institute of Municipal Engineers* (3 February 1948): 403–16.

82 See, for example, HHC: HCCM, 1946–50, and *Hull Daily Mail (HDM)*, 6 February 1950.

83 See above note 58 [check]; also HLG 79/261, meeting minutes, 16 March 1946.

84 TNA: HLG 79/261, Stephenson to Walsh, 17 July 1947.

85 Ibid., technical planning meeting, 15 July 1947. In fact the city was caught between the MTCP and the MOT; see Bullock to Secretary, MTCP, 25 February 1949, re: roadways approval. Replies internally show officials worried that they 'won't be able to complain of the ineptitude of Hull' if MOT is a problem, Walsh to Vince, 1 March 1949.

86 For example, HLG 79/261, Gatliff to Vince (no date but October 1947).

87 Ibid., Vince to Bullock, 8 October 1947.

88 Ibid., Gatliff to Bullock, 2 July 1948.

89 TNA: HLG 79/260, Tetlow to Vince, 25 January 1949; Vince to Walsh, 25 February 1949, also shows the MTCP intends to tell the Chamber of Trade that they will only deal with city officials. Later the MOT rebuffs the Chamber by noting their objections to road proposals but stating that they would negotiate only with the Corporation on the matter, MOT letter (copy), 7 April 1949. Also Chamber to MOT, 12 March 1949.

90 Ibid., planning technique notes, 5 March 1949; draft letter to Bullock, unsigned, 31 March 1949.

91 Ibid., Bullock to Walsh, MTCP, 11 July 1949.

92 *HDM*, 6 February 1950.

93 *HYT*, 4 March 1950, 'The New Hull: Official Reconstruction Proposals'. This was apparently not sent to the MTCP who claimed in May that they had seen nothing more than an outline, nothing was yet formally submitted in advance of (or with) impending CPOs (awaiting appeal in the courts).

94 TNA: HLG 79/260, see memos and meeting minutes dated 20 and 22 May 1950.

95 Ibid. To be clear, the amount shown was a licence limit, not funding or grants given to the city.

96 Ibid., Coates to MTCP, 22 January 1951.

97 Ibid., Tetlow to Gilliem, 14 March 1951.

98 Ibid., Tetlow claimed also that after the MTCP had agreed to changes suiting the Chamber, the Chamber had still continued to battle new perceived issues.

99 Ibid.

100 *HDM*, 19 and 25 June 1951.

101 *HDM*, 19 June 1951; *The Manchester Guardian*, 22 June 1951 'Changes in Investment Plan'; *The Times*, 22 June 1951, 6, Issue 52034, col. G 'Cuts in Civil Investment'.

102 TNA: T 229/521, Ellis (Works) to Blaker (Treasury), 18 December 1951.

103 HC Deb, 25 November 1952, vol. 508, cc35-6W, 'Bombed Cities (Reconstruction)', Hull received £400,000.

104 HC Debs, 2 March 1953, vol. 512, cc42-109, 'Blitzed Towns', Morley (Southampton) col. 45-6.

105 Ibid., col. 76-7.

106 Ibid.

107 Ibid., col. 78.

108 See, for example, the report from 1954 on the ongoing issues: HHC, L.388.1, Alston report, 'Traffic volumes ...', March 1954. It was estimated that delays cost business at least £500 per day.

109 For issues with homeowners having to move for industry or roadways, see throughout the CPO files: HHC: C DBRI/6/6, C TPG 5, Orders/Proceedings. For later objections to Development Plan, C TPG/2.

110 Larkham and Lilley, 'Planning the City', 9. Also P. Jones, 'A Fairer and Nobler City', 301.

111 See *The Architects' Journal*, 21 August 1952, 222; *Express & Echo (E&E)*, 27 August 1952; *Western Morning News (WMN)*, 24 December 1952; and BBC news, 'Exeter tops BBC poll on Britain's blandest high street 2005': http://news.bbc.co.uk/1/hi/england/devon/4610965.stm (5 June 2005).

112 The term was applied by Baron Gustav von Stumm, speaking after destruction of the historic city of Lübeck in March 1942. See N. Rothnie, *The Baedeker Blitz*

(Shepperton, 1992), 131. While the British government claimed that Lübeck was a military target, news reports at the time made it clear that the targets were either false or widely missed. Historians since have tended to ascribe the bombing of cities like Lübeck, Rostock and Cologne as having been targeted to hit at the morale of the German civilian population. Therefore the subsequent raids were considered reprisal raids, and Exeter was the first hit. See also A. C. Grayling, *Among the Dead Cities* (London, 2006), 50, 51.

113 T. Sharp, *Exeter Phoenix* (London, 1946), 42.

114 These are approximate figures, all agreed by several sources. See Cmd. 8204, 60; H. Gayton, 'City Redevelopments: I. Exeter', *Town and Country Planning* 26 (1958): 378–80; W. G. Hoskins, *Two Thousand Years in Exeter* (Chichester, 2004); G. Goss, 'Exeter – A New Chapter in a Long History', *Enterprise* 2 (1957): 11–13; D. Davies, *The Bombing of Exeter* (Exeter, 1973); N. Venning, *Exeter: The Blitz and Rebirth of the City* (Exeter, 1988).

115 As they were mainly businesses they would have brought in higher business rates.

116 Excluding London, see TNA: BT 64/1111 dated 1942. See also Table 4.2. The nearest small blitzed city on the list was Norwich with losses estimated at £88,275. Exeter appears in various records with differing population figures but all are near £65,000 as of 1943. Of the blitzed cities the nearest in size to Exeter is Southampton, an industrial and port city with nearly double Exeter's population.

117 See C. Flinn '"Exeter Phoenix": Politics and the Rebuilding of a Blitzed City', *Southern History* 30 (2008): 104–27 (a preliminary version of this research).

118 Reactions to the bombing vary greatly; however, see B. Beaven and J. Griffiths, 'The Blitz, Civilian Morale and the City: Mass-Observation and Working-Class Culture in Britain, 1940–41', *Urban History* 26:1 (1999): 71–88.

119 No mention was found in local press, City Council meeting minutes or in Hansard before April of 1943.

120 Devon Record Office (DRO) and West Country Studies Library (WCSL) Exeter City Council minutes (ECCM), 20 April 1943. The deputation group included the town clerk, the mayor, an alderman, two city councillors, the chair of the Finance Committee and the city treasurer. No other city appears to have taken up the same matter of rate loss (in Parliament) until late in the war (November–December 1944). The (Conservative) MP for Exeter, A. C. Reed, spoke only immediately after the raid, on 3 June 1942, urging financial assistance for those bombed out of their homes (HC Deb, vol. 390, col. 782). Reed did not speak again on the issue in the 1942–43 session of parliament, or at all in 1943–44, although City Council minutes state their appreciation for his assistance in this matter (WCSL, ECCM, 20 April 1943). Also see TNA: CAB 102/878 (War Damage Commission).

121 See, for example, in HC Deb, 18 November 1947, vol. 444, cc988-1101; HC Deb, 29 June 1951, vol. 489, cc1855-68; HC Deb, 5 December 1951, vol. 494, cc2478-528. It is possible other cities sent similar deputations, though no evidence of this has been found.

122 WCSL: ECCM 28 September 1943.

123 WCSL: ECCM 28 September 1943, 26 October 1943; Sharp Archives University of Newcastle (hereafter SAUN): agreement signed 10 May 1944. Sharp was one of the most prolific postwar planners, completing more than ten plans for cities or counties in the 1940s and 1950s; see Larkham and Lilley, *Planning the 'City of Tomorrow'*.

124 K. M. Stansfield, 'Sharp, Thomas Wilfred (1901–1978)', rev. *Oxford DNB* (Oxford, 2004).

125 J. Brierley, 'Exeter 1939–1974: The Reconstruction of a City' (former City Engineer), unpublished MA thesis, 1980 (held by WCSL), 170. J. Pendlebury, 'The Urbanism of Thomas Sharp', *Planning Perspectives* 24:1 (2009): 3–27. While and Tait, 'Exeter', 77–97.

126 WCSL: City Council minutes, 27 February 1945. On 29 May 1945, the minutes also stated a recommendation that 'each political section in the Council should now be requested to approach their respective National Headquarters with a view to their assisting the City' (*sic*). Not in Council minutes, the local press also reported an official visit of complaint to the MTCP; see *Western Morning News* (WMN), 10 May 1950. The February 1945 delegation was composed of the same members as the prior visit to the Ministry of Health, with the addition of the Sheriff and a request for local MP Reed to accompany them; the September 1945 note does not name attendees, but does state that the new MP Maude was asked to join the delegation. The Council continued to send delegations until at least 1952, later complaining about the amounts of their allocations. (See ECCM and local news.)

127 HC Deb, 17 October 1945, vol. 414, cc1293 ff. Again, later in the 1945–46 session he inquired about housing assistance for bombed cities. HC Deb, 31 January 1946, vol. 418, c254 WA.

128 Process initiated in City Council minutes 24 July 1945 (WCSL), see also *WMN*, 28 February 1945, 29 September 1945, 15 March 1946, 26 September 1946, 5 December 1946 and 25 June 1947; *Express & Echo (E&E)*, 16 May 1945, 13 March 1946, 14 November 1946, and 26 February 1947. Note that the Board of Trade did not give business relief, the only assistance would have come from the War Damage Commission.

129 Venning, *Exeter*, 20. Venning worked in engineering for Exeter City Council for twenty-nine years.

130 Ibid., 12.

131 *E&E*, 13 March 1945. It had been sixteen months since he began the contract.

132 *E&E*, 28 December 1945, also the *WMN* reported on 15 January 1946 that 20,438 people – nearly one-third of the city's population – had attended the exhibition of Sharp's proposals.

133 Ibid. Also Sharp, *Exeter Phoenix*.

134 Sharp, *Exeter Phoenix*. Also see Pendlebury, 'Urbanism'; and While and Tait, 'Exeter'.

135 *WMN*, 3 January 1946 – Sub-heading 'But Who Will Pay? Asks City M.P.'

136 Venning, *Exeter*, 18; Brierley, 'Exeter 1939–1974', 170. *WMN*, 13 March 1946. More on this in the following chapter.

137 Cmd. 8204, 60.

138 TNA: HLG 71/2222, 2223, and MTCP Circular 39, 16 March 1948.

139 For all DO and CPO dates, see Cmd. 8204, Appendix IV, 181–95.

140 TNA: HLG 79/171 War damage redevelopment: notice of motion: Declaratory Order, Exeter CB. See also local news reports dated February 1945 through 1949 (available WCSL).

141 See D. Childs, 'Exeter: A Survey', *The Architects' Journal*, 21 August 1952, 216; G. Goss, 'Exeter – A New Chapter', *Local Government, Commercial and Industrial Enterprise* 2:2 (1957): 11; G. Goss, 'The Economics of Rebuilding', in R. Hackett, *The Municipal Journal* 61:3158 (1953): 1836.

142 Cmd. 8204, Appendixes IV and V, and Venning, *Exeter*, 21 and 30.

143 Cmd. 8204, 184.

144 Photographs of mid-1945 in Venning's publication show the city centre and state that 'some measure of orderliness had been established by the demolition of ruined walls of buildings, the random filling of basements and general clearance work. It was thus possible to look across the devastated areas where the extent of desecration was at once evident'. Venning, *Exeter*, 10.

145 Ibid., 23.

146 Ibid., 23–5.

147 TNA: HLG 71/1284, Kennedy to Meyer on 5 July 1947 and 18 September 1947, for example.

148 Ibid., Southwestern Region, Coates to Wheeldon, 8 December 1948.

149 See, for example, throughout TNA: HLG 71/1284 for Exeter and HLG 79/261 for Hull.

150 *WMN*, 13 March 1946.

151 *E&E*, 29 September 1947.

152 See Chapter 4, note 48.

153 *E&E*, 24 September 1947, also TNA: HLG 71/1284 (this Exeter planning file holds a great deal of correspondence on issues between the City of Exeter and the Ministry of Transport as well as the Ministry of Town and Country Planning).

154 *E&E*, 18 February 1949, Noted in *The Municipal Journal*, 11 March 1949, TNA: HLG 71/1284 as above shows also that local owners were displeased: see memo 27 February 1949 by Lichfield re: complaint by Co-operative Society that their development 'can't go ahead as the town doesn't know what they are doing at Eastgate yet'. (Additionally a biased account is found in the Brierley thesis.)

155 Venning, *Exeter*, 36–7.

156 Ibid., 27–8.

157 HC Deb, 1 February 1949, vol. 460, cc1485-6, 'Blitzed Cities (Steel Allocation)'.

158 Brierley, 'Exeter 1939–1974', 42.

159 Representatives of blitzed cities such as Plymouth, Coventry, Bristol, Southampton, Portsmouth, Birmingham, Hull and so on were regular speakers or questioners. Full list of debates in appendix.

160 DRO: Group G, Box 7/63. Development Plan for Exeter, 1950, 1. Also R. Hackett, 'Exeter Rebuilds', *The Municipal Journal* 61:3158 (1953): 1838.

161 TNA: CAB 134/455, HLG 71/34, HLG 71/1571, HLG 88/10, also Cmd. 8204, 57–60, and Cmd. 9559 (Appendices).

162 Ibid.

163 This may also partly explain the planning ministry's frustration with the city.

164 See TNA: HLG 71/1571, also CAB 134/982. The very small sizes of the allocations led R. Morley (MP for Southampton) to point out that at these rates the allocation might allow each city to build perhaps one or two new shops or offices per year and the time to rebuild fully at such a rate would be over 130 years. See HC Deb, 4 December 1952, vol. 508, c1906-16.

165 TNA: HLG 71/34 Conferences with Local Authorities. Transcript of question from C. Newman (Exeter) to Silkin (MTCP), October 1947.

166 See *WMN*, 6 September 1952, also Venning, *Exeter*, 58.

167 The by-pass road was finally approved in March 1952 on the south side of the city centre, not on the north as in Sharp's plan. WCSL: Exeter Planning Committee report, 6 March 1952. The first section took five years to complete, later sections were not completed until 1959–64 and some later still. Venning, *Exeter*, 66–72.

168 See: W. G. Hoskins, *Two Thousand Years*, 139–44; D. Davies and R. Fortescue-Foulkes, *Exeter, a City Saved?* (Exeter, 1977); also unpublished thesis by D. Minns, 'The Post-War Redevelopment of Exeter' 1979 (held at WCSL). Also see notes immediately below.

169 SAUN: de Cronin (of *The Architectural Review*) to Sharp (dated 25 May 1945), also Sharp to Richards (dated 3 October 1949). Additionally, in several memos found in TNA files both Transport and MTCP civil servants complain that the City Council forbade Sharp from speaking with government ministers and civil servants. See TNA: HLG 71/1284, '1944 Confidential Special Investigative Report' (handwritten, undated notes).

170 DRO: City Council minutes 21 December 1948; *WMN*, 22 December 1948; *E&E*, 3 December 1948; also Hoskins *Two Thousand Years*; and Brierley, 'Exeter 1939–1974'. Many difficult personalities stand out in the Exeter City Council but most especially C. J. Newman, the town clerk. See Rothnie, *The Baedeker Blitz*, 28, 42, 45–6; also BBC WW2 People's War Memories website: http://www.bbc.co.uk/history/ww2peopleswar/stories/37/a4005037.shtml.

171 See *E&E* for 18 August 1948, 3 December 1948, 21 March 1950; and Brierley, 'Exeter 1939–1974'.

172 Venning, *Exeter*, 20.

173 TNA: HLG 71/1284 Kennedy to Henson, 18 November 1947; *E&E*, 10 April 1951, Brierley, 'Exeter 1939–1974', 36.

174 DRO: Group G, Box 7/63, Development Plan for Exeter, December 1950, Report by H. Gayton (Approved with modifications, July 1954), and Gillie to Newman, 19 July 1954.

175 H. C. Haley, 'Financing the Rebuilding', *The Municipal Journal* 61:3158 (1953): 1831.

176 See TNA: HLG 71/1284 Exeter reconstruction file.

177 See Venning, *Exeter*, 51–2, 75, 88.

178 T. Sharp, *Cathedral City: A Plan for Durham* (London, 1945).

179 See Hoskins, *Two Thousand Years*; also Stamp, *Britain's Lost Cities* (London, 2007), chapter titled 'Exeter'.

180 Hoskins, *Two Thousand Years*, 139–44; Rothnie, *The Baedeker Blitz*, 137; TNA: HLG 79/171 includes a memo (no author, no date): Gaston of the Ministry of Works visited Exeter and stated that the area at Dix's Fields is Grade II and should be preserved, even where only facades remain. (Exeter acquired these properties after a legal battle and tore them down.)

181 Again, see Hoskins, *Two Thousand Years*; and throughout City Council minutes.

182 *E&E*, 6 December 1946 and 24 September 1947.

183 See Chapter 2 on Reith and 4 on Silkin; also TNA: HLG 71/601 1947 conference transcripts.

184 David Palliser, in John Cannon (ed.), *Oxford Companion to British History* (NYC, 1997), 360.

185 See G. Hemm et al., *Liverpool: Past, Present and Future* (Liverpool, 1948). For air raid history, see J. Hughes, *Port in a Storm: The Air Attacks on Liverpool and Its Shipping in the Second World War* (Birkinhead, 1993).

186 I. Morley, *British Provincial Civic Design and the Building of Late-Victorian and Edwardian Cities, 1880–1914* (Lampeter, 2008); based on PhD thesis, Sheffield University, 2001: chapter 4.1, Liverpool, 69–104.

187 It also was the site of the first tunnel bored under a metropolitan area to accommodate the railway to the dock area (1836). See J. Belchem (ed.), *Liverpool 800: Culture, Character & History* (Liverpool, 2006).

188 A new book on Liverpool and Manchester examines how a number of problems were perceived and dealt with in the period before the war: C. Wildman, *Urban Redevelopment and Modernity in Liverpool and Manchester, 1918–1939* (London, 2017).

189 See the first few years of *Town Planning Review* (from vol. 1 in 1910–11) for many articles on planning and improving Liverpool by figures such as Adshead, Reilly and Muir.

190 TNA: HLG 71/601 and 602. See also Table 2.2. City centre damage was said only to total sixteen acres, however.

191 A. Shennan, 'City Redevelopment', *Liverpool Trade Review (LTR)* 45:9 (1946): 123.

192 F. Thompson, *Merseyside Plan: 1944* (London, 1945). Commissioned in 1943 by the minister of town and country planning.

193 Hughes, *Port in a Storm*, 90. For another account of Liverpool in the war, and related national issues, see P. Adey, D. Cox and B. Godfrey, *Crime, Regulation and Control during the Blitz: Protecting the Population of Bombed Cities* (London, 2016), which focuses on Liverpool.

194 TNA: HLG 71/601 notes on Liverpool C.B. and *The Times*, 7 October 1952, 3, Issue 52436, col C. The TNA data on Liverpool is not as comprehensive as Hull or Exeter, but see Hughes, *Port in a Storm*.

195 See Hughes, *Port in a Storm*; and Adey et al., *Crime*.

196 LSE: BLPES HD7/324 'The post-war reconstruction of Liverpool' by A. E. Shennan, Merseyside Civil Society annual meeting, 10 December 1941, 3–4; University of Liverpool Archives (ULA): *Liverpool Daily Post (LDP)*, 13 August 1943, 'Opening of RIBA exhibition'. See Chapter 4 re: 1909 and 1932 Acts.

197 LSE: BLPES HD7/324 'The post-war reconstruction of Liverpool', 3–4.

198 Ibid., 3 and 5.

199 Ibid., 4.

200 LRO: 352 MIN RED 1/1 Post-War Redevelopment Advisory (Special) Committee, Minute Book No. 1, September 1942–December 1950 (hereafter PWRASC Mins).

201 Ibid., 21 January 1944.

202 LRO: Liverpool City Council Minutes (hereafter LVCCM) H1383: 1944–45. 7 February 1945, reiterated at meeting on 24 July 1945 and at meeting on 3 October 1945 the PWRASC agrees to submit a report; follow-up next in PWRASC Mins, 20 March 1946.

203 LRO: H74 POS, *First Report of the Post-War Redevelopment Advisory (Special) Committee on Reconstruction Proposals for the City* (Liverpool, June 1946). Minutes do not discuss a public exhibition but it seems that the model pictured with the report was made for public viewing. Note of the impending plans was made in the national press: *The Times*, 29 March 1946, 2, Issue 50413, col. B, 'Proposed New Roads For Liverpool Redevelopment Plan'. See Figure 5.11.

204 *First Report of the Post-War Redevelopment Advisory (Special) Committee*, 36.

205 Ibid., ii.

206 LRO: Proceedings of Council (henceforth LVCCM) 1946–47, Mins, 9 November 1946.

207 LRO: PWRASC Mins, 21 January 1947.

208 LRO: PWRASC Mins, 21 July 1947.

209 LRO: LVCCM, 1946–47, Mins, 4 June 1947.

210 LRO: PWRASC Mins, 20 January 1948. Also LRO: LVCCM, 1947–49, vol. 1, 4 January 1948.

211 Ibid.

212 For example, see *The Manchester Guardian*, 25 January 1947, 'Rising from the ruins' (re: the India Building, shipping business); also *The Manchester Guardian*, 21 May 1947, 'Rebuilding a Store' (re: Lewis's, which may not have had a license, or may have been sponsored by the BT).

213 LRO: LVCCM, 1947–49, vol. 1, 2 February 1949.

214 LRO: PWRASC Mins, 24 June 1948, 19 July 1948. Hearings held in late June 1948.

215 Ibid., 24 June 1948.

216 Ibid.

217 Ibid., 21 February 1949.

218 MTCP Circular 39, 16 March 1948.

219 LRO: PWRASC Mins, 21 February 1949. Files in TNA also show that the city was coordinating their ideas with the MTCP, see HLG 79/310–313.

220 LRO: LVCCM, 2 March 1949, also PWRSC Mins, 22 April 1949.

221 LRO: LVCCM, 4 May 1949.

222 Ibid.

223 TNA: HLG 79/307 and HLG 71/1289. Liverpool series is mainly in HLG 79/307 to 313.

224 LRO: PWRSC Mins, 2 September 1949.

225 Ibid.

226 Ibid.

227 Like Hull the city had been granted powers of a corporation by Parliament in the nineteenth century.

228 The same firm that had problems with a CPO in Hull.

229 LRO: PWRSC Mins, 29 November 1949.

230 *Hull Daily Mail*, 19 December 1949.

231 LRO: PWRSC Mins, 25 April 1950, 20 July 1950.

232 LRO: PWRSC Mins, 27 September 1949.

233 See Cmd. 8204, 193. Section 38 applied to land under a DO that was not necessarily war-damaged, but was needed to carry out plans as approved by the planning ministry.

234 LRO: PWRSC Mins, 25 April 1950.

235 Powers were also given to local authorities under the War Damaged Sites Act 1949 to enable them to prevent sites becoming hazardous (as well as rubbish tips, etc.).

236 LRO: PWRSC Mins, 20 July 1950.

237 Ibid.

238 LRO: PWRSC, 24 October 1950. Officials did in fact eventually make plans and tender bids for the work, presumably completing the screens for the Festival.

239 LRO: LVCCM, 5 April 1950, PWRSC Mins, 20 July 1950, show the officials had already been consulting with the Liverpool Stores Committee (a traders' group) on the proposed temporary or permanent developments.

240 LRO: PWRSC, 24 October 1950.

241 Ibid., and throughout 1951. LRO: LVCCM, 3 January 1951, also mentions negotiations with railways to build an underground system, which did eventually get built.

242 HC Deb, 11 May 1950, vol. 475, c90W; HC Deb, 20 June 1950, vol. 476, c103W.

243 Cmd. 8204, 46–8; LRO: PWRSC Mins, 24 October 1950. This of course was not funding or grants, only a capped allowance for building license values.

244 The £1,00,000 was 2.5 per cent of the total for all blitzed cities.

245 LRO: PWRSC Mins, 20 July 1950. City officials also unsuccessfully attempted to negotiate a higher number after the announcement. Ibid., 24 October 1950 and 21 December 1950.

246 Ibid., 13 February 1951 and 21 November 1951. The PWRSC had to reallocate the licence distribution twice.

247 LRO: PWRSC Mins, 13 February 1951.

248 Ibid., for example.

249 LRO: PWRSC Mins, 28 January 1952, 24 April 1952.

250 LRO: PWRSC, 'Car Parking, Central Area', September 1951; 'Report of the PWRSC on Car Parking', 30 November 1951. Some of this was incorporated into the 'Report and Recommendations of the Housing Committee on Slum Clearance and Central Area Redevelopment' dated 2 December 1951.

251 J. Murden in *Liverpool 800*, 395ff. The Development Plan was rejected initially for having left off areas added to the city by the Liverpool Extension Act 1951 (the land had been included on the Development Plan for Lancashire), LRO: PWRSC Mins, 24 February 1953.

252 One minor exception was a land exchange at the Lord Street site, still not settled and so not yet under construction. LRO: LVCCM, 4 November 1953.

253 For example, the volume of LVCC reports for 1953–54 contains an elaborate report with photographs titled 'Multi-Storey Housing in the USA', March 1954, which is a report of a deputation sent to several large American cities.

254 *Liverpool 800*, 397.

255 *The Times*, 7 October 1952, 3, Issue 52436, col. C, 'Remoulding of Liverpool: Little Progress In City Centre'.

256 LRO: LVCCM, 17 December 1952, 24 February 1953. It is surprising that the Corn Exchange project was not licensed earlier out of allocations for export and trade business that operated through the Board of Trade. The minutes do not give any hints, and the project does not appear to have been discussed before the allocation.

257 Ibid.

258 Ibid., 17 December 1952, 24 February 1953 and 1 October 1953.

259 Discussion of the open space runs throughout several years of minutes, but see LRO: PWRSC Mins, 24 February 1953 for construction discussion.

260 *LDP*, 23 June 1954, supplement, 2. The area is now part of the forty-four acre Liverpool One shopping centre site, built in 2003–2008.

261 LRO: PWRSC Mins, 23 December 1953. Letter to Mr. Alker, Liverpool Municipal Buildings from Vince, MHLG, dated 9 December 1953.

262 *LDP*, 23 June 1954, Special supplement. The image was of the 1952 plan, from the official Development Plan

263 Ibid.

264 Ibid., 1.

265 Ibid., 2. Also see the article by Shennan from September 1949, 'Liverpool: Some Reconstruction Problems', *LTR* v 48 n 9, 1949, 113–23.

266 *LDP*, 23 June 1954, 2. By contrast in his article for the *LTR* in 1946 Shennan had stated that 'the only solution is to be found in a coordinated scheme embracing both vacant and occupied sites within the area of extensive war damage'. Adding that he expected 'Liverpool's proposals will be considerably more extensive than

those made by Plymouth' which of course did not come to pass. Shennan, 'City Redevelopment', 123–4.

267   Osborn (ed.), *Making Plans*, 38–9. Other local architects had agreed: 'A Haussman technique is required in reshaping [Liverpool]', said Gordon Hemm (co-author of *Liverpool: Past Present & Future*) in *LDP*, 16 August 1943, and *Evening Express*, same date, same letter to the editor.

268   *LDP*, 23 June 1954, supplement, 9.

269   Unusually compared to the other cities investigated, the town clerk seem barely to have made himself – or his views – known. Only the city engineer and city architect show in historic records as being occasionally insistent on preferred policy or issues of redevelopment.

270   R. Hattersley, *Who Goes Home? Scenes from a Political Life* (London, 1995).

6 Postwar Rebuilding: Hopeful Plans, Different Realities

1   ULA: Papers of William, Baron Holford; Visits Abroad: Harvard University-School of Design; D147/V15/4 lecture: 'Architecture and the Public in Postwar Britain' (n.d., but January 1952).

2   Authors are cited in previous chapters, particularly Chapter 1, for example, Hasegawa, Tiratsoo, and Essex and Brayshay. Essex and Brayshay, it should be noted, do discuss the issues with obtaining labour and materials, but do not have room to give more detail about various Plymouth projects – see 'Boldness', 458–9.

3   Marriott, *Property Boom*, chapter 5.

4   Ibid., 74; 'A property knight and his men' (Business Diary), *The Times*, 9 January 1969, 23; Issue 57454, col. B. Also Scott, *Property Masters*, 105; Ambrose and Colenutt, *Property Machine*, 77, 132; Rose, *Dynamics*.

5   *The Times*, 9 January 1969, 23

6   Turned down at first for a large insurance company, they later negotiated their way in through that same company. Marriott, *Property Boom*, 72–6.

7   Ibid., 75–8.

8   Ibid.

9   Scott, *Property Masters*, 105. A major difference from the interwar period was that more of these companies were working at national and international, not local or regional, scales. Also Rose, *Dynamics*; and Marriott, *Property Boom*, chapter 5.

10   DRO, Group G, Box 763 (1950). Brierley, 'Exeter', 43. Also Marriott, *Property Boom*, 74–81. Land Securities still controls the Princesshay development, which was torn down and redeveloped in 2004–2007.

11   By 1965 they had also added Liverpool: *The Times*, 15 December 1965, 6; see also 'A property knight', *The Times*; Ambrose and Colenutt, *Property Machine*, 38. Also, Marriott, *Property Boom*, chapter 5.

12   'A property knight', *The Times*.

13   Ambrose and Colenutt, *Property Machine*, 38. Data on p. 39 shows LSIT by September 1974 as by far the largest UK property company (ranked by 'capitalization'). Ravenseft's holdings were valued at 2.1 million when they were absorbed by LSIT: 'A property knight', *The Times*.

14   'A property knight', *The Times*; and Land Securities website: http://www.landsecurities.com/about-us/the-land-securities-story (now archived at https://

web.archive.org/web/20150716040714/http://www.landsecurities.com:80/about-us/
the-land-securities-story).

15 'Land Securities Investment Trust: Policy of Continued Expansion', *The Times*, 18 July
   1958, 18; col. C.

16 Cmd. 8204, 193.

17 This property swallowed a small street, called Chariot Street. See *Hull Times*, 24
   May 1952.

18 HHC, L711: City Council of Kingston-upon-Hull, *Planning in Action* (undated, per
   staff: 1959), 17; Cmd. 9559. *Report of the Ministry of Housing and Local Government
   for the Period 1950/51 to 1954* (London, 1955), 68.

19 TNA: HLG 79/260, 261, 268.

20 The largest of these was Hammond's, as described in the previous chapter, as well as
   the Cooperative and Edwin Davis, now long out of business.

21 Cmd. 9559, Appendix XIV, Table B, 190.

22 HHC: L711, *Planning in Action*, 13.

23 Ibid. Hull's total city centre licence allocations were approximately £1 million, so
   much of this took place in 1954–58.

24 TNA: HLG 79/310–313 files detail the Church St/Lord St issues. Also see L.
   Balderstone, G. Milne and R. Mulhearn, 'Memory and Place on the Liverpool
   Waterfront in the Mid-twentieth Century', *Urban History* 41:3 (August 2014): 478–96.
   Related information on Liverpool can also be found on the Mapping Memory
   website: http://www.liverpoolmuseums.org.uk/maritime/research/mappingmemory/
   index.html.

25 TNA: HLG 79/310–313.

26 LRO: PWRSC Mins, 29 November 1949.

27 LRO: PWRSC Mins, 29 November 1949, 25 April 1950, 20 July 1950. Also
   LRO: LVCCM, 20 July 1950. Liverpool needed temporary shops less than other
   cities, as it was bigger, had less central bomb damage and so had more options for
   re-accommodating traders. See *LDP*, supplement, 2 'No stop-gap building'.

28 LRO: PWRSC Mins, 1950 inter alia.

29 Ravenscroft was in fact Ravenseft under a different name. Property companies often
   start small entities to distinguish their projects and keep the assets separate.

30 LRO: PWRSC Mins, 1950 and 1951, 1952, especially 20 April 1952. Also
   LRO: LVCCM, 25 July 1951, 30 April 1952.

31 LRO: PWRSC Mins, 12 July 1951. For Section 83: MTCP Explanatory Memo, 1947
   Act (London, 1947), 66–7, also Cmd. 9559, 96.

32 LRO: PWRSC Mins, 24 April 1952, 15 October 1952, 17 December 1952.

33 Ibid.

34 Ibid., 17 December 1952.

35 Ibid., 1 October 1953.

36 HLG 71/1284 Kacinek to Lichfield, MTCP (planning technique), 5 July 1949 re
   Exeter's City Architect.

37 Arndale Property Trust, c1966–67, company brochure. Arndale is one of Britain's
   largest developers; see Scott, *Property Masters*, 177.

38 Tiratsoo, 'Hull', and *Reconstruction, Affluence and Labour Politics*, for example, and to
   some extent Hasegawa, *Replanning*.

39 Little published work discusses these factors comprehensively; Essex and Brayshay
   are perhaps closest and Tiratsoo on Coventry. Though many papers included are
   planning related rather than building, see also P. Larkham and J. Nasr (eds), 'The

Rebuilding of British Cities: Exploring the Post-Second World War Reconstruction',
Working Paper, School of Planning and Housing, UCE (2004).

40 On planning costs, see P. Larkham, 'The Cost of Planning for Reconstruction',
Planning History 27:1–2 (2005): 20–6.

41 Many of these were at least partially funded by central government, for example,
Ministry of Transport granted 75 per cent of the cost of building certain roads. See
TNA: HLG 71/1284 Kennedy to Walsh, 8 February 1949 (re: Exeter).

42 See, for example, Medland in HC Deb, 18 November 1947, vol. 444, cc988-1101 'Local
Government Bill', and Morley in HC Deb, 29 June 1951, vol. 489, cc1855-68 'Blitzed
Towns (Exchequer Grants)'. Also, for example, a selection of debates on the following
dates: 12 and 18 November 1947, 16 September 1948, 27 January 1949, 21 March
1949, 8 November 1949. The year 1950 was particularly busy: 11 and 16 May 1950,
20 June 1950, 4 July 1950, then 21 June 1951, 3 July 1951, 20 November 1951, 5
December 1951, 25 February 1952, 10 April 1952, 14 October 1952, 25 November
1952, 1 and 4 December 1952 and many more.

43 See Cmd. 9559, 73.

44 HC Deb, 18 November 1947, as note 42. Medland gives numbers on loss of RV in
col. 1095.

45 See HC Deb, 29 June 1951, as note 42.

46 HC Deb, 18 November 1947 'Local Government Bill', Lewis, 1044–6. In the debate
both Lewis and Medland (Plymouth) gave many supporting figures from a number of
blitzed cities, including several other constituencies.

47 HC Deb, 29 June 1951 'Blitzed Towns (Exchequer Grants)', Morley col. 1855.

48 Ibid., col. 1859, 1861.

49 Ibid., col. 1861–63.

50 See Chapter 5, note 228.

51 A. Shennan, 'Liverpool: Some Reconstruction Problems', *LTR*, September 1949, 115.
Plymouth spent over £8 million on acquiring land between 1947 and 1958, according
to Essex and Brayshay, 'Boldness', 456.

52 For example, see Hull Property Owner's Protection Association file from the
MTCP: TNA: HLG 71/270.

53 See Chapter 5, showing that Hull and Liverpool won their cases. At Plymouth the
city council lost, but the case was regarding compulsory purchase of a building that
the plan did not actually intend to remove or demolish. See Essex and Brayshay,
'Boldness'.

54 Plymouth had over 300 alone; see Essex and Brayshay, 'Boldness', 453. Nationally
the number of objections per local authority ranged from 1 to over 7,000; see Cmd.
9559, 61.

55 After February 1950 the housing functions combined with planning and local
government, eliminating part of the coordination problem.

56 HC Deb, 16 September 1948, vol. 456, c373. Although the Labour MPs were more
vocal on blitzed city problems, Conservative MPs often noted agreement – Brigadier
Terence Clarke of Portsmouth was the most vocal among his party. It is surprising,
however, that during the Attlee governments the louder and more frequent
complaints came from the party in power, rather than the Opposition.

57 For more on the building industry, see Powell, *British Building Industry*, chapters 7–8.
Though a good overview, it is incorrect regarding building priorities.

58 See the *AJ* series on rebuilding bombed cities, 1952–53, also see Marriott, *Property
Boom*, Chapter 5; Scott, *Property Masters*, 105. Also Rose, *Dynamics*.

59 S. Ward, 'Public-Private Partnerships', in J. B. Cullingworth (ed.), *British Planning: 50 Years of Urban and Regional Policy* (London, 1999), 234. Little has been written outside Ward's work (and Marriott's journalistic take) on the historical phenomenon of public–private partnerships in city centre development, a field ripe for further investigation.

60 A. Shennan, 'Post-War Liverpool', *LTR*, September 1954, 295.

61 Arndale Property Trust, 1967, second page (unnumbered).

62 Ibid.

63 See the Liverpool example of Littlewood's discussed earlier in this chapter, and following, or the use of Sharp's conceptual facades as final designs in Exeter's Princesshay.

64 Sharp's suggestions were purposely bland, intending to give a general sense of the building mass more than specific stylistic suggestions. See While and Tait, 'Exeter', 77–97. Also P. Larkham, 'Thomas Sharp and the Post-War Replanning of Chichester: Conflict, Confusion and Delay', *Planning Perspectives* 24:1 (2009): 51–75.

65 Marriott, *Property Boom*, 79–80. Freedman added that the city architect took credit if the design was praised but blamed the developer if it was criticized.

66 Punter, 'A History of Aesthetic Control: Part 1, 1909–1953: The Control of the External Appearance of Development in England and Wales', *The Town Planning Review* 57:4 (1986): 351–81. See also J. Punter, 'Design' in Cullingworth, *British Planning*, 139–40.

67 Cmd. 9559, 75–6. It continues to say, '[I]t is not part of a local authority's function to re-design buildings for applicants', though many did.

68 Punter, 'Design', 138; also the slightly later publication by the MHLG *Town Centres: Approach to Renewal* (London, 1962). Also see Larkham, 'Thomas Sharp', 51–75. M. R. G. Conzen notes this can be seen as functional adaptation – in the wider historical sense of urban development: J. Whitehand (ed.), *The Urban Landscape: Historical Development and Management, papers by M.R.G. Conzen* (London, 1981), 57.

69 The author has made a similar argument regarding the development of speculative office buildings in London after the relaxation of building licenses: that developers were capitalizing on the changing economics of offices and the new social structure they were accommodating. This can also apply to the city centres of blitzed cities, where developers capitalized on the needs of the provincial cities, providing strictly what was needed and nothing more. Both attempt to examine why cities look the way they do, when the bulk of building is not by eminent architects. See C. Flinn 'Capitalising on Social & Economic Demands: Speculative Office Building in London 1953–1966', unpublished MSc dissertation, University of London, 1990.

70 A good example is Montague Burton, the business that had sued Hull and Liverpool over their sites. See F. Mort, 'Montague Burton, the "Tailor of Taste"', in *Cultures of Consumption: Masculinities and Social Space in Late Twentieth-Century Britain* (London, 1996), 128–44, esp. 134–5.

71 ULA: D147/LA7/9/1, Papers of William Graham, Baron Holford of Kemp Town. Guildhall seminars notes, 7 June 1966.

72 HC Deb, 10 April 1952, vol. 498, cc2987-3003, 'Blitzed Areas (Reconstruction)', col. 3003.

73 LRO: PWRSC Min Book, letter MHLG to Town Clerk, 24 November 1952, para 6. (Clearly a form letter sent to all blitzed cities.) The largest single item in the investment programme for the Ministry of Works in 1949–52 was the cement

industry at £10.5 million; see TNA: CAB 134/449 [IPC (WP) (48) 220], 21 December 1948, item 3.

74 G. Grenfell Baines, 'Substitute Materials and Their Influence on Design'. *RIBA Journal* (January 1948): 108–13. Also see W. A. Allen, 'Changes in Materials and Construction Methods', which describes some of the reasons for development of prefabrication and usage of concrete and other materials in the postwar period, in *The Times*, 3 July 1961, xv. For discussion of materials in a discussion of housing, see N. Bullock, 'Reconstruction: New Ways of Building and Government Sponsorship', in D. Goodman and C. Chant (eds), *European Cities and Technology: Industrial to Post-Industrial City* (Abingdon, 1999), 275.

75 See Nick Hayes, who attributes the large number of 'promotional' features in the architectural press on new technologies to be indicative of the rise of new technology/materials: 'Making Homes by Machine: Images, Ideas and Myths in the Diffusion of Non-traditional Housing in Britain 1942–54', *TCBH* 10:3 (1999): 282–309, esp. 288 (the article covers research as well, although it is focused on developments relating to housing). Also N. Hayes, 'Prefabricating Stories: Innovation in Systems Technology after the Second World War', *History of Technology* 25 (2004): 7–28; 'The Story of CLASP', in A. Saint, *Towards a Social Architecture: The Role of School-Building in Post-War England* (London, 1987).

76 Hall, *Cities of Tomorrow*, 221. Hayes, 'Prefabricating Stories', 24, also mentions the significance of the period's reliance on the 'authority' of science and technology.

77 W. Whyte, 'The Englishness of English Architecture: Modernism and the Making of a National International Style, 1927–1957', *Journal of British Studies* 48:2 (2009): 441–65; E. Darling, *Re-forming Britain: Narratives of Modernity before Reconstruction* (Abingdon, 2006); Bullock, *Building*.

78 See Gold, *Experience of Modernity*, esp. 2–3, and Chapter 7 'Marking Time'.

79 'There was general agreement that the architecture should be "modern", it should not ape the styles of the past and, when the architecture did arrive in the very late 1940s, it was a highly simplified version of late 1930s Modernism crossed with a sort of stripped Classicism.' J. Gould, 'Architecture and the Plan for Plymouth: The Legacy of a British City', *Architectural Review* 221:1321 (March 2007): 78–83 (online version). An excellent example of the 1950s neo-Georgian is The Queen's House in Hull.

80 See Larkham and Lilley, 'Plans, Planners', *Urban History* 30:2 (2003): 183–205.

81 But for a counterpoint to this, see Duwel, *Blessing in Disguise*; also N. Bullock 'Gaston Bardet: Post-War Champion of the Mainstream Tradition of French Urbanisme', *Planning Perspectives* 25:3 (2010): 347–64. For more on British-European comparisons, see C. Flinn, 'Forgetful or Purposeful? Memory and the Remaking of Place after the Blitz', in *Storia Urbana* 158 (2018): 61–86.

82 Note that Minister Silkin made a trip to Poland and Czechoslovakia to view reconstruction in 1947, reporting back to the Cabinet, TNA: CAB 129/22 [CP (47) 343, 31 December 1947, 'Impressions of a Recent Visit to Poland and Czechoslovakia'. For European reconstruction, see also J. Diefendorf, *Rebuilding* and his *In the Wake of War*; also for summaries, see S. Ward, *Planning the Twentieth-Century City: The Advanced Capitalist World* (Chichester, 2002), 160–5, for Germany, and other sections on France and so on.

83 A. Jozefacka, 'Rebuilding Warsaw: Conflicting Visions of a Capital City, 1916–1956', unpublished PhD dissertation, New York University, 2011; J. Goldman, 'Warsaw: Reconstruction as Propaganda', Chapter 6 in L. Vale and T. Campanella (eds), *Resilient Cities: How Modern Cities Recover from Disaster* (Oxford, 2005);

also A. Tung, *Preserving the World's Great Cities: The Destruction and Renewal of the Historic Metropolis* (New York, 2001), for Warsaw: 73–95. It is also claimed that reusing street patterns meant large cost savings; see M. Niemczyk, 'City Profile: Warsaw' (Warszawa), *Cities* 15:4 (August 1998): 301–11.

84 A. Murray, 'Al Murray's German Adventure', Part 2, air date 8 December 2010, BBC Four. Much of Dresden was more recently rebuilt, from postwar modern back to a version of the prewar city. Also see 'A German Phoenix', *Economist* 327:7808 (24 April 1993): 91; and Diefendorf, *Rebuilding*.

85 See Chapter 5, Exeter, Dix's Fields, p. 107. There were certainly a few buildings that were repaired and almost rebuilt where enough of the original remained to do so, as below, but this was rare in the cities attempting to implement new plans. See also a new view by P. Larkham and D. Abrams, 'Originality and Authenticity in the Post-War Reconstruction of Britain', in Bold et al., *Authentic Reconstruction*.

86 Sharp, *Exeter Phoenix*, 9, 10.

87 P. J. Larkham 'Changing Ideas of Urban Conservation in Mid-Twentieth-Century England', *Change Over Time* 4:1 (Spring 2014): 92–113, see 103–106.

88 LRO: PWRSC Mins, inter alia. Also see Shennan, 'Post-War Liverpool'. It is possible there will still be a move in Britain towards reconstruction of historic streetscapes: see *East Anglian Daily Times*, 6 April 2018, 'Return of market and historic buildings to be restored in Lowestoft Heritage Action Zone plans': http://www.eadt.co.uk/news/market-return-historic-buildings-restoration-planned-lowestoft-heritage-action-zone-1-5466805 (accessed 9 April 2018). Lowestoft was on the MTCP Blitzed Cities list.

89 Pendlebury, 'Planning the Historic City', 371. There is a convincing revisionist outline of preservation's timeline in P. J. Larkham, 'Changing Ideas of Urban Conservation in Mid-Twentieth-Century England', *Change Over Time* 4:1 (Spring 2014): 92–113. Also see P. Larkham, 'The Place of Urban Conservation', 295–324; and Stamp, *Lost Victorian Cities*.

90 For Betjeman as a preservationist, see Chapter 2; also Tewdwr-Jones, 'Oh, the planners', esp. 398–9. For other preservation examples of the period: R. Madgin, 'Reconceptualising the Historic Urban Environment: Conservation and Regeneration in Castlefield, Manchester, 1960–2009', *Planning Perspectives* 25:1 (2010): 29–48; and J. Pendlebury, 'Alas Smith and Burns? Conservation in Newcastle upon Tyne City Centre 1959–68', *Planning Perspectives* 16:2 (2010): 115–41.

91 Although some of the historic reconstruction came much later, Alon Confino argues that there was an emphasis on domestic German tourism from just after the war. See his Chapter 14 'Dissonance Normality and the Historical Method: Why Did Some Germans Think of Tourism After May 8, 1945?' in R. Bessel and D. Schumann (eds), *Life after Death: Approaches to a Cultural and Social History during the 1940s and 1950s* (Cambridge, 2003), 323–47. The new book mentioned above looks at this exact phenomenon in some depth: *Authentic Reconstruction*, Bold et al. (eds), particularly Part 1 with chapters on postwar reconstruction in Germany and Poland (London, 2017). Also see J. Hagen, 'Rebuilding the Middle Ages after the Second World War: The Cultural Politics of Reconstruction in Rothenburg Ob Der Tauber, Germany', *Journal of Historical Geography* 31:1 (2005): 94–112; and A. Confino, 'Travelling as a Culture of Remembrance: Traces of National Socialism in West Germany, 1945–1960', *History & Memory* 12:2 (2000): 92–121.

92 J. Whitehand (ed.), 'Introduction', in M. Conzen and J. Whitehand, *The Urban Landscape: Historical Development and Management* (London, 1981), 12. Yet this loss was also felt in Germany where modernist cityscapes replaced historic towns: J. Arnold, ' "Once upon a time there was a lovely town …" The Allied Air War, Urban Reconstruction and Nostalgia in Kassel (1943–2000)', *German History* 29:3 (2011): 445–69.

93 See P. Wright, *On Living in an Old Country: The National Past in Contemporary Britain* (Oxford, 2009), esp. 206–14; also J. Lubbock, *The Tyranny of Taste: The Politics of Architecture and Design in Britain 1550–1960* (London, 1995); and R. Hewison, *The Heritage Industry: Britain in a Climate of Decline* (London, 1987). J. Delafons discusses the 1947 Act as an 'inadequate vehicle for effective conservation' in his *Politics and Preservation: A Policy History of the Built Heritage, 1882–1996* (London, 1997), 61.

94 For issues around heritage, nostalgia and preservationism, see P. Mandler and A. Swenson (eds), *From Plunder to Preservation* (Oxford, 2013), Introduction; P. Mandler, *The Fall and Rise of the Stately Home* (London 1997); P. Borsay, 'History or Heritage: Perceptions of the Urban Past – A Review Essay', *Urban History* 18 (1991): 32–40; P. Borsay, *The Image of Georgian Bath, 1700–2000: Towns, Heritage, and History* (Oxford, 2000).

95 J. Pendlebury, 'Planning the Historic City', 387–8.

96 D. Gilbert, D. Matless and B. Short, *Geographies of British Modernity: Space and Society in the Twentieth Century* (Malden, MA, 2003), 8. The same authors note the 'inherently spatialized character of both twentieth-century modernity in general and the British experience in particular' (12).

97 See, for example, *Something Done: British Achievement 1945–47*, by the Office of Information (London, 1947). Also *Geographies* (as above), and D. Matless, 'Visual Culture and Geographical Citizenship: England in the 1940s', *Journal of Historical Geography* 22:4 (1996): 424–39.

98 *The Architects' Journal* (*AJ*) city surveys: Canterbury (14/4/52), Plymouth (12/6/52), Exeter (21/8/52), Bristol (2/10/52), Portsmouth (30/10/52), Liverpool (25/12/52), Southampton (16/4/53), Hull (2/7/53), Coventry (8/10/53).

99 D. Childs and D. Boyne, 'A Comparison of Progress in Rebuilding Bombed Cities', *AJ*, 8 July 1954, 50.

100 Though at this point the recent Liverpool work available for discussion was primarily warehouses and factories. See *AJ*, December 1952.

101 Note that Childs had worked for Sir Patrick Abercrombie and so was likely biased about some of the work.

102 *WMN*, 5 December 1956; *E&E*, 19 August 1958.

103 *WMN*, 25 November 1958. As soon as 1962, however, criticism had started; see *The Guardian*, 7 May 1962, 'Exeter Phoenix a Sorry Bird'. See also, Figures 5.5 and 6.1.

104 *YP*, 24 September 1954.

105 Liverpool 1954 *LDP* Special Issue: 'handsome' new offices, 'attractive premises', 'a clean, light building designed on modern lines' were other comments on new modernist buildings.

106 U. A. Coates, 'Progress in Redevelopment', *Journal of the Town Planning Institute* 39:1 (1952).

107 'From our special correspondent', *The Times*, 8 October 1952, 3, Issue 52437, col. D. Detail was included on the destruction, but also on new cranes, new dock construction and the investment being made – all of which provided information and publicity to attract business back to Hull's docks.

108 'Reconstruction at Coventry', *The Times*, 30 September 1952, 3, Issue 52430, col. E.

109 For discussion of personal experiences of reconstruction, see D. Adams, 'Everyday Experiences of the Modern City: Remembering the Post-War Reconstruction of Birmingham', *Planning Perspectives* 26:2 (2011): 237–60; and P. Hubbard et al., 'Contesting the Modern City', 377–97.

110 I. Nairn, *Outrage* (London, 1955). Exeter is particularly criticized; see D. McKie, 'Comment and Analysis: Elsewhere: The Best Laid Plans', *The Guardian*, 4 July 2002, 16; 'bland' is used in both M. Miller, *Princesshay Exeter: Concept, Development and Context* (Report Commissioned by English Heritage, 1998), 18, as cited by While in 'Sharp's Exeter', and BBC news, 'Exeter tops BBC poll on Britain's blandest high street 2005': http://news.bbc.co.uk/1/hi/england/devon/4610965.stm (5 June 2005).

111 Timothy Brittain-Catlin, [Review] *Architectural Review* 221:1321 (March 2007): 92. Wright, *On Living*, 212.

112 See quotation from Charles, Prince of Wales (Chapter 1), who has been famously critical of much postwar architecture. For example, *The Times*, 19 June 1984, 14, Issue 61861, col. A.

113 Sunand Prasad, 'The Past Sure is Tense', 18 October 2010, BBC Radio 3 'The Essay' series.

114 Ibid.

115 For more on the listing system and postwar conservation issues, see Delafons, *Politics of Preservation*, Chapter 8, especially 62–5.

116 See on a similar subject, W. Whyte, 'How Do Buildings Mean? Some Issues of Interpretation in the History of Architecture', *History and Theory* 45:2 (2006): 153–77.

117 'Change is forever', interview by Jenna Russell, *Boston Globe*, 13 December 2009 (online edition): http://www.boston.com/bostonglobe/ideas/articles/2009/12/13/change_is_forever/?page=full.

118 Childs, 'A comparison of progress', *AJ*, 8 July 1954, 51.

119 Ibid. Throughout the series there are examples of local architects' work, much of which is industrial or social, that is, housing, schools and so on.

120 L. Brett, 'The Developers', *Architectural Review* 143:893 (September 65): 163–7. Also see J. Boughton, *Municipal Dreams* (London, 2018) on the history of modern council housing.

121 P. J. Larkham and K. Lilley, 'Plans, Planners and City Images: Place Promotion and Civic Boosterism in British Reconstruction Planning', *Urban History* 30:2 (2003): 183–205.

122 Peter Shapely argues that – at least in large industrial cities – the local authorities played a major role in negotiating with the private sector, often implementing new plans: P. Shapely, 'The Entrepreneurial City: The Role of Local Government and City-Centre Redevelopment in Post-War Industrial English Cities', *Twentieth Century British History* 22:4 (2011): 498–520. Work on Dublin, Ireland, shows that despite planning, 'urban renewal was deferred to private interests'. E. Hanna, 'Dublin's North Inner City, Preservationism, and Irish Modernity in the 1960s', *The Historical Journal* 53 (2010): 1015–35; also see N. Moore, 'Valorizing Urban Heritage? Redevelopment in a Changing City', in N. Moore and Y. Whelan (eds), *Heritage, Memory & the Politics of Identity* (Farnham, 2007); and S. Mills, Chapter 8 in same work.

123 N. Falk (ed.) for URBED Ltd, *The Renaissance of Postwar Town Centres: Report of the Symposium* (London, 2000).

124 For the rise of property development in Britain in this period, see M. Boddy, 'The Property Sector in Late Capitalism: The Case of Britain', in M. Dear and A. Scott (eds), *Urbanization and Urban Planning in Capitalist Society* (London, 1981), 267–85.

125 An early work on the problematic nature of culture and consumerism is found in D. Bell, *The Cultural Contradictions of Capitalism* (New York, 1976, rev 1996), esp. 106–107.

126 LSIT as largest REIT according to outside sources and by self-description, see: https://www.qolcom.co.uk/ftse-100-group-land-securities-embraces-ipads/ and http://www.landsecurities.com/investors/shareholder-investor-information/uk-reit-taxation (archived, now at https://web.archive.org/web/20170606093303/http://www.landsecurities.com/investors/shareholder-investor-information/uk-reit-taxation).

127 There are also two renovated developments in Liverpool, and others that have been sold, that is, Hull's Queen's House, the Plymouth properties and more.

128 Land Securities website (now archived). Ravenseft continued to exist in name (and still does), but became a wholly owned subsidiary, and most development was thereafter carried out under the auspices of Land Securities.

129 It may be worth noting that contemporary press in the 1950s included criticisms of the high rents charged by Ravenseft, *HDM*, 27 November 1951. http://www.landsecurities.com/retail-portfolio/our-top-10-retail-properties (now archived at https://web.archive.org/web/20130820055637/http://www.landsecurities.com:80/retail-portfolio/our-top-10-retail-properties).

130 Ward, 'Public-Private Partnerships'.

131 Prasad, 'The Past Sure Is Tense'. See also on utopianism: M. Hollow, 'Utopian Urges: Visions for Reconstruction in Britain, 1940–1950', *Planning Perspectives* 27:4 (2012): 569–85.

132 An interesting source on the broader postwar city is J. Grindrod, *Concretopia: A Journey around the Rebuilding of Postwar Britain* (London, 2014). It should be added that there has more recently been an increasingly positive rhetoric around postwar development.

133 Gould, 'Architecture and the Plan for Plymouth'.

134 Ibid., 83.

135 J. Calame, 'Post-War Reconstruction: Concerns, Models and Approaches', in The Center for Macro Projects and Diplomacy, *Post-Conflict Reconstruction: Reconnecting Sites Nations Cultures*. Roger Williams University, Macro Center Working Papers. Paper 20. Volume 6, Spring 2005. Also see J. Gould *Coventry* (English Heritage, 2014).

136 A similar argument is made in a broader context by J. Gold in 'Modernity and Utopia', his chapter in Hall, Hubbard and Short (eds), *The Sage Companion to the City* (London, 2008), see 81–2. Also see P. Larkham, 'People, Planning and Place: The Roles of Client and Consultants in Reconstructing Post-War Bilston and Dudley', *Town Planning Review* 77:5 (2006): 557–82.

137 D. Dunster, 'Urban Myth: David Dunster Examines Liverpool's Powerful Urban Mythography and Civic Pride', *Architectural Review*, January 2008.

138 See also P. Shapely, 'Civic Pride and Redevelopment in the Post-War British City', *Urban History* 39:2 (2012): 310–28.

139 BBC news, 'Exeter tops BBC poll'.

140 'The £230m Princesshay development officially opened September 2007. The scheme has been heralded as the biggest single investment in regeneration in the city's

history. It contains a mix of shops, restaurants and apartments.' BBC News, dated 23 May 2008. http://news.bbc.co.uk/2/hi/uk_news /england/devon/7415831.stm.

141 See D. Littlefield, *Liverpool One: Remaking a City Centre* (Chichester, 2009).

142 Shennan, 'Post-War Liverpool', 290; and *LDP*, 23 June 1954, supplement, 4.

143 'Liverpool parade to mark May Blitz 70th anniversary', *Liverpool Daily Post*, 29 April 2011.

144 BBC Hull: Look North, 'The Hull Blitz', broadcast 5 May 2011.

145 'The Abercrombie Plan', Album: Songs for Humberside, Artist: Christopher Rowe and Ian Clark, written by Christopher Rowe, performed by Christopher Rowe and Ian Clark, Eclipse Records, copyright 1971, The Decca Record Company Limited. It is curious why – over twenty years after the plan was essentially set aside – a local folk-singer might choose to glorify it.

146 W. Holford, 'The Quiet Revolution in Design', *The Times*, 3 July 1961, ii, Issue 55123, Special section on architects.

147 See TNA: CAB 128/16 [CM (49) 65], 10 November 1949, and also in HLG 102/261 Headquarters Building Committee.

148 M. Banham and B. Hillier (eds), *A Tonic to the Nation: The Festival of Britain 1951* (London, 1976); and B. Conekin, *The Autobiography of a Nation: The 1951 Festival of Britain* (Manchester, 2003).

149 On consumerism, see Matthew Hilton, 'The Death of a Consumer Society', *Transactions of the Royal Historical Society* (Sixth Series) 18 (2008): 211–36, and his *Consumerism in Twentieth-Century Britain: The Search for a Historical Movement* (Cambridge, 2003).

Conclusion: Rebuilding Blitzed City Centres, Despite Planning

1 BOD-MPP: Macmillan dep c.273, Speeches 1953–55. Minister's Opening Address to the Annual Conference of the Town and Country Planning Association, 19 November 1953 (fols 247–53), fol. 247.

2 M. Thatcher, Conservative Party Conference speech, 9 October 1987, in M. Thatcher and R. Harris, *The Collected Speeches of Margaret Thatcher* (London, 1997), 286–7.

3 Gold, 'Modernity and Utopia', 81.

4 See Chapter 2, for example, Bourneville Village Trust, *When We Build Again*; also J. Stevenson, 'Planners' Moon? The Second World War and the Planning Movement', in H. Smith (ed.), *War and Social Change: British Society in the Second World War* (Manchester, 1986).

5 See list of debates covering blitz reconstruction issues in appendix.

6 HC Deb, 2 March 1953, vol. 512, c80 (Blitzed Towns debate col. 42–109).

7 See Macmillan's Cabinet memo in appendix.

8 TNA: HLG 71/601, C. Newman in transcript from the October 1947 conference.

9 For example, Hull complained internally about low building allowances generally, failing to realize that the city centres were treated separately from industry. See HHC: HCCM 1949ff.

10 For example, Tiratsoo, 'Labour and the Reconstruction of Hull, 1945–51', 141, who also blames central government and misses many of the internal problems in Hull. Also Hasegawa, *Replanning*, 120, who sees the MTCP as the major stumbling block; and Essex and Brayshay, 'Boldness', 458–9, who see the shortages of materials

affecting rebuilding as just that, rather than as the result of Whitehall (IPC) decisions. These are all valuable histories nonetheless.

11 MTCP, Circular 39, 1948.

12 Examples as above and to some extent Tiratsoo, *Reconstruction, Affluence.* For the IPC, see Flinn 'The City of Our Dreams?'.

13 Gold, 'Modernity and Utopia', 76.

14 See J. Rose, *Square Feet* (London, 1993).

15 ULA: Papers of William, Baron Holford; Civic Trust; D147/M15/3 speech: 'Rebuilding City Centres', 15 July 1960.

16 K. Morgan, *Britain since 1945: The People's Peace* (Oxford, 2001), esp. 'Labour's High Noon'.

17 See Gold, 'Modernity and Utopia', 81. Further, on the role of complexity generally, see G. O'Hara, *Governing Post-War Britain: The Paradoxes of Progress, 1951–1973* (Basingstoke, 2010); C. Hood and H. Margetts (eds), *Paradoxes of Modernization: Unintended Consequences of Public Policy Reform* (Oxford, 2010).

18 As noted by Mark Llewellyn, 'there are at least as many narratives as there are residents of [a] particular city'. 'Polyvocalism and the Public: "Doing" a Critical Historical Geography of Architecture', *Area* 35:3 (2003): 266.

19 For example, see comments by Medland, MP for Plymouth, in *Blitzed Areas* (Steel Allocation), HC Deb 21 March 1949, vol. 463 col. 164 on rateable value.

20 Debates on the subject were long and fairly regular after about 1949, but only planning ministry files have copies of some debates or excerpts; they are not acknowledged in IPC minutes or correspondence.

21 On the intense ambition of certain politicians, see M. Francis, 'Tears, Tantrums and Bared Teeth: The Emotional Economy of Three Conservative Prime Ministers, 1951–1963', *Journal of British Studies* 41 (2002).

22 M. Daunton, 'Britain and Globalisation since 1850: III. Creating the World of Bretton Woods, 1939–1958', *Transactions of the Royal Historical Society* (Sixth Series) 18 (2008): 1–42; Sked and Cook call this a bipartisan 'obsession'. A. Sked and C. Cook, *Post-War Britain: A Political History* (London, 1993), 143.

23 This is reflected in biographies and autobiographies of the time, with Attlee, Dalton, Cripps, Morrison and others focusing both at the time and on reflection the issues of a world power over home concerns. See bibliography for diaries, personal papers and so on.

24 Diefendorf, 'Katrina'.

25 See D. Harvey, 'The City as a Body Politic', in J. and I. Schneider (eds), *Wounded Cities: Destruction and Reconstruction in a Globalized World* (Oxford, 2003), 25–7, 43.

26 D. Gilbert, *Stumbling on Happiness* (London, 2006), 5. Gilbert is a prominent Harvard psychology professor.

27 Chick, *Industrial Policy.* Chick has skilfully analyzed the IPC in the realm of industrial policy, though his work looks at numbers rather than personalities, and at a broader area where the committee likely had less detailed impact.

28 R. Lowe, IHR seminar on the release of the official history, 23 March 2011. *The Official History of the British Civil Service: Reforming the Civil Service* (London, 2011).

29 Llewellyn, 'Polyvocalism', 265. Also see Whyte, 'How Do Buildings Mean?'.

BIBLIOGRAPHY

I. Primary Archival/Manuscript Material

Bodleian Library

> BOD-CPA Conservative Party Archive
> BOD-MSS Modern Political Papers: Attlee dep, Cripps dep, Macmillan dep.

Devon Records Office (DRO)

> Exeter City Council Minutes (ECCM)
> Group G

Hull History Centre (HHC)

> DBR series
> Hull City Council Minutes (HCCM)
> L series
> TPG series

Labour Party Archive (LPA)

> Election materials, 1945
> Michael Foot papers

Liverpool Record Office (LRO)

> City Council Minutes (LVCCM)
> Post-War Redevelopment Advisory (Special) Committee Minutes (PWRASC)

London School of Economics Archive

> Dalton papers
> LSE-BLPES series D4, HD7

The National Archive (UK) (TNA)

> BT Board of Trade
> CAB Cabinet Records
> HLG Housing & Local Government
> HO Home Office

T Treasury
WORK Ministry of Works

Newcastle University: Thomas Sharp Archive (SAUN)

Uncatalogued at time of visit (2007)

University of Liverpool Archive (ULA)

Baron Holford papers

West Country Studies Library (WCSL)

Exeter City Council Minutes (ECCM)
Uncatalogued reconstruction material

II. Primary Printed Material

Government Publications [All Published in London]

The British Imperial Calendar and Civil Service List. London: 1825ff.
Central Office of Information. *Town and Country Planning: The 1947 Act: 144 Questions and Answers*. HMSO, 1949.
Central Office of Information and Birch, Lionel. *Something Done: British Achievement 1945–47*. HMSO, 1948.
Ministry of Health. *Local Government Financial Statistics: Summary* (13 vols). HMSO, 1938–50.
Ministry of Housing and Local Government. *Cmd. 9559 Report of the Ministry of Housing and Local Government for the Period 1950/51 to 1954*. HMSO, 1955.
Ministry of Local Government and Planning. *Cmd. 8204 Town and Country Planning, 1943–1951: Progress Report by the Minister on the Work of the Ministry of Town and Country Planning*. Dalton, Hugh. HMSO, 1951.
Ministry of Reconstruction. *Cmd. 6527 Employment Policy*. HMSO, 1944.
Ministry of Reconstruction. *Cmd. 6609 Housing*. HMSO, 1945.
Ministry of Town and Country Planning. *Town and Country Planning (General Interim Development) Order 1945: Explanatory Memorandum*. HMSO, 1945.
Ministry of Town and Country Planning. *The Redevelopment of Central Areas*. HMSO, 1947.
Ministry of Town and Country Planning. *Cmd. 7006 Town and Country Planning Act, 1947: Explanatory Memorandum*. HMSO, 1947.
Ministry of Town and Country Planning. *Circular 39*. HMSO, 1948.
Ministry of Works. *Cmd. 7279 Summary Report (Annual Report) of the Ministry of Works for the Period 9th May 1945 to 31st December 1946, Etc.* HMSO, 1947.
Ministry of Works. *Cmd. 7541 Summary Report (Annual Report) of the Ministry of Works for the Period 1st January 1947 to 31st December 1947*. HMSO, 1948.
Ministry of Works. *Cmd. 7698 Summary Report (Annual Report) of the Ministry of Works for the Period 1 January 1948 to 31 December 1948*. HMSO, 1949.

Ministry of Works, Committee of Enquiry (Simon, Viscount). *Distribution of Building Materials and Components: Report of the Committee of Enquiry Appointed by the Minister of Works*. HMSO, 1948.

Treasury. *Cmd. 7268 Capital Investment in 1948*. HMSO, 1947.

Treasury. *Cmd. 7572 European Co-operation: Memoranda Submitted to the Organisation for European Economic Co-Operation Relating to Economic Affairs in the Period 1949 to [1953]*. HMSO, 1948.

Books and Articles

(Editorial). 'Exeter'. *The Architect and Building News* 205:20 (1954): 598–601.

(Editorial). 'Exeter and Plymouth Renewed'. *RIBA Journal* 61:6 (1954): 211–18.

Adshead, Stanley D. 'Liverpool: A Preliminary Survey, with Some Suggestions for Remodelling Its Central Area'. *The Town Planning Review* 1:2 (1910): 87–99.

Adshead, Stanley D. *New Towns for Old*. London: J. M. Dent, 1943.

Architectural Press. *Planning for Reconstruction*. London: Architectural Press, 1944.

Arndale Property Trust, company brochure (ca. 1966–67).

Betjeman, John. *English Cities and Small Towns*. London: William Collins, 1943.

Bondfield, Margaret. *Our Towns: A Close-Up*. Oxford: Oxford University Press, 1943.

Bournville Village Trust. *When We Build Again*. London: Allen and Unwin Ltd, 1941.

Chapman, W. Dobson. *Towards a New Macclesfield: A Suggestion for a New Town Centre*. Macclesfield: Macclesfield Borough Council, 1944.

Childs, D. Rigby. 'A Comparison of Progress in Rebuilding Bombed Cities'. *The Architects' Journal* (1954): 41–52.

Childs, D. Rigby. 'Exeter: A Survey'. *The Architects' Journal* (1952).

Clarke, John Joseph. *A Synopsis of the Town and Country Planning Act, 1947*. London: Pitman, 1949.

Cole, G. D. H. *Building and Planning*. London: Cassell, 1945.

Cole, G. D. H. *Plan for Britain: A Collection of Essays*. London: George Routledge and Sons Ltd, 1943.

Doble, R. L. *A Guide to the Town and Country Planning Act, 1947* (Current Law Guide No 2). London: Sweet & Maxwell, 1947.

Finer, Morris. 'The War Damage Act, 1941', *The Modern Law Review* 5:1 (July 1941): 54–63.

Gayton, H. 'City Redevelopments: I. Exeter'. *Town and Country Planning* 26:10 (1958): 378–84.

Gibbon, Gwilym Sir. *Reconstruction and Town and Country Planning, with an Examination of the Uthwatt and Scott Reports*. London: Architect and Building News, 1943.

Goss, G. H. J. 'Exeter – a New Chapter in a Long History'. *Local Government, Commercial and Industrial Enterprise* 2:2 (1957): 11–17.

Grenfell Baines, G. 'Substitute Materials and Their Influence on Design'. *RIBA Journal* (January 1948): 108–13.

Hackett, D. V. 'Exeter'. *The Municipal Journal* 61:3158 (1953): 1829–47.

Heap, Desmond. *An Outline of the New Planning Law: Being an Analysis of the Town and Country Planning Act, 1947*. London: Sweet & Maxwell, 1949.

Holford, William, Thomas Sharp and Frederick Gibberd. *Design in Town and Village*. London: HMSO, 1953.

Institution of Municipal & County Engineers. *Post-War Planning and Reconstruction.*
    London: The Institute, 1942.
Jackson, H. 'Problems of Planning and Reconstruction in Kingston-Upon-Hull'. *Journal of
    the Institute of Municipal Engineers* (1948): 403–16.
Lock, Max, and The Housing Centre. *Civic Diagnosis: A Blitzed City Analysed: An
    Outline Summary of Planning Research Undertaken by the Hull Regional Survey and
    a Guide to the Interim Exhibition Shown in London and Hull, July 1943.* Hull: Hull
    Corporation, 1943.
Lutyens, Edwin L., and Patrick Abercrombie. *A Plan for the City & County of Kingston
    Upon Hull.* Hull: A. Brown & Sons, 1945.
Mackinder, Halford J. 'The Round World and the Winning of the Peace'. *Foreign Affairs* 21:
    4 (1943): 595–605.
McAllister, Gilbert, and Elizabeth Glen McAllister. *Homes, Towns and Countryside: A
    Practical Plan for Britain.* London: B. T. Batsford, Ltd, 1945.
McAllister, Gilbert, and Elizabeth Glen McAllister. *Town and Country Planning: A Study
    of Physical Environment: The Prelude to Post-War Reconstruction.* London: Faber and
    Faber, 1941.
Morrell, J. B. *The City of Our Dreams.* 1st (rev. edn 1955, expanded) edn. London:
    St. Anthony's Press, 1940.
Orwell, George, and Bernard R. Crick. *The Lion and the Unicorn: Socialism and the English
    Genius.* Harmondsworth: Penguin, 1941 (1982 edn).
Osborn, Frederic J. *Making Plans: Based on the B.B.C. Series of Discussions.* London: Todd
    Publishing Company, 1943.
Osborn, Frederic J. et al. *Planning and Reconstruction Year Book, 1942.* London: Todd
    Publishing Company, 1942.
Purdom, Charles Benjamin. *Britain's Cities Tomorrow. Notes for Everyman on a Great
    Theme. [with a Portrait.].* London: King, Littlewood & King, 1942.
Royal Institute of British Architects. *Rebuilding Britain.* London: Lund Humphries, 1943.
Royal Institute of British Architects. *Towards a New Britain.* London: The Architectural
    Press, 1944.
Rushford, Frank H. *City Beautiful: A Vision of Durham.* Durham: Durham County
    Advertiser, 1944.
Sharp, Thomas. 'Building Britain: 1941: Words for Pictures Perhaps a Film Script'. *The
    Town Planning Review* 23:3 (1952): 203–10.
Sharp, Thomas. *Exeter Phoenix: A Plan for Rebuilding.* London: Architectural Press, 1946.
Shennan, Alfred E. 'City Redevelopment'. *Liverpool Trade Review* 45:9 (1946): 123.
Shennan, Alfred E. 'Liverpool: Some Reconstruction Problems'. *Liverpool Trade Review* 48
    (September 1949): 115.
Shennan, Alfred E. 'Post-War Liverpool'. *Liverpool Trade Review* 53:9 (1954): 290–5.
Smith, John Frederick B., Gordon Hemm and Alfred Ernest Shennan. *Liverpool, Past,
    Present, Future.* Liverpool: Northern Pub. Co., 1948.
Thompson, F. M. L., et al. *Merseyside Plan 1944.* London, HMSO, 1945.
Town and Country Planning Association (Great Britain). Conference (1941: Oxford
    England), and Frederick Edward Towndrow. *Replanning Britain: Being a Summarized
    Report of the Oxford Conference of the Town and Country Planning Association, Spring,
    1941.* London: Faber and Faber Ltd, 1941.
Towndrow, F. E. (ed.). *Replanning Britain: Being a Summarized Report of the Oxford
    Conference of the Town and Country Planning Association, Spring, 1941.* London: Faber
    and Faber Ltd, 1941.

Townroe, Bernard Stephen. *The Building of a New Britain*. London: National Council of Building Industries, 1941.

Watson, J. Paton, et al. *A Plan for Plymouth*. 2nd edn. Plymouth: Underhill, 1943.

III. Academic Theses

Brierley, John. 'Exeter 1939–1974: The Reconstruction of a City'. MA. University of Manchester, 1980.

Evans, Dinah M., and Bangor University of Wales. 'The Dynamics of Labour Party Politics in Swansea 1941–64'. University of Wales, Bangor, 2007.

Flinn, Catherine. 'Capitalising on Social and Economic Demands: Speculative Office Building I London 1953–1966'. London: University of London, 1990.

Jozefacka, A. 'Rebuilding Warsaw: Conflicting Visions of a Capital City, 1916–1956'. New York University, 2011.

Minns, David. 'The Post-War Redevelopment of Exeter'. BA (Hons). unknown, 1979. Held by Exeter West Country Studies Library.

Thorpe, Keir M. 'The Missing Pillar: Economic Planning and the Machinery of Government During the Labour Administration of 1945–51'. PhD University of London, 1999.

IV. Secondary Material

Books and Articles

(Editorial). 'A German Phoenix'. *Economist* 327: 7808 (1993): 91.

(Editorial). 'Historians and Public Records'. *Twentieth Century British History* 9: 1 (1998): 109–10.

Adams, David. 'Everyday Experiences of the Modern City: Remembering the Post-War Reconstruction of Birmingham'. *Planning Perspectives* 26:2 (2011): 237–60.

Addison, Paul. 'Consensus Revisited'. *Twentieth Century British History* 4:1 (1993): 91–4.

Addison, Paul. *Now the War Is Over: A Social History of Britain 1945–51*. London: Pimlico, 1995.

Addison, Paul. *The Road to 1945: British Politics and the Second World War*. London: Pimlico, 1994.

Adey, Peter, David J. Cox and Barry Godfrey. *Crime, Regulation and Control during the Blitz: Protecting the Population of Bombed Cities*. London: Bloomsbury, 2016.

Aitken, Stuart C., and Leo E. Zonn. *Place, Power, Situation and Spectacle: Geography of Film*. London: Rowman & Littlefield, 1994.

Alford, B. W. E., Rodney Lowe and Neil Rollings. *Economic Planning 1943–1951: A Guide to Documents in the Public Record Office*. London: HMSO, 1992.

Amati, Marco, and Robert Freestone. 'All of London's a Stage: The 1943 County of London Plan Exhibition'. *Urban History* 43:4 (November 2016): 539–56.

Ambrose, Peter J., and Bob Colenutt. *The Property Machine*. Harmondsworth: Penguin, 1975.

Arnold, Jörg. ' "Once Upon a Time There Was a Lovely Town ..." ': The Allied Air War, Urban Reconstruction and Nostalgia in Kassel (1943–2000)'. *German History* 29:3 (2011): 445–69.

Baigent, Elizabeth. 'Typologies of Urban History'. *Urban History* 25 (1999): 536–46.

Balderstone, Laura, Graeme Milne and Rachel Mulhearn. 'Memory and Place on the Liverpool Waterfront in the Mid-twentieth Century'. *Urban History* 41:3 (August 2014): 478–96.

Banham, Mary, et al. *A Tonic to the Nation: The Festival of Britain 1951*. London: Thames and Hudson, 1976.

Barnett, Correlli. *The Lost Victory: British Dreams, British Realities, 1945–1950*. London: Macmillan, 1995.

Beaven, Brad, and John Griffiths. 'The Blitz, Civilian Morale and the City: Mass-Observation and Working-Class Culture in Britain, 1940–41'. *Urban History* 26:01 (1999): 71–88.

Beaven, Brad, and D. Thoms. 'The Blitz and Civilian Morale in Three Northern Cities, 1940–1942'. *Northern History* 32: 1 (1996): 195–203.

Beers, Laura. 'Labour's Britain, Fight for It Now!' *The Historical Journal* 52:03 (2009): 667–95.

Belchem, John. *Liverpool 800: Culture, Character & History*. Liverpool: Liverpool University Press, 2006.

Bessel, Richard, and Dirk Schumann. *Life after Death: Approaches to a Cultural and Social History during the 1940s and 1950s*. Cambridge: Cambridge University Press, 2003.

Betjeman, John, and Stephen Games. *Trains and Buttered Toast: Selected Radio Talks*. London: John Murray, 2006.

Bold, John, Peter J. Larkham and Robert Pickard (eds). *Authentic Reconstruction: Authenticity, Architecture and the Built Heritage*. London: Bloomsbury, 2017.

Borsay, Peter. 'History or Heritage: Perceptions of the Urban Past: A Review Essay'. *Urban History* 18 (1991): 32–40.

Borsay, Peter. *The Image of Georgian Bath, 1700–2000: Towns, Heritage, and History*. Oxford: Oxford University Press, 2000.

Bowley, Marian. *The British Building Industry: Four Studies in Response and Resistance to Change*. Cambridge: Cambridge University Press, 1966.

Bowley, Marian. *Innovations in Building Materials: An Economic Study*. London: Duckworth, 1960.

Bowley, Marian. 'Review: [Untitled]'. *The Economic Journal* 71:284 (1961): 800–801.

Bowley, Marian. 'Review: [Untitled]'. *The Economic Journal* 72:285 (1962): 209–11.

Bradbury, Ronald, and Liverpool City Architect's Department. *Liverpool Builds, 1945–65: The Postwar Building Achievements of the City and County Borough of Liverpool*. Liverpool: Public Relations Office of City of Liverpool, 1967.

Brett, Lionel. 'The Developers'. *Architectural Review* 143: 893 (1965): 163–7.

Brittain-Catlin, Timothy. 'Modernist Rediscovery: Review "Mediating Modernism"'. *Architectural Review* 221:132 (2007): 92–5.

Brivati, Brian, Julia Buxton and Anthony Seldon. *The Contemporary History Handbook*. Manchester: Manchester University Press, 1996.

Brivati, Brian, and Harriet Jones (eds). *What Difference Did the War Make?* Leicester: Leicester University Press, 1995.

Broadberry, S. N., and N. F. R. Crafts. 'British Economic Policy and Industrial Performance in the Early Post-War Period'. *Business History* 38:4 (1996): 65–91.

Bullock, Nicholas. *Building the Post-War World: Modern Architecture and Reconstruction in Britain*. Abingdon: Routledge, 2002.

Bullock, Nicholas. 'Reconstruction: New Ways of Building and Government Sponsorship'. *European Cities & Technology: Industrial to Post-Industrial City*. Ed. D. C. Goodman and C. Chant. Abingdon: Routledge in association with the Open University, 1999.

Butler, Richard Austen Butler. *The Art of the Possible: The Memoirs of Lord Butler*. London: Hamish Hamilton, 1971.

Cairncross, Alec. *Years of Recovery: British Economic Policy 1945–51*. London: Methuen, 1987.

Cairncross, Alec Sir, and Nita G. M. Watts. *The Economic Section, 1939–61: A Study in Economic Advising*. London: Routledge, 1989.

The Center for Macro Projects and Diplomacy. *Post-War Reconstruction: Concerns, Models and Approaches, Paper 20*. Post-Conflict Resolution: Reconnecting Sites Nations Cultures. Roger Williams University, 2005.

Cherry, Gordon E. *The Evolution of British Town Planning: A History of Town Planning in the United Kingdom During the 20th Century and of the Royal Town Planning Institute, 1914–74*. Leighton Buzzard: Royal Town Planning Institute, 1974.

Cherry, Gordon E. *Town Planning in Britain since 1900: The Rise and Fall of the Planning Ideal*. Oxford: Blackwell, 1996.

Chick, Martin. *Industrial Policy in Britain, 1945–1951: Economic Planning, Nationalisation and the Labour Governments*. Cambridge: Cambridge University Press, 1998.

Clapson, Mark and Peter Larkham (eds). *The Blitz and Its Legacy*. Farnham: Ashgate, 2013.

Clarke, David B. *The Cinematic City*. London: Routledge, 1997.

Clarke, P. F. *The Cripps Version: The Life of Sir Stafford Cripps*. London: Allen Lane, 2002.

Coats, A. W. 'Economists in Government – an Historical and Comparative Perspective'. *Economic Papers* 7:2 (1988): 89–102.

Cole, G. D. H. *The Post-War Condition of Britain*. London: Routledge & Kegan Paul, 1956.

Conekin, Becky. *The Autobiography of a Nation: The 1951 Festival of Britain*. Manchester: Manchester University Press, 2003.

Conekin, Becky, Frank Mort and Chris Waters. *Moments of Modernity: Reconstructing Britain: 1945–1964*. London: Rivers Oram, 1998.

Confino, Alon. 'Traveling as a Culture of Remembrance: Traces of National Socialism in West Germany, 1945–1960'. *History and Memory* 12:2 (2000): 92–121.

Conzen, M. R. G., and J. W. R. Whitehand. *The Urban Landscape: Historical Development and Management*. London: Academic Press, 1981.

Cullingworth, J. B. *British Planning: 50 Years of Urban and Regional Planning*. London: Athlone Press, 1999.

Cullingworth, J. B., and G. E. Cherry. *Environmental Planning, 1939–1969*. Peacetime History. Vol. 1: Reconstruction 1939–47. London: H.M.S.O, 1975.

Cullingworth, J. B. and Vincent Nadin. *Town and Country Planning in the UK*. 14th edn. London: Routledge, 2006.

Dalton, Hugh, and Ben Pimlott. *The Second World War Diary of Hugh Dalton 1940–45*. London: Cape, 1986.

Darling, Elizabeth. *Re-forming Britain: Narratives of Modernity before Reconstruction*. Abingdon: Routledge, 2006.

Daunton, Martin. 'Britain and Globalisation since 1850: Iii. Creating the World of Bretton Woods, 1939–1958'. *Transactions of the Royal Historical Society (Sixth Series)* 18 (2008): 1–42.

Daunton, Martin. *The Cambridge Urban History of Britain*. Vol. III, 1840–1950. 3 vols. Cambridge: Cambridge University Press, 2000.

Daunton, Martin. 'The Future Direction of British History: Thinking About Economic Cultures'. *History Workshop Journal* 72:1 (2011): 222–39.

Daunton, Martin. *Wealth and Welfare: An Economic and Social History of Britain, 1851–1951*. Oxford: Oxford University Press, 2007.

Davies, D. P. *The Bombing of Exeter*. Exeter: The Regional Resources Centre, Institute of Education, University of Exeter, 1973.

Dear, M. J., and A. J. Scott. *Urbanization and Urban Planning in Capitalist Society*. London: Methuen, 1981.

Delafons, J. *Politics and Preservation: A Policy History of the Built Heritage, 1882–1996*. London: E. & F. N. Spon, 1997.

Diefendorf, Jeffry M. *In the Wake of War: The Reconstruction of German Cities after World War II*. Oxford: Oxford University Press, 1993.

Diefendorf, Jeffry M. *Rebuilding Europe's Bombed Cities*. Basingstoke: Macmillan, 1990.

Diefendorf, Jeffry M. 'Reconstructing Devastated Cities: Europe after World War II and New Orleans after Katrina'. *Journal of Urban Design* 14:3 (2009): 377–97.

Dow, J. C. R. *The Management of the British Economy, 1945–60*. Cambridge: Cambridge University Press, 1964.

Dow, J. C. R. 'Review: Cairncross, Alec. Years of Recovery'. *Journal of Economic Literature* 25:3 (1987): 1327–9.

Dunleavy, Patrick, and R. A. W. Rhodes. 'Core Executive Studies in Britain'. *Public Administration* 68:1 (1990): 3–28.

Dunster, David. 'Urban Myth: David Dunster Examines Liverpool's Powerful Urban Mythography and Civic Pride'. *Architectural Review* (January 2008).

Düwel, Jörn, and Niels Gutschow (eds). *A Blessing in Disguise: War and Town Planning in Europe, 1940–45*. Berlin: DOM, 2013.

Dyos, H. J. *Urban History Yearbook*. Leicester: Leicester University Press, 1974.

Edgerton, David. 'War, Reconstruction, and the Nationalization of Britain, 1939–1951'. *Past & Present* 210:suppl. 6 (2011): 29–46.

Ellwood, David W. *Rebuilding Europe: Western Europe, America and Postwar Reconstruction*. London: Longman, 1992.

Elwall, Robert. *Building a Better Tomorrow: Architecture in Britain in the 1950s*. Chichester: Wiley-Academy, 2000.

Esher, Lionel. *A Broken Wave: The Rebuilding of England, 1940–1980*. London: Allen Lane, 1981.

Essex, Stephen, and Mark Brayshay. 'Boldness Diminished? The Post-War Battle to Replan a Bomb-Damaged Provincial City'. *Urban History* 35:3 (2008): 437–61.

Essex, Stephen, and Mark Brayshay. 'Town versus Country in the 1940s: Planning the Contested Space of a City Region in the Aftermath of the Second World War'. *The Town Planning Review* 76:3 (2005): 239.

Essex, Stephen, and Mark Brayshay. 'Vision, Vested Interest and Pragmatism: Who Re-made Britain's Blitzed Cities?' *Planning Perspectives* 22:4 (2007): 417–41.

Falk, Nicholas (ed.). *The Renaissance of Post-War Town Centres: Report of the Symposium*. London: Urban and Economic Development Group, 2000.

Fielding, Steven. 'What Did "the People" Want?: The Meaning of the 1945 General Election'. *The Historical Journal* 35:03 (1992): 623–39.

Fielding, Steven, Peter Thompson and Nick Tiratsoo. '*England Arise!*': *The Labour Party and Popular Politics in 1940s Britain*. Manchester: Manchester University Press, 1995.

Flinn, Catherine. '"The City of Our Dreams"? The Political and Economic Realities of Rebuilding Britain's Blitzed Cities, 1945–54'. *Twentieth Century British History* 23:2 (2012): 221–45.

Flinn, Catherine. '"Exeter Phoenix": Politics and the Rebuilding of a Blitzed City'. *Southern History* 30 (2008): 104–27.

Flinn, Catherine. 'Forgetful or Purposeful? Memory and the Remaking of Place after the Blitz'. *Storia Urbana* 158 (2018): 61–86.

Fortescue-Foulkes, R., and Society Exeter Civic. *Exeter, a City Saved?* Exeter: The Society, 1977.

Forty, A. 'Being or Nothingness: Private Experience and Public Architecture in Post-War Britain'. *Architectural History* v. 38 (1995): 25–35.

Forty, A. 'Cold War Concrete'. *Constructed Happiness, Domestic Environment in the Cold War Era*. Ed. M. Kalm and I. Ruudi. Estonian Academy of Arts Proceedings 16 (2005): 28–44.

Freestone, R., and M. Amati (eds). *Exhibitions and the Development of Modern Planning Culture*. Farnham: Ashgate, 2014.

Gaitskell, Hugh, and Philip M. Williams. *The Diary of Hugh Gaitskell, 1945–1956*. London: Cape, 1983.

Gardiner, Juliet. *Wartime: Britain 1939–1945*. London: Review, 2005.

Giedion, Sigfried. *Space, Time and Architecture: The Growth of a New Tradition*. 3rd edn. Oxford: Oxford University Press, 1954.

Gilbert, Daniel Todd. *Stumbling on Happiness*. London: HarperPress, 2006.

Gilbert, David, David Matless, and Brian Short. *Geographies of British Modernity: Space and Society in the Twentieth Century*. Malden, MA: Blackwell, 2003.

Gillett, Edward, and Kenneth A. MacMahon. *A History of Hull*. 3rd edn. Hull: Hull University Press, 1989.

Gold, John R. *The Experience of Modernism: Modern Architects and the Future City, 1928–53*. London: E & FN Spon, 1997.

Gold, John R. 'In Spite of Planning'. *Journal of Urban History* 26:4 (2000): 545–52.

Gold, John R. *The Practice of Modernism: Modern Architects and Urban Transformation, 1954–1972*. London: Routledge, 2007.

Gould, Jeremy. 'Architecture and the Plan for Plymouth: The Legacy of a British City'. *Architectural Review* 221:1321 (2007): 78–83.

Gourvish, T. R., and Alan O'Day. *Britain since 1945*. Problems in Focus Series. Basingstoke: Macmillan, 1991.

Grayling, A. C. *Among the Dead Cities: Was the Allied Bombing of Civilians in WWII a Necessity or a Crime?* London: Bloomsbury, 2006.

Graystone, P. *The Blitz on Hull, 1940–45*. Hull: Lampada Press, 1991.

Greenhalgh, Paul. *Ephemeral Vistas: The Expositions Universelles, Great Exhibitions and World's Fairs, 1851–1939*. Manchester: Manchester University Press, 1988.

Grindrod, John. *Concretopia: A Journey around the Rebuilding of Postwar Britain*. London: Old Street Publishing, 2014.

Hagen, Joshua. 'Rebuilding the Middle Ages after the Second World War: The Cultural Politics of Reconstruction in Rothenburg Ob Der Tauber, Germany'. *Journal of Historical Geography* 31:1 (2005): 94–112.

Hall, Peter. *Cities of Tomorrow: An Intellectual History of Urban Planning and Design in the Twentieth Century*. Oxford: Basil Blackwell, 1988.

Hall, Peter. *Urban and Regional Planning*. 3rd edn. London: Routledge, 1992.

Hall, Tim, Phil Hubbard and John R. Short. *The Sage Companion to the City*.
    London: Sage, 2008.
Hanna, Erika. 'Dublin's North Inner City, Preservationism, and Irish Modernity in the
    1960s'. *The Historical Journal* 53:04 (2010): 1015 –35.
Harris, Jose. *William Beveridge: A Biography*. 2nd edn. Oxford: Clarendon Press, 1997.
Harvey, David. 'The City as a Body Politic'. *Wounded Cities: Destruction and
    Reconstruction in a Globalized World*. Ed. Jane Schneider and Ida Susser. Oxford:
    Berg, 2003.
Hasegawa, Junichi. 'The Reconstruction of Portsmouth in the 1940s'. *Contemporary British
    History* 14:1 (2000): 45.
Hasegawa, Junichi. *Replanning the Blitzed City Centre: A Comparative Study of
    Bristol, Coventry and Southampton 1941–1950*. Themes in the Twentieth Century.
    Buckingham: Open University Press, 1992.
Hasegawa, Junichi. 'The Rise and Fall of Radical Reconstruction in 1940s Britain'.
    Twentieth Century British History 10:2 (1999): 137–61.
Hayes, Nick. 'Making Homes by Machine: Images, Ideas and Myths in the Diffusion of
    Non-traditional Housing in Britain 1942–54'. *Twentieth Century British History* 10: 3
    (1999): 282 –309.
Hayes, Nick. 'Prefabricating Stories: Innovations in Systems Technology after the Second
    World War'. *History of Technology* 25 (2004): 7–28.
Hein, Carola. 'Urban Reconstruction in Britain and Japan, 1945–1955: Dreams, Plans
    and Realities, And: Housing in Postwar Japan: A Social History (Review)'. *Journal of
    Japanese Studies* 30:2 (2004): 481–6.
Hein, Carola, Jeffry M. Diefendorf, and Yorifusa Ishida. *Rebuilding Urban Japan after
    1945*. Basingstoke: Palgrave Macmillan, 2003.
Hennessy, Peter. *Cabinet*. Oxford: Basil Blackwell, 1986.
Hewison, Robert. *Culture and Consensus: England, Art and Politics since 1940*. London:
    Methuen, 1997.
Hewison, Robert. *The Heritage Industry: Britain in a Climate of Decline*. London: Methuen
    London, 1987.
Hillier, Bevis. *John Betjeman: New Fame, New Love*. London: John Murray, 2004.
Hilton, Matthew. *Consumerism in Twentieth-Century Britain: The Search for a Historical
    Movement*. Cambridge: Cambridge University Press, 2003.
Hilton, Matthew. 'The Death of a Consumer Society'. *Transactions of the Royal Historical
    Society (Sixth Series)* 18 (2008): 211–36.
Hitchcock, Henry Russell, and Philip Johnson. *The International Style*. 2nd edn. London:
    W.W. Norton, 1966.
Hobbs, Peter. 'The Economic Determinants of Post-War British Town Planning'. *Progress
    in Planning* 38:Part 3 (1992): 185–300.
Hollow, Matthew. 'Utopian Urges: Visions for Reconstruction in Britain, 1940–1950'.
    Planning Perspectives 27:4 (2012): 569–85.
Holman, Valerie. *Print for Victory: Book Publishing in Britain 1939–1945*. London: British
    Library, 2008.
Hoskins, W. G. *Two Thousand Years in Exeter*. Ed. Harvey, Hazel. New edn, orig edn 1960.
    Chicester: Phillimore, 2004.
Hubbard, Phil, Lucy Faire and Keith Lilley. 'Contesting the Modern City: Reconstruction
    and Everyday Life in Post-War Coventry'. *Planning Perspectives* 18:4 (2003): 377–97.
Hughes, John. *Port in a Storm: The Air Attacks on Liverpool and Its Shipping in the Second
    World War*. Birkenhead: Merseyside Port Folios, 1993.

Jackson, Gordon. *Hull in the Eighteenth Century: A Study in Economic and Social History.* London: Published for the University of Hull by Oxford University Press, 1971.

Jackson, John Brinckerhoff. *Discovering the Vernacular Landscape.* New Haven: Yale University Press, 1984.

James, Simon. *British Cabinet Government.* 2nd edn. London: Routledge, 1999.

James, Simon. 'The Cabinet System since 1945: Fragmentation and Integration'. *Parliamentary Affairs* 47:4 (1994): 613–29.

Jefferys, Kevin. 'Perspectives on Postwar Britain'. *Twentieth Century British History* 4:3 (1993): 297–301.

Johnson-Marshall, Percy. *Rebuilding Cities.* Edinburgh: Edinburgh University Press, 1966.

Jones, Harriet. ' "This Is Magnificent!": 300,000 Houses a Year and the Tory Revival after 1945'. *Contemporary British History* 14:1 (2000): 99.

Jones, Harriet, and Paul Addison. *A Companion to Contemporary Britain, 1939–2000.* Malden, MA: Blackwell, 2005.

Jones, Philip N. ' " … A Fairer and Nobler City" – Lutyens and Abercrombie's Plan for the City of Hull 1945'. *Planning Perspectives* 13:3 (1998): 301–16.

Kynaston, David. *Austerity Britain, 1945–1951.* London: Bloomsbury, 2007.

Langhamer, Claire. 'The Meanings of Home in Postwar Britain'. *Journal of Contemporary History* 40:2 (2005): 341–62.

Larkham, Peter J. 'Changing Ideas of Urban Conservation in Mid-Twentieth-Century England'. *Change Over Time* 4:1 (Spring 2014): 92–113.

Larkham, Peter J. 'The Cost of Planning for Reconstruction'. *Planning History* 27:1–2 (2005): 20–6.

Larkham, Peter J. 'Hostages to History? The Surprising Survival of Critical Comments About British Planning and Planners C. 1942–1955'. *Planning Perspectives* 26:3 (2011): 487 –91.

Larkham, Peter J. *Infrastructure and the Rebuilt City.* Working Paper 22. Birmingham: Birmingham City University, 2013.

Larkham, Peter J. 'The Place of Urban Conservation in the UK Reconstruction Plans of 1942–1952'. *Planning Perspectives* 18:3 (2003): 295–324.

Larkham, Peter J. 'Planning for Reconstruction after the Disaster of War: Lessons from England in the 1940s'. *Perspectivas Urbanas/Urban Perspectives* 6:1 (2004).

Larkham, Peter J. *The Rebuilding of British Cities: Exploring the Post-Second World War Reconstruction.* Working Paper 2004. Birmingham: University of Central England, School of Planning and Housing.

Larkham, Peter J. 'Rebuilding the Industrial Town: Wartime Wolverhampton'. *Urban History* 29:3 (2002): 388–409.

Larkham, Peter J. 'Remaking Cities: Images, Control, and Postwar Replanning in the United Kingdom'. *Environment and Planning B: Planning and Design* 24:5 (1997): 741–59.

Larkham, Peter J. 'Thomas Sharp and the Post-War Replanning of Chichester: Conflict, Confusion and Delay'. *Planning Perspectives* 24:1 (2009): 51–75.

Larkham, Peter J., and Keith D. Lilley. 'Exhibiting the City: Planning Ideas and Public Involvement in Wartime and Early Post-war Britain'. *Town Planning Review* 83 (2012): 647–68.

Larkham, Peter J., and Keith D. Lilley. *Planning the 'City of Tomorrow': British Reconstruction Planning, 1939–1952: An Annotated Bibliography.* Pickering: Inch's Books, 2001.

Larkham, Peter J., and Keith D. Lilley. 'Plans, Planners and City Images: Place Promotion and Civic Boosterism in British Reconstruction Planning'. *Urban History* 30:2 (2003): 183–205.

Lilley, Keith D., and Peter J. Larkham. *Exhibiting Planning: Communication and Public Involvement in British Post-War Reconstruction*. Working Paper Series/Faculty of Law, Humanities, Development and Society. Birmingham: Birmingham City University, 2007.

Littlefield, David. *Liverpool One: Remaking a City Centre*. Chichester: John Wiley & Sons, 2009.

Llewellyn, Mark. 'Polyvocalism and the Public: "Doing" a Critical Historical Geography of Architecture'. *Area* 35:3 (2003): 264.

Lowe, Rodney. *The Official History of the British Civil Service: Reforming the Civil Service*. London: Routledge, 2011.

Lowe, Rodney. 'Plumbing New Depths: Contemporary Historians and the Public Record Office'. *Twentieth Century British History* 8:2 (1997): 239–65.

Lowe, R. 'The Second World War, Consensus and the Foundation of the Welfare State'. *Twentieth Century British History* 1:2 (1990): 152–82.

Lowenthal, David. *The Past Is a Foreign Country*. Cambridge: Cambridge University Press, 1985.

Lubbock, Jules. *The Tyranny of Taste: The Politics of Architecture and Design in Britain 1550–1960*. New Haven: Yale University Press, 1995.

Luckhurst, K. W. *The Story of Exhibitions*. London: Studio Publications, 1951.

Macmillan, Harold. *Tides of Fortune, 1945–1955*. London: Macmillan, 1969.

Madgin, Rebecca. 'Reconceptualising the Historic Urban Environment: Conservation and Regeneration in Castlefield, Manchester, 1960–2009'. *Planning Perspectives* 25:1 (2010): 29–48.

Malpass, Peter. 'The Wobbly Pillar? Housing and the British Postwar Welfare State'. *Journal of Social Policy* 32:04 (2003): 589–606.

Mandler, Peter. *The English National Character: The History of an Idea from Edmund Burke to Tony Blair*. New Haven: Yale University Press, 2006.

Mandler, Peter. *The Fall and Rise of the Stately Home*. London: Yale University Press, 1997.

Mandler, Peter, and Astrid Swenson (eds). *From Plunder to Preservation*. Oxford: Oxford University Press, 2013.

Margetts, H. P., and C. Hood. *Paradoxes of Modernization: Unintended Consequences of Public Policy Reform*. Oxford: Oxford University Press, 2010.

Markham, John. *Hammonds of Hull: A Store of Good Things for Family and Home*. Beverley: Highgate Publications, 2004.

Marriott, Oliver. *The Property Boom*. London: Abingdon Publishing, 1967.

Marwick, Arthur. *Britain in the Century of Total War: War, Peace and Social Change, 1900–1967*. Harmondsworth: Penguin, 1970.

Matless, David. *Landscape and Englishness*. London: Reaktion, 1998.

Matless, David. 'Visual Culture and Geographical Citizenship: England in the 1940s'. *Journal of Historical Geography* 22:4 (1996): 424–39.

McCullagh, C. Behan. 'Bias in Historical Description, Interpretation, and Explanation'. *History & Theory* 39:1 (2000): 39.

McKay, David H., and Andrew W. Cox. *The Politics of Urban Change*. London: Croom Helm, 1979.

McLaine, I. A. N. *Ministry of Morale: Home Front Morale and the Ministry of Information in World War II*. London: Allen and Unwin, 1979.

Meller, Helen. 'From Dyos to Daunton: The Cambridge Urban History of Britain, Vol. III'. *Urban History* 28:2 (2001): 269–77.

Meller, Helen. *Towns, Plans and Society in Modern Britain*. New Studies in Economic and Social History. Cambridge: Cambridge University Press, 1997.

Milward, Alan S. *The Reconstruction of Western Europe 1945–51*. London: Methuen, 1984.

Morgan, Kenneth O. *Britain since 1945: The People's Peace*. 3rd edn. Oxford: Oxford University Press, 2001.

Morley, I. *British Provincial Civic Design and the Building of Late-Victorian and Edwardian Cities, 1880–1914*. Lewiston, NY: Edwin Mellen Press, 2008.

Morrison, Herbert. *Government and Parliament: A Survey from the Inside*. 2nd edn. London: Oxford University Press, 1960.

Mort, Frank. *Cultures of Consumption: Masculinities and Social Space in Late Twentieth-Century Britain*. London: Routledge, 1996.

Mort, Frank. 'Fantasies of Metropolitan Life: Planning London in the 1940s'. *Journal of British Studies* 43:1 (2004): 120–51.

Mosley, R. K. *The Story of the Cabinet Office*. London: Routledge & Kegan Paul, 1969.

Muir, Ramsay, and J. J. Bagley. *A History of Liverpool*. East Ardsley: S. R. Publishers, 1970.

Nicholas, Sian '"Sly Demagogues" and Wartime Radio: J. B. Priestley and the BBC'. *Twentieth Century British History* 6:3 (1995): 247–66.

Niemczyk, Maria. 'City Profile – Warsaw (Warszawa)'. *Cities* 15:4 (1998): 301–11.

O'Hara, Glen. *From Dreams to Disillusionment: Economic and Social Planning in 1960s Britain*. Basingstoke: Palgrave Macmillan, 2007.

O'Hara, Glen. *Governing Post-War Britain: The Paradoxes of Progress, 1951–1973*. Basingstoke: Palgrave, 2010.

O'Hara, Glen. 'A Journey without Maps: The Regional Policies of the 1964–70 British Labour Government'. *Regional Studies* 39:9 (2005): 1183–95.

O'Hara, Glen. 'Social Democratic Space: The Politics of Building in "Golden Age" Britain, c.1950–1973'. *arq: Architectural Research Quarterly* 10:3–4 (2006): 285–90.

O'Hara, Glen. '"What the Electorate Can Be Expected to Swallow": Nationalisation, Transnationalism and the Shifting Boundaries of the State in Post-War Britain'. *Business History* 51:4 (2009): 501–28.

Owen, Charles. *One Man's City: A Newcomer's View of Exeter*. Exeter: Flying Post (n.d. est. 1977).

Pendlebury, John. 'Alas Smith and Burns? Conservation in Newcastle Upon Tyne City Centre 1959–68'. *Planning Perspectives* 16:2 (2001): 115–41.

Pendlebury, John. 'Planning the Historic City: Reconstruction Plans in the United Kingdom in the 1940s'. *The Town Planning Review* 74:4 (2003): 371–93.

Pendlebury, John. 'Reconciling History with Modernity: 1940s Plans for Durham and Warwick'. *Environment and Planning B: Planning and Design* 31 (2004): 331–48.

Pendlebury, John. 'The Urbanism of Thomas Sharp'. *Planning Perspectives* 24:1 (2009): 3–28.

Pendlebury, John, and Simin Davoudi. 'Centenary Paper: The Evolution of Planning as an Academic Discipline'. *Town Planning Review* 81: 6 (2010): 613–46.

Pendlebury, John, Erdem Ertem and Peter J. Larkham (eds). *Alternative Visions of Post-War Reconstruction: Creating the Modern Townscape*. Abingdon: Routledge, 2015.

Pevsner, Nikolaus. *Pioneers of Modern Design from William Morris to Walter Gropius*. London: Penguin, 1991.

Pimlott, Ben. *Hugh Dalton*. London: HarperCollins, 1995.

Pimlott, Ben, Dennis Kavanagh and Peter Morris. 'Is the "Postwar Consensus" a Myth?'
    Contemporary British History 2:6 (1989): 12–15.
Plowden, Edwin. *An Industrialist in the Treasury: The Post-War Years.* London:
    Deutsch, 1989.
Powell, Christopher. *The British Building Industry since 1800: An Economic History.*
    Abingdon: Routledge, 1996.
Punter, John. 'A History of Aesthetic Control: Part 1, 1909–1953: The Control of the
    External Appearance of Development in England and Wales'. *The Town Planning
    Review* 57:4 (1986): 351–81.
Ravetz, Alison. *Remaking Cities: Contradictions of the Recent Urban Environment.*
    London: Croom Helm, 1980.
Reith, John Charles, with Charles Stuart. *The Reith Diaries.* London: Collins, 1975.
Richmond, Peter, and C. H. Sir Reilly. *Marketing Modernisms: The Architecture and
    Influence of Charles Reilly.* Liverpool: Liverpool University Press, 2001.
Ritschel, Daniel. 'The Making of Consensus: The Nuffield College Conferences During the
    Second World War'. *Twentieth Century British History* 6:3 (1995): 267–301.
Robinson, Austin. 'The Economic Problems of the Transition from War to Peace: 1945–
    49: Reviewing: Alec Cairncross, Years of Recovery: British Economic Policy 1945–51'.
    Cambridge Journal of Economics 10:2 (1986): 165–85.
Rose, Jack. *The Dynamics of Urban Property Development.* London: E. & F.N.
    Spon, 1985.
Rose, Jack. *Square Feet: An Autobiography.* London: Royal Institution of Chartered
    Surveyors, 1993.
Rosenberg, Nathan. *Economic Planning in the British Building Industry, 1945–49.*
    Philadelphia: University of Pennsylvania Press, 1960.
Rosenberg, Nathan. 'Government Economic Controls in the British Building
    Industry, 1945–9'. *The Canadian Journal of Economics and Political Science* 24:3
    (1958): 345–54.
Rothnie, Niall. *The Baedeker Blitz: Hitler's Attack on Britain's Historic Cities.*
    Shepperton: Ian Allan, 1992.
Rydin, Yvonne. *Urban and Environmental Planning in the UK.* Basingstoke:
    Macmillan, 1998.
Saint, Andrew. *Towards a Social Architecture: The Role of School-Building in Post-War
    England.* London: Yale University Press, 1987.
Scott, Peter. *The Property Masters: A History of the British Commercial Property Sector.*
    Abingdon: Taylor & Francis, 2013.
Scott, Peter. 'The Worst of Both Worlds: British Regional Policy, 1951–64'. *Business History*
    38:4 (1996): 41–64.
Shapely, Peter. 'Civic Pride and Redevelopment in the Post-War British City'. *Urban
    History* 39:2 (2012): 310–28.
Shapely, Peter. 'The Entrepreneurial City: The Role of Local Government and City-Centre
    Redevelopment in Post-War Industrial English Cities'. *Twentieth Century British
    History* 22:4 (2011): 498–520.
Sharp, Evelyn. *The Ministry of Housing and Local Government.* London: George Allen &
    Unwin, 1969.
Sheehan, James J. *Where Have All the Soldiers Gone?: The Transformation of Modern
    Europe.* Boston: Houghton Mifflin, 2008.
Shonfield, Andrew. *British Economic Policy since the War.* Harmondsworth: Penguin, 1959.
Sked, Alan, and Chris Cook. *Post-War Britain: A Political History.* London: Penguin, 1993.

Smith, Harold L. (ed.). *War and Social Change: British Society in the Second World War*. Manchester: Manchester University Press, 1986.

Spalding, Frances. 'Art in Dark Times. ' *History Today* 59:9 (2009): 19–22.

Stamp, Gavin. *Britain's Lost Cities*. London: Aurum, 2007.

Stamp, Gavin. *Lost Victorian Britain: How the Twentieth Century Destroyed the Nineteenth Century's Architectural Masterpieces*. London: Aurum, 2010.

Sutcliffe, Anthony (ed.). *British Town Planning: The Formative Years*. Leicester: Leicester University Press, 1981.

Swenarton, Mark. *Homes Fit for Heroes: The Politics and Architecture of Early State Housing in Britain*. London: Heinemann Educational Books, 1981.

Tanner, Duncan, Pat Thane and Nick Tiratsoo. *Labour's First Century*. Cambridge: Cambridge University Press, 2000.

Taylor, Nigel. *Urban Planning Theory since 1945*. London: SAGE, 1998.

Tewdwr-Jones, Mark. '"Oh, the Planners Did Their Best": The Planning Films of John Betjeman'. *Planning Perspectives* 20:4 (2005): 389–411.

Thatcher, Margaret, and Robin Harris. *The Collected Speeches of Margaret Thatcher*. 1st edn. London: HarperCollinsPublishers, 1997.

Thorpe, Keir M. '"Statistical Floodlighting"? The Unpublished Economic Surveys 1946–47'. *Contemporary British History* 11:4 (1997): 86–111.

Tichelar, Michael. 'Central-Local Tensions: The Case of the Labour Party, Regional Government and Land-Use Reform During the Second World War'. *Labour History Review* 66:2 (2001): 187–206.

Tichelar, Michael. 'The Conflict over Property Rights during the Second World War: The Labour Party's Abandonment of Land Nationalization'. *Twentieth Century British History* 14:2 (2003): 165–88.

Tiratsoo, Nick. *The Attlee Years*. London: Pinter, 1991.

Tiratsoo, Nick. *From Blitz to Blair: A New History of Britain since 1939*. London: Weidenfeld & Nicolson, 1997.

Tiratsoo, Nick. 'The Reconstruction of Blitzed British Cities, 1945–55: Myths and Reality'. *Contemporary British History* 14:1 (2000): 27.

Tiratsoo, Nick. *Reconstruction, Affluence and Labour Politics: Coventry, 1945–1960*. London: Routledge, 1990.

Tiratsoo, Nick, and Jim Tomlinson. *The Conservatives and Industrial Efficiency, 1951–64: Thirteen Wasted Years?* London: LSE/Routledge, 1998.

Tiratsoo, Nick, and Jim Tomlinson. *Industrial Efficiency and State Intervention: Labour 1939–51*. London: LSE/Routledge, 1993.

Tiratsoo, Nick, Junichi Hasegawa, Tony Mason and Takao Matsumura. *Urban Reconstruction in Britain and Japan, 1945–1955: Dreams, Plans and Realities*. Luton: University of Luton Press, 2002.

Tomlinson, Jim. 'After Decline?' *Contemporary British History* 23:3 (2009): 395–406.

Tomlinson, Jim. 'Balanced Accounts? Constructing the Balance of Payments Problem in Post-War Britain'. *English Historical Review* CXXIV:509 (2009): 863–84.

Tomlinson, Jim. *British Macroeconomic Policy since 1940*. London: Croom Helm, 1985.

Tomlinson, Jim. 'Correlli Barnett's History: The Case of Marshall Aid'. *Twentieth Century British History* 8:2 (1997): 222–38.

Tomlinson, Jim. *Democratic Socialism and Economic Policy: The Attlee Years, 1945–1951*. Cambridge: Cambridge University Press, 1997.

Tomlinson, Jim. 'The Labour Party and the Capitalist Firm, c.1950–1970'. *The Historical Journal* 47:03 (2004): 685–708.

Tomlinson, Jim. *Managing the Economy, Managing the People*. Oxford: Oxford University Press, 2017.

Tomlinson, Jim. 'Managing the Economy, Managing the People: Britain c.1931–70'. *Economic History Review* 58:3 (2005): 555–85.

Tomlinson, Jim. *The Politics of Decline: Understanding Post-War Britain*. Harlow: Longman, 2000.

Tomlinson, Jim. 'Thrice Denied: "Declinism" as a Recurrent Theme in British History in the Long Twentieth Century'. *Twentieth Century British History* 20: 2 (2009): 227–51.

Town and Country Planning Association. *Your Place and Mine: The Report of the TCPA Inquiry into the Future of Planning*. London: The Town and Country Planning Association, 1999.

Toye, Richard. *The Labour Party and the Planned Economy, 1931–1951*. Woodbridge: Royal Historical Society/Boydell Press, 2003.

Tsubaki, Tatsuya. 'Planners and the Public: British Opinion on Housing during the Second World War'. *Contemporary British History* 14:1 (2000): 81.

Tung, A. M. *Preserving the World's Great Cities: The Destruction and Renewal of the Historic Metropolis*. Clarkson Potter, 2001.

Vale, L. and Campanella, T. (eds). *Resilient Cities: How Modern Cities Recover from Disaster*. Oxford: Oxford University Press, 2005.

Venning, Norman. *Exeter: The Blitz and Rebirth of the City: The Reconstruction of the Central Areas of Exeter, 1945–65*. Exeter: Devon Books, 1988.

Ward, Stephen V. *The Geography of Interwar Britain: The State and Uneven Development*. London: Routledge, 1988.

Ward, Stephen V. *Planning and Urban Change*. 2nd edn. London: Sage, 2004.

Ward, Stephen V. *Planning the Twentieth-Century City: The Advanced Capitalist World*. Chichester: Wiley, 2002.

Weiler, Peter. 'Labour and the Land: From Municipalization to the Land Commission, 1951–1971'. *Twentieth Century British History* 19:3 (2008): 314–43.

Weiler, Peter. 'The Rise and Fall of the Conservatives' "Grand Design for Housing", 1951–64'. *Contemporary British History* 14:1 (2000): 122.

While, Aidan. 'Modernism vs Urban Renaissance: Negotiating Post-War Heritage in English City Centres'. *Urban Studies* 43:13 (2006): 2399–419.

While, Aidan, and Malcolm Tait. 'Exeter and the Question of Thomas Sharp's Physical Legacy'. *Planning Perspectives* 24:1 (2008): 77–97.

Whyte, Iain Boyd. *Man-Made Future: Planning, Education, and Design in Mid-20th Century Britain*. London: Routledge, 2007.

Whyte, William. 'The Englishness of English Architecture: Modernism and the Making of a National International Style, 1927–1957'. *Journal of British Studies* 48:2 (2009): 441–65.

Whyte, William. 'How Do Buildings Mean? Some Issues of Interpretation in the History of Architecture'. *History and Theory* 45:2 (2006): 153–77.

Wilkinson, Graham. *Hull*. Rev. edn. Salisbury: Francis Frith Collection, 2006.

Worswick, G. D. N., and Peter H. Ady. *The British Economy, 1945–1950*. Oxford: Clarendon Press, 1952.

Wright, Patrick. *On Living in an Old Country: The National Past in Contemporary Britain*. Oxford: Oxford University Press, 2009.

Film, Radio and Television

New Towns for Old, 1942, dir. J. Eldridge, Strand Film Productions for MOI.
Winston Churchill, Broadcast to the Nation, BBC Radio, 21 March 1943. BL Sound
  Archive T 5499.
When We Build Again, 1943, dir. R. Bond, Strand Film for Cadbury Brothers.
A City Reborn, 1945, dir. J. Eldridge, Gryphon Films with Verity Films, the Ministry of
  Information (MOI).
The People and the Plan, 1945, dir. F. Sainsbury, Realist for MOI.
Proud City, 1945 (release 1946), dir R. Keene, Greenpark Productions for MOI.
They Came to a City, 1945, dir B. Dearden, prod S. Cole (Ealing Distribution).
Land of Promise, 1946, dir. P. Rotha, Films of Fact Ltd.
The Way We Live, 1946, dir. J. Craigie, Two Cities for Rank.
A. Murray, 'Al Murray's German Adventure', Part 2, air date 8 December 2010,
  BBC Four.
Sunand Prasad, 'The Past Sure Is Tense', 18 October 2010, BBC Radio 3 'The Essay'
  series.
'The Hull Blitz', Look North by BBC Hull, broadcast on 5 May 2011.

Websites

Hansard online:
https://api.parliament.uk/historic-hansard/index.html

A History of Picture Post:

http://www.lacrossehistory.org/literature/AlltheBest(2010).pdf

BBC WW2 People's War Memories website:

http://www.bbc.co.uk/history/ww2peopleswar/stories/37/a4005037.shtml

BBC News, 'Exeter tops BBC poll on Britain's blandest high street 2005', 5 June 2005:

http://news.bbc.co.uk/1/hi/england/devon/4610965.stm

BBC News, Exeter, 23 May 2008:

http://news.bbc.co.uk/2/hi/uk_news /england/devon/7415831.stm

Boston Globe, 'Change is forever', interview by Jenna Russell, 13 December 2009:

http://www.boston.com/bostonglobe/ideas/articles/2009/12/13/
  change_is_forever/?page=full

Dictionary of National Biography (Oxford University Press)

http://www.oxforddnb.com/

Guardian play review, Lyn Gardiner, 2011:

http://www.guardian.co.uk/stage/2011/may/09/they-came-to-a-city-review

Land Securities website:

http://www.landsecurities.com/about-us/the-land-securities-story

http://www.landsecurities.com/retail-portfolio/our-top-10-retail-properties

http://www.landsecurities.com/investors/shareholder-investor-information/
    uk-reit-taxation

(above now archived at web archive)

Liverpool – Mapping Memory project:

http://www.liverpoolmuseums.org.uk/maritime/research/mappingmemory/index.html

QOL.com:

http://www.qolcom.co.uk/2011/07/ftse-100-group-land-securities-embraces-ipads/ and

This is Hull and East Riding:

http://www.thisishullandeastriding.co.uk

Newspapers Cited

East Anglian Daily Times
Evening Express
Express & Echo
The Guardian
Hull and Yorkshire Times
Hull Daily Mail
Liverpool Daily Post
The Manchester Guardian
The Times
Western Morning News
The Yorkshire Post

INDEX

loan charges 105, 131, 163
Lock, Max 185–6, 195
London 3, 15, 18, 20, 62, 68, 71–2, 96,
    124–5, 146
  treated separately 38, 58, 162
London and Coventry – The Plan and the
    People (1945) film 18, 20
'Looking Ahead' pamphlets 13, 21
Lutyens, Edwin 85–6

Macmillan, Harold 151, 190
  cabinet memo 56–7, 162–3
  as Minister of Town & Country
    Planning 55–8, 61, 77–8, 94, 153,
    157, 162–3, 190–1
'Making Plans' (radio programme and
    book) 16–18, 120
Marquis, Frederick (1st Earl of Woolton)
    21, 23, 26, 68, 178
Marriott, Oliver 124, 136, 213
Materials Committee 44, 186 n.86
Maude, J. C. (MP, Exeter) 98, 101, 204
Maynard, Fred 124–6, 144, 164–5, 213 *see
    also* Ravenseft
Ministry of Economic Affairs 38–41, 58
Ministry of Food 117
Ministry of Health (included Housing
    until 1950) 25, 27, 29, 43–4, 62, 77,
    97–8, 102, 120, 133–4, 173 n.29, 179
    n.125, 185 n.71, 186 n.96, 189 n.140,
    193 n.14, 197 n.92, 204 n.126
Ministry of Housing & Local Government
    (planning ministry from 30 October
    1951) *see* planning ministry
Ministry of Information 13, 18, 172 n.18,
    175 n.57, 176 n.62
Ministry of Local Government & Planning
    (1951 only) *see also* planning
    ministry 51, 118, 189 n.140
Ministry of Reconstruction 10, 22, 24, 26,
    178 n.99, 179 n.134, 192 n.196
Ministry of Supply 45, 184 n.58, 185
    nn.70, 77
Ministry of Town & Country Planning
    (*see also* planning ministry)
Ministry of Town & Country Planning:
    Advisory Panel on Redevelopment
    of City Centres 28–9, 67, 86, 98, 196
    n.73

Ministry of Town & Country Planning:
    formation of 28
Ministry of Town & Country Planning:
    list of blitzed cities 6, 31, 59, 72–4,
    192 n.190
  conference for blitzed cities 70, 77, 92,
    105, 154, 205 n.165, 206 n.183, 219 n.8
  technical section 29, 43, 68
Ministry of Transport 76–7, 86, 88, 91,
    102, 104, 107, 134, 136, 154, 188
    n.132, 199 n.32, 205 n.153, 212 n.41
Ministry of Works & Building *see* Ministry
    of Works
Ministry of Works & Planning 2, 28, 179
    n.122 *see also* Ministry of Works
Ministry of Works 25, 27–8, 41, 43–7, 49,
    51, 54, 59, 67, 71–6, 104, 107, 119–20,
    134–5, 137, 154, 180 n.2, 183 n.55,
    184 n.58, 185 n.70, 186 n.93, 189
    n.137, 194 n.34, 206 n.180, 213 n.73
Montague Burton 91, 116, 213
Morrison, Herbert 37, 68, 181–3
Morrison, Wm. S. 21, 28, 64, 68, 86, 97,
    176, 179, 195, 220

New Towns for Old (1942) film 18
Newman C. J. 102, 105, 154, 157, 203, 206

Orwell, George 21–2
Osborn, F. J. 16–7, 172, 175, 210

Pepler, George L. 195
Picture Post special issue 1941 11, 172 n.13
planning legislation *see under* legislation
    or individual acts
planning ministry 6–7, 28–9, 43–7, 51,
    54–5, 59, 61–80, 82, 85, 87, 89, 91–5,
    97, 101–2, 104, 107, 109, 113, 115,
    118–21, 128, 130–1, 134, 136–7, 152–
    8, 163, 165, 173 n.29, 175 n.50, 185
    n.71, 186 n.91, 187 n.107, 188 n.118,
    190 n.149 n.158 n.164, 192 n.190,
    194 n.34 n.36, 195 n.63, 196 n.78, 197
    n.88 n.92, 201 n.65, 205 n.163, 208
    n.233, 220 n.20
planning profession 1–2, 11–12, 14, 32, 62,
    68, 76, 109, 148, 168 n.10, 192 n.5
Plowden, E. (Sir) 36, 41–2, 50–1, 183,
    190–1